SOCIAL STATUS
AND LEGAL PRIVILEGE
IN THE
ROMAN EMPIRE

SOCIAL STATUS
AND LEGAL PRIVILEGE
IN THE
ROMAN EMPIRE

BY

PETER GARNSEY

OXFORD
AT THE CLARENDON PRESS
1970

Oxford University Press, Ely House, London W. 1

GLASGOW NEW YORK TORONTO MELBOURNE WELLINGTON
CAPE TOWN SALISBURY IBADAN NAIROBI DAR ES SALAAM LUSAKA ADDIS ABABA
BOMBAY CALCUTTA MADRAS KARACHI LAHORE DACCA
KUALA LUMPUR SINGAPORE HONG KONG TOKYO

PRINTED IN GREAT BRITAIN

TO
E. W. G.

PREFACE

I T has long been held that law serves the interests of the governing élite of a society. Recent studies, of which Cardascia's 'L'apparition dans le droit des classes d' "Honestiores" et d' "Humiliores" ' (1950) and Kelly's *Roman Litigation* (1966) are the most prominent, have illustrated the validity of this contention in the case of Roman society. But to my knowledge no comprehensive treatment of the subject of legal privilege in the Roman judicial system has been attempted. In the present work, the techniques of discrimination used by the Romans in the administration of the law are investigated in detail. However, legal privilege was not a purely juridical phenomenon. An attempt is made to relate patterns of discrimination to the social and political forces which produced and transformed them over a period of time.

This book is a revised version of a thesis submitted to the University of Oxford for the Degree of Doctor of Philosophy in 1967. In its original form, it was produced under the supervision of Dr. Fergus Millar. I owe him an enormous debt, for positive suggestions and ideas, for stimulating criticism, and for the generous encouragement and support he has given me at every stage. My thanks are due also to my examiners, Mr. F. A. Lepper and Professor A. H. M. Jones, for useful corrections and suggestions; and to Professors Sir Ronald Syme and W. A. J. Watson, who most kindly read the whole typescript, and enabled me to make a number of improvements. In addition, I gratefully acknowledge the friendly help I have received from Professor D. Daube, Mr. M. W. Frederiksen, Mr. J. F. Matthews, and Mr. G. E. M. de Ste Croix. Finally, I was able to pursue my work in Oxford by the kind favour of the Master and Fellows of University College, who elected me to the Salvesen Junior Fellowship.

P. D. A. G.

University of California
Berkeley

CONTENTS

ABBREVIATIONS

A–J	F. F. Abbott–A. C. Johnson, *Municipal Administration in the Roman Empire* (Princeton, 1926)
Acta Arch. Acad. Sc. Hung.	*Acta Archaeologica Academiae Scientiarum Hungaricae*
AE	*Année Épigraphique*
AJP	*American Journal of Philology*
Anal. Boll.	*Analecta Bollandiana*
Arch. Ert.	*Archaeologiai értesítö*
Archiv	*Archiv für Papyrusforschung*
Ath. Mitt.	*Mitteilungen des Deutschen Archäologischen Instituts* (Athenische Abteilung)
BGU	*Ägyptische Urkunden aus den Staatlichen Museen zu Berlin, Griechische Urkunden*
BIDR	*Bullettino dell'Istituto di Diritto Romano*
C	*Corpus Inscriptionum Latinarum*
CIG	*Corpus Inscriptionum Graecarum*
CJ	*Codex Justinianus*
CR	*Classical Review*
CTh	*Codex Theodosianus*
Coll.	*Mosaicarum et Romanarum Legum Collatio*
DACL	*Dictionnaire d'archéologie chrétienne et de liturgie*, F. Cabrol, H. Leclercq
DE	*Dizionario epigrafico di antichità romane*, E. de Ruggiero
DS	*Dictionnaire des antiquités grecques et romaines*, Ch. Daremberg, E. Saglio
Dacia	*Dacia: recherches et découvertes archéologiques en Roumanie*
Dig.	*Digesta seu Pandectae*, Justinian
EJ	*Documents illustrating the reigns of Augustus and Tiberius*[2], V. Ehrenberg, A. H. M. Jones (Oxford, 1955)
FIRA	*Fontes Iuris Romani Anteiustiniani*[2], S. Riccobono and others
IBM	*Ancient Greek Inscriptions in the British Museum*, C. T. Newton, E. L. Hicks, G. Hirschfeld

IGBulg.	*Inscriptiones Graecae in Bulgaria repertae*, G. Mihailov
IGRR	*Inscriptiones Graecae ad Res Romanas pertinentes*, R. Cagnat
IJ	*Institutiones*, Justinian
ILS	*Inscriptiones Latinae Selectae*, H. Dessau
JEA	*Journal of Egyptian Archaeology*
JHS	*Journal of Hellenic Studies*
JÖAI	*Jahreshefte des Österreichischen archäologischen Instituts in Wien*
JRS	*Journal of Roman Studies*
K–K	*Ausgewählte Märtyrerakten*[3], R. Knopf, G. Krüger (Tübingen, 1929)
MAMA	*Monumenta Asiae Minoris Antiqua*
OGIS	*Orientis Graeci Inscriptiones Selectae*, W. Dittenberger
PBSR	*Papers of the British School at Rome*
P. Fouad	*Les Papyrus Fouad I*, A. Bataille and others
P. Giss.	*Griechische Papyri im Museum des oberhessischen Geschichtsvereins zu Gießen*, O. Eger, E. Kornemann, P. M. Meyer
P. Hal.	*Dikaiomata: Auszüge aus Alexandrinischen Gesetzen und Verordnungen*, etc., Graeca Halensis.
PIR	*Prosopographia Imperii Romani*
P. Lond.	*Greek Papyri in the British Museum*, F. G. Kenyon, H. I. Bell
P. Oxy.	*The Oxyrhynchus Papyri*, B. P. Grenfell, A. S. Hunt, and others
PS	*Sententiae Receptae Paulo Tributae*
PSI	*Papiri greci e latini*, G. Vitelli, M. Norsa, and others
RE	*Real-Encyclopädie der klassischen Altertumswissenschaft*, Pauly–Wissowa (–Kroll)
REA	*Revue des études anciennes*
REG	*Revue des études grecques*
RHDFE	*Revue historique de droit français et étranger*
RIDA	*Revue internationale des droits de l'antiquité*
Rhein. Mus.	*Rheinisches Museum für Philologie*
RISG	*Rivista italiana di scienza giuridica*
SB	*Sammelbuch griechischer Urkunden aus Ägypten*, F. Preisigke, F. Bilabel
SHA	*Scriptores Historiae Augustae*
Sitz. Berl. Akad.	*Sitzungsberichte der Preussischen Akademie der Wissenschaften*

StR   *Römisches Staatsrecht*, Th. Mommsen (Leipzig, 1887–8)

Syll.³   *Sylloge Inscriptionum Graecarum³*, W. Dittenberger

TAM   *Tituli Asiae Minoris*

TAPA   *Transactions and Proceedings of the American Philological Association*

vat. fr.   *Fragmenta quae dicuntur Vaticana*

Vocabularium   *Vocabularium Iurisprudentiae Romanae*

ZSS   *Zeitschrift der Savigny-Stiftung für Rechtsgeschichte* (Romanistische Abteilung)

INTRODUCTION

ROMAN philosophers commenting on Plato's theory of punishment pointed to a motive for punishment which was not mentioned in his work. In addition to being corrective or deterrent in purpose, punishment in the Roman view could justifiably be aimed at 'the preservation of honour, when the dignity and prestige of the injured party must be protected, lest, if the offence is allowed to go by without punishment, he be brought into contempt and his honour be impaired'.[1]

Aulus Gellius, our source for the Roman view of punishment, found the absence of this motive for punishment from Plato's works, and specifically from the *Gorgias*, worthy of comment, but he did not remark on its inclusion in the writings of Roman philosophers.[2] That Roman theories of punishment were characterized by a respect for status (of which honour and prestige were attributes) would not have seemed at all remarkable to a representative of the upper stratum of a society as hierarchical in structure as Roman society. The Romans saw men as subordinated to or

---

[1] Gellius, *Noct. Att.* 7. 14. 3; cf. 9. The word τιμωρία had been applied to this aim of punishment, in supposed derivation from τιμή (*honor*).

[2] In explaining the omission of punishment *propter tuendam laesi hominis auctoritatem*, Gellius suggests, first, that Plato passed it over as trivial and worthy of contempt, and second, that he disregarded it as irrelevant in the context (Plato was writing of punishment after death). He does not deny that Plato might have entertained the concept. Nor does he state or imply elsewhere in the chapter that no other Greek philosophers before the Roman period thought of τιμή as something which in itself needed the protection of the courts. Mr. A. R. W. Harrison has suggested to me that Aristotle *may* be getting near the principle in *Nik. Eth.* 5. 4. 1131ᵇ25 ff. in his description of diorthotic justice, where on one view the status of two parties to a dispute may make a difference to the damages to be awarded in a court. This would by implication involve penalties for attacking a man's τιμή. See Harrison, *JHS* 77 (1957), 45. Further, in the γραφὴ ὕβρεως the assessed penalty would have taken account of the status of the victim of the ὕβρις which was the subject of the suit. For the *actio iniuriarum* and the importance attributed to *persona* by Roman jurists, pp. 198 ff. below. It may be suggested that τιμωρία, in Gellius' sense, had a central place in Roman penal theory and practice which it lacked in Greek. Seneca was perhaps writing in the Greek tradition when he did not include it as a motive for punishment. See *de clem.* 1. 22. 1.

raised up above one another by their involvement in conventional social relationships (so a father was placed above a son, a patron above a freedman, and a master above a slave); by their involvement in the political relationship (the magistrate was placed above the private citizen); and by their respective positions in society.

The Roman respect for status is more clearly reflected in the actions and attitudes of judicial officials than in legal theory. This book is a study of discrimination based on status in the administration of the law.[1] It does not attempt to cover all aspects of inequality before the law in the Roman setting. Virtually nothing is said about the way in which economic institutions operated to the benefit of those with property, either with the aid of the law or because of the absence of substantive legal regulation. Emphasis is placed rather on the inequalities associated with legal procedures in both civil and criminal spheres. These inequalities were of two kinds. Particular features of the legal system or procedural rules (written or unwritten) were discriminatory in effect, even if they were not designed to be so. For example, the formulary system operated under the assumption that any plaintiff could bring a defendant before the praetor at the start of a civil suit, and could, if successful, execute the sentence of the court on the defendant. No acknowledgement was made of the fact that a low-status plaintiff might find both summons and execution beyond his powers. This is an illustration of *de facto* bias in the law. In addition, men of low social rank were confronted with certain *de iure* disadvantages and disqualifications which sprang from the conscious or unconscious prejudices of judges,

---

[1] I am principally concerned with the legal privilege which derives from inequalities of prestige (*dignitas* or *honor*), rather than that which is directly connected with inequalities of wealth (see below). The class/status distinction is applied to stratification in terms of wealth and prestige respectively. It has therefore seemed proper to make use of the terminology of status rather than class in this book. In doing so, I am not committing myself to a particular standpoint on the question of whether, in the Roman case, status is reducible to economic phenomena. On class and status see *Max Weber: Economy and Society* (ed. G. Roth, C. Wittich, 1968), i. 302–7; ii. 928–36; S. Ossowski, *Class Structure in the Social Consciousness* (1963), 121–44; W. G. Runciman, in *Social Stratification* (ed. J. A. Jackson, 1968), 25 ff.

juries, and law-enforcement officers. Thus judges of criminal cases under the Empire as a regular policy applied severer penalties to defendants of low status than to defendants of high status.

The period with which I am principally concerned stretches from the age of Cicero to the age of the Severan Emperors: that is, from the mid first century B.C. to the early third century A.D. Despite the far-reaching political changes which marked this period, the structure and ethos of Roman society remained basically unaltered. The early Emperors confirmed and indeed accentuated existing social divisions. Again, although Roman legal institutions underwent transformation to suit the needs and attitudes of the new regime, there was a fundamental continuity from Republic to Empire in the spirit in which the law was administered. Thus discrimination according to status persisted, although patterns of discrimination changed in accordance with modifications in the judicial system.

Republican Romans possessed a constitution in which, theoretically, monarchical, aristocratic, and democratic elements were finely balanced. However, as Cicero acknowledged in his treatise *De Legibus*, this harmonious compromise was achieved and maintained through the submission of the people to the nobility.[1] On the democratic ideal of equality, Cicero's position was plain: 'equality is unequal when it does not recognize grades of dignity'.[2] Cicero did not enunciate any elaborate theory to support this view. He appealed, in true Roman fashion, to the *mos maiorum*, to traditional practice.

Cicero made no direct statement on the subject of juridical equality itself. At one point in the *pro Milone*, however, he reminded the jury that in Rome one set of courts existed for all criminal offenders, and that the laws which set up the courts had laid down penalties in advance for all crimes.[3] It might be thought that under a system of this kind there was little opportunity for

---

[1] Cic. *de leg.* 3. 10. 25, cf. 28.
[2] Cic. *de rep.* 1. 43: '. . . tamen ipsa aequabilitas est iniqua, cum habet nullos gradus dignitatis.'
[3] Cic. *pro Mil.* 17.

discrimination in favour of status groups, and Cicero might seem
to have sanctioned such a state of affairs. Not much is known of the
standard of justice administered by these courts, because of the
quality of the evidence. (Bribery and corruption appear to have
been rife, but this is not relevant to the present discussion, as the
Romans themselves considered bribery and corruption improper.)
But under the jury-court system favouritism could be shown to
individual defendants and to classes of defendants in two principal
ways: either the court could bring in a verdict of not-guilty
when an acquittal was not justified, or the magistrates could fail to
carry out the sentence on a defendant who had been declared
guilty. Other courts, at this time and subsequently, seem to have
taken into consideration the birth, wealth, and social position of
the parties in reaching their verdict, and it would be surprising if
juries of Republican criminal courts were oblivious of such factors.
As for the execution of sentence, there is no proof that the praetors
had low-status defendants locked up while their cases were being
considered, but allowed high-status defendants the opportunity
to go into voluntary exile before they were pronounced guilty.
But if praetors used their discretionary powers in this matter as
they used them in the realm of private law, they undoubtedly
acted in the interests of members of the higher orders, to which
they themselves belonged. Praetors, when administering the civil
laws, shielded their peers from at least one suit (the action for
fraud) which carried the risk of loss of status for the defendant,
by denying the suit to plaintiffs of low rank. Moreover, they
apparently showed no inclination to assist with the power of the
state those plaintiffs who found their attempts to summon or execute
thwarted by the superior force of more influential opponents.

   The coming of the Empire forced statesmen and theorists to
revise their political attitudes. Many senators were unable to
accept the diminished role of the Senate, and withdrew or were
forcibly withdrawn from the political scene. Tacitus was speaking
for a new breed of humbler senators when he praised the Emperor
Nerva for reconciling two irreconcilables, *principatus* and *libertas*.[1]

   [1] Tac. *Agric.* 3: '. . . Nerva Caesar res olim dissociabilis miscuerit, princi-
patum ac libertatem . . .'

Libertas means *libertas senatus*, the freedom of the Senate to operate as part of the machinery of the state. It does not stand for the democratic ideal of equality.[1] A remark of Tacitus' contemporary Pliny shows that this was still alien to the Roman political temperament. Pliny objected on one occasion that the Senate, by deciding a matter according to the wishes of the majority instead of following the views of men of wisdom (*prudentes*), was behaving like a popular assembly: 'But the majority wanted it so. For the votes were counted, not weighed. No other method can be followed in a public assembly. But nothing is so unequal as the equality associated with a public assembly, in which wisdom is not shared equally among all, but rights are.'[2] We shall see that Pliny rejected juridical equality, the equality of all citizens before the law, as easily as he rejected political equality.

With regard to the administration of the law, some features of the Republican system were not likely to survive the collapse of the oligarchy. A disguised monarchy which pursued the goals of stability, order, and efficiency would not tolerate the non-execution of judicial sentences by magistrates with the connivance of or by the instruction of the Senate, or defiance of the law on the part of powerful individuals (who, for example, refused to obey summons, ignored praetorian interdicts, or blocked the execution of a sentence). The Emperors were also, intermittently at least, hostile to bribery and corruption. Republican procedures were not abolished, however, but were allowed to die out gradually. The Emperors introduced new tribunals and a new procedure, *cognitio*.[3] This was parasitic on the jury-court system; it also proved more attractive, especially to weaker plaintiffs, than the formulary system in the civil law, administered by praetor and private judge. In time, *cognitio* was applicable in the trial of all offences, as the distinction between public crime and private delict slowly declined in importance.

[1] See Ch. Wirszubski, *Libertas* (1950), 9 ff., 136 ff.
[2] Pliny, *Ep.* 2. 12. 5: 'Sed hoc pluribus visum est. Numerantur enim sententiae, non ponderantur; nec aliud in publico consilio potest fieri, in quo nihil est tam inaequale quam aequalitas ipsa. Nam cum sit impar prudentia, par omnium ius est.'
[3] R. Orestano, *St. Cagl.* 26 (1938), 153; M. Lemosse, *Cognitio* (1944).

Jury-court procedure was accusatorial. The praetor simply presided over the contest between accuser and accused and pronounced the verdict of the jury. The *cognitio* procedure, on the other hand, was inquisitorial, and gave immense power to the judge. He sought and questioned witnesses, and interrogated the accused. Before passing sentence he regularly consulted his advisers, but was not bound by their counsel. As for the sentence itself, as Ulpian wrote, 'he may issue the sentence which pleases him, be it relatively severe or relatively mild, so long as he stays within the limits defined by reason'.[1] The judge was able to vary the penalty according to the gravity of the crime and according to his own social prejudices. Further, because limits were prescribed by reason and not law, he was free to choose penalties not recognized by the law, penalties which in earlier times had been used almost entirely against free aliens and slaves, who stood outside the civil law. The consequence was the emergence of a dual-penalty system under the Empire, according to which, broadly speaking, the 'legal' penalties were applied to the higher orders, and the administrative sanctions (which were severer and more degrading) to the lower orders.

Cognitio, as the procedure most characteristic of the Empire, receives the lion's share of attention in this study. With the introduction of courts which operated according to the *cognitio* procedure, a number of tribunals were capable of handling most cases. In Part I, the hypothesis that the choice of court was of consequence for the defendant is investigated. It may be possible to establish that there were upper-level and lower-level tribunals in Rome, which dealt with disputes involving members of the higher orders and members of the lower orders, respectively. Part II explores the dual-penalty system, which originated, as already stated, in the flexibility of penalty which was a distinctive feature of the *cognitio* procedure. Because of the nature of the evidence, the material in these two sections is drawn in large part from the criminal law.

---

[1] *Dig.* 48. 19. 13: 'Hodie licet ei, qui extra ordinem de crimine cognoscit, quam vult sententiam ferre, vel graviorem vel leviorem, ita tamen ut in utroque modo rationem non excedat.'

Part III is devoted to the formulary procedure of the civil law. It demonstrates the wide variety of ways in which the procedure itself, and the magistrates and judges who administered it, denied equal protection and equal rights to those who were regarded as socially undesirable or simply inferior. The section dealing with the private judge is not only relevant to the formulary system. It is concerned with the influences to which the judge was subjected in the course of the trial itself, as he listened to the pleas of the accused, the prosecutor, their advocates, and their witnesses. These pressures were felt equally by the private judge and the *cognitio* judge, and it is unnecessary to discuss them twice.

Legal procedures cannot be studied in isolation from the social environment which engendered them. In Part IV it is argued that the criteria for legal privilege were social and dependent upon status.

The relevant sources are both legal and non-legal. For the Antonine and Severan periods, we are dependent on the juristic writings assembled in the *Digest* of Justinian and other late compilations. The *Digest* was compiled by a commission appointed by the Emperor Justinian in A.D. 530. The editors' aim was not to transmit faithfully select portions of the works of the classical lawyers. On the contrary, their declared intention was to bring simplicity and intelligibility to a vast collection of material which, because of its size, lack of symmetry, and many inconsistencies, posed problems for the practising lawyers of the day. It took almost exactly three years to put together this massive work. Considering the conception and scope of the work and the way it was assembled, it would clearly be unreasonable for us to reject out-of-hand the hypothesis that the *Digest* as we have it is full of emendations, interpolations, and errors. (There is, moreover, no assurance that the original texts reached the compilers without undergoing alteration.) However, the search for additions and corruptions which dominated Roman legal studies in the late nineteenth and early twentieth centuries was taken to extremes. (In reaction, some modern scholars have based assertions about the attitudes and

careers of jurists entirely on stylistic usage.[1]) The contemporary
student of Roman history or Roman law has been forced by the
interpolation hunters to be cautious and critical in his investigations and reconstructions.[2] At the same time, he should recognize
that the compilers were unsuccessful if they sought to purge
anachronisms and expunge historical details which for lawyers
of the sixth century could only have had curiosity-value. For example, many administrative terms which occur in the *Digest*, and
many names of officials and institutions, are familiar from other
sources for the second and third centuries.[3] This must provide encouragement to anyone seeking to discover the drift of
Ulpian's or Paulus' thought. It may be that even the *ipsissima
verba* of a jurist are not beyond recovery, although this is inevitably a matter of dispute. Each case should be settled on its
merits.

The *Digest* contains few items of importance from the pre-
Hadrianic period, and the earliest entry in the *Code* (of Justinian)
is Hadrianic.[4] We must turn to historical and biographical (non-
legal) sources for information about the first century of the Empire.
The interests of the non-legal and the legal sources differed
markedly. While the non-legal sources (those from which we
derive any help on the relevant questions) were mainly centred on
Rome, the concerns of the Antonine and Severan jurists were
Empire-wide. For example, the sections in the *Digest* that relate

---

[1] See A. M. Honoré, *Gaius* (1962), introd. xiii ff.; 'The Severan Lawyers:
A Preliminary Survey', *Studia et documenta historiae et iuris* 28 (1962), 162 ff.
For a moderate view, W. W. Buckland, *Harvard Law Review* 54 (1941),
1273 ff.

[2] Errors and inconsistencies are to be expected. See, e.g., *Dig.* 1. 6. 2 (end),
with *Coll.* 3. 3. 4; *Dig.* 5. 1. 37 (Hadrian), with 48. 6. 5. 1 (Pius); 48. 8. 1. 5,
with 48. 5. 39. 8; 47. 21. 2, with *Coll.* 13. 3. 2; etc.

[3] e.g. *princeps, proconsul, procurator, curator, aedilis, praetor, aerarium, fiscus,
iudicium publicum, poena legis, interdictio aqua et igni, concilium* (sc. *provinciae*),
imperium, eques Romanus, ius Italicum, etc.

[4] *Cf* 6. 23. 1. But see 9. 21. 1 (Visellian law, Tib.); 9. 23. 3 (Claud.); 8. 10. 2
(Vesp.). There are one or two early items in the *Collatio* (late fourth century),
e.g. 15. 2. 1 (citing a *S.C.* of A.D. 17). Early Imperial pronouncements in the
Digest include: 14. 2. 9; 16. 1. 2 praef.; 23. 2. 14. 4; 28. 2. 26; 48. 18. 1 praef.;
ibid. 8 praef. (all Aug.); 48. 5. 39. 10 (Tib.); 4. 4. 3. 4; 16. 1. 2. praef.; 37. 14. 5;
40. 8. 2; 48. 10. 14. 2; ibid. 15 praef. (all Claud.); 37. 14. 7 praef.; 50. 4. 18. 30
(Vesp.); 48. 3. 2. 1; 48. 16. 16 (Dom.). See G. Hänel, *Corpus legum ab imperatoribus Romanis ante Iustinianum latarum* (1857).

to criminal jurisdiction deal largely with the administration of justice outside Rome, and especially in the provinces. Thus the decurion, or the local councillor of an Italian or provincial city, is taken as the type of the man of honour and dignity who was favoured in the law courts. It is not surprising that senators and equestrians, who were presumably similarly favoured, are hardly mentioned. In contrast, most of the legal activity recorded by Tacitus and other historians took place in Rome. As a result, it is these sources which provide the best evidence for the privileged position of senators and equestrians. (Their testimony is confirmed by stray references from later literary works of history or biography which share the orientation of the first-century sources but do not match their quality.) This evidence should, moreover, equip us for interpreting some of the key legal texts. To give an illustration, instances of variation of penalty in accordance with status, which occur in a few legal texts from the reigns of Hadrian and Pius, do not appear novel when set beside instances cited by Tacitus or Pliny of lenient treatment of senatorial and equestrian defendants in comparison with that of defendants of low rank. In general, most obstacles to a correct understanding of the way in which legal privilege developed during our period (and especially in the central part of it) are removed if the contrast between the emphases and approaches of the two groups of sources is kept in mind. Thus, for instance, the awareness that the interests of the first-century sources were focused on Rome should reduce any inclination we might have to believe that Hadrian's prohibition of the execution of decurions for murder transformed the decurions into a privileged order. (Such a view would not in any case survive an examination of the immediate context of the ruling and an exploration of the social background.)

One final remark should be made on the subject of the legal sources, and this also relates to the question of the evolution of certain types of legal discrimination. If legal discrimination was thoroughgoing, and the evidence suggests that it was, it is odd that there was no concentrated treatment of the subject by any classical jurist, and that no section of either *Digest* or *Code* was devoted to it. The details have to be gathered piecemeal from the writings of the jurists. It is certain that there are many omissions. How is the anomaly to be explained? The answer lies in the informal nature of a system which was grounded not in legislative enactment, but in administrative rules, customary practices, and ultimately the social attitudes of the ruling élite.

PART I
COURTS

INTRODUCTION

ACCORDING to Roman law, a defendant was impeached in his place of birth or domicile: *actor sequitur forum rei*.[1] This rule existed both during the period under consideration, the classical age of Roman law, and the late Empire. However, a great deal more is known about the content of the rule and the way in which it operated in the later period than in the earlier.[2] Excerpts from jurists of the Antonine and Severan period are cited in the chapter of the *Digest* entitled 'On courts: where it is proper to sue or to be sued', and the subject with which they are principally concerned is potentially significant. It is the question whether *forum rei*, or the *ius fori*, applied in all circumstances.[3] But the instances that are chosen for discussion are of limited interest, particularly to the legal historian.[4] Moreover, the discussion is relevant only to the civil law. Were it not for a solitary citation of Severan date in Justinian's *Code*, we should be unaware that defendants on criminal charges could be tried where their alleged crimes had been committed, rather than where they were domiciled.[5] Finally, no attention is given in the *Digest* to a variation of the *forum rei* principle, *praescriptio fori*, according to which, in the fourth, fifth, and sixth centuries, at any rate, certain kinds of offences, and certain privileged categories of offenders (for example, palatines,

---

[1] *Dig.* 2. 8. 7 praef.; 5. 1. 65; 5. 2. 29. 4; *vat. fr.* 325-6 (A.D. 293-4); *CJ* 3. 13. 2 (A.D. 293); *CTh* 2. 1. 4 (A.D. 364); *CJ* 3. 13. 5 (A.D. 397); etc. See Kipp, *RE* 7 (1912), 59 ff. s.v. *forum*.

[2] This appears to be one case where the Justinianic compilers have been relatively successful in purging the treatises of the classical jurists of items of historical interest.   [3] *Dig.* 5. 1; cf. *CJ* 2. 13-26; *CTh* 2. 1.

[4] e.g. it is asked whether provincials involved in contract-disputes, where the contracts were entered into outside their province, possessed the *ius revocandi domum* or *ius fori* (*Dig.* 5. 1. 2. 4); and whether provincials in Rome as envoys or witnesses were obliged to appear before the praetor in response to a summons (ibid. 5). Such passages cannot be compared, either in subject-matter or vitality, with the Imperial constitutions relevant to *praescriptio fori* which are preserved in the Codes of Theodosius and Justinian. See p. 14 n. 1 below.

[5] *CJ* 3. 15. 1 (A.D. 196). The closing words, *notum est*, imply that Severus and Caracalla were referring to an established rule. Cf. *CTh* 9. 1. 1 (A.D. 316).

senators, soldiers) were dealt with by special tribunals. It would be surprising if privileges of this type had no parallel in the first three centuries of the Empire.[1]

In the discussion that follows, an attempt is made to establish the existence in the classical period of the equivalent of the *praescriptio fori* of the late Empire. We can make a beginning by considering the situation that existed in Rome under the Empire where a legal contest between two residents of the city (to take the simplest case) could be decided by more than one court.[2] In the Severan age (the floruit of most of the jurists from whose works the *Digest* title on courts was compiled), if the dispute was a civil one, it could in principle be heard and settled, on the one hand by praetor and private judge (through the two-stage formulary process), and on the other hand by one of a number of magistrates and officials, including even the Emperor (through the *cognitio* procedure). Crimes in the same period were dealt with in Rome by the urban prefect, curule magistrates, the Senate, and the Emperor (the *quaestiones*, or public jury-courts, were no longer active). How were civil and criminal cases apportioned among the Imperial courts? If the first initiative in choosing a court lay with the *petitor*, or accuser, it still remained for the official who had been approached to decide whether or not to take the case—and, perhaps, for the accused to 'decline' the court and opt for another, if he had any choice in the matter.[3] An attempt is made below to discover which rules, if any, lay behind the distribution of cases,

[1] The expression *praescriptio fori* occurs in *Dig.* 2. 8. 7 praef. (Ulpian, referring to a judgement of Pius). For the fourth century and later, see A. H. M. Jones, *Later Roman Empire* (1966), 484 ff.; M. Kaser, *Das römische Zivilprozessrecht* (1966), 474, n. 19; 478, n. 28; etc.

[2] In the sphere of criminal justice under the Republic there was one set of courts, the *quaestiones*, or jury-courts, for all criminal offenders. In addition, claimants seeking redress for private injury or loss had no alternative but to approach the praetor and ask for an action according to the formulary procedure. The situation was transformed under the Empire with the emergence of courts and tribunals which administered justice by the *cognitio* procedure. These courts were competent to try cases in both areas in the law.

[3] The phrase *forum declinare* occurs in *CTh* 9. 7. 9. For the verbs *eiurare* and *reiicere* see *JRS* 56 (1966), 182–3. On *reiectio Romam* see pp. 263–4, below. This was a right of Roman citizens to defend themselves in litigation in Rome. We learn from non-legal sources that Roman citizens may still have possessed this privilege towards the end of the Republic, and perhaps even as late as the age of the Julio-Claudian Emperors.

and to ascertain whether the social position of the accused was one factor that was taken into consideration. It is also asked whether the social position of either party influenced the outcome of trials. Attention is concentrated on criminal jurisdiction, which is better documented than civil jurisdiction, and on courts in Rome and Italy, where the jurisdiction of courts overlapped to a greater degree than elsewhere, and to which the interest of most of the sources was directed.

The following courts tried criminal cases in Rome at some stage in the period from Augustus to the Severans, and receive some mention below: the courts of the Emperor, the Senate, the urban prefect, the praetorian prefect, and the curule magistrates, and the jury-courts. (The provincial governors' courts are considered in conjunction with the Emperor's jurisdiction, for reasons that will become apparent.) Not all the above courts merit lengthy consideration, and of some no detailed treatment is possible. The whole section revolves around the senatorial and Imperial courts, which are the best known to us and also of central interest and importance, both from a legal and a political viewpoint; courts such as that of the prefect of the city and the jury-courts play a minor role in the discussion. No attempt is made to describe in detail the rise or decline of any court. The history and character of a court are only investigated when they bear upon the problem of whether the court system in Rome gave unequal treatment to high-status and low-status defendants.

1

THE SENATORIAL COURT UNDER THE JULIO-CLAUDIANS

THE sources for the Julio-Claudian period, as is well known, are preoccupied with the fortunes of Emperors and their conflicts with the Senate. Moreover, the central narrative of politics and court intrigue in Tacitus' *Annals*, for example, is broken by descriptions of foreign wars rather than by discussions of administrative or legal developments. On the infrequent occasions when items of administrative interest are brought up, the office of the urban prefect, or the peculiar position of Egypt among the provinces of the Empire, they are dealt with in all too brief excursuses.[1] Only those aspects of legal affairs are discussed which are intimately related to politics.[2]

The result is an imbalance in the evidence for the administration of the criminal law. Allusions to the activities of the public jury-courts are few, just sufficient to indicate that these courts, or some of them, still existed; and the even rarer references to dispensation of justice by the urban prefect reveal the existence of a tribunal about which we should otherwise have been quite ignorant. In contrast, the senatorial court is comparatively well documented. The reason must be that judicial murder and the fall of important personages, which were directly relevant to the main theme, were commonly accomplished in the senatorial court; whereas the jury-courts and the urban prefect could not have handled political offenders, or, at any rate, those of high status, after Augustan times. Again, while a great deal can be discovered about political trials in the Senate, less is known of some subsidiary functions which the Senate undoubtedly exercised: notably, the

---

[1] Tac. *Ann.* 6. 11 (prefect); 2. 59, cf. *Hist.* 1. 11 (Egypt).
[2] The theme of *Ann.* 26–8 is misuse of law by politicians.

punishment of conspicuous or scandalous crimes committed
against senators, and the punishment of conspicuous or scandalous
crimes *tout court*. But did the Senate occupy itself with the investigation of the 'ordinary' crimes of senators (and perhaps
equestrians)? Or was this the business of other courts, those which
are normally assumed to have dealt with 'plebeian' criminals on
most charges, the prefect and the jury-courts?[1] It may be possible
to answer questions such as these, and in general to achieve a
balanced view of the relationship between the different courts.

Type of charge and status of defendant

In a recent study Bleicken has argued that the senatorial court
was no mere 'Pairsgericht'; that is to say, the court did not concern
itself exclusively with the trial of senatorial criminals. Tiberius
gave it the responsibility of punishing crimes against the state,
whether they were committed by senators, equestrians, or foreign
princes. Conversely, Bleicken observes, it was possible for senators
to be tried in the *quaestiones*, for as long as the *quaestio*-system
existed.[2]

These statements are sound, as far as they go. Bleicken is right
to admit the possibility that senators might appear as defendants
in the public courts. However, it may be felt that a more informative conclusion could be reached if a close study were made of the
evidence for the Senate's jurisdiction in the field of non-political
crime.

Again, the accounts of treason trials in the primary sources
justify the conclusion that the senatorial court was not a 'Pairs-
gericht' (in the sense defined above). But Bleicken had previously
noted that the Senate, in the reign of Tiberius, was able to try
any criminal case which a public court was competent to try.[3]
If what induced the Senate to meet as a court on any occasion was
'only its interest in the case', then the possibility is left open that,

---

[1] See, recently, W. Kunkel, *An Introduction to Roman Legal and Constitutional History* (1966), 67–70.

[2] J. Bleicken, *Senatsgericht und Kaisergericht* (1962), espec. 53–4.

[3] Ibid. 43 fin. Bleicken's account is misleading in that it is implied that the
first recorded trials for adultery, etc., were followed by others. This cannot be
shown in some cases involving, e.g., *vis* of officials and sacrilege.

standard political crimes such as treason and extortion excepted, the senatorial court was a 'Pairsgericht'. This hypothesis is surely worth investigation.

Finally, whether senatorial defendants could expect a senatorial trial in respect of any charge, or some charges, is only one issue, the interest of which is limited unless it is linked with another: to what extent was it an advantage for a senator to be tried by his peers in the period of the Julio-Claudian Emperors? It is also relevant and important to inquire into the circumstances in which non-senators were brought before the Senate as defendants, and to see how they fared in comparison with senatorial defendants.

Thus Bleicken's account provides a useful starting-point, but a more detailed analysis is called for of the issues which he raises. The first task is to arrive at some estimate of the extent of the Senate's jurisdiction, and to explain which principles governed the Senate's handling of some cases and not others.

In A.D. 15 Tiberius was asked by a praetor, presumably the praetor responsible for the *quaestio de maiestate*, whether he should accept *maiestas* charges.[1] The reply, 'the laws must be administered' (*exercendas leges esse*), seems to carry the implication that Tiberius envisaged the holding of *maiestas* trials in the *quaestio*. However, to judge by the number of such trials which were staged in the Senate, it is difficult to believe that more than the barest trickle of cases went to the *quaestio*.[2] It must have been virtually automatic for accusers to lodge accusations of *maiestas* with the consul or Emperor rather than the praetor, and for the accusations, once accepted, to be heard in the Senate. The Senate took these cases because it was pre-eminently responsible for the punishment of crimes against the state.

While members of all ranks could be and were prosecuted for *maiestas*, only a restricted circle of persons were liable to charges of

---

[1] Tac. *Ann.* 1. 72. On *maiestas* (treason) see now R. Bauman, *The Crimen Maiestatis* (1967), 1 ff.

[2] Tac. *Ann.* 3. 38: 'addito maiestatis crimine, quod tum omnium accusationum complementum erat.' For evidence of the operation of the *quaestio de maiestate* under Augustus see Dio 53. 23 (Cornelius Gallus: the Senate, sc., passed the case to the *quaestio*); 54. 3 (M. Primus); Suet. *Tib.* 8 (Fannius Caepio). One kind of case not mentioned in the sources for the post-Augustan period which might have gone to the *quaestio* is the impeachment of a plebeian for an offence committed by himself as principal (not as a mere accomplice). Cf. Suet. *Aug.* 51.

repetundae. *Repetundae* involved basically but not solely the extortion of money from provincials.[1] Naturally the men most commonly accused on this account were provincial governors. The *quaestio de repetundis*, in company with the *quaestio de maiestate*, must have been underemployed in the Julio-Claudian period.[2] *Repetundae* trials as well as treason trials were held almost entirely in the Senate.[3] The explanation in each case lies in the nature of the crime. *Repetundae* was not a crime against the state. Nevertheless, it could be regarded as a 'political' offence, as committed by an official in the course of his duties. But the assigning of extortion trials to the Imperial Senate has a special significance which should not be missed. Pro-magistrates or governors were drawn from the membership of the Senate. The posts themselves were highpoints (some more so than others) in the senatorial *cursus*. But they were sought after not simply for the distinctions which they conferred on the holders, but also for the opportunities they afforded for recouping financial losses incurred in campaigning for and holding office in Rome. The senators who sat in judgement over a particular governor were well aware of the temptations to which all governors were subject. Most of them would have anticipated facing the same temptations at some time in the future, if they had not faced them already. Thus even if they disapproved of the conduct of the man impeached by his provincial subjects, they might none the less have felt for him a measure of tolerance and understanding. It must have been a source of some comfort to a governor under the Empire to know that he would be tried by his peers, just as it would have been for a Republican governor before the reforms of Gaius Gracchus to know that the Senate or senators would be sitting in judgement over him.[4] As Gracchus'

---

[1] For the content of the *repetundae* law see, e.g., P. A. Brunt, *Historia* 10 (1961), 191–3.

[2] For early signs of senatorial jurisdiction in *repetundae* cases see *S.C. Calvisianum* (*EJ* 311. v (5 B.C.): procedures for compensation), and probably the trial of Volesus Messalla (Tac. *Ann.* 3. 68: Tiberius wrote *libelli* concerning his behaviour to the Senate, which at some stage passed an *S.C.* against him. The charge was *repetundae* plus *saevitia*, cruelty).

[3] Exception: Dio 60. 33. 5, and see p. 86.

[4] Gracchus transferred control of the jury-court (set up by the Calpurnian law of 149 B.C.) from senators to equestrians. See Vell. Pat. 2. 6. 3; 2. 13; 2. 32; App. *BC* 1. 22; etc.; and P. A. Brunt, *2nd Intern. Conf. of Econ. Hist. 1962*

legislation struck a blow at the narrow senatorial interest, so the Senate's recapture of control over *repetundae* trials in the Imperial period was a victory for that interest.[1]

A third crime which was tried in the Senate with some degree of regularity was adultery.[2] Why were adultery trials held in the Senate? Adultery was not a political crime in any obvious sense, although Augustus had emphasized that adultery with a princess of the royal house was akin to *maiestas*.[3]

We should note first that an adultery charge was sometimes linked with more sinister charges like magic or *maiestas*.[4] In Tiberius' reign such counts were easily tacked on to the main one, and, when the Emperor was in command of the situation and of himself, as easily discarded.[5] During his prolonged absence at Capri, however, the additional charges tended to stand, and were the means of securing either the execution or the suicide of the accused. Behind most adultery cases of this kind lay the private animosity towards the defendants of men whose political star was for the time being in the ascendant. Sejanus engineered the impeachment of Agrippina's cousin, Claudia Pulchra, and Macro was responsible for the attack on Mamercus Aemilius Scaurus and Albucilla (together with her bevy of followers of senatorial rank).[6]

(1965), i. 141 ff. (= *The Crisis of the Roman Republic*, ed. R. Seager, 1969, 107 ff.). For most of the first century B.C. and under the Empire, the majority of jurors in the *quaestio de repetundis* (as was the case in other *quaestiones*) were non-senators. For *repetundae* trials before the Imperial Senate see Dio Chrys. *Or*. 34. 9: the accusation is περὶ ἡγεμόνων . . . πρὸς ἡγεμόνας.

[1] Cf. Brunt, *Historia* 10 (1961), 199.

[2] The only references to adultery trials in the *quaestio de adulteriis* are Dio 54. 30. 4 (Aug.), and probably Tac. *Ann*. 38 (Tib.).

[3] Tac. *Ann*. 3. 24. Cf. 2. 50: the accuser of Appuleia Varilla included adultery as part of the *maiestas* charge on the grounds that Varilla was a niece of Augustus' sister. But Tiberius ruled that the adultery charge should be considered separately, under the adultery law. See also ibid. 11. 12: adultery of C. Silius with the wife of Claudius, Messalina, could clearly be regarded as treason, even before it led into marriage (11. 26 ff.). See also 15. 50: Tigellinus' charge against Faenius Rufus.

[4] See nn. 3 and 6 for references to trials of Appuleia Varilla, Claudia Pulchra, Mamercus Aemilius Scaurus, Albucilla *et al*.

[5] See pp. 37 ff., below. The *maiestas* charge against Varilla was dropped.

[6] Pulchra: ibid. 4. 52 (note that after Agrippina had taken her life, Tiberius taunted her for having committed adultery with Asinius Gallus, ibid. 6. 25); Scaurus: ibid. 6. 29; Albucilla, etc.: ibid. 6. 47–8, cf. Dio 58. 27. 2. Cf. 6. 40: the Aemilia Lepida who schemed with Sejanus for the removal of her husband

In short, while adultery may have been in essence a non-political crime, an adultery trial could be launched for political ends.[1]

Yet the adultery trial would not have been an effective weapon of political intrigue if the Senate had not been interested in the punishment of conspicuous moral lapses in themselves. In A.D. 19, according to Tacitus, a certain Vistilia was tried by the Senate and exiled to the island of Seriphos. A daughter of a senator of praetorian rank, she had tried to register herself with the aediles as a prostitute.[2] In the same chapter Tacitus mentions the expulsion of 'Egyptian sacred rites' from Italy. This is an oblique reference to a scandal described in some detail by Josephus, which involved an equestrian Decius Mundus, a noble Roman lady Paulina, and priests of the cult of Isis. The culprits were punished presumably under the adultery law, and the cult expelled.[3] Again, Suetonius refers to an undated trial involving one Gaius Laetorius. Nothing is known of the background to the trial. He was a patrician, and this may be sufficient explanation of the bringing of the indictment.[4] Finally, Aquilia and her lover Varius Ligur were condemned in what was apparently a simple adultery trial.[5]

I would suggest that adultery cases went to the Senate primarily because of the special significance which first Augustus and then Tiberius attached to the adultery law. It seems that the law, which was Augustus' creation, was seen by both Emperors as of outstanding importance for the preservation of the social and political order. Augustus made the law the basis of his social legislation designed to rehabilitate marriage; he wrote into the law sanctions

Drusus Caesar was a victim of the enemies of Sejanus. No political charge against her is recorded. Yet she took her own life—perhaps adultery with a slave was a more serious crime than simple adultery and earned a capital sentence.

[1] Cf. ibid. 14. 62–4: Octavia, wife of Nero, was exiled and later forced to die. Whether the Senate or the Emperor condemned her is not known; ibid. 11. 2 ff.: Valerius Asiaticus was tried by Claudius on charges that included adultery. Presumably both charges were baseless.   [2] Ibid. 2. 85.

[3] Jos. AJ 18, 65 ff. Josephus' account implies that Tiberius himself tried the offenders and pronounced judgement on them. It is more likely that he sent the case to the Senate and took a leading part in the investigation.

[4] Suet. Aug. 5.   [5] Tac. Ann. 4. 42.

of enhanced severity; and he enforced the law within his own family. Tiberius, for his part, showed a preparedness to punish offenders with some strictness.

But not all adultery trials are likely to have been held in the Senate. Almost all the cases referred to above involved defendants of senatorial stock, as far as can be ascertained.[1] This would suggest that the Emperors were primarily concerned with the morals of the nobility; and the fact that the Augustan marriage laws forbade only marriages between members of the senatorial order on the one hand, and freedmen, freedwomen, and those of degraded family or profession on the other, serves to reinforce this notion.[2]

The alternative is to hold that the sources omitted to mention a whole group of senatorial trials involving non-senators as principals in cases covered by the Julian law on adultery. The scandal of A.D. 19 offers no support to this theory, even though the accused on this occasion were an equestrian, a freedwoman, and presumably foreign priests. The dignity of a noble woman and her distinguished husband (probably one of the consular Sentii Saturnini) had been outraged, and a prompt revenge was due. Moreover, Tiberius and the Senate saw the cult of Isis, which in the person of its priests had connived at the crime, as a menace to the state religion.[3] The prosecution of Sextus Marius, the Spanish provincial, for incest (a crime probably punished under the adultery law at this time) also had special features. We may not believe Dio's story that Marius' daughter was desired by Tiberius and kept from him by the father. But the earlier friendship between the two men, the measures taken against the property of the condemned man, and his cruel punishment strongly suggest that Tiberius was deeply involved in Marius' destruction, if he was not actually behind it. If so, it is not at all surprising that the case was, first, sent to Rome from the province, and second, tried before the senatorial

---

[1] This is true certainly of C. Laetorius, Scaurus, Varilla, Vistilia, Pulchra, and Lepida, and probably of Aquilia. Albucilla's status is not known, nor that of her ex-husband, Satrius Secundus (described simply as Sejanus' henchman, e.g. ibid. 4. 34). But in any case her lovers included several eminent senators.

[2] *Dig.* 23. 2. 44.

[3] On the case see Jos. *AJ* 18. 65 ff., and R. S. Rogers, *Criminal Trials and Criminal Legislation under Tiberius* (1935), 34 ff.

tribunal.[1] I would conclude that the fates of the bulk of the defendants from the lower orders were settled, like that of the Macedonian Antistius Vetus, in the *quaestio de adulteriis*, if by a court at Rome at all.[2]

Finally, the relative absence of reference to simple adultery indictments against ordinary members of the senatorial order deserves comment. Perhaps the sources were selective and passed over the more routine senatorial investigations. Even allowing for a few such indictments, it still seems likely that there was no even enforcement of the adultery law within the senatorial order—if 'enforcement' is the word, for Tiberius launched no 'crusade' against adultery in the higher orders, and the private prosecutors, who alone could have carried out such a project, were already fully employed in a more lofty mission, that of protecting the Emperor against challenges to his *maiestas*.[3] Some political scores were settled, as we have seen, through adultery trials. Otherwise probably only those offenders were punished who caught the eye: on the one hand, those whose immorality was conspicuous because of their distinguished birth and ancestry, and on the other hand those who openly advertised their dissolute lives.[4]

There are some grounds for believing that with treason, extortion, and adultery, we have exhausted the list of crimes in which the Senate showed a regular interest. This is supported by the account of the trial of Cn. Calpurnius Piso in A.D. 20 to be found in Tacitus' *Annals*. Piso expected to be tried before the *quaestio de (sicariis et) veneficiis* on the charge of poisoning Germanicus. For when Vibius Marsus urged him in a letter to come to Rome to plead his cause, Piso wrote in reply:

> adfuturum ubi praetor qui de veneficiis quaereret reo atque accusatoribus diem prodixisset.[5]

---

[1] Tac. *Ann.* 6. 19, cf. Dio 58. 22. We may conjecture that the Senate might have been prepared to take up cases against non-senators which arose out of a specific *S.C.*, such as that relating to equestrians in Tac. *Ann.* 2. 85. 1.

[2] Ibid. 3. 38 (Vetus). I take it as probable that *iudicibus* here refers to the jurymen of a *quaestio*. It is not known why Vetus was tried at Rome for adultery.

[3] Cf. Dio 76. 14. 4 (Septimius Severus).

[4] Apart from Tac. *Ann.* 2. 85, see Suet. *Tib.* 35.

[5] 'that he would be there when the praetor in charge of poisoning cases had fixed a day for the accused and his prosecutors'. Tac. *Ann.* 2. 79.

But the investigation was held in the Senate as a concession to Germanicus, although Tiberius recognized that this was irregular. In his own words (or those attributed to him by Tacitus) he acknowledged that in ordering it he was not acting in accordance with the dictates of the law:

id solum Germanico super leges praestiterimus, quod in curia potius quam in foro, apud senatum quam apud iudices de morte eius anquiritur . . .[1]

This statement would have been without point if the procedure had not been not only irregular, but also out of the ordinary.

The charge against Piso was certainly an unusual one. His alleged victim was Tiberius' adopted son, to whom the Senate had granted *imperium* superior to that of any provincial governor. Moreover, Tiberius was inclined to believe that Piso's military activities in the East were not far removed from *civile bellum*. *Maiestas* seems to have been a subsidiary charge. It is therefore surprising, not that the case was referred to the Senate, but that the case was not automatically sent to the Senate. At any rate, it seems legitimate to infer from the statements of Piso and Tiberius that a murder trial of lesser importance involving a senator as defendant would have been held in the *quaestio*.[2]

It is instructive to compare the trial of Piso with trials of other alleged murderers before the Senate. Livilla was convicted in A.D. 31 of a crime committed eight years earlier, the murder of Drusus, her husband and Tiberius' natural son. She was also suspected of complicity in the 'conspiracy' of Sejanus.[3] In A.D. 23 Rhescuporis, the Thracian king, was brought to Rome and condemned in the Senate. The murder of his nephew and rival Cotys was only one

---

[1] 'In this only we raise Germanicus above the laws, by inquiring into his death in the senate-house rather than in the forum, before the Senate rather than before a jury.' Ibid. 3. 12. Tiberius was asked to undertake the investigation himself, but after a preliminary hearing, he passed the whole matter to the Senate. Ibid. 3. 10.

[2] The Augustan evidence shows that the *quaestio* was used in the earlier period. See Sen. *Contr.* 2. 5. 13 (Moschus, c. 20 B.C.); Suet. *Aug.* 56 (Nonius Asprenas); Dio 56. 24 (a quaestor, under A.D. 10).

[3] Dio 58. 11. 7; 57. 22. 2 and 4; Suet. *Tib.* 62. 1. Cf. Tac. *Ann.* 12. 65: the destruction of Domitia Lepida, Nero's aunt, for allegedly seeking to kill the Emperor's wife, Agrippina, by magic (and for offences against order). The location of the trial is not known.

of his crimes—he had upset Augustus' settlement of Thrace by taking up arms, and had disregarded Tiberius' order to lay them down again.[1] In A.D. 24, the urban praetor M. Plautius Silvanus threw his wife out of a window. An irate father-in-law reported the crime to the Emperor. The matter was referred to the Senate, once Tiberius had satisfied himself that the woman had not committed suicide. What followed is unclear: perhaps a trial in the Senate, perhaps an investigation by a committee of the Senate.[2] Finally, from the reign of Nero, in A.D. 61 the murder of the urban prefect Pedanius Secundus by one of his slaves led to a senatorial investigation.[3]

The charges against Livilla and Rhescuporis bear some resemblance to those which Piso faced, and were 'political' in an obvious, accepted sense. That they were heard in the Senate is not hard to understand. Next, the murder of any master by a slave was traditionally regarded as an outrage which threatened the existence of the Roman social order. It was therefore punished with the utmost cruelty. But presumably not every case of this kind was investigated by the Senate. On this occasion a *consularis vir* had been killed, and the retaliatory execution of the slaves 'under the same roof' (*sub eodem tecto*) was carried out by the senators to deter others from attacking their dignity (*sua dignitas*).[4] Murder by a praetor, while perhaps insignificant in the eyes of senators beside the murder of a prefect, was hardly an admirable example of magisterial conduct. In passing the case to the Senate Tiberius might have been guided, both by the conviction that the crime was a grave one (because of the person of the criminal), and by the feeling that only the Senate should try a magistrate (as it habitually tried pro-magistrates).[5]

---

[1] Tac. *Ann.* 2. 64–7.

[2] Ibid. 4. 22. The correct interpretation of 'refert ad senatum, datisque iudicibus' is uncertain. For the trial of Numantina that followed see n. 5 below.

[3] Ibid. 14. 42 ff.

[4] For other indications that the Senate was concerned to guard its dignity see p. 32.

[5] After Silvanus committed suicide, his former wife Numantina was accused of driving him mad through the use of magic. This trial was conducted in the Senate presumably because of its close relationship with the previous one. Numantina's alleged offence fell under the Cornelian law *de sicariis et veneficiis*.

In sum, the Senate can only be shown to have handled murder charges which were coupled with *maiestas* charges and were themselves not far removed from *maiestas* charges, or which were unusual because of the status or office of the victim or agent. That senators accused of 'simple' homicide were also tried in the Senate in this period is theoretically possible. The large lacunae in the narrative of Tacitus may account for their absence. Or Tacitus and the other sources might not have bothered to mention such cases because of their relative unimportance. However, the excerpts quoted from Piso's letter to Marsus and from Tiberius' speech to the Senate appear to contradict that hypothesis. Most of those accused of homicide, whatever their status, would seem to have met their trial in the court where Piso anticipated facing his accusers, the *quaestio*.[1]

To turn now to *falsum*, a trial of A.D. 61, described by Tacitus, is of central importance. The will of an old and wealthy senator had been forged. The prosecutor, Valerius Ponticus, had approached the praetor in charge of the *quaestio de falsis*, but was caught negotiating with the defence, and the case was transferred to the senatorial court. There is an oddity in the fact that while Ponticus was obeying the letter of the law in taking the case to the *quaestio* —this he did, in Tacitus' words, *specie legum*—it was necessary for him to avoid the prefect's court to do so. The crucial sentence runs:

> pari ignominia Valerius Ponticus adficitur quod reos ne apud praefectum urbis arguerentur ad praetorem detulisset, interim specie legum, mox praevaricando ultionem elusurus.[2]

One point which cannot fail to strike the reader of Tacitus' narrative is the degree of freedom which potential litigants (in

---

[1] According to Sen. *Contr.* 9. 5. 15 ff., Numisia Galla was tried for the attempted murder of her father before the centumviral court. This is the only sign that the *centumviri* ever sat over criminal cases of any description.

[2] 'Valerius Ponticus suffered the same degradation for having indicted the defendants before the praetor to save them from prosecution in the court of the prefect of the city, with the aim of defeating justice first by feigning legality and then by collusion.' Tac. *Ann.* 14. 41. I take it as certain that the affair which went to the praetor and not to the prefect was the *falsum* case. The use of *alter* shows that 14. 40–2 concerns two *insignia scelera* and not more than two. *Falsum* is forgery, of whatever kind. The Cornelian law on *falsum* embraced other offences also, such as bribery of a judge or witnesses and false testimony. See *Dig.* 48. 10.

falsum, at any rate) possessed in selecting a court. It appears that they were guided towards one court rather than another not by any regulation, but by customary practice, which could be readily modified to suit a particular end. Here the praetor in charge of the *quaestio* was evidently approached because his court was thought to provide the most suitable setting for the transaction of a shady deal. Similarly, the senatorial court was bypassed because neither party wanted publicity. It may also be inferred that if a speedy and just settlement had been desired (if, for example, Ponticus had been anxious to protect the rightful heirs against loss of money), the prefect's court would have been chosen.

Further, the court of the prefect was apparently the regular court for *falsum*.[1] That is to say, if no special approach was made either to the praetor in charge of the *quaestio de falsis*, or to the consul who presided over the Senate, a case of *falsum* would be brought up in the prefect's court.

Another aspect of the case deserves comment: the fact that the defendants were treated as one group for the purpose of the trial. It is true that Tacitus distinguished between senators and equestrians on the one hand and *alii minus illustres* on the other, but this was his own division and corresponded to his own interests. Tacitus introduced the crime as one committed through 'senatoris . . . audacia', and his attention throughout the narrative is given to the ringleaders or most conspicuous offenders. There is no sign that only *alii minus illustres* were destined for the prefect's court and then diverted to the praetor; or that those of higher status were, from the first, set apart for trial by the Senate. Reversion to the Senate came only when the dubious designs of the prosecution had been exposed, and then it seems that all the defendants were sent before the Senate.

The following conclusions can be drawn from Tacitus' account of the trial. First, it is confirmed that it was no novelty for high-status defendants to appear before either the prefect's tribunal or the jury-courts; and also that low-status defendants were not excluded from the senatorial court, at any rate when they were

---

[1] The significance of this point for the relationship of the jurisdictions of the prefect and the jury-courts is touched upon at a later stage. See p. 92.

involved as accomplices in the crimes of their social superiors. Second, three courts had concurrent jurisdiction over *falsum* cases, but such jurisdiction was not normally exercised by the Senate (or by the *quaestio*) in the Neronian period at least, whatever the status of the accused. Valerius Ponticus might of course have approached the consul in the first instance with a request for a trial in the Senate. Nevertheless, it was not considered worthy of note that he did not, despite the dimensions of the crime and the status of the victim and some of the criminals. Those factors, which so impressed Tacitus, ultimately led to a senatorial trial, but only after the negotiations of prosecution and defence were brought to public notice.

Such direct evidence as we possess for senatorial trials for *falsum* in the earlier period suggests that the above conclusions do not apply to the Neronian age alone. First, Aemilia Lepida, arraigned in the Senate in A.D. 20 for falsely claiming to have given birth to a son by the rich and childless P. Sulpicius Quirinius, was no ordinary high-status defendant.[1] A descendant of both Sulla and Pompey, she had been betrothed by Augustus to the young prince Lucius Caesar. Her status increased the enormity of the crime and made it more likely that Quirinius would request a senatorial investigation (even if he would not have done so anyway). In any case, other charges quickly followed, adultery, attempted poisoning, consulting astrologers about the fortunes of the ruling house. Second, the case of testamentary forgery which the Emperor Gaius sent to the Senate was unusual in that one of the witnesses to the allegedly fraudulent will was the future Emperor Claudius.[2] Suetonius told the story to illustrate Gaius' contempt for his uncle, and it is likely that the case was referred to the Senate for the purpose of embarrassing Claudius as much as possible in public. This affair is not good evidence for regular senatorial *falsum* trials. There may have been a few other trials: we possess only senatorial decrees extending the Cornelian law on *falsum*, some of which may have arisen out of *falsum* investigations. But not much can be made of evidence so

[1] Tac. *Ann.* 3. 22 ff. Cf. Suet. *Tib.* 49. 1.
[2] Suet. *Div. Cl.* 9.

shadowy and indirect.[1] In general, our knowledge of the way *falsum* in all its various forms was punished before A.D. 61 is insubstantial. I submit that the only significant change in that period was the emergence of the court of the prefect as the main court for *falsum*, and that this advance was made at the expense not of the Senate but of the *quaestio de falsis*.

Finally, the Senate conducted a number of judicial investigations involving miscellaneous offences. Individuals were punished for crimes ranging from *vis publica* and *privata*, *sacrilegium*, *iniuria* and *calumnia*, to negligence which led to the death of thousands of spectators at gladiatorial games.[2] The public courts were competent to deal with only some of the above cases, and it is not difficult to understand why these found their way into the Senate. For example, the trial in the Senate in A.D. 23 of Vibius Serenus, governor in Spain, for *vis publica*, is to be explained on the analogy of the *repetundae* trials involving governors.[3] The trial before the Senate of a prefect of a cavalry troop for *vis et rapina* is paralleled by that of the procurator Lucilius Capito on a similar charge. A jury-court trial was hardly a possibility in either case, as both defendants were equestrian officials directly responsible to

---

[1] *Coll.* 8. 7. 1–2 is in places corrupt, but may refer to decrees of A.D. 16 (cons. of Taurus and Libo), 20 (cons. of Cotta and Messalla), 29 (cons. of two Gemini, sc. C. Fufius and L. Rubellius), and 44 (cons. of Licinius II and Taurus). There may be a confusion between the first and the last of these. The *S.C. Libonianum* (see *Dig.* 48. 10 passim) is perhaps identical with the first. Its substance was repeated in an edict of Claudius (*Dig.* 48. 10. 14. 2; ibid. 15 praef.), and a similar measure is ascribed to Nero (Suet. *Nero* 17), along with other enactments, which may have been either *S.CC.* or Imperial edicts. Imperial edicts on *falsum* might of course have followed Imperial *falsum* trials (for one such trial see Suet. *Div. Cl.* 15. 2). On the other hand, the whole idea that the decrees (or edicts) followed *falsum* trials is suspect. The *S.CC.* associated with A.D. 20 and 29 are concerned, and then only secondarily, with the bribery of witnesses, a form of corruption not specially related to *falsum* trials.

[2] For refs. see following notes. In addition, sanctions were invoked by the Senate against various groups whose existence and activities were considered a threat to the political and religious life of the state (e.g. Jews, devotees of Isis, astrologers) and against other groups for acts of disorder and violence (e.g. actors and their supporters, citizens of Italian Pollentia and Pontic Cyzicus). Selected refs. include Tac. *Ann.* 2. 85; 2. 32, cf. *Coll.* 15. 2. 1; 1. 77; Suet. *Tib.* 37. 2–3. In such cases the senatorial decrees issued did not come at the end of formal trials. They were administrative acts, not judicial sentences, promulgated by the Senate acting in its traditional capacity as an administrative organ of government, rather than in its new-found role as court.

[3] Tac. *Ann.* 4. 13. 2. His province was Hispania Ulterior.

the Emperor. Tiberius' decision not to punish them himself was a private one, and his choice of the Senate a special compliment to that body.[1] Next, Calpurnius Salvianus was exiled by the Senate, perhaps for sacrilege. He had chosen a (literally) inauspicious moment to lodge a criminal charge against Sextus Marius, a day of the *feriae Latinae*. Accusers were not uncommonly tried in the Senate in the reign of Tiberius (false accusation, or *calumnia*, was the most frequent charge), probably because their trials arose directly out of prosecutions or attempted prosecutions (like that of Calpurnius Salvianus) in that court.[2]

Thus, as with homicide and *falsum*, so with *vis publica*, *vis privata*, sacrilege, and other crimes for which a *quaestio* was available, the Senate took probably only a handful of the cases which cropped up. The rest must have been left to the proper *quaestio*, or perhaps to the urban prefect.

The other *cognitiones* listed above fell outside the official or statutory criminal law. The freedman-profiteer Atilius, who was responsible for the Fidenae disaster of A.D. 27, might in theory have been punished by the urban prefect rather than the Senate.[3] Similarly, the abuse of a senator by a woman who had been convicted for fraud might have led to a suit for *iniuriae* by the formulary process.[4] Why did the Senate take these cases?

The Fidenae affair of A.D. 27 was a scandal, and the Senate's predilection for investigating scandals has been remarked upon already. Yet obviously there are different kinds of scandals. It would be misleading to place in the same category, for example, the collapse of an amphitheatre which allegedly killed 50,000 people and the forgery of a rich old senator's will. The former was

---

[1] Suet. *Tib.* 30; Tac. *Ann.* 4. 15. Both authors indicate that the trial in the Senate was unexpected.

[2] Ibid. 4. 36 (Salvianus). *Calumnia* charges: ibid. 3. 37; 4. 31; 6. 7; 12. 42, fin.; 13. 33, etc. Cf. ibid. 6. 30 (*praevaricatio*). Not all the accusers punished in the Senate were senators, but this is not remarkable, especially considering that their opponents were. It was senatorial policy to punish crimes of non-senators against senators. Calpurnius Salvianus (*PIR*² C 315) was probably a Spaniard from Corduba, as was his enemy Sextus Marius. The nature of the projected charge is not known.

[3] Tac. *Ann.* 4. 62–3. The prefect was frequently called upon to punish low-status criminals. See pp. 90 ff.

[4] Ibid. 3. 36 (Annia Rufilla).

a scandal of the highest order, whatever the status of the man responsible; the latter was a serious crime but no scandal in itself: it was only the status of some of the accused and of the victim which made the case of A.D. 61 a *cause célèbre*—and brought it into the Senate.

This distinction between crimes which are self-evidently scandalous or outrageous, and crimes which can be called scandalous solely because of the status of those involved, makes it possible to explain the appearance of Annia Rufilla before the Senate in A.D. 21. The substance of C. Cestius' complaint was that he could not pass through the forum and into the senate-house without encountering the threatening abuse of this woman (who thought that she could protect herself from punishment by carrying an image of the Emperor). Cestius had little difficulty in convincing his peers that if such conduct was allowed to go unpunished, 'the laws were annulled and completely overturned'. Rufilla was clapped into gaol. It is safe to assume that a nonsenator who had been subjected to like abuse would have had to proceed against his tormentor by the cumbrous processes of the civil law.

The prosecution of the Cretan, Claudius Timarchus, makes an enlightening comparison.[1] Tacitus introduced Timarchus as representative of a class of provincials who used their wealth to oppress those weaker than themselves. It is not to be imagined that the Senate normally bothered with such men—their petty crimes could be satisfactorily dealt with by the governor. But Timarchus had on more than one occasion uttered a boast to the effect that whether a proconsul was ceremoniously thanked by the Cretan Provincial Assembly depended on his, Timarchus', attitude—and not, by implication, on the governor's own acts or reputation. This remark was seen as an insult to the Senate (*ad contumeliam senatus*), and Timarchus was sent off to face that body.

We may now sum up our findings to this point. First, there is a strong presumption that some senatorial defendants appeared before the public courts or the prefect's court rather than the

---

[1] Tac. *Ann.* 15. 20 ff.

Senate for crimes other than *maiestas*, crimes ordinarily non-political but shading into *maiestas* in exceptional cases, for *repetundae*, and adultery (and kindred crimes). The argument rests chiefly on Tacitus' accounts of two trials, the trial of Cn. Calpurnius Piso in A.D. 20, and the *falsum* trial of A.D. 61. Piso expected a trial before the jury-court which dealt with poisoning, and words of Tiberius imply that this would have been normal. In the forgery case, the accused might have been tried either by the prefect or by the proper jury-court. These cases prove, to my mind, that senatorial jurisdiction was selective, and they make it possible to formulate principles of selection that can be tested in the light of the available evidence.

The next point concerns the status of the defendants who came before the senatorial court. The Senate did not try only senators, but it tried mainly senators. Most of the non-senatorial defendants who appeared in the Senate were charged with *maiestas*. Yet even *maiestas* was predominantly a senatorial crime. Moreover, among crimes which might be committed by men of any status, *maiestas* was apparently unique in that it was punished exclusively (or nearly exclusively) by the Senate. In effect, with respect to all crimes apart from *repetundae* (in any case virtually a high-status crime, the trial of which was monopolized by the Senate) and *maiestas*, the Senate practised only a restricted and selective jurisdiction.[1] In the first place, it handled shocking or outrageous crimes of high-placed persons, notably adultery, but other offences as well. In some of these affairs non-senators were involved, but only in minor roles—it was not their participation which gave them the air of scandals. Secondly, some non-senators were condemned and punished by the Senate for their own scandalous crimes. Of these crimes, a small minority were self-evidently scandalous. Of the rest it can be said that it was only the status of the injured party which made them at all remarkable or significant.[2]

The principles which governed the Senate's selection of cases were thus more complex than might have been imagined. The

[1] *Calumnia* (and other crimes of accusers) was a special case, as it arose out of attempted prosecutions (normally) of senators. See next note.

[2] This category includes indictments of non-senators for offences against senators, among them, *calumnia* or false accusation.

Senate did not try only senatorial defendants; it was not a 'Pairs-gericht' in the sense in which Bleicken uses the term. Nor, however, did it try only those crimes which were scandalous in themselves and/or dangerous to the state. For some of the crimes punished by the Senate were scandalous and dangerous only by the Senate's own definition. In its selection of cases for its judgement, the Senate showed that it was not immune to considerations of status.

Treatment of defendants

Next we must try to decide to what extent the Senate, in the actual judgement of the cases with which it dealt, showed itself attentive to the narrow senatorial interest. Granted that a majority of the defendants who came before the Senate (for whatever reason) were senators, was it an advantage for senators to be tried by the Senate; and conversely, was a senatorial trial a disadvantage for non-senators?

There is more than one indication that non-senators were subject to more summary treatment than senators. It is doubtful whether the Senate would have proceeded against a senator as it proceeded against the equestrian Clutorius Priscus, who was tried and immediately executed on a trifling charge that was treated as *maiestas*.[1] Further, the speed with which Annia Rufilla was dispatched to gaol by order of the consul for molesting C. Cestius, far from convincing us of her guilt, makes us wonder whether she did not have a legitimate grievance against her enemy.

As far as punishments are concerned, no elaborate differential penalty-system can be shown to have operated in this period. However, it seems that at least on occasion low-status defendants were punished more harshly than high-status defendants on the same charges. One suspects that Priscus and Rufilla might have received not only less summary treatment but also less severe penalties if they had been of senatorial rank. Similarly, it was not normal to hurl down the Tarpeian rock astrologers or men convicted of incest. This was a sanction which custom reserved for slave-criminals (or public enemies), but which the Senate

[1] Tac. *Ann.* 3. 49–51. See p. 40 below.

decreed for a plebeian citizen and a leading provincial.[1] (In general, there was little to prevent a judge proceeding *extra ordinem* from invoking any penalty whatsoever against defendants of free birth but humble status. It is likely that other penalties that were in origin slave-penalties were being increasingly employed at this time against humbler defendants. There is, however, little reflection of this development in the evidence relating to the senatorial court.) Finally in the matter of penalties, it is appropriate to cite the account given by Suetonius of the trial of Laetorius in the Senate for adultery.[2] C. Laetorius, a young patrician (*adulescens patricii generis*), pleaded for a mild punishment on the grounds of age and birth (*praeter aetatem atque natalem*), and because Augustus had been born in a house he at present owned. It is not known whether the plea was successful, and if it was successful, for what reasons.[3] For us it is enough that Laetorius would not have been able to introduce the argument from his birth in the senatorial court if he had been anything less than a senator. The rhetoricians state that such arguments appealed to judges and juries in general, drawn as they were from the upper stratum of society, and there is no reason to doubt the truth of their testimony.[4]

Further, not a few senators and senatorial officials who were tried in the Senate, especially on *repetundae* charges, were either acquitted outright, or condemned and later restored.[5] In contrast, the acquittal of non-senatorial defendants was something of a rarity.[6] It seems as if there was in the minds of the judges a heavy presumption of guilt in their cases.

All this leads to the not very remarkable conclusion that there was a difference of attitude among senators to senatorial defendants and non-senatorial defendants which worked in favour of the

---

[1] Ibid. 2. 32 (astrology, L. Pituanius; P. Marcius received the 'traditional penalty', cf. Suet. *Nero* 49); ibid. 6. 19, cf. Dio 58. 22 (incest). The regular penalty for incest, in the later period at any rate, was *deportatio*. See *Dig.* 48. 18. 5. Conspirators were thrown down the rock: Dio 58. 15. 3; 60. 18. 4. A man declared a public enemy forfeited his rights as a free man or citizen.

[2] Suet. *Div. Aug.* 5.

[3] Suetonius relates only that the Senate ordered the consecration of that part of the house where the birth took place.

[4] See p. 229.   [5] See p. 36.   [6] See p. 39 n. 1.

former. More noteworthy is the fact that senatorial discrimination in favour of senators was not permitted to function smoothly and regularly in the Julio-Claudian period. The chief reason for this was the participation of the Emperor in the activities of the senatorial court. This may now be documented.

A glance at the acquittals and post-condemnation restorations in *repetundae* cases will reveal that many of the former and most of the latter were the result of Imperial intervention. Admittedly, direct evidence of such intervention is lacking in the cases of Fonteius Capito, Cestius Proculus, and Eprius Marcellus (who, Tacitus expressly states, was freed unjustly).[1] But Nero was personally responsible for the acquittal of two proconsuls of Africa and a special legate (of praetorian rank) to Cyrene.[2] Moreover, Otho's *potentia* won from Nero the return of a consular to his previous status, though not without cost, while Cossutianus Capito regained his seat in the Senate through the good offices of his father-in-law, Nero's notorious praetorian prefect Tigellinus.[3]

It is not always apparent which factors decided an Emperor in favour of an individual defendant. Nero seems most often to have been influenced by the appeals of men whom he respected or needed, although he did not always grant concessions gratis.[4] Naturally senators were more likely to have powerful friends than men of lower ranks. Isolated exceptions, however, are known. The equestrian Vibius Secundus secured a milder penalty than was due for *repetundae* because his brother Crispus interceded for him.[5] In general, however, non-senators were not well placed, as is indicated by a story in the *Annals* relating to the future Emperor Vespasian.[6] It was the occasion of the quinquennial games, and Rome was full of men from Italian and provincial cities. Many came because they feared that absentees would be punished. It was an offence for spectators to show any signs of gloom (*tristitia*). Of those who offended, says Tacitus, the more in-

---

[1] Tac. *Ann.* 4. 36 (Capito; but the charge might not have been *repetundae*); 13. 30 (Proculus); 13. 33 (Marcellus).
[2] Ibid. 13. 52 (*absolvit Caesar*: sc. a vote for acquittal); 14. 18.
[3] Suet. *Otho* 2; Tac. *Ann.* 13. 33, cf. 14. 48 and 16. 21.
[4] Suet. *Otho* 2; Tac. *Ann.* 13. 52 (*ambitus*; cf. 13. 33).
[5] Ibid. 14. 28.   [6] Ibid. 16. 5.

conspicuous (*tenuiores*) were dealt with on the spot, while the notable (*inlustris*) were passed over for the moment. Vespasian got into trouble at the festival because he fell asleep, and was only saved from ruin (*pernicies*) at the hands of Nero by the intervention of men close to the throne.

Nero could also be impressed by exceptionally high rank. Asinius Marcellus escaped scot-free in the forgery scandal of A.D. 61 because of the fame of his ancestors (he was great-grandson of Asinius Pollio) and the intervention of Nero.[1]

A number of men and women of senatorial rank benefited from the interventions of Tiberius, when, for example, penalties were reduced or nullified, or charges waived. His motives for intervening were various. On some occasions he was probably influenced by the conspicuous *dignitas* of the defendant. The suicide of Cn. Calpurnius Piso led Tiberius to express regret at the terrible calamity (however deserved) that had fallen upon a house of such high *nobilitas*. At the same time he excused the part that M. Piso had played in his father's *civile bellum*. Subsequently, when the consul proposed that M. Piso should be exiled for ten years and should be stripped of rank and fortune (with the exception of five million sesterces), Tiberius ruled that he should retain his rank and his share of his father's property.[2] Again, Appuleia Varilla suffered the traditional penalty for adultery rather than the harsher penalty prescribed by the Julian law. That is to say, she was merely escorted by relatives beyond the two-hundredth milestone. Tiberius had previously quashed the treason charges against her. Appuleia Varilla was the niece of Augustus' sister.[3] Similarly, it may have been the illustrious family-background of Aemilia Lepida which induced Tiberius to ask the Senate to drop the *maiestas* charges against her.[4] Finally, Tiberius stated that rank itself was sufficient reason for placing C. Iunius Silanus on the island of Cythnus rather than Gyaros:

atque ille prudens moderandi, si propria ira non impelleretur, addidit insulam Gyarum immitem et sine cultu hominum esse: darent Iuniae

[1] Ibid. 14. 40.   [2] Ibid. 3. 17–18.
[3] Ibid. 2. 50. Her lover, Manlius, was forbidden entry into Italy and Africa.
[4] Ibid. 3. 22: 'deprecatus primo senatum ne maiestatis crimina tractarentur'.

familiae et viro quondam ordinis eiusdem, ut Cythnum potius concederet.[1]

Tiberius concluded the same speech by observing that the concession he was granting Silanus had been requested by Torquata, Silanus' spotless sister. Tiberius was susceptible no less than Nero to the pleas of men or women of influence. The acquittal of Cn. Piso's wife Plancina was sought and obtained by none other than the Augusta.[2] Again, the pardoning of the equestrian C. Cominius, who was accused of slandering Tiberius, was won by the prayers of his brother, a senator.[3]

Often Tiberius' private likes and dislikes were of direct consequence. He revived the trial of Vibius Serenus with new charges, based on a personal grudge of eight years' standing, when it had all but collapsed following the flight of the prosecutor from Rome.[4] That prosecutor was Serenus' son of the same name, one of a group of infamous accusers of high rank who attained a position of 'sacrosanctity' through their special relationship with the Emperor.[5] This man seems to have specialized in lodging rash and groundless accusations. His attempt to inculpate two highly respectable senators in his father's 'conspiracy' against the Emperor was a major blunder, for the two men were Tiberius' close friends. There was a moment of embarrassment, and the charge was dropped.[6] Indictments against L. Arruntius and M. Aurelius Cotta Maximus Messallinus came to nothing for similar reasons.[7]

[1] 'He, knowing how to be moderate when he was not carried away by personal resentment, said further that Gyaros was a cruel and uninhabited island, and that, as a favour to the Junian family and to a man once of the same order as themselves, they should allow him to retire instead to Cythnus.' Tac. *Ann.* 3. 69. Previously (3. 68) Tiberius had agreed that the property which Silanus inherited from his mother should not be confiscated.

[2] Ibid. 3. 17, cf. 4. 52 (Agrippina's influence could not save Claudia Pulchra); 6. 40 (Aemilia Lepida was safe from prosecution as long as her father lived).

[3] Ibid. 4. 31.

[4] Ibid. 4. 28 ff. Perhaps Tacitus has exaggerated the extent of Tiberius' hatred. Would he have blocked punishment 'more maiorum' simply 'quo molliret invidiam' (and then substituted the more civilized Amorgos for Gyaros or Donusa as a place of exile)?   [5] Ibid. 4. 36.

[6] The men were Cn. Lentulus and Seius Tubero, the former an old man and the latter unwell, ibid. 4. 29.

[7] Ibid. 6. 7, cf. Dio 58. 8. 3 (L. Arruntius); Tac. *Ann.* 6. 5 (Cotta). Note that Plautius Lateranus got off lightly for his part in the affair of Messalina and

Tiberius sometimes quashed charges of *maiestas* for a quite different motive. Given the confused state of the *maiestas* law, it was not always easy to decide whether an alleged offence came within the scope of the law. It was in the Senate that the process of interpreting the law took place, under Tiberius' direction. His attitude, as it happens, was liberal: he made an effort to keep the definition of *maiestas* within bounds. Several charges against equestrians were dropped because Tiberius considered that the *maiestas* law had not been broken.[1]

This last explanation for the waiving of indictments by the Emperor holds in only a few cases. When treason charges came to nothing, it was normally because the Emperor decided, out of personal or political considerations, that it should be so; and it was regularly the rank or connections of the defendant concerned which saved them.[2]

Thus the senatorial court was not always free to favour whom it chose. The clue to its behaviour lay in the attitude of the Emperor. Nero does not appear to have been a frequent attender at senatorial investigations, but he showed considerable interest in their outcome. Claudius' conduct and policy are less well-documented; but he earned a reputation both for his keen appetite for the law and for the extent to which he was subject to the influence of those around him. Until his retirement to Capri, Tiberius not only regularly sat in on senatorial investigations, but also took an active part in them.[3] The result was that even if the Senate was allowed to arrive at a free decision—and this may not

Silius because of the services rendered Claudius by his famous uncle, Aulus Plautius (who the year before, A.D. 47, had celebrated an *ovatio* for his victories in the British campaign of A.D. 43). Ibid. 11. 36. Seven years later he recovered his place in the Senate (ibid. 13. 11).

[1] Ibid. 1. 73; 3. 70.
[2] But see ibid. 11. 36 (Suillius Caesoninus) and 13. 22 (Paris). Political considerations were perhaps relevant in the postponement by Tiberius (probably indefinite) of the trial of C. Annius Pollio and L. Annius Vinicianus (ibid. 6. 9), and in the passing over (for a time) by Nero of Rubellius Plautus (13. 22). There were some genuine acquittals: ibid. 6. 9 (C. Calvisius Sabinus, C. Appius Iunius Silanus); 6. 8–9 (Terentius); perhaps too 3. 37 (Caecilianus); 4. 13 (Sacerdos and Gracchus); 4. 31 (the sister of Firmus); etc.
[3] Tiberius' interest in the judicial investigations of the Senate did not die during the time of his sojourn in Capri. In addition, the Senate had to put up with first Sejanus and later Macro.

have been a common occurrence—that decision was frequently modified by the Emperor. The trial of Clutorius Priscus was an exception among treason trials because the Senate made a decision and carried it out in Tiberius' absence and without his knowledge. Tiberius showed his disapproval by fixing for the future a ten-day gap between the passing of sentence and the execution of sentence. Thereafter there could be no doubt that the decisive factor in a trial in the Senate was the operation or inoperation of Imperial *clementia*. The Senate had no power of reconsideration: 'sed non senatui libertas ad paenitendum erat . . .'[1]

Such interference in the working of the senatorial court might not have mattered, if Emperors could have been relied upon to pursue a course consistently favourable to senators. But Tiberius, for example, was as capable of inclemency as clemency;[2] and the concern for truth which he displayed in the early days of his reign was by no means a virtue in the eyes of Tacitus, for whom it represented a threat to freedom—the freedom of *potentes* to influence the course of trials.[3] As for Nero, an Emperor who required to be consulted by the Senate before it made decisions was conceding that body at best a semblance of freedom.[4] Tacitus was constantly aware of the contrast between the attitudes and behaviour of Nerva and Trajan and those of their predecessors. In the matter of senatorial trials, Trajan seems to have attended them only when required to as consul, and to have shown little interest in the proceedings. His Senate, left to its own devices, was able systematically to favour members of the senatorial order.[5]

Conclusion

In the Julio-Claudian period, conditions were far from ideal for the promotion of the interests of the senatorial order. In the first place, a large part of the Senate's judicial time was given to

---

[1] Tac. *Ann.* 3. 49–51. Gaius allowed his Senate little room to manœuvre. See Dio 59. 18. 2.

[2] See, e.g., Tac. *Ann.* 4. 42; cf. 3. 23, where Drusus rejects a milder penalty suggested by some senators.

[3] Ibid. 1. 75.

[4] Nero's behaviour in the case of Antistius Sosianus (ibid. 14. 48 ff.) is to be compared with Tiberius' in the case of Clutorius Priscus (ibid. 3. 49–51).

[5] See pp. 50 ff.

the trial of political crimes and scandalous crimes (*insignia scelera*) committed by men of all classes. It was only when the Emperors built up their own jurisdiction that the senatorial court lost its monopoly over cases of this sort, and was more free to turn its attention to the trial of senators. Secondly, again until the Emperor's tribunal operated on a regular basis, the senatorial court was unable to function without Imperial interference.

On the other hand, non-senatorial defendants in the senatorial court were a clear minority. Their cases were carefully selected. The crimes for which they were tried were almost without exception either scandalous in themselves or scandalous in the eyes of senators. They could thus expect no mercy, and to my knowledge they received virtually none. The Senate would certainly give them less consideration than high-status defendants. And when Imperial generosity (*beneficium*) worked to cancel or mitigate a sentence, or to reject an indictment, the gainer was normally a member of the senatorial order. In most of those cases, the favour was granted because of the personal influence or social prestige of the defendant or his supporters.

Is it legitimate to conclude that senatorial defendants as a whole saw any real advantage to be gained by trial before their peers? This question cannot be answered satisfactorily while we can only draw upon evidence for the working of the senatorial court. It is of course impossible to make a comparison between the way defendants of status were treated in the Senate and the way they were treated in jury-courts or in the court of the prefect. To judge from the evidence at our disposal, senatorial defendants as a whole did not expect more lenient treatment than the law prescribed. Much seems to have depended on the nature of the offence and the status of the injured party. The outcome of *maiestas* trials (and quasi-*maiestas* trials) was often quite unpredictable, because in these cases the attitude of the Emperor was vital. One senator might be benefited, while another might be hastened to his destruction. Only firm friends of the Emperor could be sure of their survival. Adultery was not a crime against the life or dignity of the Emperor, but it was thought to threaten the moral fabric of society. This explains the Emperor's interest in the crime, and, in Tiberius' case, his unwillingness to grant concessions to any defendant, apart from the niece of Augustus' sister. In contrast, acts of mercy towards those accused of *repetundae* were frequent. Here, as with *maiestas*, 'chance factors' counted, especially the possession of powerful friends. But *beneficium* could be more readily distributed to offenders where the victims of crime were merely provincials. On the other hand, if the Senate agreed to investigate a crime of a man or woman of senatorial status against one of like status, the offence might well be considered outrageous and deserving of strict punishment. In practice in such cases *clementia* was shown only to those of the most illustrious family.

Thus, because the Senate was more of an 'Imperial court' ('Kaisergericht') than a 'senatorial court' ('Senatsgericht'),[1] and because Imperial *beneficium* was not offered regularly to senatorial defendants on the grounds of their senatorial rank, a trial before the Senate is likely to have been considered by senators a doubtful privilege in this period. With the possible exception of provincial governors on *repetundae* charges, senators would have viewed their coming trial in the Senate with as much apprehension as hope.

[1] Bleicken, op. cit., 61.

2

THE SENATORIAL COURT FROM THE FLAVIANS TO THE SEVERANS

In a familiar passage in Dio's History[1] Maecenas is made to give Augustus the following advice: in respect of serious charges involving senators and their families, and calling for the penalties of disfranchisement (ἀτιμία),[2] exile (φυγή), and death (θάνατος), the Emperor should allow the matter to be brought before the Senate without having made a prior decision, and should leave the entire judgement to that body.

The statement in Dio probably represents the opinion of moderates in the Senate of the early third century. It is necessary to inquire how far the policy of Emperors up to and including the Severan period approximated to the views of this group, and to show why senators might have favoured a trial in the Senate.

The death penalty and 'maiestas' trials

We may begin with charges which might carry a death sentence, and especially maiestas. It was, understandably, the use of the death penalty which the Senate was most anxious to control.

Emperor and Senate had long fought over the question whether it was proper for the Emperor to try senators for crimes which might lead to execution. The seeds of the controversy were sown in the Julio-Claudian period. No Emperor of the first dynasty claimed or practised a regular criminal jurisdiction. However, individual Emperors from time to time disposed of individual senators without regard for the legal processes which had become customary. The classic attack on behaviour of this kind was delivered not by an ordinary senator, but by Nero, in his first

---

[1] Dio 52. 31. 3–4, cf. 9–10; 52. 32. 1.
[2] On ἀτιμία see p. 58 n. 5.

appearance in the Senate as Emperor.[1] In the speech, Claudius was castigated for, among other things, judging 'all cases' (*negotiorum omnium*), and behind his palace-doors (*unam intra domum*). Nero probably exaggerated the extent of Claudius' shortcomings.[2] In any case, his own promise to avoid the practice of his predecessor was broken after the Pisonian conspiracy of A.D. 65, if not before.[3] Moreover, in the last months of his reign, if we are to believe Dio and Suetonius, Nero threatened to extinguish the whole senatorial order.[4]

The crisis in the relations between Senate and Emperor was delayed until the reign of Domitian (by which time the senatorial court and the Emperor's court existed side by side).[5] Dio's epitomator, under A.D. 81, reports[6] that Domitian's Senate passed repeated decrees to the effect that the Emperor should not destroy anyone of his own rank. It seems to have been the aim of those who framed the decrees to avoid executions of senators by preventing Domitian from condemning senators independently of the Senate. It is difficult to decide on the evidence available whether the Senate acted in this way in uneasy anticipation of its future insecurity, or whether an attack on its membership had already occurred and had galvanized it into action. Nor is it known to what extent the imputation of Dio/Xiphilinus that Domitian disregarded the senatorial decrees was justified.[7] But at any rate, Domitian did not resign any claim to independent capital jurisdiction over senators. Some later Emperors, however, in effect did this, by declaring on oath that they would kill no senator.

It has recently been argued that the Emperor's oath not to execute senators originated in the reign of Vespasian.[8] It is true that an oath was introduced at a meeting of the Senate and ad-

---

[1] Tac. *Ann.* 13. 4. No doubt Seneca composed the speech.

[2] Valerius Asiaticus was tried *domi*, Tac. *Ann.* 11. 1 ff., and probably Appius Silanus also, Suet. *Div. Cl.* 37, cf. Tac. *Ann.* 11. 29 and Dio 60. 14. 3. Evidence of other trials of this kind is lacking. Contrast Dio 60. 16. 3; Suet. *Div. Cl.* 40. 2.

[3] But Tac. *Ann.* 14. 50 (under A.D. 62) shows that before the conspiracy Nero normally sent criminal cases to the Senate.

[4] Suet. *Nero* 37. 3; 43. 1; Dio 63. 27. 2.

[5] See Quint. *Inst. Or.* 7. 2. 20. Quintilian wrote in the closing years of Domitian.

[6] Dio 67. 2. 4.

[7] See pp. 46–7.

[8] A. R. Birley, *CR* 12 (1962), 197–9.

ministered to those present. Its terms were, 'that they had committed no action tending to anyone's hurt, and had gained neither reward nor preferment from the downfall of fellow Romans'.[1] Vespasian and Titus were not present at the meeting, but perhaps they would have been compelled to swear the oath if it had remained in force. However, the oath was purely retrospective; it was designed specifically to embarrass those informers or accusers who had endangered the lives of senators under Nero. No open request was made of Vespasian as Emperor to give his word or swear an oath to respect senators' lives; and as far as we can tell he made no such pledge. He took the more positive measure of refusing to entertain charges of treason.[2]

Titus did not swear not to kill senators. He followed Vespasian's policy of rejecting *maiestas* charges. Further, he is said to have banished informers. He put no senator to death, and was praised for it.[3]

Nerva freed those on trial for *maiestas*, restored exiles, forbade *maiestas* accusations, and punished informers. He also swore that he would kill no senator (μηδένα τῶν βουλευτῶν φονεύσειν),[4] and Trajan followed suit.[5] It was prudent for the successor of a tyrant to do so; Trajan was close enough to Domitian's reign to make capital out of it also. Of the Emperors that followed, Hadrian, Pertinax, and Septimius Severus can be shown to have sworn the oath.[6] We might have been able to add Pius' name, had there not been a lacuna in Dio's narrative. In his reign, according to the Biographer, no senator lost his life—even a parricide escaped with exile.[7] Moreover, it was apparently Pius' policy to allow the Senate to try senators—one of the two conspirators against his rule was

---

[1] Tac. *Hist.* 4. 41: 'nihil ope sua factum quo cuiusquam salus laederetur, neque se praemium aut honorem ex calamitate civium cepisse.'

[2] Dio 66. 9. 1. The execution of Helvidius Priscus by order of Vespasian was represented as an error, Suet. *Div. Vesp.* 15. But see Epict. 1. 2. 19 ff.

[3] Dio 66. 19; 67. 2. 4; Suet. *Div. Tit.* 9.

[4] Dio 68. 1. 1–2; 2. 3. It was to Nerva's credit that he kept oath despite plots against his life. Dio 68. 2. 3, cf. 16. 2.

[5] Dio 68. 5. 2. Trajan's oath had one peculiar feature. See p. 58.

[6] *SHA Hadr.* 7; Dio 69. 2. 4–6; 70. 1 (Hadrian); Dio 74. 5. 2 (Pertinax); *SHA Sev.* 7. 5; Dio 74. 2. 1–2 (Severus). Birley, art. cit. 197–9, thought all Emperors from Nerva to Severus, except perhaps Commodus, took an oath. Cf. Bleicken, op. cit. 118 ff.

[7] *SHA Pius* 8. 10.

prosecuted in the Senate (and the other committed suicide).[1]
The only oath recorded for Marcus is placed near the end of his
reign, when he is said to have sworn that no senator had been
killed with his knowledge.[2]

Thus Dio would have been able to support his plea for the
senatorial trial of senatorial criminals in cases involving the death
penalty by appealing to the professed or apparent policies of a
good proportion of the Emperors who followed Domitian.[3]

Dio would have known, from the past history of the senatorial
court, that no senatorial defendant was guaranteed any advantage
from the mere fact that he was to be tried by his peers. Yet he
would not have pressed for senatorial trials of senatorial criminals
if he had not considered that such an arrangement could favour
senators. The real danger, as Dio appreciated, lay in interference
from above. Thus he requested, through Maecenas, not simply that
the Emperor should surrender a senatorial criminal to the Senate;
but that having done so, he should hold himself aloof from the case.
He should give no prior judgement, and resist the temptation to
influence the Senate's decision.

Dio (Dio/Xiphilinus) reports that the senatorial decrees designed to prevent Domitian from acting independently against
senators caused that Emperor no anxiety.[4] Yet Domitian did not
disregard them entirely. If the references to Domitianic trials are
assembled, it will be seen that many if not most of the senators who
were killed or exiled in his reign were condemned in the Senate.[5]

[1] *SHA Pius* 7. 3–4, cf. 6. 3 (Hadrian's enemies).

[2] *SHA Marcus* 29. 4. See also ibid. 25. 6; *Av. Cass.* 8. 7: Marcus pressed the
Senate not to pass the death sentence on those involved with Avidius Cassius
in his rebellion. Dio thought it worthy of note that Marcus did not slay or
imprison the associates of Cassius, or bring them before his own court (71. 28. 2).
It is not clear why Dio was impressed. He may have felt that, in the face of open
military revolt, a threatened Emperor would have been justified in taking the
(sc. irregular) step of dealing with the rebel and his followers himself. See Dio
52. 31. 10. Despite *SHA Marcus* 24. 2 (on which see p. 59 n. 1), I do not
believe that Marcus regularly handled capital cases involving senators.

[3] Of the Emperors who followed Septimius Severus, Alexander is said to
have killed no senators (*SHA Sev. Al.* 52, quoting Herodian; cf. Her. 6. 1. 7;
6. 9. 8), and Macrinus begged off Aurelianus by insisting that it was impious
to put a senator to death (Dio 78. 12. 2).

[4] Dio 67. 2. 4.

[5] See Dio 67. 3. 3[2] (A.D. 83, first Vestal Virgin case); 67. 4. 5, cf. Suet. *Dom.*
11. 2 (general statements about *maiestas* cases); Pliny, *Ep.* 4. 11 (second Vestal

This was true even of the victims of the 'purge' which began in A.D. 93. Tacitus in the *Agricola* confesses that the Senate bore a corporate responsibility for the elimination of men such as Helvidius Priscus the Younger:

mox nostrae duxere Helvidium in carcerem manus; nos Maurici Rusticique visus ⟨adflixit⟩; nos innocenti sanguine Senecio perfudit.[1]

Thus Domitian, on some occasions at least, was cynical enough to get rid of his enemies without breaking the letter of the senatorial decrees. There was more than one way of destroying a senator, as Dio fully appreciated. He commented with bitterness that the decrees were futile and innocuous because, with an Emperor like Domitian, it made no difference whether a senator was condemned by an Emperor in person or by a Senate under his domination.

It might be supposed that senators living under Emperors who had sworn not to execute them would be better placed. If this was ever so, it was not by virtue of the fact that the Emperors concerned had taken oaths. In the first months of Hadrian's reign, before his arrival in Rome, four conspicuous consulars were put to death. Hadrian, according to the Biographer, claimed that they died by the Senate's order and against his will (*senatu iubente, invito Hadriano*).[2] The Biographer goes on to say, apparently without irony, that Hadrian incurred odium because he 'allowed'

Virgin case, see pp. 57–8); ibid. 7. 33 (Baebius Massa, *repetundae*, see pp. 57–8). Suet. *Dom.* 10 ascribes a host of murders to Domitian personally, not however to his court. Similarly, when Iulius Bassus is said by Pliny to have been *a Domitiano relegatus* (*Ep.* 4. 9. 2), this does not rule out a senatorial trial (such as occurred when he was acquitted under Vespasian). No doubt his recall (*revocatus a Nerva*) was inspired by Nerva but effected by a *S.C.* On the other hand, Salvius Liberalis was tried by a private judge appointed, presumably, by Domitian (ibid. 3. 9. 33; both charge and year are unknown). Again, the executions after the military revolt of A.D. 89 did not take place in Rome at all. Dio complains (67. 11. 3) that Domitian did not bother sending a report to the Senate. For the 'purges' beginning in A.D. 93 see next note.

[1] 'Soon our hands led Helvidius to prison; the look of Mauricus and Rusticus put us to shame; Senecio sprinkled us with his innocent blood.' Tac. *Agric.* 45. The detail supplied by Pliny (*Ep.* 7. 19. 6) that Senecio's books were burned by order of the Senate perhaps supports Tacitus, if support is necessary. For the idea of the corporate responsibility of senators cf. Dio 59. 16. 2 (the taunt of Gaius over Tiberius' reign) and Tac. *Hist.* 4. 8 (Eprius Marcellus on Nero's reign).

[2] *SHA Hadr.* 7. 2, citing Hadrian's Autobiography.

the men to die.[1] If the Emperor had not in fact ordered the executions (and the Epitomator of Dio records that he denied this on
oath),[2] he had at least let slip the opportunity to veto them.
Hadrian followed his self-exoneration with an oath that he would
never punish a senator with execution except by the Senate's
decision (*nisi ex senatus sententia*).[3] It will be obvious that this
oath would not have satisfied his more intelligent critics. It did
not rule out the possibility that senators might be executed,
stipulating only that any death sentence had to be ratified by the
Senate. The death of the four consulars had apparently followed
a *senatusconsultum*.

The Emperor Septimius Severus took advantage of the same
anomaly. He swore an oath, and insisted that it be reinforced by a
senatorial decree prohibiting the death of a senator by the Emperor's agency without prior consultation of the Senate.[4] After
referring to the oath and the decree, Dio charges Severus with
being the first to violate them, by destroying many senators,
including the framer of the decree. (These were followers of
Julianus.)[5] But, as the Biographer shows, the action took place in
the Senate:

> alia die ad senatum venit et amicos Iuliani incusatos proscriptioni ac
> neci dedit.[6]

Severus could presumably have claimed that he had observed the
formal requirement of 'consulting' the Senate. No doubt he obtained a senatorial decree of condemnation in this case. When
dealing with most of his other foes, notably the followers of

[1] *SHA Hadr.* 7. 3: 'quod occidi passus esset uno tempore quattuor consulares.'
Cf. *SHA Marcus* 26. 10: 'Ipsum Cassium *pro clementia* occidi *passus est*, non
occidi iussit.' The murder of Trajan's friends had been accomplished suddenly
and hastily, so as to encourage the belief that their crime was imaginary.
But the crime of Cassius was public, for all to see.

[2] Dio 69. 2. 6. Ibid. 2. 4 may point to an earlier oath, perhaps immediately
following the accession.

[3] *SHA Hadr.* 7. 4.

[4] *SHA Sev.* 7. 5: 'ne liceret imperatori inconsulto senatu occidere senatorem.'
This text mentions no oath. But see Dio 74. 2. 1–2 and perhaps Her. 2. 14. 3;
and p. 62.

[5] See next note. The death of Julianus himself was decreed by the Senate:
Her. 2. 12. 6; Dio 74. 17. 4.

[6] *SHA Sev.* 8. 3: 'On another day he came to the Senate, accused Julianus'
friends, and gave them to proscription and death.'

Clodius Albinus, he showed less 'scruple'.[1] The oath could hardly survive such a reign.[2]

Thus Dio knew from first-hand experience that the Imperial oath not to kill senators guaranteed only a senatorial trial for senatorial defendants, and was no protection against the death penalty. He must have had his own Emperor Severus, among others, in mind when he put into the mouth of Maecenas the demand that a senatorial trial should be free from any intervention from the Emperor, however well-intentioned it might be.

The battle between Emperor and Senate, which, as I have suggested, lies behind the passage in Dio, arose principally from the threat posed to the lives of senators by Imperial misuse of the *maiestas* law. But the passage reflects an anxiety among senators to protect their status as well as their lives: it was no doubt felt that a senator should no more lose his citizenship and property and homeland than his life because of the personal hostility which an Emperor bore to him.[3] The discussion must thus be broadened to embrace penalties less severe than the death penalty, and crimes less serious than *maiestas*.

[1] The supporters of Pescennius Niger were not put to death, according to Dio 75. 8. 4 (cf. *SHA Sev.* 9. 3: one man was slain), but at least one senator, Cassius Clemens, was brought before Severus himself (Dio 75. 9). The Biographer emphasizes that this generosity was only extended to senators, though not to the senatorial generals of Niger's army (*SHA Sev.* 9. 6–8). No mercy was shown to the senators who followed Clodius Albinus. Twenty-nine were slain, perhaps without trial (Dio 75. 8. 4, cf. the less reliable account of *SHA Sev.* 13: forty-one men, all named, executed *sine causae dictione*). Regarding *maiestas* charges of less importance see Dio 76. 8–9. 2 (Apronianus, governor of Asia, was condemned by *the Senate*; an alleged confederate, Marcellinus, lost his head before Severus learned that *the Senate* had condemned him); contrast 76. 4. 4–5 (Plautianus, a summary execution); 76. 5. 3 (deaths which followed that of Plautianus; perhaps these trials were held in the Emperor's court); 76. 7. 3 (Quintillus, tried by the Emperor); etc.

[2] Elagabalus was not averse to using the Senate. Silius Messalla and Pomponius Bassus were sentenced to death by that body for alleged dissatisfaction with the Emperor's actions. But this followed the receipt of a written charge from the Emperor—and their death. See Dio 79. 5. On the other hand, no statement was made to the Senate about his murder of a governor of Syria (Dio 79. 3. 4) and other followers of Macrinus in Rome, the governors of Arabia and Cyprus (Dio 79. 3. 4–5), and an ex-governor of Cappadocia (79. 4. 5). Caracalla is said to have killed countless prominent men. See Dio 77. 4; 77. 5. 5; 77. 6; 77. 11. 6; 77. 20. 4; 77. 22–3; etc. For Macrinus and Severus Alexander see p. 46 n. 3, above.

[3] For possible reflections of these feelings in Imperial oaths see pp. 58, 62.

Other penalties and crimes: Flavian and Trajanic evidence

The best evidence for the trial of crimes other than *maiestas* is provided by letters of the Younger Pliny, and relates mainly to *repetundae* trials under Trajan.

Pliny's account of the few trials which he describes is coloured by the fact that he was, as an advocate, a leading actor in them and no mere eyewitness. What is lost in evenness and objectivity in narrative is gained in the insight provided into his reaction to the events and to his own part in them. Pliny appeared more often for the prosecution than for the defence. This was not the way he would have liked it, for three reasons. First, the Roman Senate had just emerged from a prolonged period of insecurity ending in a brief 'reign of terror', when its ranks had been purged of actual or imagined enemies of the state. A number of senators had compromised themselves by co-operating with Domitian in his war against individuals and parties within the Senate. Any senator who had survived this experience untarnished and who was sensitive to his reputation would think twice before proceeding against a fellow senator in the senatorial court. Second, the prosecution of a senator was to be avoided because the accused was unlikely to lack powerful supporters who were capable of creating trouble for the prosecutor. Third, rank-and-file senators felt a natural sympathy for a senator under attack, and antipathy for any assailant, especially if he was a non-senator or a representative of non-senators.

Pliny attacked a senator willingly once, and, considering what has just been said, his choice of opponent and his tactics on that occasion deserve scrutiny.[1] First, Pliny singled out a senator who had played some part in the prosecution and condemnation of Helvidius Priscus. Pliny never specifies the exact charge he proposed to lay against Publicius Certus; it is said only that Certus had committed the ultimate in crimes: 'Moreover, though many crimes had been committed by numerous persons, none seemed so shocking as the violent attack in the Senate-house made by a senator on a fellow senator, by a praetorian acting as judge on a

[1] Pliny, *Ep.* 9. 13.

consular who had been brought to trial.'[1] If Certus' action was that of a common *accusator*, Pliny had only the public interest in mind when he called for his punishment (§ 21). Next, Pliny took the first steps towards instituting legal proceedings, but soon let the matter drop. He presumably listened to the advice of his consular friends, who warned that Certus had both influence (*gratia*) and support (*amicitia*) (§ 11). But Pliny was too circumspect not to have been aware of this from the first (§ 12). It is unlikely that he seriously intended to bring Certus to trial. Finally, Pliny must have known that whatever odium (*invidia*) he incurred would be more than balanced by the credit he gained with two groups in the Senate, those who approved of his attack and those who applauded his withdrawal.

Thus Pliny did not prosecute senators idly. It is no surprise to find that he acted as counsel to provincial plaintiffs only when 'drafted' by the Senate at their request. In Pliny's eyes the enterprise was unsafe, and *periculum*, or the danger of arousing odium, is a regularly recurring theme in the letters relating to trials. It is not too harsh a judgement to say that performing this duty (*munus*) brought him some mental conflict but little risk. If as counsel for the prosecution he painted the crimes of a governor black, it was expected that he would do so, and his efforts would not necessarily have any bearing on the Senate's decision. The Senate could still treat the defendant with leniency. As is revealed by the aftermath of the trial of Baebius Massa, an advocate in a *repetundae* case was only really in danger if it was considered that he was going beyond his brief. A senatorial advocate was expected to go so far but no further in his service to his non-senatorial clients.[2]

---

[1] 'Porro inter multa scelera multorum nullum atrocius videbatur, quam quod in senatu senator senatori, praetorius consulari, reo iudex manus intulisset.' (§ 2.)

[2] Pliny's rather empty forebodings contrast with the terror of the advocate Tuscilius Nominatus at the prospect of doing battle in the Senate, on behalf of the people of Vicetia, with the praetorian Sollers (who wanted to hold a fair on his property). He had been advised by friends 'not to be too persistent in opposing the wishes of a senator (and especially in the Senate), who was no longer fighting the case on account of the proposed market, but because his influence, reputation and position were at stake; otherwise Nominatus would make himself more unpopular than on the last occasion'. *Ep.* 5. 13. 2.

E

Baebius Massa in A.D. 93 was condemned for *repetundae*.[1] His assets were placed in the care of the consuls. It seems that there was a risk that Massa would recover them before compensation was paid to the provincials. This, at any rate, was the opinion of Pliny's co-advocate Herennius Senecio, who persuaded a reluctant Pliny to go with him to the consuls. The difference of attitude in the two men is marked. Senecio was truly concerned with the interests of the Spaniards whom Massa had oppressed, and was prepared to fight on until they were fully compensated; Pliny, on the other hand, felt that his job was done at the conclusion of the trial proper—he was evidently less troubled about the provincials' rights than about his own popularity in the Senate. Senecio was charged by Massa with *impietas*, that is to say, with having gone beyond the responsibilities of an advocate.[2] Pliny, to his credit, quashed the charge by pointing out that he himself must be either Senecio's accomplice in *impietas* or Massa's in *praevaricatio* (collusion). That this manœuvre was successful, together with the fact that the complaint was filed against Senecio alone, is surely proof that Pliny's conduct in this case was not such as to expose him to the enmity of Massa or anyone else.[3]

There was not much danger involved for Pliny in his prosecution of Caecilius Classicus on behalf of the Baeticans, because Classicus was dead.[4] As a result Pliny does not question the *utilitas* of the proceedings (§ 8), which were devoted in the main to the prosecu-

[1] *Ep.* 7. 33. On the inequitable aspects of the *repetundae* trials see P. A. Brunt, *Historia* 10 (1961), 217 ff.

[2] See A. N. Sherwin-White, *Commentary* 446. It is of course true that *impietas* towards *an Emperor* is equivalent to *maiestas* (e.g. Tac. *Ann.* 6. 47; cf. Pliny, *Pan.* 33. 3), but the context suggests a different object of *impietas* here: 'Massa questus Senecionem non advocati fidem sed inimici amaritudinem implesse impietatis reum postulat.'

[3] Pliny speaks twice of the *periculum* which he ran as a result of his prosecution of Massa. See *Ep.* 3. 4. 6: 'Praeterea cum recordarer, quanta pro isdem Baeticis superiore advocatione etiam pericula subissem'; also ibid. 7. 33. 3 (to Tacitus): 'iucundum mihi futurum si factum meum, cuius gratia periculo crevit, tuo ingenio tuo testimonio ornaveris.' The reference to *gratia* reveals that in fact Pliny gained credit (at least in his own judgement) from his advocacy, as he did from attacking Publicius Certus.

[4] The trial is described in *Ep.* 3. 9. For his feelings on the death of Classicus see ibid. 3. 4. 7: 'Ducebar etiam quod decesserat Classicus, amotumque erat quod in eiusmodi causis solet esse tristissimum, periculum senatoris'. Pliny suffered brief, minor discomfiture in the course of the trial. Ibid. 3. 9. 25–6.

tion of Classicus' associates. No doubt both Pliny and the Senate were relieved that the two chief confederates of Classicus were provincials. The Senate overruled their plea that they had been compelled to obey their governor's orders—although the defence of superior orders was, it seems, usually effective in Roman courts[1] —and exiled them for five years. Four other defendants are referred to, and of them three were acquitted and one exiled from Italy for two years. It may not be accidental that the three who went free were all of senatorial family—they were Classicus' wife, Casta, his daughter, and his son-in-law—while the exile was an equestrian. The acquittal of Casta, for one, was not a foregone conclusion. The provincial prosecutor Norbanus Licinianus was charged with collusion with her. But if he was guilty, Casta was no less so; and if she had tried to come to an arrangement with him, she must have had something to hide. Pliny saw the implications of her collusion, and claims to have emphasized them in his speech, but without success (§ 34).[2] But Pliny's own account of the third stage of the trial, the stage in which the debate over Casta took place, casts suspicion on the truth of this claim. Pliny explains to his correspondent that it was decided to group together several defendants in this third phase of the trial, lest the length of the case and the tedium of it caused the judges to lose a strict sense of justice (*iustitia . . . severitasque*) (§ 19). We can see from his report that it was his own insistence on Casta's alleged innocence rather than the Senate's boredom which was responsible for her acquittal. We can also be sure that the Senate would never have been too much asleep to fail to pounce on Licinianus, convict him of collusion by an irregular procedure, and sentence him to a more severe penalty than was normal or warranted.[3] He was a mere provincial, one, moreover, who had not kept his hands clean in the reign of Domitian.[4]

---

[1] D. Daube, *The Defence of Superior Orders in Roman Law* (1956).

[2] Pliny comments that it was quite without precedent for the accuser to be condemned for collusion and the accused to get off.

[3] Ibid. 29 ff. The trial of Licinianus should have followed the main trial, as Pliny says. Licinianus was forced to defend himself on the spot, his requests for time and for a statement of the charges against him having been refused. The penalty for collusion according to the *S.C. Turpilianum* was a ban on activity as an advocate. See Sherwin-White, op. cit. ad loc.

[4] Compare the treatment of Theophanes, ibid. 4. 9. 14, cf. 3; 20–1. See Dio

In prosecuting Marius Priscus on behalf of the Africans, Pliny felt he had to tread more carefully.[1] He stresses in his letter to Arrianus that he and Tacitus were conscripted for the task (*adesse provincialibus iussi*). Pliny in fact had begged unsuccessfully to be excused, on the grounds that he was at the time prefect of the public treasury.[2] Priscus pleaded guilty to *repetundae* and asked for a committee of assessors to decide what compensation was due. But the two advocates blocked this move by bringing to the notice of the Senate crimes of *saevitia* or cruelty (as opposed to the mere extortion of money) which Priscus was attempting to hide. Pliny finds it necessary to explain to his correspondent that he and Tacitus had judged it their duty so to act (*existimavimus fidei nostrae convenire*), and Arrianus was clearly meant to admire their courage in pressing for a full hearing of the provincials' complaints against a man of such fame (*claritas*). By the time Pliny was called upon to make his major speech against Priscus, the difficulty of the case (*causae difficultas*) had increased—the defendant who was once a consular and a member of a priestly college was now neither. It was a heavy task (*perquam onerosum*) to attack someone already condemned and deprived of status. Pliny knew that sympathy aroused by Priscus' situation would draw attention away from the serious nature of the remaining charges against him (*atrocitas criminis*). There was, in fact, a strong body of support for Marius Priscus. The proposal even to consider the charges had been passed only with difficulty;[3] and at the conclusion of the hearing, when there could be no doubt about his guilt, a majority seriously considered voting against any additional punishment, apart from the payment into the treasury of the 700,000 HS Priscus had received for flogging, condemning to mines, and strangling a Roman equestrian. It should be noted that the penalty finally decreed for Priscus, exile from Rome and Italy, was thought to be severe (§ 1). The implication is that similar crimes at this period were normally punished even more leniently, by loss of

Chrys. *Or.* 34. 9, for the bad reputation won by provincials who prosecuted their governors.

[1] Pliny, *Ep.* 2. 11.   [2] Ibid. 10. 3A. 2.

[3] Ibid. 2. 11. 6: *favor et misericordia* had had an initial impact of considerable proportions.

status, payment of compensation, and perhaps a short period of exile; and that permanent exile was not inflicted, much less capital exile (or permanent exile with loss of citizenship and property). Again, it is significant that Marius Priscus was penalized no more harshly than Marcianus, the African from Lepcis who had paid over the 700,000 HS. The crimes of Priscus and Marcianus were hardly comparable in gravity; but neither were the criminals alike in status.

Pliny defended Iulius Bassus, proconsul of Bithynia, on a charge of *repetundae*. Now at last he could show a real enthusiasm for his task.[1] To his great satisfaction, the Senate voted for Bassus (who had undeniably broken the *repetundae* law by accepting 'gifts') a milder penalty than was prescribed in the law: he retained his seat in the Senate, and was required only to pay compensation. Caepio Hispo, the mover of the victorious motion, argued that Bassus' action was illegal but not without precedent, and that in such cases it was open to the Senate to adjust the penalty:

licere senatui . . . et mitigare leges et intendere (§ 17).

It is interesting to watch Pliny—who, incidentally, agreed with Hispo's reasoning (*sicut licet*)—at work as chief advocate for Bassus. Not that his technique is likely to have been at all remarkable: the special pleading for the defendant, the appeal to the defendant's family background (to excite admiration) and to his chequered career (to arouse compassion), and the abuse of the provincial prosecutors were presumably stock features of any speech for the defence. They were no less effective for that, as is shown on this occasion not only by the generous treatment of the defendant, but also by the way the regular animosity of the Senate towards provincial prosecutors erupted into the attempted prosecution of their leader, Theophanes. Senatorial partisanship is nowhere more graphically demonstrated than in the trial of Iulius Bassus.[2]

---

[1] Pliny, *Ep.* 4. 9.

[2] It is not known whether Varenus Rufus, governor of Bithynia, was brought to trial. An accusation was lodged by a Bithynian delegation, but rival envoys attempted to quash it, and the Emperor was approached. No further details are known. Even during these preliminaries the Senate (and Pliny) made its prejudices plain. First, the law was stretched (cf. 4. 9. 17) to allow the accused

Thus Pliny has left us an exceptionally vivid picture of the operation of the senatorial court in his heyday. The relevant letters illustrate the various ways in which the Senate showed partiality towards senatorial defendants. In addition, the freedom with which the court functioned is striking. Trajan was apparently disinclined to intervene in its proceedings. He is mentioned in connection with two cases. First, in the Varenus Rufus case, he was asked to break the deadlock caused by the presence of two rival Bithynian delegations, one seeking to impeach Rufus, the other anxious to withdraw the accusation.[1] Second, Trajan attended the main hearing of the trial of Marius Priscus, but only as presiding consul. Beyond urging Pliny in the midst of his five-hour speech not to overstrain himself, he seems to have taken no active part in the trial.[2]

Letters of Pliny also throw light on the pre-Trajanic period. The Publicius Certus affair, which Pliny discussed in a letter to Ummidius Quadratus, belongs to Nerva's reign.[3] The suggested prosecution did not eventuate. But Pliny claims that his boldness in attacking Certus was applauded in the Senate:

Almost the entire Senate embraced me with open arms and overwhelmed me with enthusiastic congratulations for having revived the practice, long fallen into disuse, of bringing measures for the public good before the Senate at the risk of incurring personal enmities; I had in fact freed the Senate from the odium in which it was held amongst other orders for showing severity to the rest while sparing its own members by a sort of mutual connivance.[4]

himself to summon witnesses from the province, e.g. 5. 20. 2 ff. espec. 7: 'impetravimus rem nec lege comprehensam nec satis usitatam, iustam tamen.' When this was contested by the provincials, they lost the support of those who had had doubts about the move in the first place. See 6. 13, espec. § 2, where Pliny attacks Claudius Capito for his 'irreverence' in challenging a *S.C.* in the Senate. See also 5. 20. 4 ff., cf. 7. 6. 2 for Pliny's opinions of another provincial prosecutor, Fonteius Magnus. In 7. 6. 2 Pliny complains that Magnus pestered the senatorial advocate, Nigrinus, until the latter asked the consuls to force Varenus to show his accounts. Why did Magnus have to apply any pressure at all?

[1] Ibid. 7. 6. 14, cf. 6. See also ibid. 6. 13. 2: the Bithynians approached the Emperor to complain about the concession given to Varenus (see last note). He merely passed the matter back to the Senate.

[2] Ibid. 2. 11. 10 ff., espec. 15.

[3] Ibid. 9. 13.

[4] § 21: 'non fere quisquam in senatu fuit, qui non me complecteretur

This remark, for all its tendentiousness, gives us a rare opportunity of savouring something of the dissatisfaction of men outside the senatorial order with the abuses of senatorial privilege. Pliny, of course, was commenting on the period which preceded the inauguration of the 'Golden Age' by Nerva.

Ironically, perhaps, we must turn to two Domitianic trials for examples of senatorial favouritism to senators in the pre-Nervan age. The trial of Baebius Massa took place in A.D. 93.[1] We saw that the consuls of the year could not be trusted to ensure that the provincials of Baetica recovered what Massa had extorted from them; and that the Senate's concept of 'legal aid' to provincials was so circumscribed that senatorial advocates were not expected to take any interest in their provincial clients' welfare after the termination of the trial proper. In such ways as these the rights and interests of the provincials were neglected by the senatorial court. The second Vestal Virgin affair preceded this trial by perhaps three years. Celer, an equestrian, was beaten to death with rods in the assembly (*comitium*) for incest. Valerius Licinianus, a senator of praetorian rank, was advised by those whose business it was (*ab iis quibus erat curae*) that he might avoid the same fate by a confession. He took the hint, confessed, and was permitted a 'soft' exile (*molle exilium*). Nerva made the exile even 'softer' by transferring him to Sicily.[2]

The two cases make an interesting comparison. The Vestal Virgin trial for incest was the culmination of a campaign waged by Domitian, as corrector of public morals, against immorality in the higher orders and in the state religion.[3] We may be sure that he watched over the Vestal Virgin trial from beginning to end, and that each penalty was sanctioned by him. The only doubtful point is whether he granted Licinianus a milder sentence purely because of his status, or in response to the requests of friends of

exoscularetur certatimque laude cumularet, quod intermissum iam diu morem in publicum consulendi susceptis propriis simultatibus reduxissem; quod denique senatum invidia liberassem, qua flagrabat apud ordines alios, quod severus in ceteros senatoribus solis dissimulatione quasi mutua parceret.'
[1] Ibid. 7. 33.
[2] Ibid. 4. 11. 13. On the date see Sherwin-White, op. cit. 283. The first Vestal Virgin trial probably belongs to A.D. 83-4.
[3] See the summary in Suet. *Dom.* 8. 3 ff.

Licinianus in close proximity to him.[1] Be that as it may, Domitian was as much involved in this trial as in his senatorial *maiestas* trials. The trial of Baebius Massa, however, resembles the trials of Classicus, Priscus, and Bassus in atmosphere. Pliny gives the impression that in all these trials the Senate was in complete control of the proceedings. There is no hint of imperial interference in Massa's trial, at least in its aftermath, which alone is described in any detail by Pliny.[2] It cannot, of course, be inferred that Domitian followed a consistent policy of non-interference in *repetundae* trials,[3] or in all senatorial trials which did not involve his policies or his own person as Emperor. But at least it seems legitimate to conclude that Domitian, for whatever motive, did not constantly subject the Senate to his paralysing influence.

The preceding discussion, ostensibly about crimes of less gravity than *maiestas*, has dealt in the main with *repetundae* with or without *saevitia*. This was unavoidable, as Pliny, our major authority, has little to say about other crimes.[4] However, it does not follow that Trajan's Senate could not try senators on other charges, more particularly, on charges which involved higher penalties than *repetundae* carried. Trajan swore not to kill *or disfranchise* senators on his own authority, and this is an indication, however indirect, that the Senate was entitled to pass sentences of death or capital exile on senatorial defendants.[5]

---

[1] The status of *iis quibus erat curae* is not clear. They were men close to the Emperor, but probably not the defendant's personal friends.

[2] It is unlikely that the attempted prosecution of Senecio was inspired by the Emperor; or that the consuls were under his orders. It is equally improbable that Domitian intervened in the trial itself to reduce Massa's penalty. Massa was not yet the formidable accuser he was to become.

[3] Suetonius (*Dom.* 8. 2) refers briefly to a *repetundae* charge which, he says, was brought by tribunes against an aedile at the Emperor's request.

[4] One senatorial investigation not yet mentioned followed the murder or suicide of the consul of A.D. 105, Afranius Dexter. Pliny, *Ep.* 8. 14. 12. See ibid. 4. 13 for a similar case.

[5] Dio 68. 5. 2: ὡς δὲ αὐτοκράτωρ ἐγένετο, ἐπέστειλε τῇ βουλῇ αὐτοχειρίᾳ ἄλλα τε καὶ ὡς οὐδένα ἄνδρα ἀγαθὸν ἀποσφάξοι ἢ ἀτιμάσοι, καὶ ταῦτα καὶ ὅρκοις οὐ τότε μόνον ἀλλὰ καὶ ὕστερον ἐπιστώσατο. Disfranchisement, for senators, automatically followed a sentence of capital exile. See p. 115. Disfranchisement is only one possible meaning of the word ἀτιμία, but perhaps the most likely in the context. (ἀτιμία means dishonour or disgrace, or the loss of civic privileges. In the Roman context, therefore, it could conceivably stand for either *infamia* or loss of rank, or loss of citizenship.)

Post-Trajanic evidence

The history of the senatorial court after the close of Trajan's reign is known only in the most shadowy outlines. Some have even argued for the virtual disappearance of senatorial jurisdiction by the Severan age. But they reach this conclusion on the basis of a few texts from the Augustan History (in judicial matters, at least, a source of dubious value), which show, at the most, that the Emperors sometimes tried senators.[1] Besides, positive evidence of the continued functioning of the court is provided by the two suits against the famous Athenian sophist Herodes Atticus, by

---

[1] (1) Mommsen (*Strafrecht*, 220) thought, on the basis of *SHA Marcus* 24. 2 ('capitales causas hominum honestorum ipse cognovit'), that Marcus brought to an end the capital jurisdiction of the Senate. Ibid. 10. 1 perhaps contradicts ('senatum multis cognitionibus et maxime ad se pertinentibus iudicem dedit'). See also Dio 71. 30. 1–2, cf. *SHA Marcus* 25. 5; and see below, pp. 60–1 (Herodes). There were certainly treason trials (at least) in the Senate in later reigns.

(2) Bleicken (op. cit. 117 ff.) appears to believe, first, that *maiestas* trials were ruled out both in the Senate and in the Emperor's court (but see above, pp. 47 ff.); second, from *SHA Hadr.* 8. 8, *Marcus* 10. 6, *Alex. Sev.* 21. 5, that non-political cases (as a concession to the Senate) were dealt with by the Emperor with a *consilium* made up exclusively of senators. The second text is the most explicit, but it is not clear whether it implies that the Emperor followed this procedure in all capital cases involving senators, or in all which were brought before him ('quotiens de quorum capite esset iudicandum'). The former interpretation seems less likely, considering the other evidence for Marcus (above). Of course, the text does not refer to non-capital cases. The first and third texts carry no implication of the universality of the practice, and the kind of cases is not specified. All three texts are generalizations.

(3) Some other passages from *SHA* are ambiguous or unspecific, and not much can be inferred from them with safety. On *repetundae*, one cannot argue for the termination of senatorial *repetundae* suits in the second century (sc. after Trajan) from *SHA Ant. Pius* 10. 7 ('si quos repetundarum damnavit, eorum liberis bona paterna restituit') and *SHA Sev.* 8. 4 ('accusatos a provincialibus iudices probatis rebus graviter punivit'). Of course, no Emperor was directly responsible for all the actions which his Biographer(s) ascribed to him. In judicial matters there is the added complication that an Emperor could influence directly a decision made in the Senate.

(4) *Dig.* 48. 5. 2. 6 ('nam Claudius Gorgus vir clarissimus uxorem accusans cum detectus est uxorem in adulterio deprehensam retinuisse, et sine accusatore lenocinio damnatus est a divo Severo') does not rule out the existence of senatorial trials in the Severan age (let alone under the Antonines), even if we can be sure that Severus personally tried and condemned Gorgus. (Severus was particularly concerned to fight adultery and kindred crimes, or at least for a time. But there were certainly too many cases for him to cope with in person. See Dio 76. 16. 4.) Cf. *Dig.* 48. 13. 12. 1, on sacrilege ('Divus Severus et Antoninus quendam clarissimum iuvenem, cum inventus esset arculam in templum ponere ibique hominem includere convictum in insulam deportaverunt').

the senatorial *maiestas* trials in the reigns of Hadrian, Pius, Marcus, and Septimius Severus, and by the portion of the speech of Maecenas which deals with senatorial jurisdiction.

Herodes Atticus was indicted in A.D. 144 by Athenians on a number of counts, probably in the Senate.[1] In a revealing series of letters between an advocate for the prosecution, Fronto, and Herodes' friend and patron, the young Marcus, Marcus is shown to have exerted his influence strongly, though with tact, in favour of Herodes before the trial took place. Fronto was not prepared to gloss over the facts which bore on the case—one free man killed and others beaten and robbed, a son's lack of respect for his father's prayers, cruelty, avarice, butchery—but he agreed not to go beyond those facts, not to speak on the defendant's 'character, and the other aspects of his life'.[2] This was apparently sufficient for Marcus—'you have taken my advice' (*comprobasti*)—who professed himself anxious only for Fronto's reputation: no harm would be done to his good faith (*fides*) or honour (*modestia*) if Fronto left his private feelings unspoken and kept to what was relevant to the case.[3] Why was Marcus so restrained? He was well aware that every advocate mindful of his career must put a strong case in order to keep faith with his clients and attract public attention. Marcus was simply reminding Fronto that he had a second obligation, to his patron. No doubt Fronto took the point, and chose to give up the small chance he had of influencing the outcome of the case rather than run the risk of forfeiting the friendship of the prospective Emperor. We have no record of the trial itself, but it seems that Herodes was acquitted—perhaps Marcus did more for Herodes than hold Fronto in check.[4] Later,

---

[1] *ad M. Caes.* 3. 2–6 (ed. van den Hout, pp. 36–40); *M. Caes. ad Front.* 4. 2 (pp. 54 ff.). There is no proof that the case went before the Senate. But the rhetorical note struck by Fronto suggests he is preparing for a major speech before a large gathering in public. For Ti. Claudius Herodes Atticus see *PIR*² C 802.

[2] *ad M. Caes.* 3. 3 (pp. 37 ff.). For the origin of the indictment see Philostr. *Vit. Soph.* 549 (Loeb, pp. 142 ff.). Later the two Quinctilii (in Achaea as proconsul and legate A.D. 148–50, joint consuls 151) took up the cause of the Athenians. See ibid. 559 ff. (Loeb, pp. 166 ff.).

[3] *ad M. Caes.* 3. 5 (p. 39).

[4] In A.D. 165 Fronto refers to Herodes as *summus nunc meus*. See *ad Anton. imp.* 3. 4 (p. 106), cf. *ad Ver. imp.* 2. 9 (p. 130).

at the beginning of Marcus' reign, Herodes was accused of murdering his wife, Regilla. His opponent was formidable, a consular like himself and the brother of the dead woman. Herodes was again freed by the Senate. But this time, if we believe Philostratus, 'the truth prevailed'.[1]

The senatorial *maiestas* trials have already been discussed in some detail. Here it is simply necessary to stress that they, and especially the Severan trials, form an essential part of the background of the passage in Maecenas' speech, and help to establish its contemporary relevance.[2]

Dio began working on his History in the reign of Septimius Severus, when executions for *maiestas*, more often than not following senatorial hearings, were relatively frequent.[3] When Dio insisted, through the mouth of Maecenas, that an Emperor should both pass to the Senate cases involving the death penalty, and leave the Senate free to reach its own decision in such cases, he could not but have had Severus in mind. Severus by his oath (backed by a senatorial decree) had acknowledged the first of these requirements only, and had circumvented it by forcing the senatorial court to pass death sentences on his enemies. Moreover, if Severus' hypocritical behaviour helped Dio formulate his demands, Caracalla's blatant murders in the opening years of his reign gave Dio a target at which to aim them.[4] Thus it can be asserted with some confidence that the reference to the death penalty in the passage is pointed, and pertinent to Dio's age.

What of the reference to loss of citizenship (or political position)[5] and capital exile in the same passage? Had the Senate lost the power to inflict these penalties, and was Dio requesting its return?

---

[1] Philostr. *vit. soph.* 555–6 (Loeb, pp. 158 ff.). The consular was Appius Annius Atilius Bradua. Philostratus later records how an attempt by Herodes to indict his political opponents at home on criminal charges before the proconsul was turned against him. See ibid. 560 ff. (Loeb, pp. 168 ff.); and below, p. 69.

[2] The speech as a whole is a political broadsheet. See Fergus Millar, *A Study of Cassius Dio* (1964), 102 ff.

[3] For the date of the composition of the History, ibid. 28 ff.; on Severan *maiestas* trials see above, pp. 48–9.

[4] Millar (op. cit. 104) suggests plausibly that Caracalla was the addressee of the speech, which may have been written in A.D. 214.

[5] See p. 58 n. 5 on the meaning of ἀτιμία.

According to Herodian, Severus swore neither to kill senators *nor to confiscate their property* without a (sc. senatorial) trial. The latter sanction, moreover, is presented not as a mere adjunct of the former.[1] This is of consequence, as confiscation of property was regularly associated with the sentence of capital exile.[2] We saw that Trajan's oath mentioned death and disfranchisement, which was also a necessary concomitant of capital exile.[3] In Trajan's case we have the correspondence of a senator to prove that his Senate was concerned to protect senators against lesser sanctions than death, and that it was permitted to administer those sanctions against senatorial defendants. Herodian's version of the oath of Severus may be a sign that the Senate of Severus had lost neither its concern with the penalties of disfranchisement and exile (and associated sanctions) nor its power to administer them to its own members.

In general, it is difficult to see what motive any of the Antonine or Severan Emperors could have had for bringing to an end the jurisdiction of the Senate. The Senate had long since lost its role as the High Court of the Empire. The scope of its jurisdiction had been limited by the development of the Emperor's court, and it could not compete with that court as a rival. Dio's plea was for a senatorial trial for senatorial defendants in cases of any gravity, and few senators of his time would have wished for more. It cost the Emperor nothing to concede to the Senate a court of this type, and there were compelling political reasons for doing so. Above all, the Senate would undoubtedly resent the withdrawal of a privilege exercised almost from the inception of the Empire, and prized not only for the real benefits it brought to senatorial defendants, but also as a status-symbol. Senators could never argue for the maintenance of their jurisdiction with reference to specific legal enactments. But in the course of a century or more of judicial activity they had come to regard it as a permanent

[1] Her. 2. 14. 3: μήτε δὲ ἄκριτόν τινα φονευθήσεσθαι ἢ δημευθήσεσθαι. The wording of the original oath (and *S.C.*) is probably beyond recovery. The different versions both contribute something. Herodian's ἢ δημευθήσεσθαι is a new detail and should probably be accepted. (Contrast ἄκριτον, which is perhaps an inaccurate translation of 'inconsulto senatu', *SHA Sev.* 7. 5.)

[2] See pp. 115 ff.   [3] Dio 68. 5. 2. See p. 58.

prerogative to which they were entitled, rather than as a revocable concession which they were allowed by the Emperor's kind favour.

I would propose, then, that the senatorial court maintained a meaningful jurisdiction into the Severan age;[1] and that the point of conflict between Senate and Emperor was the control of the senatorial court rather than its continued existence. Control became an issue primarily because of the overuse or misuse of the *maiestas* law. Had it not been for the arraignment of political criminals, the disengagement of the Emperor from the senatorial court, which was encouraged by the growth of his own jurisdiction, might have been more or less complete.[2] The policy of some Emperors probably varied according to the circumstances of the particular trial. This was suggested tentatively above in the case of Domitian; Hadrian is perhaps a less controversial example. For all we know, Hadrian may have permitted his senatorial court to operate in relative freedom when it met to try offences which did not directly involve him as Emperor. The prohibition of appeals from the Senate to the Emperor which is associated with his name is an indication of a general unwillingness on his part to overrule the Senate in judicial matters.[3] Yet his reputation was tarnished by the judicial murders of leading senators and his involvement of the Senate in those murders. An Emperor who was well regarded in senatorial circles was likely to be one who followed a policy of non-intervention consistently, from *maiestas* trials down, if he did not rule out *maiestas* trials altogether.

---

[1] It is not proposed that the Senate tried *all* senatorial defendants on serious charges. An Emperor might take a case if requested to do so.

[2] i.e. an Emperor would have found it easier to allow the Senate a large measure of autonomy in its jurisdiction if cases in which his own dignity and safety were involved had been effectively excluded from its sphere of interest. Of course, the Emperor's overriding discretionary powers would not have been curtailed under such conditions. Thus Trajan showed only a remote, fatherly interest in the Senate's judicial activities, while retaining ultimate authority over them. See Pliny, *Ep.* 3. 20. 10 and 12 (not specifically on judicial matters).

[3] *Dig.* 49. 2. 1. 2: 'sciendum est appellari a senatu non posse principem idque oratione divi Hadriani effectum.' Despite Bleicken, op. cit. 118, it is not obvious why the rule should have referred to civil and not criminal cases.

Conclusion

Different Imperial attitudes and policies towards the senatorial court, from reign to reign and in individual reigns, produced different discrimination patterns within that court in the period from the Flavians to the Severans. One pattern is more characteristic of the Julio-Claudian age, when the senatorial court functioned under the Emperor's active supervision. Under such conditions the fate of senatorial criminals was likely to be influenced by chance factors, especially the presence of Imperial favour and Imperial fear. A second pattern is exemplified in the Trajanic *repetundae* trials, in which the Emperor apparently played no part, while the Senate was left free to favour senatorial defendants because of their rank, that is, because they were senators. Dio/ Maecenas envisaged that an Emperor would follow a policy of non-intervention for political considerations, because he was mindful of his position and of the desirability of maintaining good relations with the Senate. But in addition he might very well approve of the use that the Senate made of its freedom, because of his own aristocratic prejudices.

3

EMPEROR, GOVERNORS, AND DELEGATED JURISDICTION

THERE was widespread dissatisfaction at the beginning of the Principate with the existing state of both the civil and the criminal law. The *ius ordinarium*, built up by the praetor through edicts, was felt to be excessively formalistic and inflexible, and its delays were notorious; the criminal jury-courts, meanwhile, were slow-moving and corrupt. The Emperor's subjects looked to him to remedy the situation, to bring equity into the legal system, and in general to provide a higher authority for law.

Imperial jurisdiction, then, was less a conscious creation of Emperors than a response to popular needs and discontents. One consequence of this was that the Emperor's field of interest in law was open-ended: of necessity it embraced the whole range of legal problems which were brought to him by large numbers of would-be litigants, all of whom in theory had some chance of gaining his attention.

The accessibility of the Emperor to his subjects is a remarkable phenomenon. But, of course, to gain access to the Emperor through a petition was not the same as to gain access to his tribunal. No Emperor, however hardworking, could hope to act as judge in all the disputes which were referred to him by subjects. Inevitably the great majority of requests for litigation were passed on to subordinate authorities, whether to individuals appointed to make *ad hoc* decisions in single cases, or to special officials empowered to settle either single cases or whole classes of cases, or, finally, to officials whose jurisdictions were already competent to try cases of the type now sent down to them. Moreover, if the volume of cases was one problem, the sheer size of the Empire created another. It was plainly more difficult and expensive for a provincial than for an Italian or a Roman, and for a poor provincial than for a rich one, to bring his grievance in person to the Emperor. But there are grounds for thinking that a plaintiff's chance of gaining the Emperor as adjudicator were very slim if he did not make a personal appearance at the Emperor's court. A less obvious but equally important point is that in all probability principles of selection operated which virtually excluded certain types of cases and certain types of people from the Imperial tribunal. Thus the Emperors, rather than trying a wide variety of cases on an *ad hoc* basis, may have confined themselves to a restricted and clearly demarcated area of the law. Again, some or all cases may have been taken less because a potential plaintiff or defendant managed to awake the Emperor's interest or arouse his feelings than because he held a certain position or rank.[1]

The discussion that follows seeks to establish the character of the Emperor's judicial court. It is concerned in the main with the period from the Flavians to the Severans, not because the Imperial tribunal did not function earlier (evidence from the Julio-Claudian period will be drawn upon), but because the responsibilities of the Emperor for criminal justice do not seem to have grown to any marked extent until about the Flavian period.[2]

[1] In the field of civil law (no systematic treatment of civil law is attempted here) little is known about whether the Emperor took disputes involving men of high rank as defendants. In general, the Emperor probably preferred *ad hoc* decision-making in a variety of cases to specializing within a narrow area. He took cases covered by the *ius ordinarium* (an early example, Val. Max. 7. 7. 3–4; Augustus) and also cases outside it. Particular attention may have been paid to the latter, but the normal practice of Emperors seems to have been not to assume responsibility for specific problems themselves, but to pass them on to special officials. Thus, in the matter of trusts, Augustus established a consular jurisdiction over them rather than directing litigants to approach himself. See *IJ* 2. 23. 1. Status disputes may be the exception to the rule—but the granting of the citizenship was regarded as an Imperial prerogative. See Suet. *Div. Aug.* 40. 3–4; *Div. Cl.* 15. 2; Pliny, *Ep.* 10. 5 ff.; etc. The less scrupulous and less sensitive Emperors might have sat over property disputes in which the Imperial treasury was involved, but this is not likely to have happened frequently. References in Pliny and Tacitus show that a controversy was raging about suits of this kind in their day. But the issue seems to have been over whether they should be settled by Imperial agents, especially procurators, by *cognitio*, or by the praetor and the formulary process. See Tac. *Ann.* 4. 6; 4. 15; Pliny, *Pan.* 36. 3 ff. In *Dig.* 28. 4. 3, the Emperor settles a point before passing the case to a prefect of the treasury. On the Emperor's accessibility see F. Millar, *JRS* 56 (1966), 156 ff.; 57 (1967), 9 ff., *pass.*

[2] At the close of Domitian's reign, when Quintilian was writing, the Imperial tribunal was a fully-fledged court, existing side by side with the senatorial court:

The Emperor's jurisdiction can be broken down into three main compartments: primary jursidiction, cases remitted from lower tribunals (especially the governor's court) after a preliminary investigation, and criminal appeals.[1] The willingness of the new Flavian dynasty to extend and display its powers over a reorganized Senate and increasingly dependent governors led to a greater involvement in primary jurisdiction (especially as the activities of the jury-courts were further contracted) and a rise in the number of cases remitted from the provinces; while the volume of appeals to the Emperor from the ever-expanding body of citizens must have continued to swell.

Provincials

We may begin by examining in more detail the situation of the provincials, who of course formed the greater part of the population of the Empire.

The ordinary provincial with a grievance which he wanted the Emperor to investigate would send off a *libellus* or petition. In due course, presumably, an answer would come to the petitioner in the form of a rescript. But the rescripts would very often contain the formula, 'You may approach the man in charge of the province' (*eum qui provinciae praeest adire potes*), or a variant. So regularly was this formula used, that Antoninus Pius was accustomed to say, when he himself used it, that the governor, if subsequently approached, was not obliged to undertake an investigation himself, but only to decide whether to do so or to name another judge.[2]

'. . . et sunt re vera secundum forense ius duae lites. potest tamen hoc genus in cognitionem venire senatus aut principis.' *Inst. Or.* 7. 2. 20.

[1] Emperors also gave written replies, or rescripts, to queries about legal points. See p. 174.

[2] *Dig.* 1. 18. 8 (Julian, an eyewitness): 'saepe audivi Caesarem nostrum dicentem hac rescriptione: "eum qui provinciae praeest adire potes" non imponi necessitatem proconsuli vel legato eius vel praesidi provinciae suscipiendae cognitionis, sed eum aestimare debere, ipse cognoscere an iudicem dare debeat.' Cf. *FIRA*[2] i, no. 74, p. 422 (Vespasian, A.D. 77): 'de his proconsulem adire debebitis.' See also *Dig.* 22. 5. 3. 3 (Hadrian). Trajan, when once approached directly by letter, agreed to undertake a *falsum* investigation. But the defendants were a freedman-procurator and an equestrian, and the plaintiffs

Some litigants would have been satisfied if the Emperor, rather than consent to inquire into the case himself, was prepared to issue a ruling which could then be flourished in the face of an opponent in a local law-court. The Emperors, however, were probably less free in offering their authoritative opinions to individuals than is sometimes imagined. Trajan, if the story is authentic, refused to issue rescripts in reply to *libelli*, lest they should be used as precedents in other cases, while Pius was warned by Fronto not to comment on the decision of a governor in a case over a will that was referred to him, 'lest you should provide a rule for all magistrates of all provinces for deciding all cases of this sort'.[1] A number of rescripts to private individuals survive in the legal sources. It is noteworthy that those relevant to the criminal law do not relate to disputes still *sub iudice*, but are in the main replies to protests against sentences passed or sanctions applied.[2] The rest deal with civil-law matters or problems of administration, and most of these do little more than guide the petitioner to another tribunal, as Pius' rescripts were wont to do.[3]

On at least one occasion Pius broke his habit. Instead of merely referring one Domitius Silvanus to the governor of his province, he wrote to the governor, Geminus, a strong letter describing the substance of Silvanus' complaint (a savage attack on his uncle's son) and bidding him to listen to it, inquire into it, and punish the offender heavily. It is noteworthy that the *libellus* was actually handed over to the Emperor by Silvanus. To judge from the tone

---

perhaps related to the ex-praetor whose codicil had allegedly been forged. See Pliny, *Ep.* 6. 31. 7 ff., and p. 87.

[1] *SHA Macr.* 13. 1: 'fuit in iure non incallidus, adeo ut statuisset omnia rescripta veterum principum tollere, ut iure, non rescriptis ageretur, nefas esse dicens leges videri Commodi et Caracalli et hominum inperitorum voluntates, cum Traianus numquam libellis responderit, ne ad alias causas facta praeferrentur, quae ad gratiam conposita viderentur'; Fronto, *ad M. Caes.* 1. 6. 3, cf. 2 (pp. 10 ff., ed. van den Hout): 'quare, si hoc decretum tibi proconsulis placuerit, formam dederis omnibus omnium provinciarum magistratibus, quid in eiusmodi causis decernant.' The date is A.D. 144–5.

[2] e.g. *CJ* 2. 11. 1–3 and 5; 9. 47. 2 and 9; *Dig.* 1. 19. 3. 1–2; 42. 1. 33; 48. 19. 27 praef. (2 cases). See also *FIRA*² i, no. 103, p. 495 (*coloni* of saltus Burunitanus; Commodus).

[3] *CJ* 2. 12. 2; 5. 25. 2–3; 5. 62. 18; *Dig.* 1. 7. 39; 1. 18. 8; 25. 3. 5. 9; 25. 3. 6 praef.; 35. 1. 50; 49. 1. 1. 3; 49. 9. 1; *vat. fr.* 168; 247. See M. Kaser, *Das römische Zivilprozessrecht* (1966), 352, with bibl.

and content of the Emperor's letter, the personal approach by the representative of the injured party had paid dividends.[1]

An early case of Imperial *cognitio* in a dispute involving provincials followed the arrival of the prosecution, and probably also of the accused, in Rome.[2] In 6 B.C. two ambassadors from Cnidos in Asia brought to Augustus an accusation against a man (who died at some stage during the investigation) and his wife, both Cnidans, for the murder of another citizen of the place. Augustus conducted his own inquiry, with the assistance of the proconsul of Asia, Asinius Gallus, who had the slaves of the defendants interrogated. The woman was acquitted, and the city and its magistrates were castigated for persecuting the accused. The trial is interesting from several points of view. For present purposes what is relevant is that the Emperor conducted the investigation. It seems possible to infer that a plaintiff (or plaintiffs) would greatly improve his chances of obtaining a *cognitio* from the Emperor if he took his case to Rome either in person or through representatives.[3] This point is confirmed by a later case. Herodes Atticus, the Athenian sophist, was thwarted in his attempt to indict his political enemies before a friendly proconsul in Athens, when the defendants escaped to Marcus at Sirmium. In the trial that followed, Herodes was less accuser than accused.[4]

Two Trajanic trials may be considered next. It is uncertain how Claudius Aristion and Trebonius Rufinus, the defendants, came to be tried by Trajan.[5] If it can be supposed that the two men were both accused *ab initio* before the Emperor,[6] then two things seem to be relevant. First, we can assume that both the defendants

---

[1] *Dig.* 48. 6. 6. Cf. 42. 1. 33: a personal approach to Hadrian by Iulius Tarentinus, in search of *restitutio*. See also Suet. *Div. Aug.* 40 (citizenship); and Epict. 3. 9. 1 ff. (on which see p. 70 n. 1).   [2] *FIRA*[2] iii, no. 185, pp. 582 ff.

[3] If, as is likely, the defendant also on this occasion made her way to Rome, in order to present her side of the case, this, together with the verdict, serves as a reminder that Imperial assistance (*auxilium*) was available to threatened defendants as well as to outraged plaintiffs.

[4] Philostr. *vit. soph.* 560 ff. (Loeb, pp. 168 ff.). The charge was of rousing the people against him (Herodes), and the chief defendant was Demostratus. See *PIR*[2] C 849.

[5] Pliny, *Ep.* 6. 31. 2 ff. (Aristion); 4. 22. 1 ff. (Rufinus).

[6] The other possibility, that the defendants were sent to the Emperor by their respective governors, is considered below, pp. 72 ff.

and the prosecutors could have paid for a journey to Rome, as the Domitii Silvani, Herodes' rivals, and the city of Cnidos evidently could, and as the average provincial just as evidently could not.[1] The defendants were powerful and therefore wealthy men in their respective communities, Ephesos and Vienne.[2] Their opponents, who are unknown, are not likely to have been far behind in prominence. The indictments of both defendants probably originated in the jealousy of their rivals, that is to say, of men strong enough to compete with them for pre-eminence. Second, both offences were of a serious kind. Aristion was probably charged with public violence (*vis publica*).[3] The second trial seems to have revolved around the prerogatives of local magistrates. Rufinus had suppressed the local gymnastic games in his capacity as chief magistrate, and he was accused of misusing his powers. It should be noted that the offences complained of by Domitius, Herodes, and the Cnidans were also serious.

A direct approach to the Emperor was apparently not out of the question for appellants.[4] The regular procedure (in the Antonine and Severan periods at any rate) by which the governor forwarded the appellant's petition to Rome was of course considerably slower.[5] Moreover, if an appellant merely sent a petition

[1] One man who could certainly afford to go to Rome was a leading citizen of Cnossos in Crete, who on the way encountered Epictetus. The object of his journey was to win the position of *patronus* of his city by way of a lawsuit. See Epict. 3. 9. 1 ff. The financial position of the Cnidan woman, Tryphera (supposing that she did in fact travel to Rome), is unknown. She was not a Roman citizen. Sicinius Aemilianus (below, p. 96) was a prosperous landowner in Tripolitania and well able to pay his way to Rome for a trial before the urban prefect.

[2] Aristion was three times Asiarch and Archiereus of Asia, as well as a leading magistrate of Ephesos. *PIR*[2] C 788; *AE* 1898, no. 66; 1906, nos. 28–9; *JÖAI* 45 (1959), Beiblatt 23, 329–30; *JÖAI* 46 (1960), Beiblatt 24, 83, no. 9; etc. Rufinus was duumvir at Vienna in Narbonese Gaul, and is described by Pliny as *vir egregius, nobisque amicus*.

[3] The charge of *vis publica* is suggested by the words *innoxie popularis* in the text of Pliny. It is stated that the impeachment sprang from *invidia*. The description of the defendant as *homo munificus* hints at the reason for his unpopularity (in some quarters), and makes it likely that the trial was brought on by rivals for local honours and esteem.

[4] See *Dig.* 49. 1. 25 (= *P. Oxy.* 2104): ὅποτε ἔξεστιν τήν ἑτέραν ὁδὸν τρεπόμενον ταὐτὸ ποιεῖν (i.e. ἐκκαλεῖσθαι) καὶ θᾶττον πρός με ἀφικνεῖσθαι (Severus Alexander to the koinon of the Bithynian Greeks). Also, *Dig.* 42. 1. 33 (Hadrian approached by a *condemnatus* seeking a *restitutio*).

[5] See last note (θᾶττον). An appeal was lodged with the governor two or three days after he passed sentence, whether in civil or in criminal disputes. See *Dig.*

(*libellus*), and the governor in his accompanying letter (*litterae*) chose to twist the facts, the former was in no position to expose the latter's mendacity. Proconsular distortion must have frequently gone undetected because unchallenged. Again, there was no guarantee that a governor would co-operate even to the extent of permitting a would-be appellant to lodge a formal appeal. It was commonly his judgement which was being disputed.[1]

In practice few would have been able to bypass the governor. The problem was not simply the financial one of finding money for the journey. Most appellants would have been under some sort of restriction from the time of their arrest, and their situation would not have changed until the final judgement was handed down from the appellate court. Only a defendant who was a member of the higher orders had any freedom of movement. 'Concerning the custody of defendants', wrote Ulpian, 'the proconsul usually decides whether someone should be put in prison or handed over to a soldier *or entrusted to guarantors or to himself*'. It turns out that the governor's decision was normally influenced by such factors as the gravity of the crime, and the wealth, position, and rank of the accused.[2]

To sum up: first, there is a strong supposition that a provincial plaintiff or defendant was much more likely to gain the Emperor's effective intervention if he was ready and able to go to Rome and ask for it in person than if he stayed at home and merely sent off a *libellus*. Ordinary provincials would have found the way to Rome barred by obstacles of a physical or material kind.[3] Second, the Emperor would not necessarily accept every request for

49. 4 *pass.* If accepted by the governor, it (i.e. the appellant's *libellus*) was sent off with a letter from the governor including, no doubt, a full statement on the trial and a copy of the judgement. See *Dig.* 28. 3. 6. 9, etc.

[1] See *Dig.* 49. 1. 1. 1, for proconsular distortion; for a fuller discussion of defects of the appeal system see below, pp. 82 ff.

[2] *Dig.* 48. 3. 1, cf. ibid. 3 (rescript of Pius). Severus Alexander (for the reference see above, p. 70 n. 4) protested against the action of governors and procurators in preventing by force the departure of appellants for Rome. Perhaps he was defending the freedom of movement of just such high-status defendants. (The fact that his rescript is addressed to the koinon of Bithynian Greeks, that is, in effect, the leading men of the cities of Bithynia, perhaps supports this hypothesis.)

[3] On the financial side, the litigant had to provide money for travel, board and lodging, and advocate's fees. The burden would become heavier the longer the trial went on. Postponements were easy to obtain. See Fronto, *ad M. Caes.* 1. 6. 3.

litigation which was brought to him by a provincial. It no doubt made a difference if the stakes were high. In criminal cases, they normally were.

As was indicated earlier, nothing is known about the preliminaries of the trials of Aristion and Rufinus. It is quite possible that they were examples not of cases brought to the Emperor in the first instance, but of cases remitted to the Emperor by a provincial governor. The question arises whether the latter class of cases provided for the average provincial, whether as plaintiff or as defendant, an alternative avenue of access to the Emperor. The evidence available suggests that this was not the case. The explanation is to be sought partly in the attitude of the governor, who in most cases must have been responsible for the dispatch of a prisoner to Rome; and partly in the attitude of the Emperor, who was normally in a position to dictate policy to the governor, and as time went on was more and more inclined to do so. There is no sign that any governor was ever persuaded by an ordinary provincial plaintiff to send a case out of his jurisdiction to a higher tribunal. As for provincial defendants of low status, when they did appear before the Emperor's judgement-seat, it was hardly by choice, and hardly in circumstances favourable to them. Again, when the governor lost some of his discretionary authority as a result of Imperial intervention, the situation may have improved for the provincial élite, but the condition of the mass of provincials remained the same.

The evidence for cases remitted may now be reviewed. I include in this category cases in which the governor surrendered final judgement to the Emperor, at first voluntarily and later under compulsion, while holding the defendants concerned in his province. This was probably a procedural change introduced deliberately in the course of the second century to take the pressure off the prisons and tribunals in Rome.

It seems that the bulk of the defendants sent to the Emperor by governors in the first century were charged with serious political crimes, rebellion or subversion, or offences against the Emperor.[1]

---

[1] For a discussion of cases remitted see F. Millar, *JRS* 56 (1966), 159 and 165. The cases referred to in this section are from the first or early second

In 7 B.C., two citizens and a freedman were sent up to Augustus by one P. Sextius Scaeva, probably the governor of Cyrene. They were said to possess knowledge pertaining to the welfare of the Emperor and the safety of the state. Augustus investigated separately an allegedly treasonable offence committed by one of them.[1] Three years later Quinctilius Varus, as legate of Syria, quelled a Jewish revolt and sent off the leaders of one group of rebels to Augustus.[2] Later governors intervened in a similar way to send off leading rebels or leaders of opposing factions in Judaea (and even procurators accused of cruelty).[3] At the close of Nero's reign, Fonteius Capito, the legate of Lower Germany, arrested two leading Batavians of royal blood (*regia stirpe*), perhaps for suspected complicity with Vindex the rebel. One of them, Iulius Civilis, was put in irons and sent to the Emperor.[4] Finally, Apollonius and Larginus Proculus were sent to Rome for foretelling the days of Gaius' and Domitian's deaths, respectively.[5] Of this group of prisoners it can be said that they were dispatched to Rome less because of their rank—they were representative of most sections of the provincial populations—than because of their crime. That such cases were set aside for the Emperor's *cognitio* is easily explained. It seems to have been recognized from the

century. But there were no doubt parallels in the later period. Cf. the first one listed (next note) with *Dig.* 48. 19. 6 praef. (Ulpian). Three cases are not discussed in the account that follows: Tac. *Ann.* 16. 10. 2 (*ob flagitia*); Pliny, *Ep.* 10. 56–7 (illegally returned exile); ibid. 10. 74 (slave with information about the Dacian and Parthian kings).

[1] *EJ* 311. ii. 42–7. In Suet. *Div. Aug.* 51. 2, the man from Corduba may have been sent to Augustus by the governor of Baetica. The two defendants of 51. 1 are perhaps plebeians from Rome.

[2] Jos. *AJ* 17. 297; cf. *BJ* 2. 77.

[3] Jos. *AJ* 18. 88–9 (Pilate); *BJ* 2. 243–4 = *AJ* 20. 135 ff. (Cumanus, Celer, leading Jews—including two high-priests and the son of one of them—and Samaritans; I take Josephus' version of these events and not that of Tacitus in *Ann.* 12. 54, despite E. M. Smallwood, *Latomus* 18 (1959), 560); cf. *BJ* 3. 398 (Vespasian, though not of course as governor of Syria, intended to send to Nero Josephus himself); *vita* 408 ff. (Philip ben Jacimus).

[4] Tac. *Hist.* 4. 13, cf. *Ann.* 6. 40. 2 (Tigranes); ibid. 12. 21 (Mithridates).

[5] Dio 59. 29. 4; 67. 16. 2. Domitian's prisons were filled with prisoners charged with capital crimes (mostly alleged offences against the Emperor). The provincials among them may have been sent to Rome by governors. See Philostr. *vita Ap.* 7. 22 ff.; for Apollonius himself see ibid. 7. 10 ff. (Apollonius anticipated a summons from Domitian via the proconsul of Asia.)

beginning of the Principate that the Emperor had the right to protect himself and his rule.[1]

A smaller group of cases involved religious offenders, specifically, Christians. Christianity, as Pliny discovered, had attained a position of some strength in the province of Bithynia by the reign of Trajan. Pliny had no sooner shown a willingness to accept criminal indictments against Christians than prosecutors began to come from all sides. The situation was not an easy one to handle. Pliny, as he confessed to Trajan, had never before attended a trial of Christians. Furthermore, his doubts, as expressed in his letter to the Emperor,[2] covered virtually everything: punishments, mitigating circumstances, pardons, the nature of the crime, and whether Christianity should be made the object of an official investigation. Pliny goes on to detail the steps he had taken to deal with those Christians who had been brought before him. The aliens had simply been led away and executed once their guilt was determined. The Roman citizens were treated differently. 'I have put them down for dispatch to the city.'[3]

Would it be accurate to say that the primary reason for the sending to Rome of the citizen Christians was their citizen-status?[4] It was certainly their citizenship which separated them from their brethren in the first place and saved them from immediate execution. (Roman citizens, as distinct from aliens, were

[1] This is reflected in the Emperor's primary jurisdiction in *maiestas* cases. Tiberius' policy of refusing to try in person any *maiestas* charge was a reversal of the practice of Augustus, who seems himself to have considered charges against plebeians (Suet. *Div. Aug.* 51. 1), and perhaps also against higher-placed persons (Dio 55. 10. 14 ff.; 55. 4. 3, cf. 15. 4). Tiberius' example was not followed by later Emperors. The right of an Emperor to try senatorial criminals was alone contested. Even Domitian took some notice of the Senate's feelings on the subject, while arraigning before his own court men of lower status on political charges (Philostr. *vita Ap.* 7. 22: the fifty-odd prisoners included men of Rome and Italy. See e.g. 7. 24).

[2] Pliny, *Ep.* 10. 96.

[3] The whole sentence runs: 'Fuerunt alii similis amentiae, quos, quia cives Romani erant, adnotavi in urbem remittendos' (§4).

[4] A. H. M. Jones, *Studies in Roman Government and Law* (1960), 55, argues from this case that appeal in Trajan's reign was automatic—the decline of *provocatio* (soon to be replaced, in his view, by *appellatio*) was all but complete. See *JRS* 56 (1966), 180 ff., for a discussion of the theory that *provocatio* and *appellatio* were two different systems of appeal. In any case, these particular defendants were *confessi*, and *confessi* forfeited their rights of appeal (ibid. 173).

not subject to execution without trial, unless they had been declared enemies of the state.) But it was not at all automatic that they should be sent to Rome for trial. Pliny had to decide whether he was sufficiently knowledgeable about Christianity and the sense in which it was a crime to sit in judgement over them. He did not think he was, and the men were sent to a higher authority. To sum up, these Roman citizens were guaranteed a full trial rather than the summary execution meted out to aliens, but not trial in Rome.[1]

We come now to the case of St. Paul.[2] In the course of the investigation of his case by the prefect Festus at Caesarea, Festus proposed to try Paul at Jerusalem. At this stage Paul took the initiative and 'appealed' to be sent to Rome for trial by the Emperor. The reference of Paul to Nero's tribunal has usually been explained purely in terms of his status as a Roman citizen. This explanation might have been sufficient if an appeal had been lodged, and indeed this has been treated as a model case of criminal appeal.[3] But the appeal was not an orthodox one if appeal was normally after sentence, for no sentence was passed by Festus on Paul.[4] Again, Paul's citizenship might have been decisive if there had existed a rule according to which a governor was required to send to Rome any citizen on a capital charge, or any citizen on one of a certain select group of capital charges. There were, however, no such rules.[5]

---

[1] Over sixty years later the governor of Gallia Lugdunensis was no better informed about the way Christians who were citizens should be punished, and he wrote to his Emperor, Marcus Aurelius, for instructions. He did not, however, send the prisoners off to Rome, but in due course punished them in the way the Emperor directed him. (The Romans were beheaded and the aliens sent to the beasts. Attalus, however, although a citizen, was punished as if an alien.) See Eus. *EH* 5. 1.

[2] Acts 25: 9–10; 26: 32. See *JRS* 56 (1966), 182–5.

[3] See Jones, op. cit. 55; A. N. Sherwin-White, *Roman Society and Roman Law in the New Testament* (1963), 57 ff.

[4] If Paul's appeal is *'provocatio-before-trial'* in the sense assumed by Jones and Sherwin-White, there is no parallel which is of any use, and consequently the case has to be explained in the light of itself. Again, citizenship is not mentioned as a factor here, but only in connection with the earlier beating (Acts 22: 24, cf. 16: 37). It is pertinent to ask if the 'appeal' would have been refused automatically if it had *not* been known that Paul was a citizen.

[5] The first position was held by Mommsen, *GS* iii. 431 ff., cf. *Strafr.* 242 ff. See also Bleicken, op. cit. 178 ff. Was it illegal of Festus to invite Paul, a citizen

On the other hand, it can be agreed that the *persona* of Paul, his record and his status (including his possession of the citizenship), did influence Festus in reaching his decision. We may perhaps allow that the Roman citizenship was more highly regarded in Judaea in the mid first century than in Bithynia in the early second; further, that Paul, in comparison with the Bithynian citizen Christians, was a more prominent representative of his faith, and a greater danger in the eyes of the Roman authorities, both to the state religion and to the peace and order of the Empire. It may also be the case that Paul, in requesting trial before the Emperor, was exercising a little-used if not virtually obsolete prerogative of provincial citizens to choose between courts and seek to have their case referred to Rome (*reiectio Romam*).[1] However, if, as I hold, Festus was under no obligation to grant Paul his request, then a complex of causes must be acknowledged to lie behind his decision. Festus' personality and attitudes, his uncertainty about the basis of the allegations against Paul,[2] and the strain of Jewish pressure—as well as Paul's status—were probably relevant factors.

Maiestas could easily be regarded by governors as primarily the Emperor's affair. Christianity raised special problems, and it might be claimed that it fell to the Emperor, as Pontifex Maximus and guardian of the state religion, to solve them. But the Emperor was also commander-in-chief, and as such was from time to time called upon to deal with offences committed in a military context. A consular legate sent Trajan an adultery case involving the wife of a military tribune *laticlavius* (that is, of senatorial rank) and a centurion.[3]

The adultery case was a flagrant breach of military discipline. However, it is doubtful if it would have been regarded as seriously

on a capital charge, to face trial under him at Jerusalem? See also Acts 26:32, where Agrippa's comment seems to assume the feasibility of a trial. It is not difficult to show that governors did take capital cases involving citizens—only to give a convincing explanation of how this was possible. I have attempted this in *JRS* 58 (1968), 51 ff. The second alternative is favoured by Jones (op. cit. 56 ff. and 90 ff.) and Sherwin-White (op. cit. 60 ff.). It is criticized in *JRS* 56 (1966), 167 ff.

[1] On *reiectio Romam* see pp. 263–4.   [2] See Acts 25:19–20, 25–7.
[3] Pliny, *Ep.* 6. 31. 4 ff.

by the legate (and passed on to the Emperor at all) if the injured party had not been an officer, and one whose candidature for senatorial office was imminent. Thus, in seeking to explain why this case was referred to the Emperor, it would not be sufficient to talk merely in terms of the *qualitas causae*, the nature of the crime and its gravity. *Condicio personae*, the status of the persons involved, was also relevant. *Condicio personae* was equally important in the cases of Claudius Aristion and Trebonius Rufinus, assuming for the moment that they did pass through the hands of their governors, and in that of Jason, a magnate of the province of Lycia.[1] As already stated, the opponents of Aristion and Rufinus are shadowy figures, but they are likely to have been their equals or near-equals in rank and wealth. Jason was accused of misusing the office of Lyciarch, and Pius considered and dismissed the charge. We have only the name of his attacker, Moles, and he too was probably a personal enemy and rival. The rank of either party or both parties in all these cases was one factor influencing the governor to transfer the trial to Rome.

There are two reasons why this might have been so. First, many governors would have admitted the social importance of the provincial élite, which, by the Trajanic period, had forged strong links of kinship, friendship, and common origin with the Roman aristocracy. We have seen that the *novus homo* Pliny approved of the Senate's maltreatment of those provincial envoys who prosecuted ex-governors for extortion and other crimes.[2] But Pliny was not unwilling to ascribe *dignitas* to the provincial gentry, from which class the envoys were drawn, and to acknowledge that they merited privileged treatment. In a letter to his friend Calestrius Tiro, who was about to take up office as proconsul of Baetica in Spain (in succession to another governorship), he wrote as follows:

> You have done splendidly—and I hope you will not rest on your laurels—in commending your administration of justice to the provincials

---

[1] Ibid. 6. 31. 3 (Aristion); 4. 22. 1 ff. (Rufinus); *IGRR* iii. 704 (Jason). There is no positive evidence that Jason appeared before the Emperor Pius. The charge was brought against him in the first instance before an Imperial official, Iunius Paetus, who was probably the *legatus* of the province. See W. Williams, *Historia* 16 (1967), 476–7, with nn.   [2] See p. 55.

by your great tact. This you reveal particularly in the consideration you show for the best men, yet in such a way as to win the reverence of the lower orders at the same time as you hold the affection of their superiors. Many men, in their anxiety to avoid seeming to show excessive favour to men of influence, succeed only in gaining a reputation for perversity and malice. I know there is no chance of your falling prey to that vice, but in praising you for the way you tread the middle course, I cannot help sounding as if I were offering you advice: namely, that you should maintain the distinctions between ranks and degrees of dignity. Nothing could be more unequal than that equality which results when those distinctions are confused or broken down.[1]

Pliny's position is only superficially inconsistent. He could both sincerely praise Tiro for respecting provincial *dignitas* above provincial *vilitas* (lack of status), and despise provincial *dignitas* for not only competing with but also attacking senatorial *dignitas*, on its home ground. A request for transference to Rome from a distinguished provincial, either as plaintiff or defendant, might have been given careful consideration by a governor such as Pliny or Tiro, out of respect for status.

Pliny's notions were probably too advanced for some governors, who were less ready to admit that the provincial aristocracy had moved closer, socially, to the aristocracy of Rome. But even those governors who emphasized the traditional subservience and inferiority of provincials could not be ignorant of the fact that the provincial aristocracy was a force to be reckoned with in their own provinces. Any governor who had been at all exposed to local power struggles, as had most governors, was aware of this.[2] It was well within the capabilities of individuals or factions to create trouble for a governor both during and after his term of office, and often this could be avoided only by skilful diplomacy. One effective way of avoiding odium (*invidia*), it may be proposed, was to refer a contentious lawsuit to the Emperor. Moreover, if either defendant or plaintiff had himself taken the initiative and requested trial before the Emperor, a governor, in granting this request, would be making a concession to one party without

---

[1] Pliny, *Ep.* 9. 5.
[2] Speeches of Dio of Prusa, and, to a lesser extent, letters of Pliny, reveal the complexity of the relations which could pertain between a governor and rival factions within the provincial aristocracy. See espec. Dio, *Or.* 38. 33–8; 43. 11.

necessarily antagonizing the other. To sum up, one can envisage political considerations as well as private prejudices entering into a governor's decision to remit a case involving a member of the provincial aristocracy to the Emperor.

Of the Emperor's role little has been said. It was passive, in the sense that the cases came to him as a result of the initiative of others, the governor and/or the plaintiff (or defendant). It need hardly be said that the Emperor was under no obligation to try every case sent to him from the provinces. Equally obviously there were ways in which he could change the type of cases which were sent by issuing direct instructions to a governor or governors. This was probably only ever done in very modest ways. According to Pliny, Trajan hinted in his postscript to the sentence passed on the centurion and the tribune's wife that he was not anxious to accept cases of this sort on a regular basis.[1] But there is no sign that Trajan or Pius was averse to judging distinguished provincials, and we may take it that they and other Emperors not infrequently did so.

By the Severan period the relationship between the Emperor and the provincial aristocracy had taken a new turn. A passage of Ulpian's treatise on the duties of a proconsul indicates that in the early third century the Emperor's ratification was required for any sentence of *deportatio*, or capital exile, passed by a governor.[2] Among provincials, only the aristocracy was punished with deportation.[3] Moreover, deportation was the only capital penalty to which the provincial aristocracy was subject.[4] Thus what was required of a governor was, in effect, the reference to the Emperor of any capital case which involved a member of the provincial aristocracy. The text of Ulpian is as follows:

The right to deport to an island is not granted to governors of provinces, although it is granted to the urban prefect: for this is stated in a letter of the Divine Severus to Fabius Cilo the urban prefect. Thus

---

[1] 'Caesar et nomen centurionis et commemorationem disciplinae militaris sententiae adiecit, ne omnes eius modi causas revocare ad se videretur.' Pliny, *Ep.* 6. 31. 6. See also Fronto, *ad M. Caes.* 1. 6 (ed. van den Hout, pp. 10 ff.). Here Pius is strongly advised to discourage governors from remitting cases of disputed wills to him.

[2] *Dig.* 48. 22. 6. 1.   [3] See p. 121.

[4] *Dig.* 48. 19. 15; 48. 22. 6. 2; and see p. 155.

whenever governors think that someone should be deported to an island, they should accordingly note this down, but then send his name to the Emperor in order to secure his deportation. They should write to the Emperor and include a full opinion, so that the Emperor may make up his mind as to whether the sentence passed should be executed and the man deported to an island. In the meantime, while the letter is being written, he should give orders for the imprisonment of the accused.[1]

Two matters concern us here, the means by which the Emperors were able to introduce this change, and their motives for doing so.[2]

It is plain that the governor's judicial independence was far from complete even in the early days of the Principate, and that in the course of time Imperial interference in the governor's sphere of influence mounted. What needs to be stressed is that governors bore part of the responsibility for their growing dependence on the Emperor, by their readiness, first, to pass on to him cases which they might have decided, and second, to consult him in matters which they nevertheless retained for their own jurisdiction. The first point is illustrated by the four cases last considered. The consular legate was fully competent to punish any offence against military discipline, and indeed Trajan indirectly reminded him of the fact. Similarly, the charges against Claudius Aristion, Trebonius Rufinus, and Jason at the least would not have lacked parallels, and for all we know formed part of the staple diet of governors in the preceding period.[3] Meanwhile, *sua sponte*

---

[1] 'Deportandi autem in insulam ius praesidibus provinciae non est datum, licet praefecto urbi detur: hoc enim epistula divi Severi ad Fabium Cilonem praefectum urbi expressum est. praesides itaque provinciae quotiens aliquem in insulam deportandum putent, hoc ipsum adnotare debeant, nomen vero eius scribendum principi ut in insulam deportetur: sic deinde principi scribere missa plena opinione, ut princeps aestimet, an sequenda sit eius sententia deportarique in insulam debeat. modo autem tempore, dum scribitur, iubere eum debet in carcere esse.'

[2] About the antecedents of the system little can be discovered. Callistratus quoted from and referred to *mandata* which instructed particular governors to follow the procedure outlined by Ulpian (see *Dig.* 48. 19. 27. 1–2). He did not connect the *mandata* with any particular Emperor, but the singular *mihi* points to Caracalla rather than to Severus and Caracalla, unless Callistratus quoted from *mandata* of a past Emperor (the *de cognitionibus* was written after A.D. 197. See *Dig.* 1. 19. 3. 2; 50. 2. 11; 50. 4. 14. 4; Bonini, *I 'Libri de cognitionibus' di Callistrato* (1964), 14–15). With this, the direct evidence seems to be at an end.

[3] It is not possible to decide whether the cases of Aristion and Rufinus were sent to the Emperor by the governor, or whether the defendants were accused

(voluntary) consultation of Emperors by governors was regular, in judicial as in administrative matters, and this only facilitated and encouraged increased interference from the centre.[1] Such consultation by governors, in addition to the administrative and judicial activity of the Emperor[2] and his agents,[3] led to a situation where detailed instructions, or *mandata*, were regularly given to all governors by the Emperor.[4] This made the climate even more

ab initio before Trajan. The issue is not crucial, to the extent that the two alternative explanations illustrate in different ways the same fact, the subjection of the governor to the Emperor. For either the governors concerned passed the cases on to Trajan (supposing that the indictments were brought in the provinces in the first instance), or Trajan chose not to remit them to the governor (supposing that the plaintiffs had bypassed the governors). Yet these governors were clearly competent to deal with the charges against the two men. For another case (civil) unnecessarily remitted to the Emperor, see Fronto, *ad M. Caes*. 1. 6.

[1] The principle of consultation *sua sponte* is stated clearly by Aelius Aristides in his Roman Oration of A.D. 143 or 156, § 32, ed. J. H. Oliver, *Trans. Am. Phil. Soc*. N.S. 43. 4 (1953), 871. The practice had a long history. Republican proconsuls may have consulted the Senate on *ad hoc* matters, especially in relation to war, peace, and treaties, although there is no echo of this in the sources. Nor is there any evidence that they sought advice in a judicial issue. The comparative independence of the governor could not last in a situation where one man controlled foreign policy and was pre-eminent in the field of justice.

[2] e.g. his practice of advising and instructing governors in response to petitions from local communities and individuals. See F. Millar, *JRS* 56 (1966), espec. 163 ff. In the legal sphere note the Emperor's usurpation of the power of *restitutio in integrum*, the reinstatement of a condemned man to his former legal position. Rescripts of the *divi fratres* show that by their reign governors did not and could not alter their sentences (*Dig*. 48. 19. 27 praef.). If a condemned man was shown later to be innocent, the governor had to write to the Emperor: 'principi eum scribere oportet' (48. 18. 1. 27 fin.). Again, the Emperor's permission was required before a man awarded the wrong penalty could be freed or the penalty altered (48. 19. 9. 11). But *restitutio* was originally an extraordinary praetorian remedy (W. W. Buckland, *Textbook of Roman Law from Augustus to Justinian*[3] (1963), 719 ff.), and the Senate and proconsuls are found exercising the same power as late as Trajan's reign (Pliny, *Ep*. 10. 56).

[3] e.g. procurators, see F. Millar, *Historia* 13 (1964), 180 ff.; 14 (1965), 362 ff.; P. A. Brunt, *Latomus* 25 (1966), 461 ff. Cf. *curatores*, sent first to individual cities. The first known are in Italy and the West: Philostr., *vita soph*. 512 (p. 66, Loeb; Nero); *ILS* 1017 (Dom.); 5918a, 6725 (Traj., Hadr.). Their sphere was primarily financial administration, and their typical tasks were control of investment of city funds, management of city lands, enforcement of the payment of debts owed to the city or of promises made (*Dig*. 22. 1. 33; 50. 10. 5; etc.).

[4] *Mandata* were certainly issued to proconsuls by A.D. 135–6 (*Dig*. 48. 3. 6. 1 and F. Millar, *JRS* 56 (1966) 158), and were presumably given to legates, at any rate, at a much earlier date. *Dig*. 29. 1. 1 praef. seems to take the practice back into pre-Trajanic times, and these *mandata* were not necessarily for legates alone.

favourable to requests and replies, or rescripts (which, probably from the early Empire, were intended and taken as orders).[1] Hence there followed a prohibition on action in specific areas without consultation (the system described by Ulpian). At the end of the process the governor had been relegated to the status of a functionary, whose reduced, but still substantial, punitive powers were held to be delegated to him by the Emperor.[2]

The development of the system of referring to the Emperor capital cases involving provincials of status can thus be placed in the general context of relations between Emperor and governor. The causes of the institution of the system are still to seek.

Part of the explanation of the Emperor's intervention lies in the inadequacies of the legal remedies which were available to provincials. One might have thought that the institution of appeal would offer protection to high-status provincials, or at least to those among them who were citizens. The whole purpose of appeal, according to Ulpian, was to correct the injustice or inexperience of judges (*iniquitatem iudicantium vel imperitiam*).[3] Ulpian wrote elsewhere that appeal was useful against a crafty judge (*adversus iudicis calliditatem*).[4] But an appeal could be held up or blocked. This possibility was envisaged by the Julian law on violence, as Maecianus indicated:

lege Iulia de vi publica cavetur, ne quis reum vinciat impediatve, quo minus Romae intra certum tempus adsit.[5]

---

[1] Pliny displayed the mentality of a governor who operated on the basis of *mandata*. See, e.g., 10. 96 ('solemne est mihi, domine, omnia de quibus dubito ad te referre'). Cf. 10. 56 (Pliny fails to make even slight inferences from his *mandata* concerning *relegati*). Trajan did not encourage Pliny to be independent, and reacted unfavourably to a request only once (10. 117). Compare the exasperation of Hadrian in a reply to a query relating to a kidnapping charge (*Dig.* 48. 15. 6 praef.: 'non me consuli de ea re oportet . . . plane autem scire debet . . .'). See Eus. *EH* 5. 1. 44; 47, for a good example of consultation from the reign of Marcus.

[2] See *JRS* 58 (1968), 51 ff.   [3] *Dig.* 49. 1. 1 praef.

[4] *Dig.* 49. 4. 1 praef.

[5] 'In the Julian law on public violence it is stipulated that no one should put an accused man in bonds or prevent him from being present in Rome within the specified time.' *Dig.* 48. 6. 8. According to a papyrus (dated variously to the reigns of Tiberius and Nero and to the third century), the *certum tempus* in capital cases was nine months for cases coming from Italy, and eighteen months for those coming from transalpine and transmarine areas. *BGU* 628 r (= *FIRA*[2] i, no. 91, p. 452). On the date see *JRS* 56 (1966), 189 n. 209.

A spirited letter of Severus Alexander to the koinon of the Bithynian Greeks condemned governors and procurators who prevented by force the departure of appellants for Rome.[1] Another danger was that misstatement or deception in the letter of the governor which accompanied the appellant's petition would render that petition ineffective.[2] Again, some governors would have denied the right of appeal outright. Gessius Florus, the Neronian prefect of Judaea, flogged and crucified equestrian Jews without trial. Appeals by his victims were obviously out of the question.[3] Towards the turn of the first century, the Senate was informed of the scandalous conduct of Marius Priscus, proconsul of Africa, towards African provincials.[4] It was disclosed at his trial that he had exiled a Roman knight and executed seven of his friends for the price of 300,000 sesterces. Priscus obtained 700,000 sesterces for having another equestrian provincial beaten, sent to the mines, and finally strangled in prison. It is not known whether Priscus bothered to stage 'trials' on these occasions. It can be assumed that any appeals were swept aside.

Thus the ineffectiveness or breakdown of the system of appeal may have been one factor which led to the demand for the reference to the Emperor of every case in which a provincial of status was threatened with a capital penalty.

Appeal, however, was not even in theory a defence against all the injustices which provincials might suffer at the hands of governors. For instance, as far as can be ascertained, there was no provision for an appeal against an over-harsh penalty. The actions of Florus and Priscus were outrageous partly because their victims suffered penalties which were customarily inflicted on men of considerably lower status. Nor could there have been much room for doubt as to which punishments were appropriate for high-status criminals in the provinces, at least by the Hadrianic period. Hadrian himself made it clear that capital exile was the highest penalty that decurions should suffer for ordinary capital

---

[1] *Dig.* 49. 1. 25 (=*P.Oxy.* 2104).
[2] *Dig.* 49. 1. 1. 1, cf. *Dig.* 48. 19. 27 praef. For this aspect of the mechanism of appeal see *Dig.* 28. 3. 6. 9.
[3] Jos. *BJ* 2. 308.
[4] Pliny, *Ep.* 2. 11.

crimes.[1] The institution of the new system suggests that abuses in the punishment of decurions (and other high-status provincials) for capital offences at least persisted in post-Hadrianic times.

If provincials of status were in need of protection against severe or arbitrary governors, the second-century Emperors also judged them to be worthy of protection. That Emperors were well disposed at least to individual representatives of the provincial gentry may perhaps be deduced from the sympathetic consideration that was given to Aristion and Rufinus by Trajan—provincials were not accustomed to such treatment from the senatorial court.[2] Pronouncements of later Emperors confirm Imperial favour and show that it was directed not merely towards individuals, but towards the whole curial order. Hadrian's statement on the subject of the death penalty is a good example.[3] The later reform which we have been considering suggests that the desire of post-Hadrianic rulers to protect the privileged position of the curial order did not wane.

Finally, a brief comment is called for on the divergent attitudes of Emperors and governors to the curial order. The Emperors in general were more sharply aware than the Senate as a whole or many individual governors that the security of the Empire depended in large measure upon the prosperity and relative contentment of the local gentry. Legal privileges such as the reference of capital cases to the Emperor were considered their due because of their status and the political and economic functions they were performing. Governors might minimize the differences between

---

[1] *Dig.* 48. 19. 15: 'Divus Hadrianus eos, qui in numero decurionum essent, capite puniri prohibuit, nisi si qui parentem occidisset: verum poena legis Corneliae puniendos mandatis plenissime cautum est.' On the interpretation of this text and the penal system in the Hadrianic period see pp. 155 ff.

[2] Senatorial trials of provincials were not unheard of in the early Empire (see pp. 31–2), although after the Julio-Claudian period they seem to have occurred only as part of investigations into crimes of senators, in particular, senatorial governors (e.g. p. 53). It is clear that the Senate treated the appearance of a provincial defendant before it as an opportunity to reaffirm its traditional supremacy over the 'subject peoples'. Thus, e.g., Thrasea Paetus burned with self-righteous wrath at the arrogance (*superbia*) of the Cretan notable, Claudius Timarchus. For his offence see p. 32 above, and Tac. *Ann.* 15. 20. On Pliny's attitude and that of Trajan's Senate see p. 53. It is thus significant that capital cases involving decurions were referred to the Emperor and not to the Senate. [3] *Dig.* 48. 19. 15, cf. 48. 22. 6. 2 (*divi fr.*).

decurions and other provincials. Emperors, however, needed to be more realistic, if they wanted co-operation in government.

To sum up the discussion so far: the accessibility of the Emperor to all his provincial subjects was not a reality, if by this it is implied that all had equal access to his tribunal. The Emperor's tribunal was in practice available to those plaintiffs (or defendants) who could afford the expense and the inconvenience of a journey to Rome, to those with friends and connections in high places in Rome, and to those capable of winning reference to Rome through their influence with governors. To point out the importance of the individual's initiative and the governor's discretion is not, of course, to make light of the Emperor's own role. It was for him to decide whether to adjudicate or delegate or even return a case to its place of origin. The fact that he frequently, if not regularly, settled disputes involving members of the provincial aristocracy is itself an indication of his readiness to make special allowance for their status. Imperial respect for curial status was also reflected in Imperial constitutions, and was strikingly advertised in the annunciation of the rule that final judgement in capital cases for which the appropriate penalty was deportation lay with the Emperor.

Equestrians

If it was primarily consideration of the *condicio personae*, the social status or official position of a party or parties, which led Emperors to involve themselves in lawsuits concerning members of the curial order, a similar explanation is appropriate for the Emperor's primary jurisdiction over members of the equestrian order.

Two passages of Dio suggest that in Severan times defendants of equestrian rank were directly subject to the Emperor's jurisdiction, at least in serious criminal cases. Although almost no information which is relevant survives from the second century, there is just enough from the first century to suggest that the same principle might have operated in earlier times.[1]

It can be inferred from words attributed to Marcus Aper in

[1] Dio 52. 33. 2; 53. 17. 6. See *Dig.* 47. 18. 1. 2 (Marcus).

the *Dialogus* of Tacitus that Imperial freedmen and Imperial procurators were regularly tried by the Emperor in Vespasian's reign.[1] But the practice was older than the Flavian period. Licinus, whose conduct in Gaul was reported to and investigated by Augustus, and Pallas, who was tried by Nero, were Imperial freedmen; and Iunius Cilo and P. Celer, who went before Claudius and Nero respectively, were procurators of equestrian rank.[2] In the Julio-Claudian age only one equestrian procurator is known to have been tried and sentenced by the Senate. This was Lucilius Capito, Tiberius' procurator in Asia. For Tacitus, writing in the early second century, the incident served to illustrate the extensive use which Tiberius made of the Senate. His words imply that the trial of Capito was without parallel in later reigns.[3]

Tiberius is also the only Emperor known to have sent to the Senate for trial an equestrian official who was not a procurator. The man, a prefect of a cavalry troop, was indicted for robbery and violence. The incident had for Suetonius the same significance as the senatorial trial of Capito had for Tacitus. It can be assumed that he knew of no analogous case from the later period.[4] We have record of a few trials of equestrian officials (apart from procurators) by Emperors. Claudius punished a procurator (Cumanus) and a military tribune (Celer) for their crimes in Judaea, Nero 'tried' his praetorian prefect Afranius Burrus, and Gaius and Septimius Severus each tried and condemned a prefect of Egypt. The equestrian Sempronius Senecio who was charged before Trajan in company with the Imperial freedman Eurythmus may have been an official.[5]

---

[1] Tac. *Dial.* 7. 1: '... aut apud principem ipsos illos libertos et procuratores principum tueri et defendere datur.'

[2] Dio 54. 21 (Licinus); Tac. *Ann.* 13. 23 (Pallas); Dio 60. 33. 5 (Cilo); Tac. *Ann.* 13. 33. 1, cf. 13. 1. 3 (Celer).

[3] Ibid. 4. 15: 'patres decrevere, apud quos etiam tum cuncta tractabantur, adeo ut procurator Asiae Lucilius Capito accusante provincia causam dixerit.' For possible exceptions involving procuratorial governors see ibid. 13. 30. 1; 14. 28. These trials belong to the period when Nero's senatorial *amici* were still powerful. However, Tacitus may not have set out to record only trials held in the Senate in the relevant passages.

[4] Suet. *Tib.* 30. A doubtful case is the trial of Clodius Quirinalis, Tac. *Ann.* 13. 30. 2 (cf. previous note).

[5] For Cumanus and Celer see p. 73 n. 3; Tac. *Ann.* 13. 23 (Burrus); Philo, *in Flacc.* 125 ff. (Avillius Flaccus); *Dig.* 48. 10. 1. 4 (prefect of Egypt); Pliny, *Ep.*

It was predictable and natural that an Emperor would wish
to deal with freedmen in his own employ and equestrian officials
who were responsible to him. It is worth inquiring whether either
category of defendant could hope or expect to receive preferential
treatment from the Emperor as judge.

Eurythmus and Senecio were accused of forging the codicil
of the ex-praetor Iulius Tiro.[1] Pliny's account of the case is
illuminating for what it reveals about the behaviour expected of
an Emperor who sat in judgement over his own freedmen. The
heirs of Tiro had lodged the accusation by a special approach to the
Emperor, but later had second thoughts and tried to withdraw it.
Trajan interpreted their reluctance to press the charge as due to
an assumption on their part that he would inevitably decide for
his freedman—as if he were a Nero and Eurythmus a Polyclitus.
Yet even an Emperor of good reputation was capable of showing
partiality to his freedman, as the affair of Licinus, the notorious
freedman-procurator of Gaul under Augustus, had demonstrated.
The whole incident seems to indicate that it was thought normal
for an Emperor to show leniency to his freedman.

It may be doubted whether Emperors were more inclined to be
generous to freedman officials than to officials of equestrian rank.
One advantage which equestrian officials, and indeed the whole
equestrian order, held over freedmen was their rank. Even the
Senate gave equestrian *dignitas* some recognition, and this was
probably reflected in judgements returned by the senatorial
court.[2] For example, it is likely that equestrian defendants before
the Senate received milder punishments than defendants of lower
rank. Direct evidence for this is lacking, but confirmation of a
sort comes from an unexpected source. As we have seen, Marius
Priscus as proconsul of Africa exiled a Roman knight and executed

6. 31. 7 ff. (Senecio: forgery of a codicil; cf. Tac. *Ann.* 14. 40–1, not before
Nero).
   [1] Probably C. Iulius Tiro Gaetulicus, *PIR*[2] I 603.
   [2] After the reign of Tiberius equestrians seem to have been rarely subject
to senatorial jurisdiction. When they did appear before the Senate it was
normally as accomplices in the crimes of senators. See Tac. *Ann.* 11. 4; 11. 35. 6;
14. 40; 16. 8, cf. 12; Pliny, *Ep.* 3. 9. 18; 4. 11. 10 ff. For doubtful cases see
p. 86 nn. 3–4. For recognition of equestrian *dignitas* see pp. 237 ff. Imperial
freedmen were without *dignitas*, but did not lack influence.

seven of his friends for 300,000 sesterces. Priscus may be said to
have had at least token regard for the status of the former, if,
as is likely, the latter suffered a higher penalty because of inferior
rank. Again, when another equestrian was beaten, sent to the mines,
and strangled in prison, Priscus was rewarded with a considerably
higher fee, 700,000 sesterces, presumably for the greater *invidia*
which attended the punishment in 'plebeian' fashion of a man of
rank.[1] But if equestrians gained by comparison with plebeians,
they suffered by comparison with senators. Senators obtained less
severe penalties and more frequent acquittals.[2]

The view taken by Emperors of the equestrian order was, by
and large, broader than that taken by the Senate.[3] In the first
place, Augustus and his successors saw the equestrian order as
the source of army officers, jurymen, administrators—as well as
of senators and magistrates. The membership of the order was
subject to their regular review and scrutiny. As for equestrian
officials, they were a particularly select group, who had caught
the Emperor's eye and gained posts in his service normally by
merit. Their careers were watched and guided by the Emperor
from their inception. Second, the social importance of the order
was considerably enhanced by the Augustan reforms, which had
transformed it into an aristocracy in its own right.[4] By the Flavian
period the social distance between the equestrian and senatorial
orders had narrowed, following the eclipse of most of the illustrious
Italian families which had dominated the Senate. In the years
following the civil wars of A.D. 68–9 it would have been difficult
to regard the Senate as a closed clique of superior families, even
if the Flavian Emperors had sympathized with such an attitude.
Suetonius records a judgement made by Vespasian, himself a
first-generation senator, relevant to the comparative positions of
the senatorial and equestrian orders. Vespasian refused to penalize
an equestrian for returning a senator's insults, while granting that

---

[1] Pliny, *Ep.* 2. 11. 8.   [2] See pp. 34 ff.
[3] Isolated cases are known of the imposition of 'plebeian' or 'servile' penalties
on equestrians by Emperors. Tiberius condemned an equestrian to the treadmill (Suet. *Tib.* 51). Gaius sentenced *multos honesti ordinis* (sc. including
equestrians) to labour in the mines or to road-work, and threw an equestrian
to the beasts (Suet. *Gaius* 27).   [4] See pp. 238 ff.

in principle it was wrong to abuse senators. As Suetonius interpreted the decision, Vespasian did not repudiate the traditional
status distinction between the two orders, but showed that he
considered it of no great importance, because he pronounced their
libertas, perhaps 'privileges', to be equal.[1] Suetonius reports this
incident after briefly reviewing Vespasian's activity as censor,
when he reformed and rebuilt the senatorial and equestrian orders
by drafting into their membership the most eminent of the Italian
and provincial nobility. The demands of politics strengthened
the conviction of this unpretentious soldier that the gap between
the orders, in social terms, was insignificant.

Thus it is reasonable to suppose that, if Emperors as judges
took into account the *condicio* of defendants, this would have
worked to the advantage of equestrians, because of their vital
administrative, political, and military functions, and because of
their standing in Roman society.

It is of course not possible to make a positive statement, based
on an empirical analysis, about the standards which the Emperors
followed in their jurisdiction. Yet, allowing for considerable
variation in their conduct,[2] it does seem likely that Imperial
decision-making was characterized by the observance of principles
which were particularistic rather than egalitarian. That is to say,
the Emperors did not follow a general policy of prescribing like
treatment for like offences irrespective of the status or position
of the defendant. Rather, in general, their decisions were affected
by their social prejudices; and, in particular, they showed a
natural tendency to favour those defendants with whom they
were acquainted, whose careers they had fostered, and who had

---

[1] Suet. *Div. Vesp.* 9. 2: 'Atque uti notum esset, utrumque ordinem non tam
libertate inter se quam dignitate differre, de iurgio quodam senatoris equitisque
Romani ita pronuntiavit, non oportere maledici senatoribus, remaledici civile
fasque esse.'

[2] It is conceivable, for example, that an Emperor might impose an aggravated penalty on an equestrian official obviously guilty of extortion and other
crimes against provincials. He might do so for worthy motives: because of his
devotion to the welfare of his subjects, or out of a conviction that his officials
should set a good example, or through a feeling that the official had been
personally disloyal to him and had abused his trust. On the other hand, personal
friends or favourites of Emperors among his freedmen or officials might have
been virtually immune from punishment.

promoted their (the Emperors') interests even if they had simultaneously advanced their own.

This tentative conclusion is fully consistent with the central argument of this section. To say that the Emperor's court operated on egalitarian principles would be to imply not only that the Emperor inflicted like penalties for like offences, but also that he was concerned equally with the fortunes of all his peoples, and that this was reflected in the kind of defendants who came before his tribunal. But the criteria of selection for at least a proportion of the cases which he tried were evidently non-egalitarian—if he regularly heard charges against his own officials, equestrians in general, and members of the provincial aristocracy (and occasionally against senators[1]). Precisely how large a part of his judicial time was spent trying freedmen, equestrians, decurions, and senators is of course unknown. But considering the attention given to these cases, and to others against political[2] or religious offenders, not much provision could have been made for the settlement of disputes involving men of low status or little influence.[3]

Delegated jurisdiction: the urban prefect

The Emperor's delegated jurisdiction is an important subject in its own right. In so far as it was exercised by new tribunals through a new procedure, *cognitio*, it made inevitable the gradual replacement of the jurisdictions and procedures which had flourished in Republican times; and in so far as it was exercised by older jurisdictions by Imperial sanction, it reduced the degree of their independence and separation from the power of the state.

Delegation of the second kind has been touched upon in connection with the relationship between the tribunals of the Emperor and the governor. It was pointed out that the Emperor's practice of referring provincial petitioners to their governors, and of directing governors to hear complaints and to carry out investigations, were part of the process by which the governor

[1] See pp. 59 ff.
[2] On the Emperor's primary jurisdiction in *maiestas* cases, p. 74 n. 1; cases remitted, pp. 72 ff.
[3] The status of some defendants is unknown. See, e.g., Suet. *Div. Aug.* 33 (parricide, *falsum*); Suet. *Div. Cl.* 15. 2 (*falsum*).

was reduced to a functionary of the government at Rome, whose punitive powers were themselves held to be delegated. The other aspect of the subject of delegation has also been broached. The jurisdiction exercised by the Senate was delegated jurisdiction, both in the particular sense that individual cases were sometimes passed down by the Emperor to the Senate for trial, and in the general sense that the senatorial court was promoted by the Emperor and remained under his direct or remote control. Of other delegated jurisdictions, that of the urban prefect was the most significant.[1] The courts of the Senate and urban prefect provide an interesting comparison. The senatorial court reached its zenith early. In Tiberius' reign it was nothing less than the High Court of the Empire. Thereafter it fell into decline, and by the Severan period had no higher ambition than to protect the interests of its own membership. At the time when the prestige of the senatorial court was at its highest, the urban prefect is not known to have handled offences more serious than a freedman's petty theft of clothes from his patron.[2] However, within two centuries he had built up a wide jurisdiction and had emerged as the Emperor's deputy in judicial affairs.

Accounts of the development of the prefect's jurisdiction usually begin with a citation of *Annals* 6. 11. 3. Here Tacitus appears to associate the office with the task of bringing order to a crowded city. This passage and the Tiberian case against the freedman are held to show that the prefect was appointed as an 'urban chief of police',[3]

[1] A full study of jurisdiction delegated by the Emperor would have to include (amongst other things) the administrative or quasi-judicial courts of Imperial agents such as procurators (see p. 81 n. 3 above), the *extra ordinem* civil jurisdiction of magistrates at Rome (over trusts, guardianship, etc.; see M. Kaser, op. cit. (cited p. 68 n. 3), 350 ff.), and *ad hoc* tribunals of individuals appointed over particular cases (e.g. Pl. *Ep.* 7. 6. 8-10, a *falsum* case). On the urban prefect see E. Sachers, *RE* 22 (1954), 2521 ff., s.v. *praefectus urbi*; G. Vitucci, *Ricerche sulla praefectura urbi in età imperiale (sec. I–III)* (1956), 50 ff.; T. J. Cadoux, *JRS* 49 (1959), 152 ff. (review of Vitucci, op. cit.). The traditional debate over the origin of the office and the source of its powers may be passed over here. For the praetorian prefect see refs. on p. 97 n. 4.

[2] Jos. *AJ* 18. 169. The patron was Herod Agrippa and the prefect Piso (A.D. 26–32).

[3] See, e.g., W. Kunkel, *Introduction to Roman Legal and Constitutional History* (1966), 66; see also Kunkel, *Zur Entwicklung des römischen Kriminalverfahrens in vorsullanischer Zeit* (1962), 75–7. Kunkel sees the prefect as the official who took over the police responsibilities of the Republican *tresviri capitales*. But see

to keep the lower orders under control. After such beginnings, the *falsum* case of A.D. 61, with its revelation that by Nero's reign the regular court for *falsum* was apparently the court of the prefect and not the *quaestio de falsis*, comes as a complete surprise.[1] The punishment of *falsum* is a far cry from the maintenance of security and the preservation of public order. Nor does *Annals* 6. 11. 3, as commonly interpreted, prepare us for open competition between the court of the prefect and the *quaestiones*.

Perhaps something of Tacitus' meaning has been missed. Augustus, he wrote, created the post of urban prefect because of the size of the populace (*ob magnitudinem populi*) and the slow-moving remedies of the law ((*ob*) *tarda legum auxilia*). The first phrase suggests that Augustus' aim was to provide for the citizens of Rome on-the-spot protection against a vast and potentially unruly populace; the second may well contain an implied criticism of existing civil and criminal procedures. The securing of compensation for private injury or loss by the formulary process could be a long-drawn-out business, while interminable delays were an ever-present feature of the jury-court system.[2] The *cognitio* procedure which Augustus introduced made possible a more efficient and streamlined justice. The urban prefect was often experienced in law as well as in government,[3] and he was able to call upon men of like distinction and record for advice and assistance.[4] It is not unlikely that Augustus from an early stage thought of the

P. A. Brunt, *Tijdschrift voor Rechtsgeschiedenis* 32 (1964), 445 (review of Kunkel, *Zur Entwicklung*).

[1] Tac. *Ann.* 14. 40–1, and see pp. 27 ff.

[2] It may be that Augustus' creation of the office of city prefect was motivated also by his disapproval of other aspects of praetorian justice, in particular, its susceptibility to corruption. J. M. Kelly, *Roman Litigation* (1966), 91 ff., has argued that some of the changes in civil jurisdiction which were introduced at the beginning of the Principate were due to Augustus' dissatisfaction with 'low praetorian standards'. He suggests (94 ff.) that a similar motive lay behind the institution of the office of the city prefect. (For a brief discussion of some of the weaknesses of the *quaestio* system see Kunkel, *RE* 24. 777; *Introduction*, 66–7.) But to my mind what principally weighed with Augustus was not the alleged unreliability of a judicial magistrate, but the limitations of the legal procedures with which he was associated.

[3] The jurist Pegasus was urban prefect under Domitian (*PIR*[1] P 164). He is the *optimus atque interpres legum sanctissimus* in Juv. 4. 78.

[4] See Apul. *Apol.* 2. 11: *de consilio consularium virorum* (forgery of a will, before Lollius Urbicus, about A.D. 150).

prefect as rather more than the police-chief of Rome; and that he foresaw that the prefect would build up a criminal jurisdiction under Imperial direction which would supersede that of the public courts.

Be that as it may, the process of displacement of the public courts by the prefect was well under way by the reign of Nero. One is forced to ask whether there were not already in addition to *falsum* other crimes both statutory and non-statutory which the prefect was empowered to punish and which he punished with some regularity. It may be that only the political discretion of the Emperor and the private conscience of the holder of the office set limits to his jurisdiction.[1] The office was not universally approved of within the senatorial order in its early days at least, and this fact had to be weighed against the popularity it must have quickly acquired for swift and impartial judgement.

Septimius Severus informed his prefect Fabius Cilo, in a letter containing perhaps the first comprehensive statement on the powers of the urban prefect, that 'all crimes' (*omnia crimina*) were within his compass, so long as they were committed in Rome and Italy. Caracalla limited his jurisdiction to within one hundred miles from Rome.[2] Cases of *falsum* still went to the prefect;[3] he may have tried adulterers;[4] and it was his special prerogative to deal with kidnappers.[5] Of these crimes *falsum* was, and kidnapping might be, capital. It is highly unlikely that the prefect was excluded from trying other capital crimes which had received definition by *leges publicae*, especially as these were all tried *extra ordinem*, at least in Severan times.[6] Curule magistrates may also have dealt

---

[1] On the attitude of M. Valerius Messalla Corvinus to the post see *StR* ii. 1063 n. 6, with Kunkel, *Zur Entwicklung* 77 n. 294. I favour Mommsen's view that Corvinus thought the offer unconstitutional (*incivilem potestatem*).

[2] *Dig.* 1. 12. 1 praef. (all Italy); but cf. ibid. 4; and *Coll.* 14. 3. 2 (no further than 100 miles from Rome); Dio 52. 21. 2; 22. 1 (750 stades, or about 120 miles); *StR* ii. 1075 ff.; Vitucci, op. cit. 51 ff.

[3] *Dig.* 45. 1. 135. 4; 48. 10. 24; Apul. *Apol.* 2. 11.

[4] *Dig.* 48. 8. 2 (Ulp. *libro primo de adulteris*; the son is presumably accused of adultery).

[5] *Coll.* 14. 3. 2 (Ulp.). The penalty could be capital. See *Dig.* 48. 15. 1. Previously the praetor had been responsible for the punishment of this crime. See Kunkel, *RE* 24. 747–8.

[6] *Dig.* 48. 1. 8.

with some. But their tribunals were considered inferior to that of the urban prefect.[1]

The non-capital *quaestiones* had also faded out by the Severan period.[2] One liability of those courts was the fact that they were wedded to a pecuniary penalty. It must have become obvious at an early stage that an alternative penalty was required, just because not all condemned men could pay a fine. Courts which operated *extra ordinem* could cope with this situation. The intrusion of the prefect's court into the sphere of *pecuniariae causae* dates at least from Hadrianic times. Paulus refers briefly to a letter of Hadrian in these words:

> (praefectum urbi) adiri etiam ab argentariis vel adversus eos ex epistula divi Hadriani et in pecuniariis causis potest.[3]

A passage of Ulpian is more detailed and gives attention to the difficulty caused by the pecuniary penalty:

> generaliter placet, in legibus publicorum iudiciorum vel privatorum criminum qui extra ordinem cognoscunt praefecti vel praesides, ut eis, qui poenam pecuniariam egentes eludunt, coercitionem extraordinariam inducant.[4]

The text of Ulpian shows that the praetor had lost ground not only in the administration of the criminal law, but also in the sphere of *ius ordinarium*. Ulpian wrote in another passage that any offence which gave rise to a pecuniary *actio* could be treated as a *crimen* (as opposed to *delictum*) and brought before an *extra ordinem* court.[5] Theft, for example, was mostly punished

---

[1] See Dio 52. 20–1. The prefect tried cases remitted or sent on appeal from magistrates. For consular jurisdiction cf. *JRS* 57 (1967), 57–8.

[2] Ibid. 56–60. For an opposing view see R. Bauman, *Antichthon* 2 (1968), 68 ff.

[3] 'The urban prefect may be approached by bankers or their opponents, according to a letter of Divine Hadrian, also in pecuniary cases.' *Dig.* 1. 12. 2 (Paulus, *de off. pr. urbi*). Other civil jurisdiction: 1. 12. 1. 6; ibid. 1. 9; 27. 1. 45. 3; *IJ* 1. 20. 4 (ed. brackets *praefectus urbis*); 1. 23. 3; 1. 24. 4. The prefect's involvement in manumission dates from the time of Marcus. See *CJ* 4. 57. 2; *Dig.* 4. 4. 11. 1; 26. 4. 3. 2; 40. 1. 20 praef. The sphere of the *iuridici* must have overlapped to a degree. See p. 97 n. 3, below; and Rosenberg, *RE* 10 (1919), 1147 ff., s.v. *iuridicus*.

[4] 'It is a general rule that those prefects or governors who judge *extra ordinem* in their administration of the laws governing public or private crimes bring *extra ordinem* punishment to bear on any who escape a monetary penalty because of poverty.' *Dig.* 48. 19. 1. 3.

[5] *Dig.* 47. 1. 3.

criminaliter in his day. None the less, *si qui velit, poterit civiliter agere.*[1]

It is not known how the various *extra ordinem* courts divided the load of non-statutory crimes (*privata* or *extraordinaria crimina*). The prefect's sanctions were the most potent, and a number of serious cases were referred to him from lower tribunals. For example, the prefect of the watch (*praefectus vigilum*) had general responsibility for the punishment of arson, theft, burglary, receiving, and abduction, at least in the city of Rome, but particularly bad cases and particularly notorious criminals were sent to the urban prefect.[2] Similarly, the praetor in charge of providing guardians (*praetor tutelaris*) punished run-of-the-mill offences committed by guardians, but the more serious offenders were dispatched to the prefect for *extra ordinem* punishment.[3] In cases of this kind the prefect was more like a higher policeman than a higher judge.[4]

We may now ask what was the status of the defendants who came before the urban prefect. To begin with the 'private' crimes: if the prefect exercised first-instance jurisdiction in this area, it is likely that he came in contact with men of means—those for instance who could pay a fine—and therefore some men of rank. As for those remitted to the prefect for harsh punishment, presumably *honestiores* were among them, if the prefect dealt with all serious offences committed in fields covered by such officials as the *praefectus vigilum* and the *praetor tutelaris*. A

---

[1] 'If anyone wants it, he can sue according to the civil law.' *Dig.* 47. 2. 93. Levy, *ZSS* 53 (1933), 166, considers *criminaliter* an interpolation, and Jolowicz, *ed. of Digest XLVII.* 2 (1940), 128–9, thinks the last sentence quoted to be an addition. For *expilata hereditas*, procedure by *ius ordinarium* is still a possibility. See *Dig.* 47. 19. 3 (cf. ibid. 1: an *extra ordinem* procedure goes back at least to the reign of Marcus). On *iniuria* see *Dig.* 47. 10. 45. See also 47. 9. 1 praef. ff. and ibid. 4. 1 (plundering a shipwreck, etc.). In the former text an *actio* and a fine is envisaged, in the latter the *cognitio* procedure. In *Dig.* 48. 19. 28. 12, *fortuita incendia* are to be treated *civiliter* or punished *modice*, sc. *extra ordinem*. The same principle might have operated in the case of theft.

[2] *Dig.* 1. 15. 3. 1–2; ibid. 5.

[3] The post of *praetor tutelaris* was created by Marcus and Verus. See *SHA Marc.* 10. 11. For reference of serious cases to the urban prefect see, e.g., *Dig.* 26. 10. 3. 15; and below. The urban prefect sometimes tried and condemned Christians. See Justin, *Apol.* 2. 1–2; Euseb. *EH* 4. 17 (Lollius Urbicus).

[4] *Dig.* 1. 12. 1 is mostly about the prefect's police duties in the city. For the prefect as higher judge see *Dig.* 4. 4. 38 praef.; 45. 1. 122. 5; Dio 52. 21. 1–2.

passage of Ulpian relating to offences of guardians does not rule this out; it simply specifies that certain severe sanctions were not properly applied to *honestiores*:

Those who stubbornly persist in their refusal to contribute or deposit money for the purchase of property until an opportunity for purchase is found are to be held in a public prison by order, and in addition are regarded as 'suspect'. But it must be recognized that not all ought to be treated with such severity, but only men of low rank; it is my judgement that those of some standing should not be held in a public prison.[1]

It may be conjectured that *honestiores* were punished with *infamia* and perhaps seizure of property.[2]

Next, the prefect inherited from the praetor the type of offender who in the past had gone before the non-capital *quaestiones*, which issued a monetary penalty. This group probably also contained some wealthy or comparatively wealthy men.

We saw that in Nero's reign the urban prefect was competent to deal with high-status defendants as well as low-status defendants on *falsum* charges (and presumably other charges carrying a capital sentence).[3] The defendants in the case of A.D. 61 included senators and equestrians. Later, the prefect drew *falsum* cases even from the provinces. Q. Lollius Urbicus, prefect of the city under Pius, heard and dismissed a charge of forgery of a will brought by Sicinius Aemilianus, the enemy of Apuleius, and a prosperous landowner of Oea in Tripolitania.[4] It is likely that Urbicus was directly approached on this occasion, perhaps because *falsum* was an acknowledged speciality of the prefect. But some

---

[1] *Dig.* 26. 10. 3. 16: 'Qui pecuniam ad praediorum emptionem conferre neque pecuniam deponere pervicaciter perstant, quoad emptionis occasio inveniatur, vinculis publicis iubentur contineri, et insuper pro suspectis habentur. sed sciendum est non omnes hac severitate debere tractari, sed utique humiliores: ceterum eos, qui sunt in aliqua dignitate positi, non opinor vinculis publicis contineri oportere.' In 26. 10. 1. 8 (cf. ibid. 2), Ulpian says that plebeians and freedmen were sent to the prefect 'for grave punishment'. (For an early case of the reference of a freedman to the prefect see Jos. *AJ* 18. 169 (A.D. 26–32).) But no classes of defendants are specified in 1. 12. 1. 7.

[2] Ulpian (*Dig.* 26. 10. 7. 2) refers to a letter of Severus which rules 'ut . . . pupillus in possessionem mittatur eius, qui suspectus sententia sua factus est . . .'. Perhaps this time Ulpian was thinking of men of property, who might have included *honestiores*. The sanctions in this case were directed against 'qui ad alimenta pupillo praestanda copiam sui non faciat'.

[3] See pp. 27 ff.   [4] Apul. *Apol.* 2–3. 23–4.

capital cases involving provincials of status were probably passed on to the prefect by the Emperor, especially in the Severan period, when the Emperor reserved for himself final judgement over all such cases. It is significant that the prefect still possessed the *ius deportandi* under the Severans, retaining it when provincial governors lost it.[1] Deportation, or capital exile, was a penalty for defendants of rank in this period.[2]

Another isolated incident from the prefecture of Lollius Urbicus brings us back to Italy and further illustrates the prefect's capacity to hear cases involving local gentry. A dispute came to Urbicus concerning eligibility for the senate of Concordia.[3] The jurisdiction of the urban and praetorian prefects in Rome and Italy must indeed have been in some ways comparable with the jurisdiction of governors in the provinces.[4] That governors were able to try members of the curial and equestrian orders can hardly be questioned. Nor should it be assumed that the courts of the prefects, and in particular the court of the urban prefect, were exclusively for men of low status. It is essential to look beyond the prefect's role as chief of police of Rome to his judicial activities, which were carried out under the Emperor's supervision. He must have taken on or shared responsibility for passing sentence on prominent provincials on trial for capital crimes and on members of the *honestiores* nearer home for non-capital crimes as well. Nevertheless, the great majority of the defendants who passed through his hands were undoubtedly plebeian or servile. After all, *honestiores* were a small slice of the total population; and it is unlikely that he tried and sentenced senators and equestrian officials with any frequency.[5]

---

[1] *Dig.* 1. 12. 1. 3; 32. 1. 4; 48. 19. 2. 1 (*ius deportandi*); cf. 1. 12. 1. 10 and 48. 19. 8. 5 (*ius in metallum damnandi*); cf. Dio 52. 21. The fact that the prefect was required to ask the Emperor to name a place of exile indicates that the *ius deportandi* was exercised under the Emperor's supervision. See *Dig.* 1. 12. 1. 3.

[2] See pp. 117 ff.

[3] Fronto, *ad am.* 2. 7. 12. The same case was later heard by a *iuridicus*, ibid. 2. 6 ff. For an earlier reference to litigation of the prefect in Italy see Statius, *Silv.* 1. 4. 11 ff.

[4] On the praetorian prefect, *StR* ii. 968 ff., 1113 ff., 1120 ff.; W. Ensslin, *RE* 22 (1954), 2391 ff., 2415 ff.; M. Kaser, op. cit. 365. We know little about his first-instance jurisdiction in the classical period, and not much more about his appellate jurisdiction.

[5] Senators, from the fourth century, were tried by the urban prefect of their city (Rome or Constantinople). See *CTh* 2. 1. 4, A.D. 364 (civil cases); 9. 40. 10,

We cannot know whether high-status and low-status defendants were afforded different treatment by the prefect. Given the dual character of his court, there must have been considerable variation in his manner of handling cases. When patrons brought their freedmen to him for castigation, and masters their slaves, when acknowledged criminals or enemies of order were sent up to him, the prefect was expected to do little more than administer appropriate sanctions. It was presumably only when he turned from the petty offences of an urban plebs to the more sophisticated crimes of the propertied that his adjudication was carried out in a truly judicial setting. The plaintiffs might still have looked to him for instant punishment of their opponents, but first they had to persuade him and his *consilium*, against opposition from a now coherent defence, of the justice of their case. (Sicinius Aemilianus utterly failed to convince Lollius Urbicus and his distinguished consular advisers that his uncle's will had been forged.) A second suggestion should be no more controversial: when the prefect did proceed as a judge rather than as a policeman, he reached his verdict after considering the *personae* of the parties as well as the facts of the case.

A.D. 366; 9. 16. 10, A.D. 371 (criminal, examined by prefect, sentenced by Emp.); 9. 1. 13, A.D. 376; 2. 1. 12, A.D. 423 (criminal, prefect with quinqueviral court).

CONCLUSION

IN this section an attempt has been made to determine whether there were high-level and low-level courts under the Empire, and whether the courts of the Emperor and Senate fitted the first category and the jury-courts and the courts of the prefect and governors the second. There are many gaps in our evidence, and such evidence as we have is chiefly concerned with high-status offenders and capital offences. But as far as we can tell, there was no sharp dichotomy between these two sets of courts. Trials of equestrians or senators before jury-courts on charges of a non-political nature were not unheard of in the Julio-Claudian age at least (the later history of those courts is lost to us); the urban prefect dealt with litigants of status or influence with some degree of regularity; and provincial governors, although they lost final judgement over high-status provincials in capital cases towards the end of our period, retained non-capital jurisdiction over them. Again, neither the Senate nor the Emperor's court was closed to men of little status or influence. We can say only that the average defendant before a jury-court (for as long as the jury-courts were active) and before the court of the urban prefect was of humble station, and that senators and equestrians accused of serious crimes went normally but not exclusively before the Senate or the Emperor. Provincial aristocrats were less well off because of their physical separation from Rome. The concession they were granted came late, in the late Antonine or early Severan period, and was relevant only in the most serious criminal cases. But if as a group they were denied regular access to the Emperor's court, it was always open to enterprising and affluent individuals from their ranks to bypass the governor and launch prosecutions or defend suits before the Emperor or a delegate.

This section also aimed at investigating the treatment given to defendants of different status in the various courts. It was found that low-status defendants were brought before the Senate or Emperor more often for punishment than for trial, and that if they were subjected to a relatively full examination and found guilty, they received harsher penalties than high-status defendants on the same charges. Moreover, low-status plaintiffs had small chance of success if their opponents were of higher status (as in these courts they commonly were). The urban prefect, it was suggested, would not have taken up the same stance towards high-status and low-status defendants. Alleged forgers of wills from the upper stratum of society would not have been deprived of status and property without a prior investigation of some thoroughness. But the numerous crimes of theft and violence committed by those without property against the propertied would have been dealt with by the prefect in more summary fashion. In general it can be said that judges and juries were suspicious of, if not resentful towards, low-status plaintiffs who attacked their 'betters' in court, and were prepared to believe the worst of low-status defendants, while the pleas of high-status plaintiffs or defendants, who in any case were likely to be more coherent and better-versed in the law, were given more credence. Further, as the next section shows in some detail, all courts which were not bound by an inflexible penalty system, that is, all which tried cases *extra ordinem*, applied more degrading and more severe penalties to condemned men of low status and power than to those better placed in the stratification system.

PART II

THE DUAL-PENALTY SYSTEM

4

PENALTIES AND THE TREATMENT
OF THE ACCUSED

sed enim sciendum est discrimina esse poenarum neque
omnes eadem poena adfici posse.[1]

UNDER the jury-court system characteristic of the late Republic
and early Empire, the task of the court was to issue a verdict, and
not to decide upon a penalty. The penalty was already fixed by the
law which set up the court. By contrast, the *cognitio* judge was
entitled to choose which penalty to prescribe. The trial, in this
matter as in other matters, was entirely in his hands: no law
governed his actions. Further, in choosing a penalty, he was not
restricted to those that the law recognized, the death penalty,
outlawry (*interdictio aqua et igni*), and the monetary fine. He could
make use of sanctions which had previously served as administrative measures of coercion against aliens and slaves.

An edict and a rescript, both Hadrianic, list and grade most
of the penalties that were commonly used in the Antonine and
Severan period. They are cited in the sixth book of the *de cognitionibus* of Callistratus:

in exulibus gradus poenarum constituti edicto divi Hadriani, ut
qui ad tempus relegatus est, si redeat, in insulam relegetur, qui relegatus
in insulam excesserit, in insulam deportetur, qui deportatus evaserit,
capite puniatur. ita et in custodiis gradum servandum esse idem princeps rescripsit, id est ut, qui in tempus damnati erant, in perpetuum
damnarentur, qui in perpetuum damnati erant, in metallum damnarentur, qui in metallum damnati id admiserint, summo supplicio ad-
ficerentur.[2]

---

[1] *Dig.* 48. 19. 9. 11 (Ulpian): 'But it should be known that there are differences
in penalties, and not all can suffer the same penalties.'

[2] Ibid. 28. 13–14: 'With regard to exiles, grades of penalties were established
by an edict of Divine Hadrian, so that a man who is relegated for a term
and returns [illicitly] should be relegated to an island; a man who is relegated

The fact that there are two Imperial pronouncements rather than one is fitting. Each presents a scale of penalties separate and complete in itself. Other evidence shows that corresponding to each separate penalty scale there was (at least in the Severan age) a broad social category. Roughly speaking, the edict dealt with penalties for high-status offenders, the rescript with penalties for low-status offenders. For the first group, *capite puniri* or execution was in fact rare, the standard penalties being *deportatio* and *relegatio*, two forms of exile, and *motio ordine*, or expulsion from the Senate (if the offender was a Roman senator), or from the local council (if a decurion). Disqualification from office-holding was also known. The monetary fine was a common minor sanction. The most serious penalty for offenders of low status was *summum supplicium*. This covered several aggravated forms of the death penalty, including exposure to wild beasts (*bestiis dari*), crucifixion (*crux*), and burning alive (*vivus uri*, or *crematio*). Condemnation to live and fight as a gladiator would normally involve the death of the condemned (at some juncture). *Metallum* was a life sentence to hard labour in the mines. A less grave penalty of the same type was *opus publicum*, or labour on public works and services. Corporal punishment was applied to *humiliores*. Torture traditionally was reserved for slaves, but free men of low rank were not immune in the second and third centuries. With respect to the treatment of defendants before trial, *honestiores* were able to avoid imprisonment in most cases.

The first part of this section will deal with the penalties mentioned in the edict, execution and exile; the second with those that occur in the rescript, *summum supplicium*, *metallum*, and *opus publicum*; and the third with other sanctions, beating, the fine, torture, and finally imprisonment.[1]

to an island and leaves that island should be deported to an island; finally, a man who is deported to an island and escapes should be executed. Also, with regard to those kept in custody, the same Emperor laid down in a rescript that the following order was to be observed: men condemned to public labour for a time are to be condemned for life, men condemned for life are to be condemned to the mines, and men condemned to the mines are to be condemned to the highest penalty [in each case, if they have escaped].'

[1] On penalty variation see F. de Robertis, *RISG* 1939, 59 ff.; *Ann. Bari* 4 (1941), 1 ff.; 281 ff.; G. Cardascia, *RHDFE* 27 (1950), 305 ff., 461 ff.

1 (a) Execution

Of the penalties recognized and prescribed by the late-Republican laws which set up the jury-courts, the death penalty (*capite puniri*) was the most serious.[1] There is little evidence, however, that it was actually inflicted on members of the citizen population, or, at any rate, on members of the higher orders. This is probably the truth behind Caesar's accusation that Silanus, in calling for the execution of the Catilinarian conspirators, was threatening to introduce a 'new kind of penalty';[2] and behind the disingenuous reply of Silanus that by 'the ultimate penalty' he had meant imprisonment, the ultimate penalty for a Roman senator (Silanus does not say Roman citizen).[3]

A similar opinion (with the substitution of 'exile' for 'imprisonment') was expressed by Thrasea Paetus, as is recorded in a fragment of Dio, which runs: (ὅτι) Θρασέας τις γνώμην ἀπεφήνατο ἀνδρὶ βουλευτῇ ἐσχάτην εἶναι τιμωρίαν τὴν φυγήν.[4] No precise context is given, but the general background is clear enough: virtually from the beginning of the Empire, death sentences were expected to follow convictions for *maiestas*, whatever the status of the defendant. This was the situation not only in the case of conspiracies and plots, but also in the case of less serious, but still treasonable, acts (*facta*), and treasonable words (*dicta*).[5] Such a

---

[1] *Capite puniri* normally means the simple death penalty, or death by decapitation (by the sword, *Dig.* 48. 19. 8. 1). The term can have a broader connotation. In *Dig.* 48. 8. 3. 5 it apparently includes *bestiae* (dealt with below under *summum supplicium*); cf. *PS* 5. 25. 1. In *Dig.* 48. 19. 15 and ibid. 28. 13–14, it is reasonable to suppose it does not include any of the penalties that made up *summum supplicium*. See E. Levy, *Die römische Kapitalstrafe* (1931), 47 ff. (= *Ges. Schr.* (1963) ii. 356 ff.). On the death penalty see also Mommsen, *Strafr.* 939 ff.

[2] Sall. *Cat.* 51. 18: 'genus poenae novum'.

[3] Plut. *Cic.* 21. 3: ἐσχάτην γὰρ ἀνδρὶ βουλευτῇ 'Ρωμαίων εἶναι δίκην τὸ δεσμωτήριον. The much briefer version in *Cato min.* has ἀνδρὶ 'Ρωμαίῳ (22. 5). Citizens were not legally immune from judicial execution, but were allowed to appeal against it. See *JRS* 56 (1966), 167 ff. For the evasion of execution by voluntary exile see below, pp. 111 ff.

[4] 'One Thrasea declared the opinion that the extreme punishment for a senator was exile.' Dio 62. 15. 1a. The statement could belong to the senatorial reaction immediately after the reign of Claudius; or to the troubled period in Nero's reign towards the end of which Thrasea himself fell a victim. The wording Θρασέας τις might indicate that this is the first mention of Thrasea in the history. But are they Dio's words or those of the Epitomator?

[5] See, for example, in the reign of Tiberius, Tac. *Ann.* 3. 49; 4. 21; 4. 34;

policy, condoned or imposed by Emperors, was bound to provoke a hostile reaction in a section of the Senate. What is striking is not that Thrasea's γνώμη (opinion) was voiced, as an assertion of the prerogatives of senators in the face of an Imperial power subject to few restraints, but rather that it is never heard of again (there is at least no record of it).[1] Even the senatorial decrees passed against Domitian were not phrased in this way.[2] Nor was the γνώμη embodied in any edict or law.

It is not difficult to understand why the γνώμη was never translated into legislation. The Emperor could only have issued it, or permitted it to be issued, against himself, and he was not likely to divest himself of the power to execute would-be assassins. Unpopular or suspicious Emperors, at any rate, would have looked upon this power as the ultimate weapon of self-defence; even Emperors who were generally popular were aware of the possibility of assassination,[3] and the most likely conspirators were men of senatorial rank. On a deeper level, it should be remembered that if Imperial power was virtually unrestricted, it was also legitimate and based on the consent of the majority of senators, as well as on that of other orders. Even when Imperial authority as a whole, or the authority of an individual Emperor, was at its weakest, senators were not moved to try to 'constitutionalize' the Principate, in the modern sense of the word; that is to say, they did not seek (they did not conceive of seeking) systematically to redefine and limit Imperial authority by making it accountable to rules which embodied their own rights.

The most that the Senate secured, and this was by Imperial generosity, was an oath that senators would not be put to death through the Emperor's own agency. Some of the drawbacks of the oath have been touched upon already.[4] It has been pointed out that the whole purpose of the oath could be thwarted (and without an overt breach of faith on the Emperor's part) by interference in

6. 9; 6. 29; etc. In all but the first of these a death sentence was anticipated by suicide. The men concerned evidently did not expect to be pardoned.

[1] The closest approximation is Dio 55. 20. 1–2 (words attributed to Livia).

[2] See p. 44.

[3] For Nerva see Dio 68. 2. 3; 68. 3. 2, with Aur. Vict. *Epit.* 12. 6; for Trajan, Dio 68. 5. 2, with Eutr. 8. 4; for Pius, *SHA Pius* 7. 3–4.

[4] See pp. 47 ff.

senatorial trials. But in any case, the oath imposed only a moral obligation on the swearer. Moreover, it was optional, was taken on the Emperor's own initiative (normally for political reasons), and could not be forced upon him.

Senatorial immunity from execution, then, was always precarious, because it rested on the self-interest and self-restraint of a discretionary ruler rather than on the established rights of the most elevated of his subjects. The situation could not have been otherwise, given the extent of Imperial power, the general acceptance of the regime by the Emperor's subjects, and what might be called the 'constitutional illiteracy' of the Senate.

Hadrian was one Emperor who bound himself by an oath not to kill senators. He also ruled, as the jurist Venuleius Saturninus reported, that decurions were not to be executed (apparently for homicide) except for parricide. Instead, the correct penalty was the penalty of the Cornelian law, by which was meant deportation. A rescript of Marcus and Verus half a century later shows that the exemption covered other capital crimes apart from homicide, for example, arson (which, in any case, was punished under the same Cornelian law).[1]

How does the Hadrianic constitution relate to the γνώμη of Thrasea? Quite apart from the substitution of local senator for Roman senator in the Hadrianic constitution, the two were not equivalent. The γνώμη admitted of no exceptions, if, as was suggested above, it was Thrasea's reply to the execution of senators for the most serious crime, *maiestas*. In contrast, the constitution of Hadrian (and also the rescript of Marcus and Verus) could only have applied to some capital offences: *maiestas*, at any rate, would always have been a practical exception to it.

Thus the singling out of decurions in the constitution presents no special problems. Hadrian was not awarding a privilege to one group which he was withholding from another. If decurions were not to be executed for ordinary capital crimes, it can be assumed that other privileged orders, including of course senators, enjoyed the same favour. Further, the issuing of a constitution

[1] *Dig.* 48. 19. 15 (Hadrian; this ruling is discussed later. See pp. 155, 169); *Dig.* 48. 22. 6. 2 (Marcus and Verus).

referring to decurions, rather than an edict embodying the γνώμη referring to senators, by no means indicates that the Emperor was ready to limit his authority with respect to the former but not with respect to the latter. Relations between Emperor and senators, and Emperor and decurions, did not develop along the same lines. In particular, capital jurisdiction over decurions in the Hadrianic period belonged to governors, and the constitution of Hadrian was directed towards governors; whereas an edict embodying the γνώμη would have been aimed at the Emperors themselves, who overtly or covertly exercised the power of life-and-death over senators.

The curial order did not possess any final guarantee of immunity from execution, any more than did the senatorial order. Ultimately their fate depended upon the benevolence of the governor or Emperor. But how far were decurions (and all *honestiores*) protected from the death penalty in the second and third centuries even in theory? Hadrian's constitution seems to have made specific reference only to homicide, and was certainly not a general prohibition of execution.[1] The rescript of Marcus and Verus laying down penalties of deportation and relegation for 'capital crimes' has apparent claims to generality; yet it is clear that it did not embrace parricide, excluded by Hadrian, or *maiestas*, punished with death throughout the period (even if no legal source before *Paul's Sentences* records the fact).[2] The case which the rescript

---

[1] See pp. 169–70.

[2] The literary non-legal sources leave no doubt that a death sentence was customary in the Severan period. The passage in *Paul's Sentences* (5. 29. 1) runs: 'His antea in perpetuum aqua et igni interdicebatur: nunc vero humiliores bestiis obiciuntur vel vivi exuruntur, honestiores capite puniuntur. Quod crimen non solum facto, sed et verbis impiis ac maledictis maxime exacerbatur.' What period is indicated by 'antea'? The legal sources are uninformative on when the change of penalty took place. It is arguable whether *interdictio* was ever *the* legal penalty; there is a case for saying that the death penalty was never formally abolished in the last century B.C., but was simply not inflicted. (Some of the important texts are Cic. *pro Caec.* 100; Sall. *Cat.* 51. 22, cf. 40; Cic. *Phil.* 1. 23; Suet. *Div. Iul.* 42; *Dig.* 48. 24. 1 (Ulp./Aug.); 37. 14. 10.) Thus the use of the death penalty in the early Empire may have been less a breach of law than of traditional practice. (By this theory, members of the Senate in the Julio-Claudian period who deprecated the use of the death penalty for *maiestas*, and supported their case with arguments recalling the *poenae legibus constitutae*, were speaking only half-truths. See Tac. *Ann.* 3. 49–51 (Lepidus); ibid. 14. 48 (Paetus); and Cic. *pro Caec.* 100: '. . . vincula, neces, ignominiasque vitant, quae

settled concerned a decurion who had confessed to homicide and arson.

Arson, like homicide, was subsumed under the Cornelian law *de sicariis et veneficiis*. A statement of the Severan jurist Marcianus shows that deportation was still in his time the penalty imposed upon *honestiores* for breaches of the Cornelian law.[1] Modestinus substantiates this for homicide, and Marcianus himself enables us to check his statement in relation to miscellaneous offences also covered by the law.[2] On the other hand, no fewer than three Severan jurists note that in their time arson in its most dangerous form, that is, arson in a city and for plunder (or simply *dolo malo*), earned the death penalty.[3] One of them, Ulpian, acknowledged that the legal penalty for arson was deportation.[4] Here, then, is one exception to the rule as stated by Marcianus.

Recourse to or practice of magic was punished under the same Cornelian law, and may have constituted another exception to Marcianus' rule, if, as is generally supposed, the penalty for magic was death.[5] However, the section in the *Institutes* where Marcianus discusses magic, which almost directly precedes the statement on penalty, implies that this was not the case. Marcianus cites a clause in the law stating that anyone who makes, sells, or possesses a potion (*venenum*) for the killing of someone, 'is punished' (*plectitur*). Presumably the penalty was the penalty of

---

sunt legibus constitutae'). In short, the *antea* clause might be a description of the *practical* situation in days gone by, just as the *nunc* clause undoubtedly is a statement of contemporary legal practice.

[1] *Dig.* 48. 8. 3. 5: 'Legis Corneliae de sicariis et veneficiis poena insulae deportatio est et omnium bonorum ademptio. sed solent hodie capite puniri, nisi honestiore loco positi fuerint, ut poenam legis sustineant: humiliores enim solent vel bestiis subici, altiores vero deportantur in insulam.' Some scholars would read *aquae et ignis interdictio* for *insulae deportatio*, others *in crucem tolli* for the second *solent*. The suggestion of Albertario (*Studi di diritto romano*, vi (1953), 125 ff.) that *hodie* is Justinianic and the whole passage thus an interpolation should be rejected. See *Index Interpolationum*, ad loc.

[2] Ibid. 3. 1–4 (Marc.); ibid. 16 (Mod.).

[3] *Coll.* 12. 6. 1 (Paulus); *Dig.* 48. 19. 28. 12 (Call.); *Coll.* 12. 5. 1 with *Dig.* 47. 9. 12. 1 (Ulpian; in *Dig.*, and probably in *Coll.*, where there is a lacuna, *capite puniri* and *deportatio* are alternatives for *honestiores*; in *Coll.* the city is identified as Rome, confusingly, as the passage is taken from the *Duties of a Proconsul*.   [4] *Coll.* 12. 5. 1.

[5] Mommsen, *Strafr.* 643, has been generally followed. Most recently, R. MacMullen, *Enemies of the Roman Order* (1967), 124–6.

the law: at any rate, the next clause, covering virtually the same ground (the seller and possessor of a *medicamentum malum* for the purpose of murder) is specific about this. After a short discussion of accidental death through a potion designed to prevent conception (for which offence the penalty was no more than relegation) there follows a list of miscellaneous offences which were all punished 'with the penalty of the law'. Next, to close the section, comes the stipulation that the penalty of the law was deportation plus confiscation, but that 'today' this was applied only to *honestiores* (*honestiore loco positi*).[1] (*Humiliores* were sent to the beasts.)

The accusation against Apuleius, on trial in A.D. 158–9 for magic, was 'capital' (*capitis*), but this could just as easily point to exile as to death.[2] On one occasion the defendant speaks of the trial as one of the many *pericula vitae* which had beset him.[3] But unless the 'dangers' were of the order of attempted assassinations or previous impeachments (or threats of impeachment) for which execution would follow a verdict of guilty, it would be best not to take this sentence as evidence that on this occasion his life was in danger.

The earlier evidence, such as it is, shows only that recourse to magic and the practice of magic were punished by death when linked with potential or actual conspiracy against the Emperor. Libo, who allegedly consulted the Chaldaeans about his Imperial horoscope, avoided execution only by suicide, while two magicians, perhaps the chief consultants, were cruelly executed, one thrown over the Tarpeian rock, the other beaten to death in public (the 'traditional punishment'). At this time the other 'mathematicians' and 'magicians' were simply banished from Italy under a sentence of *interdictio*, unless they were aliens.[4] A magician in the reign of

---

[1] *Dig.* 48. 8. 3.

[2] *Apol.* 26. 9; 100. 9. Apuleius was a member of the provincial aristocracy.

[3] Ibid. 66. 3: 'Neque enim ulla alia causa praeter cassam invidiam reperiri potest, quae iudicium istud mihi et multa antea pericula vitae conflaverit.'

[4] Tac. *Ann.* 2. 27 and 32 (Libo); cf. Dio 57. 15 and *Coll.* 15. 2. 1. See also Tac. *Ann.* 6. 29 (Scaurus); 12. 22 (Lollia); 12. 59 (Taurus). Here, consulting magicians is an additional charge to add a touch of the sinister to the accused's activities, and to guarantee his condemnation and death. The situation had not changed by the late third century. According to *Paul's Sentences*, the death penalty was awarded for consulting *mathematici, harioli, haruspices*, or *vaticinatores* 'de salute principis vel summa rei publicae'. *PS* 5. 21. 3.

Septimius Severus suffered no higher penalty.[1] However, a century later, as *Paul's Sentences* reveals, magicians were burned alive, and participants in magic arts did not escape *summum supplicium* in one of its forms, notably exposure to the beasts or crucifixion.[2] Thus the stiffening of penalty took place after the period of the classical jurists.

The cases of 'simple' homicide and adultery are parallel: the penalty of deportation had been replaced by death by the late third or early fourth century, but not by the Severan period.[3]

The conclusion is that, where the position of *honestiores* can be shown to have deteriorated through the substitution of death for exile as the penalty for capital offences, the change took place in the post-Severan age almost without exception.[4] In the period with which this study is principally concerned, *honestiores* were liable to execution only for killing a parent or for violating the *maiestas* of the Emperor.

1 (*b*) *Exile*

The terms most commonly used for exile were, for non-capital exile, *relegatio*, and for capital exile, *interdictio aqua et igni*, *deportatio* and *exilium*.

'*Interdictio aqua et igni*', '*exilium*', '*deportatio*'. For most of the Republic the Romans had no official penalty of exile. Exile was

---

[1] Dio 77. 17. 2 (Sempronius Rufus; exact status unknown).

[2] *PS* 5. 23. 17; cf. ibid. 16 (human sacrifice and pollution of temple earns *bestiae* for *humiliores* and *capite puniri* for *honestiores*). Constantine decreed that consulting a *haruspex* would be punished with deportation and confiscation, while the soothsayer himself would be burned alive. *CTh* 9. 16. 1, A.D. 319. But see ibid. 4, A.D. 357.

[3] *Homicide*: *PS* 5. 23. 1; cf. *Dig.* 48. 8. 16 (Mod.). It is stated in *PS* that *honestiores* suffered *poena capitis* (death), *humiliores* crucifixion or exposure to beasts. *Adultery*: The Julian law stipulated non-capital exile and partial confiscation as the penalty (*PS* 2. 26. 14), but by the Severan period the death penalty was inflicted, not necessarily, however, on criminals of any status (*CJ* 9. 9. 9, A.D. 224; cf. 2. 4. 18, A.D. 293). By the reign of Constantine all adulterers may have been liable to the death penalty: he regarded adulterers, along with sorcerers and homicides, as unpardonable (*CTh* 9. 38. 1, A.D. 322), and pressed for the enforcement of the adultery law (ibid. 9. 7. 2, A.D. 326). See also 11. 36. 4, A.D. 339; Ammianus 28. 1. 16 (A.D. 371–2). The case of *vis publica* is more problematic. Constantine raised the penalty from exile to death. See ibid. 9. 10. 1, A.D. 317 (?). But was it enforced on high-status criminals?

[4] The exception is arson in its most serious form (above).

voluntary, imposed on themselves by defendants on capital charges in order to escape the penalty of the law, that is, death. *Interdictio aqua et igni* was an administrative measure, issued regularly to prohibit the re-entry of exiles into Roman territory on pain of death. The transformation of exile into a penalty belongs to the closing decades of the Republic.[1] A jurist of the Augustan age, Labeo, was able to refer to exile and death as two capital penalties.[2]

Labeo's words were cited by a later jurist, and it is impossible to be sure whether he used the word *exilium* and not the phrase *interdictio aqua et igni*.[3] The two terms are virtual synonyms in the first-century literary texts.[4] They stand for the exile which involved loss of citizenship, loss of property, and commonly, though not invariably, banishment to an island.[5] This was the regular penalty laid down by the Senate for *maiestas* when death was not

[1] A *terminus post quem* is provided by Cicero's *pro Caecina*, which was written in B.C. 69. See espec. § 100. The attempt of Levy (*Ges. Schr.* ii. 332 ff.) to date the change to 63 B.C. is unconvincing.

[2] *Dig.* 37. 14. 10 (Ter. Clem.): 'Labeo existimabat capitis accusationem eam esse, cuius poena mors aut exilium esset.'

[3] Africanus, a contemporary of Clemens (through whose writings Labeo's 'opinion' comes to us), makes a statement comparable to Labeo's: 'rei autem capitalis damnatus intellegitur is, cui poena mors aut *aquae et ignis interdictio* sit.' *Dig.* 37. 1. 13.

[4] See, for example, p. 113 n. 1 (beginning).

[5] The content of the penalty was not yet fixed under Augustus. Dio (56. 27. 2–3) under A.D. 12 writes of some new regulations of Augustus on the subject of exile. Augustus is said to have been critical of exiles for several reasons. One was that some were living outside the districts to which they had been banished. Evidently the decision to confine exiles in certain places or areas antedated the legislation which Dio is reporting. Under Augustus both banishment from a certain area and confinement in a particular place are known. The exile of Cornelius Gallus in B.C. 26 (Suet. *Aug.* 66; cf. Dio 53. 23–4) is an example of the former, and the exile of the elder Julia in B.C. 2 (Tac. *Ann.* 1. 53; etc.) the first example I have found of the latter. In the passage of Dio, elements of both kinds of exile may be present. The account is very confused. One difficulty is that the rule that exiles should not inhabit islands closer to the mainland than fifty miles (except for Cos, Rhodes, Samos, and Lesbos) was rarely observed in practice. And does the choice of these exceptions mean that the regulations concerned the area of Asia Minor only? Perhaps we have before us an amalgam of regulations issued at several times, and tied only loosely to A.D. 12. Tiberius' enactment about exiles and inheritance (Dio 57. 22. 5) is just as difficult to interpret. Both Mommsen (op. cit. 974–5) and Levy (op. cit. 337 n. 96) constructed implausible theories around this passage—which, incidentally, stands alone, and is apparently unrelated to what precedes and succeeds it in Dio's History. (It is part of Xiphilinus' epitome.)

exacted.¹ The penalty of exile stood also for *vis publica*,² crimes of accusers³ (although *relegatio* is also known), and *repetundae* with *saevitia* (cruelty).⁴

Deportatio as a technical term does not seem to have made headway until the early second century.⁵ Trajanic and early-Hadrianic writers are surprisingly ignorant of it. Pliny the Younger

¹ The formulae are various: *interdictio aqua et igni* (and variations): Tac. *Ann.* 3. 38. 2; 3. 50. 4; 4. 21. 3; 6. 18. 1. *exilium*: ibid. 4. 20. 1; 6. 18. 2; 12. 52. 1; 15. 71. 3; 16. 9. 1. *Italia pulsa est*: ibid. 12. 8. 1. This case bears resemblance to 6. 18 (*aqua et igni interdictum*); see also, for the language, 2. 32. 3 (cf. *Coll.* 15. 2. 1: *aqua et igni interdicatur*—same event described); cf. 14. 50. 2; 16. 33. 2 (Epict. 1. 1. 30 establishes that this is the exile (φυγή) which was the alternative to death). Two likely instances of capital exile are ibid. 14. 48. 4 (*in insula publicatis bonis*; cf. 3. 49–50) and 12. 22. 2 (*publicatis bonis cederet Italia*). The above selection is not complete.

² Tac. *Ann.* 4. 13. 2; cf. 4. 28. 1; etc. On the penalty for *vis publica* see *PS* 5. 26. 1; *Dig.* 48. 6. 10. 2.

³ Ibid. 6. 9. 1 (*exilium*—alternative to death); 6. 30. 1 (*interdictio*); 12. 42. 3 (*interdictio*), cf. Suet. *Dom.* 9. 2 (*exilium*, but not in antithesis with *mors*); Tac. *Ann.* 4. 36, 1 with 13. 33. 3; 4. 31 (?) (*Italia arceri*; cf. 6. 30. 2: *urbe exigi*).

⁴ On the penalty for *repetundae* see A. N. Sherwin-White, *PBSR* 17 (1949), 5; M. I. Henderson, *JRS* 41 (1951), 71; P. A. Brunt, *Historia* 10 (1961), 189. In the Severan age the basic penalty was *exilium* (sc. non-capital exile, see p. 115 n. 5), but if more serious crimes were involved (e.g. execution of an innocent man), a higher sanction was applied, normally *deportatio*. See *Dig.* 48. 11. 7. 3 (Macer). In the early Empire Silanus was sentenced to capital exile (Tac. *Ann.* 3. 68) because the charge included *saevitia* (if not treason). Vibius Secundus (ibid. 14. 28: *Italia exigitur*) was saved from a *gravior poena*, presumably capital exile. The nature of the punishment of Flamma in Tac. *Hist.* 4. 45 is unclear. Brunt (art. cit. 204) thought it was *relegatio*. Marius Priscus' punishment is described in two ways by Pliny: '. . . urbe Italiaque interdicendum' (*Ep.* 2. 11. 19) and 'relegatus est' (ibid. 6. 29. 9). See also Juv. 1. 47 ff. If *repetundae* was the only formal charge, the penalty was severe. The rival *sententia* reveals that the regular punishment for *repetundae* was simply *infamia* (plus reparation). Pliny, *Ep.* 2. 11. 20; cf. ibid. 12. Cadius Rufus (Tac. *Ann.* 12. 22. 3) and Cossutianus Capito (ibid. 13. 33. 3) probably suffered loss of *dignitas* or expulsion from the senate. (Cf. 14. 18. 1, for Pedius Blaesus.) Iulius Bassus escaped even this penalty by the good offices of Pliny (*Ep.* 4. 9. 16–18).

Adultery, when joined with other charges, might be punished by exile. See Tac. *Ann.* 2. 50: exile, in all probability, was the first of three possible penalties, ruled out when the treason charges were dropped; 3. 23–4: a famous precedent; Julia's adulterers were punished *morte aut fuga*; cf. ibid. 1. 53; 4. 42. 3: *exilium* for Aquilia.

⁵ This is overlooked by Mommsen, *Strafr.* 974–5. It may be that allowance should be made for unwillingness of historians such as Tacitus (see Syme, *Tacitus* 343–4) to use technical terms. Moreover, it may be felt that, given the absence of a *Digest* for the first century, it is dangerous to infer too much from the silence of literary texts. But it seems to me that our authors' avoidance of the term *deportatio* is too thoroughgoing to be fortuitous.

uses neither *deportatio* nor its cognates. The punishment of Valerius Licinianus for incest, which can only have been equivalent to *deportatio*, is referred to as *exsilium*. Pliny also classes him with those *quibus aqua et igni interdictum est*, and writes of him as *relegatum*.[1] Elsewhere in the *Letters*, the terms *exsilium* and *relegatio* are interchangeable.[2] Tacitus, writing still in the early years of Hadrian, reports L. Piso's recommendation for the punishment of C. Silanus, proconsul of Asia, with these words:

> ille (L. Piso) . . . aqua atque igni Silano interdicendum censuit ipsumque in insulam Gyarum relegandum.[3]

His use of the verb *deportare* four times for the process of transporting a criminal to an island, or away from Italy or his homeland, is likely to be no more technical than his use of *relegare* here.[4] *Deportare* is found frequently in Suetonius' *Lives* with a literal rather than a technical meaning, for the carrying of goods of different kinds, or bodies, dead or sleeping.[5] On the other hand, the jurist Julian seems to have discussed the effects of *deportatio*.[6] He served Hadrian as well as Pius. Again, Pius himself made several statements on the condition of *deportati*, which may in-

---

[1] Pliny, *Ep.* 4. 11. 3; 15. For the use of *relegare* for *deportare* cf. ibid. 3. 11. 3: 'cum septem amicis meis aut occisis aut relegatis, occisis Senecione Rustico Helvidio, relegatis Maurico Gratilla Arria Fannia.'

[2] Cf. ibid. 7. 19. 4 and 6 (Fannia goes into *exilium* with loss of property) with 3. 11. 3 (last note); also 1. 5. 5 and 13; 6. 22. 5 (?); 9. 13. 5. For the milder *relegatio*, 2. 11. 20; 3. 9. 17; 22; 31 (?).

[3] Tac. *Ann.* 3. 68.

[4] Ibid. 4. 13 ('et Vibius Serenus . . . in insulam Amorgum deportatur'; cf. 4. 30. 2: 'ita Serenus Amorgum reportatus', where the verb is clearly non-technical); 6. 48 ('Carsidius Sacerdos . . . ut in insulam deportaretur . . .' Another man simply lost his seat in the Senate, which would be odd if Sacerdos suffered capital exile. A third received the 'same penalties' (whatever that means)); 14. 45 ('ut liberti . . . Italia deportarentur'. In the later idiom *deportari* is coupled with *in insulam*. These freedmen were simply banished from Italy); 16. 9 ('Cassio et Silano exilia decernuntur . . . deportatusque in insulam Sardiniam Cassius . . . Silanus tamquam Naxum deveheretur Ostiam amotus . . .' *Exilium* is the sentence and technical term. It, and Silanus' later death, tells us the nature of the penalty, not the words chosen to describe the transportation of the two men).

[5] Suet. *Div. Iul.* 43. 2; *Div. Aug.* 78. 2; 100. 2; *Tib.* 18. 1; 75. 3; *Gaius* 39. 1; *Nero* 31. 3. Pliny the Elder uses the word twice in similar contexts (*n.h.* 7. 36 and 69). This emphasizes its suitability; but the usage is not yet technical. Cf. Quint., *Inst. Or.* 5. 2. 1 (*in reis deportatis*: this may or may not be technical).

[6] *Dig.* 46. 1. 47 praef.

dicate that the term had been recently introduced.[1] We are thus
entitled to hold that Hadrian knew of *deportatio*, and that the
in insulam deportetur in Hadrian's *gradus poenarum* for exiles as
reported by the Severan jurist, Callistratus, was not anachronistic.[2]
As the century progressed, the use of *deportatio* became more
regular and the other terms fell out of use.[3]

'*Relegatio*'. The word *exilium* is used ambiguously in the sources.
Exilium and *exul* occur as 'umbrella terms,' covering both *relegatio*
and *deportatio*;[4] or again, *exilium temporarium* (*ad tempus*) and
exilium perpetuum are contrasted with *deportatio*.[5] On the other
hand, Paulus firmly distinguished between 'capital' penalties such
as *mors* (death) and *exilium* (which he equated with *aquae et ignis
interdictio*) and *cetera*, 'the rest', which were properly called *non
exilia sed relegationes*.[6] The Augustan poet, Ovid, long before made
the same distinction, when he indicated that he was merely 'relegated', and not 'exiled': 'ipse relegati, non exulis utitur in me/
nomine'. Augustus deprived him of 'nec vitam nec opes nec ius . . .
civis'.[7]

Relegatio in the Republic was a measure of coercion (*coercitio*).
It might be employed by a father against his wife and family, by

[1] Dig. 48. 18. 9. 2; 48. 22. 2; *CJ* 6. 24. 1; 9. 47. 1. *Deportati* should not be
tortured, might not manumit or inherit, and were similar in status to those
condemned to *opus*.
[2] *Dig.* 48. 19. 28. 13. The extent of its use under Hadrian is difficult to gauge.
Hadrian prescribed the 'penalty of the Cornelian law' for some offences (*Dig.*
48. 8. 4. 2; 48. 19. 15), but it is not clear whether he thought of this as *interdictio* or as *deportatio*. See 48. 8. 3. 5 (Marcianus; *deportatio*); cf. Gaius, *Inst.* 1,
128; *Coll.* 12. 5. 1 (Ulp.; *interdictio*).
[3] *Dig.* 48. 19. 2. 1 and 48. 13. 3 imply that *deportatio* supplanted *interdictio*.
But see 28. 1. 8. 1–2; 32. 1. 2; *CJ* 5. 17. 1 (A.D. 229). Brasiello (op. cit., chs. 4
and 10) holds (in my view, erroneously) that *interdictio* was exclusively a penalty
of jury-courts as opposed to *extra ordinem* courts, and that its decline coincided
with the decline of the former.
[4] *Dig.* 48. 19. 28. 13 (*exul*); Isid. *orig.* 5. 27. 28 (*exilium*).
[5] Cf. *Dig.* 48. 22. 4–5 and ibid. 6; 48. 19. 6. 2 (*exilium* which is not *deportatio*);
PS 5. 4. 11; 5. 17. 2; 5. 22. 5 (as an alternative to *relegatio in insulam*).
[6] *Dig.* 48. 1. 2: 'capitalia sunt, ex quibus poena mors aut exilium est, hoc est
aquae et ignis interdictio: per has enim poenas eximitur caput de civitate. nam
cetera non exilia, sed relegationes proprie dicuntur: tunc enim civitas retinetur.'
('Hoc . . . interdictio', 'nam . . . retinetur' are condemned as glosses by Volterra,
BIDR 40 (1932), 104 n. 2.)
[7] Ovid, *Tristia* 5. 11. 21 (cf. 2. 137: 'quippe relegatus, non exul dicor in
illo . . .'); ibid. 15.

a patron against his freedman, or by a master against a slave. In addition, non-citizens and occasionally citizens were relegated by magistrates—but as an administrative measure, rather than as a penalty prescribed by the laws.[1] Augustus, however, made *relegatio* the legal penalty for adultery;[2] and the sentence of *relegatio* was passed on offenders appearing before the new criminal courts that emerged in the early Principate.

Relegation as a penalty might involve banishment to a place (normally an island), or simply exclusion from Rome, Italy, or particular provinces.[3] The sentence might be restricted in time (*ad tempus*) or lifelong (*in perpetuum*).[4] But even a life sentence did not involve loss of citizenship;[5] nor was the power to make a will taken away.[6] Liberty too remained.[7] A *relegatus* could receive from a will,[8] own property,[9] and possess rights over his sons.[10]

Did the *relegatus* lose his property on condemnation? The evidence is meagre and scattered. By the adultery law of 17 B.C. a woman found guilty was deprived of half her dowry and a third of her goods. The male co-respondent surrendered half his property.[11] (Both were relegated to islands.) Cotta the consul proposed for Piso's son Marcus relegation for ten years with five million sesterces of his father's property, a generous sum.[12] Augustus' errant family either lost their property or were forbidden access to it.[13] In contrast, a rescript of Trajan implies that to

---

[1] Mommsen, *Strafr.* 23; 968 (family, freedmen); Cic. *pro Sest.* 29 (68 B.C.) (citizens: Cicero does not mention any illegality, nevertheless this must have been a rare occurrence. In general, Mommsen, op. cit. 48, and n. 1).

[2] *PS* 2. 26. 14. This marks the emergence of *relegatio* as a penalty in a criminal court.

[3] *Dig.* 48. 22. 7 praef. For *relegatio ab* (as opposed to *relegatio ad*), *Dig.* 47. 14. 3. 3 (Trajan); 47. 18. 1. 2 (Marcus); 48. 22. 7. 10 ff.; ibid. 18.

[4] *Dig.* 48. 22. 7. 2; ibid. 14 praef.

[5] Ibid. 7. 3; ibid. 14.

[6] *PS* 3. 4A. 9; *Dig.* 28. 1. 8. 1; 34. 5. 5 praef.; 48. 20. 7. 5; 48. 22. 7. 3.

[7] e.g. *Dig.* 50. 13. 5. 2.   [8] *PS* 3. 4a. 9.

[9] *Dig.* 37. 1. 13.

[10] *Dig.* 48. 22. 4 (note: 'et alia omnia iura sua'); ibid. 17. 1.

[11] *PS* 2. 26. 14.

[12] Tac. *Ann.* 3. 17. Tiberius quashed the sentence altogether (ibid. 3. 18). For Cotta's proposal of a *viaticum* of 5,000,000 HS for Lollia cf. ibid. 12. 22.

[13] Agrippa Postumus lost his property to the *aerarium militare* (Dio 55. 32. 3; for Agrippa's downfall cf. Suet. *Div. Aug.* 65. 1; Tac. *Ann.* 1. 6). Augustus' daughter, Julia, was allowed no wine or luxury (Suet. *Div. Aug.* 65. 3; cf. Dio

confiscate the property of *relegati* was irregular: 'I know that the property of men relegated has been made over to the Fiscus through the avarice of former times. But other policies are in keeping with my clemency . . .'[1]

Over a century later Ulpian refers to Imperial rescripts which prohibited the confiscation of either the whole or a part of the property of those who were relegated for a limited period. This rule, if it was a rule, had been broken, for Ulpian makes the point that the rescripts were issued as reprimands, and not with the intention of cancelling the sentences which had given offence.[2] Of the *relegati in perpetuum* Marcianus has this to say: 'They also keep all their property, save any which has been confiscated; for the sentence can deprive those sent into life exile, or those relegated, of part of their property.'[3] The second clause states that part of the property could be confiscated; the first suggests that this did not invariably happen.[4]

The status of the exile. The legal texts of the Antonine and Severan periods, and the post-classical texts, make it plain that

55. 10. 14 ff.). The younger Julia was permitted a *peculium* until Tiberius took even that away (Suet. *Tib.* 50; cf. ibid. 11. 4; and Tac. *Ann.* 4. 71. 5: 'Augustae ope sustentata'). Neither Julia, it seems, had the use of her property.

[1] *Dig.* 48. 22. 1: 'scio relegatorum bona avaritia superiorum temporum fisco vindicata. sed aliud clementiae meae convenit . . .'. There is another possible interpretation of Trajan's rescript. The key words are *relegatorum* and *fisco*. *Deportatio* was not yet a technical term in Roman law. Pliny used the word *relegatio* and its cognates for the process known later as *deportatio* (see p. 114). Might Trajan have been thinking of the property of those subsequently known as *deportati*? It might also be urged that Trajan was intending to brand as avaricious the seizure of *bona damnatorum* for the Fiscus rather than for the Aerarium. To oppose all confiscation would have been to cast a slur on all predecessors, not just on Domitian. Hadrian perhaps took up this point (*SHA Hadr.* 7. 7). But see *Dig.* 48. 8. 4. 2; 48. 20. 7. 3. On the destination of *bona damnatorum* see F. Millar, *JRS* 53 (1963), 36–7; P. A. Brunt, *JRS* 56 (1966), 81–2.

[2] *Dig.* 48. 22. 7. 4: 'reprehensaeque sunt sententiae eorum, qui ad tempus relegatis ademerunt partem bonorum vel bona, sic tamen, ut non infirmarentur sententiae quae ita sunt prolatae.' This is odd. Perhaps the recovering of the money was a problem. See Tac. *Hist.* 1. 90; *Dig.* 26. 7. 57. 1.

[3] *Dig.* 48. 22. 4: 'et bona quoque sua omnia retinent praeter ea, si qua eis adempta sunt: nam eorum, qui in perpetuum exilium dati sunt vel relegati, potest quis sententia partem bonorum adimere.'

[4] See also ibid. 14. 1; *PS* 2. 26. 14; 5. 22. 2; *Coll.* 1. 7. 2. *Relegatio* was aggravated by confiscation in the Decian and other persecutions. H. Leclercq, *DACL* 10 (1932), 'Martyr, xxix, Les supplices des martyrs', 2426.

where a man of low rank was sent to the mines or executed, a man of high rank was sentenced to *relegatio* or *deportatio*.[1] (There were other variations.) An early text is Hadrian's decree in favour of decurions. For capital crimes, decurions could expect the *poena legis Corneliae*, that is, the most serious form of exile, whether it be called *exilium, deportatio,* or *interdictio*.[2]

In addition, it is not without significance that *relegatio* was frequently bracketed with *motio ordine*, or expulsion from the council, a penalty naturally suffered only by decurions.[3] Ulpian, in fact, presented *motio* as a milder form of *relegatio*, the main distinction being that the man condemned to *relegatio* was required to leave his city.[4]

Not every *relegatus* was a decurion. Ulpian wrote: 'Qui ad tempus relegatus est, *si decurio sit*, desinet esse decurio.'[5] Papinian advised that an advocate who was a plebeian should be sent into *exilium temporarium* for reading a document containing false evidence.[6] For the same offence a decurion was suspended from the council for ten years. Augustus passed a sentence of *leve*

---

[1] *Capite puniri/deportatio*: *Dig.* 48. 19. 15; ibid. 28. 9; 48. 22. 6. 2 (by implication); etc. For deportation of decurions see p. 121. *Metallum/relegatio*: *Dig.* 47. 17. 1; 47. 20. 3. 2; *PS* 1. 21. 4; 5. 20. 2; ibid. 5. *Relegatio* is grouped with penalties for non-plebeians in *Dig.* 50. 13. 5. 2. Relegation of a decurion in Fronto, *ad am.* 2. 7, e.g. 12 (ed. van den Hout, 181 ff.). See Leclercq, ibid., for the exile of popes, bishops, and saints.

[2] *Dig.* 48. 19. 15. It is not clear whether Hadrian issued all the *mandata* referred to there. He surely issued some.

[3] e.g. *Dig.* 47. 14. 1. 3 = *Coll.* 11. 8. 3; 47. 18. 1. 1; 50. 2. 3. 1 (cf. *CJ* 10. 61. 1 (A.D. 212)); 50. 13. 5. 2; *PS* 5. 20. 6. For Roman senators, Pliny, *Ep.* 2. 12. 2, cf. 2. 11. 3 and 20; 4. 9. 16; etc.

[4] *Dig.* 50. 2. 2 praef. (this passage reveals another difference: the *relegatus* finds it more difficult to recover his position in the *ordo*). *Motio* was a penalty for *atrox iniuria* (*Dig.* 47. 10. 40; and see p. 203), deserting an embassy (*Dig.* 50. 7. 1), and extortion, for a Roman senator (p. 113 n. 4; last note, fin.). *Prohibitio honorum* was a milder penalty. *Dig.* 50. 2. 3. 1; 50. 13. 5. 2. See Kübler, *RE* 4. (1901), 2329 ff., s.v. *decurio*.

[5] *Dig.* 50. 2. 2 praef.: 'The man relegated for a time, if he is a decurion, will cease to be one.' Sometimes no alternative punishment to exile is given: *Dig.* 24. 2. 8 (*releg.* for three years); 40. 12. 39. 1 (*modus exilii*); 47. 14. 3. 3 (*releg.* for ten years from Italy); 48. 10. 32. 1 (*releg.*); ibid. 21 (*releg.*); 48. 19. 30 (*releg. in insulam*); ibid. 39 (*temp. exilium*); *PS* 2. 26. 14 (*releg.* for adultery). Or the status of the exile is not given: *Dig.* 22. 5. 3. 3. It is not inconceivable that there was a range of minor crimes such as those dealt with here, where the *honestiores/humiliores* distinction was less relevant because the most serious penalties were not applied.

[6] *Dig.* 48. 10. 13. 1.

exilium on a man *e plebe* for libel.[1] A letter of Pliny indicates that *relegatio* (temporary or for life) was a penalty regularly enforced by governors.[2] The rank of those condemned is not given, but some may have come from low-status groups.

The above are examples of *relegatio* as a *poena*, penalty. *Relegatio* in its most primitive form is also relevant. *Relegatio* appears in the *Digest* as an aspect of the authority of a *paterfamilias* over his children and wife, or of that of a patron over his freedmen.[3] Slaves were not relegated as a penalty, partly because *relegati* normally could choose their place of residence outside Italy or a province.[4]

Thirdly, reference is made in both literary and legal sources to the magisterial use of *relegatio* or *leve exilium* as a coercive measure against trouble-makers. The former tell of actors,[5] Jews,[6] philosophers,[7] the latter of soothsayers (*vaticinatores*),[8] astrologers[9] and simply gangs of youths (*iuvenes*)[10] expelled in this way. Most of these enemies of order would have been low in rank.

As for the more serious brand of exile, a few instances are known of its use against plebeians or freedmen. Ulpian spoke of the *interdictio* inflicted wholesale on astrologers in A.D. 17. The story is preserved in the *Collatio:*

denique extat senatus consultum Pomponio et Rufo conss. factum, quo cavetur, ut mathematicis Chaldaeis ariolis et ceteris, qui simile inceptum fecerunt, aqua et igni interdicatur omniaque bona eorum publicentur, et si externarum gentium quis id fecerit, ut in eum animadvertatur.[11]

---

[1] Suet. *Div. Aug.* 51. 1. The other man was also *e plebe*, and was fined.

[2] Pliny. *Ep.* 10. 56; cf. *Dig.* 47. 9. 4. 1: Pius ruled that free men were to be beaten and 'relegated' for three years for plundering a wreck (etc.). The prescription of corporal punishment here poses problems. See pp. 163–4. In *Dig.* 48. 22. 7 *pass.* little is said about the status of the culprits.

[3] See p. 161 n. 1 above.   [4] Mommsen, op. cit. 968.

[5] Suet. *Div. Aug.* 45. 4; *Tib.* 37. 2; *Nero* 16. 2; Tac. *Ann.* 1. 77. 4; 4. 14. 3; 13. 25. 4.

[6] Ibid. 2. 85. 4; cf. Jos. *AJ* 18. 65 ff.; Suet. *Div. Cl.* 25. 4.

[7] Pliny. *Ep.* 3. 11. 2, cf. Tac. *Agr.* 2 (*professores*); etc.

[8] *Coll.* 15. 2. 3; 5; *PS* 5. 21. 1.

[9] *Coll.* 15. 2. 1; Tac. *Ann.* 2. 32. 3; Dio 57. 15.   [10] *Dig.* 48. 19. 28. 3.

[11] *Coll.* 15. 2. 1: 'Again, a S.C. of the consulship of Pomponius and Rufus survives, in which interdiction is decreed for mathematicians, Chaldaeans, soothsayers, and others of similar professions, and in addition total confiscation of property and execution for any aliens among them.'

Other information is derived from Tacitus and Pliny. Anicetus, Nero's freedman, agreed to go into exile on Sardinia for 'adultery' with Octavia.[1] The alternative was death. Atilius, a freedman, who was responsible for the disaster at Fidenae under Tiberius, was driven into exile.[2] Atimetus, also a freedman, did not escape death for his share in Silana's intrigue against Agrippina. Silana's two henchmen Calvisius and Iturius, who were perhaps plebeian citizens, were 'relegated'.[3] Finally, when Afranius Dexter the consul was assassinated, some senators pressed for the banishment, some for the execution, of his freedmen. The alternatives were *relegatio in insulam* and *mors*.[4]

This last case alone would seem to put paid to the supposition that only criminals of better standing were relegated or deported to islands—the argument is that only they could support themselves adequately in exile, and that in this way the state was saved expense.[5] But there were other forms of confinement which were applicable to *humiliores*, for example *metallum* and *opus publicum*. When, as was usually the case, the possessions of *humiliores* did not amount to much, they would certainly have lived at state expense. The lot of exiles could have been made more disagreeable. Their travel allowances, or *viatica*, might have been cut, or simply disallowed. But the memory of their former *dignitas* was normally[6] sufficient to prevent their downgrading, and to ensure that, while losing their property, they lived in greater comfort than their inferiors.[7] This is the crux of the matter.

---

[1] Tac. *Ann.* 14. 62. 4.

[2] Ibid. 4. 63; the penalty involved *interdictio*, or this is an abnormal use of *exilium* by Tacitus.

[3] Ibid. 13. 22; cf. 14. 12. 4. Prima facie, Silana's punishment (*exilium*), and not that of the others, involved *interdictio*. This is not certain.

[4] Pliny, *Ep.* 8. 14. 12. This so-called *relegatio* was equivalent to *deportatio*. See pp. 113 ff.

[5] Mommsen, op. cit. 968–9.

[6] Gaius' attitude was abnormal. See Dio 59. 18. 3.

[7] Large *viatica*: Dio 56. 27. 3 (Augustus' regulations); Tac. *Ann.* 3. 17. 4 (M. Piso, the first *sententia*); ibid. 12. 22. 2 (Lollia). See also Sen. *ad Helv.* 12. 4: '. . . ut maius viaticum exulum sit, quam olim patrimonium principum fuit'. Avillius Flaccus bought an estate in Andros although he had lost all his property: Philo, *in Flacc.* 168; cf. 184 (exiles in general). Gaius had exiles put to death for financial gain although they had all lost their property: Dio 59. 18. 3. Piso was allowed slaves: Dio 59. 8. 8. Tiberius took away the allowance (*peculium*) of the younger Julia: Suet. *Tib.* 50. 1. See also Pliny, *Ep.* 4. 11. 13.

Exile was an alternative to what was still more unpleasant—either execution or penalties of a servile character such as *opus publicum* and *metallum*.

Thus the extreme thesis, that exile, mild or severe, was exclusively for *honestiores*, cannot stand. The more modest assertion, that the officials who administered criminal justice in the extraordinary courts of the Empire normally deported and relegated offenders of high status and found harsher punishments for criminals from the lower ranks of society, is upheld. It is unnecessary to repeat in this connection evidence already cited or referred to.[1] But one development which has so far been passed over should be mentioned. Governors lost the right to deport, perhaps in the reign of Severus: they might execute a sentence of deportation only after reference had been made to the Emperor.[2] We should probably see a link between this measure and the Hadrianic edict on the subject of execution. Both appear to have been aimed primarily at governors and to have served the interests of decurions. It may not seem obvious that the Severan reform was intended to be advantageous to decurions. But the passage of Ulpian in which the procedure of reference to the Emperor is outlined reveals that the offenders who were envisaged were decurions. After describing the new system, Ulpian went on: 'The Divine Brothers laid down in a rescript that decurions of cities were to be deported or relegated for capital offences. Thus they ordered Priscus, who had confessed before an investigation to homicide and arson, to be deported to an island.' There is another point. No restriction seems to have been placed on the powers of the governor to execute humbler citizens or send them to the mines. But both these penalties were more severe than deportation.

Confiscation as a regular part of the sentence of *exilium*: Silanus was outlawed and 'relegated' to Gyaros: '*eadem* ceteri, nisi quod Cn. Lentulus separanda Silani materna bona . . .', Tac. *Ann.* 3. 68. Cf. ibid. 3. 23, where confiscation was waived as a special concession. Paconius retained his property, see ibid. 16. 33, with Epict. 1. 1. 30. Egnatia Maximilla lost hers only at a later stage, ibid. 15. 71; *Syll.*³ 811–12 suggests the reason (see Furneaux, ad loc.). She perhaps retained her property originally as simply accompanying her husband. Other refs. to confiscation: Tac. *Ann.* 3. 50; 4. 21. 3; 14. 48; 16. 33 (Soranus). Legal references include *Coll.* 15. 2. 1; *Dig.* 48. 22. 14.

[1] See p. 120 nn. 1–4, and text there.
[2] *Dig.* 48. 22. 6 praef.–1. See pp. 79 ff.

One problem remains, which is quite intractable: this concerns the fate of citizen-criminals of low rank, firstly, in the late Republic, and, secondly, in the early Empire. The earlier discussion implied that in Republican times only offenders of high rank were able to escape the penalty of the law (death) by voluntary exile. This is plausible, but cannot be shown to be correct.[1] We simply do not know how the law (which in theory guaranteed equal treatment for all citizens) was administered. The early Principate was a period of transition, in the course of which the jury-courts lost ground to courts which investigated criminal accusations *extra ordinem*. Low-status criminals were sometimes exiled, by both kinds of courts,[2] until the time came when judges had recourse to the harsher penalties which were now at their disposal.

2 (a) 'Summum supplicium'

In non-legal literary sources *supplicium* has three main meanings, torture, death, and punishment generally. The suggestion has been made that it is the first meaning that is preserved in the legal term *summum supplicium*.[3] It would follow that the real content of the penalty is torture; and that *summum supplicium* is not to be thought of as a form (an aggravated form) of the death penalty, as it has commonly been supposed to be.

This conclusion is reached by the following argument: *supplicium* means death only when it is associated with verbs such as *ducere, dare, rapere*, or when it is linked with the adjective *ultimum*. The legal texts in which it appears to stand for punishment are corrupt. Thus *supplicium* stands mostly for torture, and *summum supplicium* is the most serious kind of torture.

But, in the first place, it is not proven that *ultimum supplicium* means, invariably, death simple. Celsus wrote: 'ultimum supplicium esse mortem solam interpretamur.'[4] Yet *mortem solam* might mean not 'death simple', but 'only death.' Celsus might be

---

[1] See pp. 105, 111–12.
[2] *The quaestio de adulteriis*, at any rate, would have sentenced to exile. Mommsen, op. cit. 211 n. 1, thought that exile was the highest penalty inflicted by the jury-courts, and cited Pliny, *n.h.* 29. 18.
[3] See U. Brasiello, op. cit., ch. 9, 'I Summa Supplicia', 246–71.
[4] *Dig.* 48. 19. 21.

thinking not of death without the preliminaries of flogging or torture, but of the death penalty in one of its forms, as opposed to the other penalties. Besides, *ultimum supplicium* and *summum supplicium* are both applied to slaves and to free men.[1] There is thus no certainty that the former term can never mean the same as the latter.

Secondly, *supplicium* by itself does seem to stand both for death[2] and for penalty in general;[3] and there is no passage in the *Digest* where it clearly stands for torture.[4]

Finally, death by torture was just as illegal as death by beating.[5] It is therefore unlikely that *summum supplicium* was ever officially thought of, or defined, as torture which brought death.

---

[1] *Ultimum supplicium* for slaves: *Dig.* 29. 5. 1. 28 (Hadr./Ulp.); 48. 8. 4. 2; 48. 10. 1. 13 (suspected by Brasiello, op. cit. 251). For the free: *Dig.* 1. 5. 18 (Hadr./Ulp.); 48. 5. 39. 8 (Pius/Pap.); 48. 6. 5. 2; 48. 9. 9. 1 ('capitis poena plectentur aut ultimo supplicio mactantur'. The second alternative is ruled out by Brasiello, op. cit. 251–2, following Levy, op. cit. 363, because of the rarity of the verb *mactare*. The only other occurrence of the word in legal texts is *CTh* 9. 16. 7, A.D. 364); 48. 19. 29.

   Summum supplicium for slaves: *Dig.* 12. 4. 15; 48. 10. 8; *PS* 3. 5. 8; 5. 12. 12; 5. 21. 4; *Coll.* 1. 6. 4. For the free (or for those of unspecified status): *Dig.* 47. 11. 1. 2 = *PS* 5. 4. 14; 48. 19. 28 praef.; ibid. 28. 14; ibid. 38. 5 = *PS* 5. 23. 14; *PS* 2. 24. 9; 5. 23. 17.

[2] *Dig.* 38. 2. 14. 3, where the term bears this meaning, was rejected by Brasiello on flimsy grounds (op. cit. 100 ff., 254). But 48. 9. 2 has not been noticed. Cf. perhaps 2. 1. 12 and 49. 1. 6. In 47. 18. 1 praef.; 48. 19. 19; 49. 16. 13. 6, the term might mean death or penalty generally.

[3] Brasiello (254–6) found four places where the term means penalty, but dismissed them as additions: *Dig.* 28. 3. 6. 7; 48. 19. 16. 4 and 10; ibid. 28. 16; but again there are others. See 1. 18. 14; 40. 12. 7. 4; 48. 3. 3; ibid. 12 praef.; 48. 18. 7; 48. 19. 6 praef.; *PS* 5. 4. 7; and see n. 2 above. If these too are to be rejected, then there are grounds for questioning the criteria of interpolation.

[4] The argument is one of elimination, and Brasiello finds it unnecessary to argue at length for the possible meaning which remains after the other two have been ruled out (ibid. 256–7). He is content to refer to passages in the *Digest* concerning the *S.C. Silanianum*, and to comment, vaguely, that the 'finalità' of the *S.C.* cancels out the possibility that *supplicium* here indicates a punishment which consists in, or culminates in, death. See *Dig.* 29. 5. 1. 12; 13; 21; 30; ibid. 3. 16–17; 5. 2; 14. In these texts *supplicium* is used in combination with *quaestio*, a common word for torture—a surprising usage if the words are synonyms—and otherwise it is joined with *sumere* in a construction which could mean 'to exact a punishment' or 'to exact (a punishment which is) death'. (For *supplicium sumere* see also 2. 1. 12; 28. 3. 6. 7; 47. 18. 1 praef.) In the following passages *supplicium* could possibly, but only possibly, stand for torture: 2. 9. 5; 30. 53. 8; 35. 2. 39; 40. 12. 7. 4. In the last three cases the phrase *supplicio adficere* occurs, a formula which crops up in 1. 18. 14 and 48. 19. 6 praef., where, however, *supplicium* means penalty.   [5] *Dig.* 48. 19. 8. 3.

What then can be said of *summum supplicium*? In the Hadrianic constitutions[1] *summum supplicium* and *capite puniri* are placed at the head of two distinct groups of penalties. Thus the former term is not likely to have been identical with the latter, which normally stood for simple death. There is no definition of the former term in the sources, but they enable us to identify it with penalties such as crucifixion, burning alive, and perhaps condemnation to the beasts. These were all aggravated forms of the death penalty, which, in the sources, are set off against simple death by decapitation.[2]

Our knowledge that *honestiores* escaped *summum supplicium* (in the Severan age at least) derives largely from a passage of Ulpian, which runs: 'Those are the penalties which are customarily imposed. But it should be recognized that there are differences in penalties, and not all condemned men can be sentenced to the same penalties. Above all, decurions cannot be condemned to the mines nor to any labour connected with mines, nor to the fork, nor to be burned alive.'[3] He cites no Imperial rescript or edict relating to *furca* or *crematio* or *bestiae* or *crux*. Nor does any other lawyer. Much later, Diocletian and Maximian issued the pronouncement: 'Sons of decurions ought not to be thrown to the beasts.'[4] It would be wrong to regard this as the first Imperial comment either on the exemption of decurions from *bestiae* or

---

[1] *Dig.* 48. 19. 28. 13–14.
[2] *Coll.* 8. 4. 1 (= *Coll.* 1. 2. 1–2 = *PS* 5. 23. 1); *Coll.* 12. 5. 1; *PS* 5. 23. 16; 5. 25. 1; 5. 29. 1; *Dig.* 49. 16. 3. 10–11. In the last reference torture is a preliminary to *bestiae* and *furca*. This would be odd if *bestiae* and *furca* were held to be forms of torture rather than forms of death. In *Dig.* 48. 10. 8 (Ulp.) *bestiae* is apparently contrasted with *summum supplicium*; in 48. 19. 29 (Gaius) it is treated as an instance of *ultimum supplicium*, in a passage where *summum supplicium* could probably have been used. *Dig.* 48. 19. 28 praef. and *PS* 5. 17. 2 include decapitation among penalties which make up *summum supplicium*. The plural *summa supplicia* in the second text indicates a non-technical use. The alternative would be to hold that the term *summum supplicium* was at some stage after the classical legal period applied to any penalty at all which involved death (see Brasiello, op. cit. 267); or simply that the sources are inconsistent.
[3] 'istae fere sunt poenae, quae iniungi solent. sed enim sciendum est discrimina esse poenarum neque omnes eadem poena adfici posse. nam in primis decuriones in metallum damnari non possunt nec in opus metalli, nec furcae subici vel vivi exuri.' *Dig.* 48. 19. 9. 11; cf. 28. 3. 6. 10, where the exemption of decurions from *damnatio ad bestias* is cited as an example of a general principle. On *furca* (and *crux*) see p. 128.
[4] 'decurionum filii non debent bestiis subici.' *CJ* 9. 47. 12. Relevant also to sons of decurions are 9. 41. 8 and 9. 41. 11. 1 (both Diocl. and Max.).

on the exemption of their sons. It would be similarly out of place to infer from the passage of Ulpian that decurions were liable to those penalties which he recorded until he wrote those words. In fact the whole system of privilege in the field of penalties can be deduced from Hadrian's edict which rules out *capite puniri* in the case of decurions.[1] At the moment it is enough to make the first step in the deduction: if decurions could not be executed (*capite puniri*), then it is reasonable to suppose that they also escaped *summum supplicium*. So we may take it that the general principle which Ulpian illustrates in the passage quoted was incorporated into Roman legal practice well before the time of Caracalla.

We may now look more closely at the individual penalties which are instances of *summum supplicium*.

'Vivus exuri' or *'crematio'*. This penalty stands with *furca* (the 'fork') and *capitis amputatio* (decapitation) at the top of the table of penalties compiled by Callistratus.[2]

Occurrence of the penalty is rare in the Republic and early Empire. In the *Twelve Tables* it is a penalty for arson:

qui aedes acervumve frumenti iuxta domum positum combusserit, vinctus verberatus igni necari iubetur, si modo sciens prudensque id commiserit.[3]

The cremation of the Pompeian Fadius was one of the atrocities committed by Balbus in Spain.[4] The fact that the victim pleaded that he was a citizen may indicate that the use of the penalty against citizens was irregular. But Fadius could have appealed only to tradition, and not law. In a Giessen papyrus the Emperor Gaius gives orders for an accuser καῆναι. The penalty envisaged might be branding rather than burning to death, although Musurillo was led to favour the latter by the brevity of phrase and by the wider context.[5]

---

[1] *Dig.* 48. 19. 15, and see p. 155.   [2] *Dig.* 48. 19. 28 praef.

[3] *Dig.* 47. 9. 9: 'A man who burns a house or a heap of corn next to a house is to be bound, beaten, and burned alive, provided he knew what he was doing and foresaw the consequences.' On this passage see Mommsen, op. cit. 837 n. 1.

[4] Cic. *ad fam.* 10. 32. 3.

[5] *P. Giss.* 46 = H. A. Musurillo, *The Acts of the Pagan Martyrs*, III. iii. ll. 24–5, pp. 14 and 112 ff. There is no parallel elsewhere in the *Acts*.

Nero burned Christians in Rome after the Fire.[1] Subsequently *crematio* was a common punishment for Christians. The cases of Polycarp and Pionius are conspicuous.[2] Vespasian tortured and burned alive the leader of the Jewish revolt in Cyrene, Jonathan.[3]

Commodus gained a belated revenge on the descendants of Avidius Cassius, the rebel against Marcus, by giving them to the flames: 'quasi in factione deprehensos'.[4] Finally, Macrinus, according to the biographer, had a reputation for being blood-thirsty, and made frequent use of slave penalties. He is said to have always burned adulterers alive.[5]

The legal evidence shows that *crematio*, at least in the period of the classical lawyers, was for slaves and free *humiliores*. Callistratus wrote: 'Mostly slaves are burned alive, slaves who have plotted against the life of their masters; also, on occasions, free men of the plebeian order and men of low status.'[6] According to Ulpian, those guilty of sacrilege were sometimes burned alive,[7] and the penalty was still in use in his time for arson.[8] Subsequently *crematio* was extended to other crimes. In *Paul's Sentences* it is prescribed for deserters,[9] magicians[10] and for *humiliores* found guilty of *maiestas*.[11]

'*Crux*'. The lawyer Macer wrote of slaves that they were punished after the example of men of low rank: 'In servorum persona ita

---

[1] Tac. *Ann.* 15. 44.

[2] *Mart. Polyc.* (= K–K, no. 1, p. 1) 13 ff. (On the date see T. D. Barnes, *Journ. Theol. Stud.* 19 (1968), 510 ff.); *Pass. Pionii* (K–K, no. 10, p. 45; Decius), 21. 2; 7; 9. See also *Pass. Perp. et Fel.* (K–K, no. 8, p. 35; A.D. 203), 11. 4 (i.e. deaths of Iocundus, Saturninus, and Artaxius); *Pass. Montani et Lucii* (K–K, no. 16, p. 74; A.D. 259), 3; *Acta Fruct.* (K–K, no. 17, p. 83; Valerian), 2. 4; 4. 3-4; *Acta Carpi, et al.* (K–K, no. 2, p. 8; *divi fratres* or Decius), 4 (Latin text); 23 and 36 (Greek text); *Acta Kononis* (K–K, no. 14, p. 64; Valerian), 5. 5; Cypr. *de hab. virg.* 6 fin.; Tert. *ad Scap.* 4; 11; *ad nat.* 1. 18 fin.; *ad mart.* 5; Eus. *EH* 5. 1. 52; 6. 41. 7-8 and 21; 8. 8 and H. Leclercq, *DACL* 5 (1922), 1456 ff., s.v. 'Feu'.

[3] Jos. *BJ* 7. 450 (c. A.D. 73).

[4] *SHA Avid. Cass.* 13. 7.

[5] *SHA Macr.* 12. 1-2; 10.

[6] *Dig.* 48. 19. 28. 11: 'Igni cremantur plerumque servi, qui saluti dominorum suorum insidiaverint, nonnumquam etiam liberi plebeii et humiles personae.'

[7] *Dig.* 48. 13. 7.

[8] *Dig.* 48. 19. 28. 12. The text is suspect. See *Index Interp.*, ad loc.

[9] *Dig.* 48. 19. 38. 1.   [10] *PS* 5. 23. 17.

[11] *PS* 5. 29. 1.

observatur, ut exemplo humiliorum puniantur.'[1] The sequence might have been reversed. When one examines the forms of punishment used on *humiliores*, one is struck by the connection with, and the derivation from, typical slave punishments. By the end of the second century some penalties, which in the late Republic and early Empire had been applied to slaves, were commonly used in the punishment of ordinary free men of humble origin and status, including, presumably, citizens. Crucifixion was the standing form of execution for slaves.[2] When Asiaticus the freedman received a *servile supplicium* at the hands of Mucianus, we can take it as probable that he was crucified.[3] Galba, when governor of Baetica, crucified a Roman citizen.[4] Suetonius represents the action as outrageously cruel. The victim is reported to have 'implored the laws' and 'testified to his Roman citizenship'. The implication is not that there was a law prohibiting the crucifixion of citizens, but rather that the punishment was properly and normally employed against slaves and perhaps humble aliens. Galba's act had been foreshadowed by Verres' treatment of Gavius in Sicily.[5] Furthermore, in the reign of Nero, Gessius Florus scourged and crucified some Jews in Jerusalem, including some equestrians.[6] On other occasions Jewish rebels suffered crucifixion. Quadratus, the governor of Syria, crucified some during a troublesome disturbance in the procuratorship of Cumanus.[7] Felix crucified many brigands in quelling more strife.[8] A political charge was at least aired in the trial of Christ;[9] later, the cross was frequently used for the punishment of Christians, at least from the time of Nero.[10]

---

[1] *Dig.* 48. 19. 10 praef.

[2] For crucifixion of slaves see Cic. *pro Cluentio* 187; Val. Max. 8. 4. 2; Livy 22. 33. 2; Suet. *Dom.* 10; *SHA Pert.* 9. 10. Tarquinius Priscus crucified citizens: Pliny, *n.h.* 36. 107; Servius on *Aen.* 12. 603. In general, see Mommsen, *Strafr.* 918 ff.; Hitzig, *RE* 4 (1901), 1728–31, s.v. *crux*; Leclercq, ibid. 2429.

[3] Tac. *Hist.* 4. 11.   [4] Suet. *Galba* 9.

[5] Cic. *in Verr.* 5. 162, cf. 12.   [6] Jos. *BJ* 2. 301 ff.

[7] Jos. *AJ* 20. 129.   [8] Jos. *BJ* 2. 253 ff.

[9] On the nature of the charge see A. N. Sherwin-White, op. cit. (see p. 75 n. 3), ch. 2, 24–47.

[10] Tac. *Ann.* 15. 44; Sen. *ad Marc.* 20. 3; *de vita beata* 19. 3; *ep.* 14. 5; Justin, *dial.* 110. 4; Tert. *apol.* 12. 3; 50. 12; *de praescr.* 3 with *scorp.* 15 (Peter); *ad mart.* 4. 2 and 9; *ad nat.* 1. 3; 1. 18 fin.; Cypr. *de hab. virg.* 6 fin.; Eus. *EH* 2. 25. 5, cf. 3. 1. 2; 3. 32. 6; 8. 8; *Acta Carpi, et al.* (K–K, no. 2, p. 8;

The *crux* was banned by Constantine, and the *furca* put in its place.[1] (The criminal apparently hung by the neck from a wooden fork until he was dead.)[2] Thus the Severan jurists, as emended by the Justinianic compilers, record exemption from the *furca* for decurions and soldiers.[3] In *Paul's Sentences*, however, which is pre-Constantinian, we read that kidnappers who were *humiliores* were crucified or sent to the mines.[4] Murderers of the same status were either thrown to the beasts or crucified,[5] and those found guilty of *impia* or magic faced the same alternatives.[6] Any offender against the Cornelian law on *falsum* was punished with *metallum* or *crux* if of low birth, according to *Paul's Sentences*.[7] No exemption from *crux* is recorded explicitly, then, in this source, but it is implicit in the variant penalties set for *honestiores* and *humiliores*.

There is some doubt about the form of physical apparatus used for the punishment in the Severan period. Mommsen thought that the Republican brand of *furca* was identical with *crux*, but this is implausible. Traditionally, the man condemned to the *furca*, commonly a slave, was bound to a wooden apparatus with a fork and perhaps a crosspiece.[8] He was then made to carry the wood on his neck around the neighbourhood, thus earning the nickname of *furcifer*.[9] He was often, if not always, beaten in addition. But this beating was normally only a preparation for a death brought on by other means, for example, crucifixion—which had a separate existence in Republican times.[10]

divi fr. or Decius), 3–5 (Latin text). There are a few references to crucifixion (not of Christians) in the *SHA*; see, e.g., *Avid. Cass.* 4. 2 ff. and 6; *Pert.* 9. 10; *Sev.* 4. 3; *Macr.* 12. 2; *Al. Sev.* 28. 5.

[1] Aur. Vict. *Caes.* 41. 4; Sozomenus, *EH* 1. 8; etc. The last reference to crucifixion is *CTh* 9. 5. 1, A.D. 314. On *furca*, Mommsen, op. cit. 919 ff.; Hitzig, *RE* 7. 1 (1910), 305–7, s.v. *furca*; Brasiello, op. cit. 458; R. Bonini, *I 'Libri de cognitionibus' di Callistrato* (1964), 87 n. 19. For the substitution of *furca* for *crux* in the *Digest* cf. 48. 19. 38. 2 and *PS* 5. 22. 1.

[2] Isid. *orig.* 5. 27. 34 and Mommsen, op. cit. 921 n. 2.

[3] *Dig.* 48. 19. 9. 11 (Ulp.); 49. 16. 3. 10 (Mod.). Other refs. to *furca* include 48. 13. 7; 48. 19. 28 praef.; ibid. 38. 1.

[4] *Coll.* 14. 2. 2.   [5] *PS* 5. 23. 1.   [6] Ibid. 15; 17.

[7] *PS* 5. 25. 1.   [8] Hitzig, op. cit. 306–7.

[9] e.g. Plaut. *Most.* 69 and 1172.

[10] Crucifixion in Republican times: Pliny, *n.h.* 18. 12 (*XII Tables*); Mommsen, op. cit. 918 n. 6; Livy 1. 26. 6; Cic. *pro Rab.* 5. 16, etc.; *in Verr.* 5. 162 ff. The 'traditional' (*more maiorum*) punishment seems to have been a variation of the

However, it is safe to regard crucifixion, whatever precise form it took, as traditionally a slave penalty,[1] from which *honestiores* were exempt under the Empire, but not *humiliores*.

'Bestiae'. An excerpt from Ulpian seems to provide a scale of severity for capital punishments.[2] It may be deduced that condemnation to the mines ranked lowest of the capital penalties to which men of low status were subject; that exposure to wild beasts was the least severe of those penalties mentioned which caused death (decapitation is omitted from the passage); that it was a more common punishment for sacrilege than burning alive or the fork (that is, in the classical period, crucifixion); and that for the less serious forms of sacrilege it was the highest rung on the ladder of possible penalties.[3]

Damnatio ad bestias was little known in Republican times. Scipio Africanus, victorious over Carthage, followed the example of his father Aemilius Paullus, who triumphed in Macedonia, when he held games and threw deserters and runaway slaves to the beasts.[4] The victims were of alien, not Roman, origin.[5] Further, it seems to have been common practice for a governor to supply human victims to a Roman aedile for his games. Piso sent some for Clodius, and Cicero was asked to provide them for Caelius, presumably for the same purpose. These were again

punishment of *furca*, and was not identical with *crux*. See Suet. *Nero* 49. 2; Aur. Vict. *epit*. 5. 7; Livy *per*. 55.

[1] A second assertion of Mommsen, that crucifixion was the oldest form of magisterial execution for free citizens, has little to support it. The punishment of the lovers of the Vestal Virgins, which he cites, belongs to the realm of family law, not public law. See refs. in Mommsen, op. cit. 919 n. 1, and Hitzig, op. cit. 306. And if traitors were crucified, it was because they were deemed to have forfeited their rights as citizens.

[2] *Dig*. 48. 13. 7: 'Sacrilegii poenam debebit proconsul pro qualitate personae proque rei condicione et temporis et aetatis et sexus vel severius vel clementius statuere. et scio multos et ad bestias damnasse sacrilegos, nonnullos etiam vivos exussisse, alios vero in furca suspendisse. sed moderanda poena est usque ad bestiarum damnationem eorum, qui manu facta templum effregerunt et dona dei in noctu tulerunt. ceterum si qui interdiu modicum aliquid de templo tulit, poena metalli coercendus est, aut, si honestiore loco natus sit, deportandus in insulam est.'

[3] The same passage may seem to imply that *crematio* was less severe than *furca* ('nonnullos etiam vivos exussisse, alios vero in furca suspendisse'), but the order is reversed in *Dig*. 48. 19. 9. 11.

[4] Livy, *per*. 51.

[5] Val. Max. 2. 7. 13 (146 B.C.: *exterarum gentium transfugas*).

non-Romans.[1] On the other hand, Balbus' action in throwing Roman citizens to the beasts in Spain is regarded by Cicero's correspondent Pollio as highly irregular.[2] But there was no law to prevent it.

In the same way, if an Emperor wished to subject someone of high status to this undignified and cruel form of death, there were no legal means of preventing him. Gaius condemned to the beasts men of high rank, *honesti ordinis*, and not always for offences of any gravity.[3] At least one Roman knight met his end in this way. The next Emperor, Claudius, is said to have had men thrown to the beasts for serious breaches of the law:

et in maiore fraude convictos legitimam poenam supergressus ad bestias condemnavit.[4]

Under Nero Christians were torn to pieces by dogs.[5] More 'scruple' was shown by the governor of Lugdunensis in Marcus' reign—he sorted out citizens from aliens and sent the latter to the beasts.[6] Other references from the pre-Severan period demonstrate that the penalty was employed against slaves,[7] foreign foes,[8] and free men guilty of a few very serious or notorious offences.[9]

---

[1] Cic. *in Pis.* 89 (*socios stipendiariosque*); cf. *ad fam.* 8. 4. 5.

[2] Ibid. 10. 32. 3.

[3] Suet. *Gaius* 27. 3–4; cf. Dio 59. 10. 3.

[4] Suet. *Div. Cl.* 14: 'he condemned to the beasts those found guilty of relatively grave crimes, exceeding the penalty set by the law.'

[5] Tac. *Ann.* 15. 44.

[6] Eus. *EH* 5. 1. 47. Christians were often condemned to the beasts. See *Pass. Perp. et Fel.* (K–K, no. 8, p. 35; A.D. 203), 6. 4; *Acta Kononis* (K–K, no. 14, p. 64; Valerian?), 5. 5; Cypr. *de hab. virg.* 6 fin.; Eus. *EH* 8. 7. 4–6; Tert. *apol.* 12. 4; 40. 2; 50. 12; *ad mart.* 4; *ad Scap.* 3. 6; *ad nat.* 1. 3 fin. Polycarp narrowly escaped this form of death: *Mart. Polyc.* (K–K, no. 1, p. 1), 11. See H. Leclercq, *DACL* i (1924), 452 ff., s.v. *ad bestias*.

[7] The freedom of masters to send slaves to the beasts was restricted somewhat, in theory, by the Petronian law of (probably) Tiberian date. *Dig.* 48. 8. 11. 2; cf. Apion in Gellius 5. 14. 27.

[8] See S. Aurigemma, *I Mosaici di Zliten* (1926), 180 ff., fig. 111ª, 111ᵇ, 112; also Aurigemma, *L'Italia in Africa: Le scoperte archeologiche, 1911–43; Tripolitania*, vol. i, pt. 1 (1960), tav. 151–2, 154. The author associates these mosaics with the punishment of the Garamantes in Flavian times (see vol. i, pt. 1, p. 14, and vol. i, pt. 11, p. 56).

[9] e.g. Hadrian prescribed this penalty for parricide as an alternative to the traditional 'penalty of the sack', but presumably only for those of low birth or position. See *Dig.* 48. 9. 9, praef., cf. 48. 19. 15. See Cicero's comment on

The Severan sources indicate that men were thrown to the beasts in that period for rustling,[1] murder (and other offences covered by the Cornelian law),[2] and sacrilege.[3] The application of the penalty in all these cases was probably a recent development, although this is only demonstrable in the case of rustling.[4] Severan texts also include reference to exemptions from *bestiis subici*. Ulpian considered that a decurion condemned to the beasts was *damnatus illicite*.[5] In another passage he stated that for the crime of arson those *in aliquo gradu* were executed or deported, but those *in humiliore loco* went to the beasts.[6] Veterans[7] were spared the beasts, and soldiers[8] also, unless they were traitors.

By the end of the third century, *bestiis subici* and *crux* were the sole penalties prescribed for accomplices in magic[9] and for those who indulged in *sacra impia nocturnave*.[10] There was apparently no alternative to *bestiis subici* for armed burglary of a temple at night.[11] It seems that the area of privilege receded, as certain crimes were adjudged too serious to warrant a 'moderate' penalty.

2 (b) 'Metallum' and 'opus publicum'

In the Hadrianic rescript, the penalties *in custodiis* are placed in the following order: *summum supplicium, metallum*, (sc. *opus*) *in perpetuum*, (sc. *opus*) *in tempus*.[12] The rescript, then, recognizes after *summum supplicium* only two important categories, *metallum* and *opus publicum*. The first task is to assess the state to which the two penalties brought the condemned man. An attempt will be

---

damnatio ad bestias as a possible penalty for parricide, *Sex. Rosc.* 71. See also *SHA Comm.* 18. 10 (*delatores*); Dio 73. 16. 5, with *SHA Sev.* 14. 1 (murderer of Commodus).

[1] *Coll.* 11. 8. 4.   [2] *Dig.* 48. 8. 3. 5.
[3] *Dig.* 48. 13. 7; cf. *PS* 5. 19.
[4] Hadrian had recommended condemnation to mortal combat and to the mines as the harshest penalties for these criminals. See *Coll.* 11. 7. 1–2. Cf. 11. 8. 4 (Ulp.). For *damnatio ad gladium, damnatio in ludum gladiatorium*, ibid. 11. 7. 4; *Dig.* 48. 19. 8. 11–12. Other references include *Dig.* 29. 2. 25. 3; *Coll.* 4. 3. 2; and see Brasiello, op. cit. 382 ff.
[5] *Dig.* 28. 3. 6. 10.   [6] *Dig.* 47. 9. 12. 1; cf. *Coll.* 12. 5. 1 ff.
[7] *Dig.* 49. 18. 3; cf. ibid. 1.   [8] *Dig.* 49. 16. 3. 10.
[9] *PS* 5. 23. 17.   [10] Ibid. 15.
[11] *PS* 5. 19. For this offence *bestiae* was the maximum, and not the sole, penalty, when Ulpian wrote. See p. 129 n. 2, above.
[12] *Dig.* 48. 19. 28. 14.

made at the same time to explain the various terms used for these penalties by the jurists.

Metallum comes next after death in severity: 'Deinde proxima morti poena metalli coercitio.'[1] The condemned man lost not only citizenship, if he possessed it, but also liberty.[2] He was a 'slave of the penalty' (*servus poenae*), with no right of making a will or receiving from a will.[3] He was loaded with chains, and beaten like a slave.[4]

The phrase *in perpetuum*, in Hadrian's usage, covered both *opus perpetuum* and *opus metalli*. In another rescript he made a precise distinction between *opus metalli* and *metallum*, while insisting that *opus metalli* like *metallum*, was a life sentence. *Metallum* but not *opus metalli* deprived a man of his freedom. Callistratus quotes the rescript: 'No one ought to be condemned to work in mines [*opus metalli*] for a restricted term; rather, he who has been condemned for a restricted term, even if he does work in mines [*metallicum opus*] should not be held to have been condemned to the mines [*metallum*]. For his freedom remains, as long as the freedom of those condemned to public labour for life [*perpetuum opus*].'[5] By the Severan period, however, it was evidently felt that no man could perform *metallicum opus* and retain his freedom. Both *metallum* and *opus metalli* were held to deprive free men of freedom,[6] and Callistratus placed them together among penalties by which *existimatio* or *dignitas* were 'consumed' rather than 'diminished', and by which *magna minutio capitis* was suffered.[7] In addition,

---

[1] *Dig.* 48. 19. 28. praef. As the text suggests, the punishment was originally not a 'legal' penalty, but an aspect of *coercitio*. See *Dig.* 1. 12. 10 and 37. 14. 1 (*metallum* as *coercitio* for a freedman for physical injury to his patron). On *metallum* and *opus publicum* see Mommsen, op. cit. 949 ff.; Brasiello, op. cit. 360 ff.

[2] *Dig.* 40. 5. 24. 6; 48. 19. 8. 4; 49. 14. 12.

[3] *Dig.* 28. 3. 6. 5–7; 29. 1. 13. 2; 49. 14. 12. For other disabilities see *Dig.* 34. 1. 11; 40. 1. 8 praef. On *servus poenae* see Brasiello, op. cit. 416–46; below, p. 165.

[4] *Dig.* 48. 19. 8. 6 (chains); *Dig.* 49. 14. 12 (beating). He was probably also branded. See Suet. *Gaius* 27. 3; *CTh* 9. 40. 2, A.D. 315.

[5] *Dig.* 48. 19. 28. 6: 'In opus metalli ad tempus nemo damnari debet sed qui ad tempus damnatus est, etiamsi faciet metallicum opus, non in metallum damnatus esse intellegi debet: huius enim libertas manet, quamdiu etiam hi, qui in perpetuum opus damnantur.' Brasiello (op. cit. 380) brackets 'quamdiu . . . damnantur'.   [6] *Dig.* 48. 19. 8. 4.

[7] *Dig.* 50. 13. 5. 3. This is not a homogeneous group. The loss of *libertas* cannot be its distinguishing feature, as *deportati* retained *libertas*.

Ulpian thought the only difference between *opus metalli* and *metallum* was the weight of the chains used.[1] Thus for the Severans *perpetuum* in the (first) Hadrianic rescript could have stood only for forced labour (*opus*) elsewhere than in the mines.

The jurists placed *opus publicum* among the penalties by which *existimatio* was diminished. The condemned man lost *dignitas* but not *libertas*. This explains the irregularity which Papinian detected in sending a slave into *opus publicum temporarium* or *perpetuum*. These penalties were normally for free men, and they remained free men even after sentence.[2]

This interpretation of *opus perpetuum* is confirmed by a rescript of Pius, asserting that this penalty and *deportatio* had the same consequences for the status of the condemned man.[3] The jurist Marcianus puts these two penalties side by side, as equally depriving the condemned man of his citizenship.[4] Freedom, however, was not lost, certainly not in the case of *deportati*, nor in all probability in the case of those sent to *opus perpetuum*. A passage of Ulpian raises a slight doubt.[5] He links *opus perpetuum* with *opus metalli* as alternative, stiffer penalties for the fugitive from *opus publicum (temporarium)*. But it does not follow from his remarks that *opus metallum* and *opus publicum perpetuum* were equally severe.

To sum up, *opus perpetuum* had in common with *opus metalli* and *metallum*, but also with *deportatio*, the fact that it was a life sentence. Like *deportatio*, but unlike the other penalties, it did not take away freedom. It is best to regard *opus perpetuum* as an extended *opus publicum temporarium*. A man who was transferred from the latter to the former did not undergo a change in status. Hence the series of penalties in the Hadrianic rescript runs: *in*

---

[1] *Dig.* 48. 19. 8. 6.

[2] *Dig.* 48. 19. 34 praef.; but see ibid. 10 praef. (Macer): when a free man is beaten and sentenced to *opus publicum*, the slave suffers *poena vinculorum*, is whipped with *flagella*, and sent back to his master. Only if he is not received by his master is he dispatched into *opus perpetuum*.

[3] *CJ* 9. 47. 1: 'etiam in opus perpetuum damnati non dissimilis condicionis sunt ab his qui deportantur in insulam.'

[4] *Dig.* 48. 19. 17. 1: 'item quidam ἀπόλιδες sunt, hoc est sine civitate: ut sunt opus publicum perpetuo dati et in insulam deportati, ut ea quidem, quae iuris civilis sunt, non habeant, quae vero iuris gentium sunt, habeant.'

[5] Ibid. 8. 7.

tempus (a species of *opus*), *in perpetuum* (again a species of *opus*, but including, for Hadrian, *opus metallicum*), *in metallum*. *Opus publicum* and *metallum* are the two main categories. By the former the *dignitas* of the condemned was affected, by the latter his *libertas* also.

The early history of forced labour as a criminal sentence in Rome is badly documented.[1] *Metallum* and *opus* were both recognized penalties under Tiberius and Gaius. Both Emperors are said to have imposed them on men of rank, and this was clearly considered outrageous.[2] A Trajanic governor of Africa, Marius Priscus, had an equestrian (probably a member of the local gentry) beaten, condemned to the mines, and strangled in prison.[3] It has already been suggested that the action of Priscus was irregular, not just because of the presumed innocence of the victim, but also because of the degrading punishments which were inflicted on him.[4] The condemnation to the mines of Flavius Archippus for *falsum* in Domitian's reign by the governor of Bithynia, Velius Paulus (apparently without irregularity), is not necessarily inconsistent with the theory that this penalty, when used at all of capital offences, tended to be applied to ordinary citizens or plebeians even as early as the latter half of the first century.[5] Nothing is known of the status of Archippus before his condemnation. It is not certain that he was already a Roman citizen. Domitian subsequently gave him roughly the census required for the decurionate, but there is no sign that Archippus had lost a similar amount at the time of his conviction through confiscation. Further, his profession as a philosopher may tell against any theory that he had already been a local politician.[6]

Condemnation to *opus* was known in Bithynia in Pliny's time.[7] The status of the offenders is not recorded.

[1] For the treatment of men condemned to mines see Mommsen, op. cit. 949 ff.

[2] Suet. *Tib.* 51. 2 (an equestrian sentenced to the treadmill); Suet. *Gaius* 27. 3 ('multos honesti ordinis deformatos prius stigmatum notis ad metalla et munitiones viarum . . . condemnavit').

[3] Pliny, *Ep.* 2. 11. 8.　　　　　[4] See pp. 54 ff.

[5] Pliny, *Ep.* 10. 58 ff. Cf. *Dig.* 49. 15. 6: a slave woman is sent to hard labour in the British salt mines in A.D. 84–6 (see E. Birley, *Roman Britain and the Roman Army* (1953), 87 ff.).

[6] On the other hand, it might imply that he was a man of means.

[7] Pliny, *Ep.* 10. 31–2.

The exemption of decurions from *metallum* and *opus metalli* is not explicitly mentioned in our texts until Ulpian touches on the topic in his treatise on the duties of a proconsul: 'For, above all, decurions cannot be sentenced to the mines [*metallum*] or mine work [*opus metalli*], nor to the fork, nor to be burned alive.'[1] No reference is made to any authorities, and Ulpian is in fact describing current practice, which, I suggest, had its roots well in the past.

Pius issued an edict about the punishment of those who stole gold or silver from Imperial mines. The penalty was exile or *metallum*, according to the *dignitas* of the offender:

> si quis ex metallis Caesarianis aurum argentumve furatus fuerit, ex edicto divi Pii exilio vel metallo, prout dignitas personae, punitur.[2]

If this edict is set beside other pronouncements of the same Emperor, it can be deduced that decurions would not have gone to the mines.[3] Nor is Pius likely to have been the first Emperor who took this view.

Caracalla, in a rescript, spoke of exemptions from *metallum* and *opus publicum* for the sons of veterans.[4] They could expect relegation to islands. Caracalla did not award the privilege, but treated it as an established fact. According to Marcianus, veterans and their sons had *honor* equal to decurions, 'and therefore will not be sentenced to the mines or to public labour, nor are they exposed to the beasts, nor beaten with rods.'[5]

Metallum and *opus metalli* were 'plebeian' penalties, in the view of Marcianus' contemporary Callistratus.[6] The crime of *stellionatus*, or cheating, was normally punished *extra ordinem*, Ulpian wrote, and specified that *opus metalli* was the maximum penalty *in plebeiis*.[7] *Metallum* was the penalty for commoners who had committed theft (with arms), or tampered with the banks of the Nile, for

---

[1] *Dig.* 48. 19. 9. 11: 'nam in primis decuriones in metallum damnari non possunt nec in opus metalli, nec furcae subici vel vivi exuri'; cf. 50. 2. 2. 2 (Ulp.); *CJ* 9. 47. 9 (Sev. Al.). The second text is about sons of a decurion, the third about a daughter of a decurion.

[2] *Dig.* 48. 13. 8. 1, cf. 48. 19. 38 praef.   [3] e.g. *Dig.* 50. 2. 14.

[4] *CJ* 9. 47. 5.

[5] *Dig.* 49. 18. 3: 'igitur nec in metallum damnabuntur nec in opus publicum vel ad bestias, nec fustibus caeduntur.'

[6] *Dig.* 50. 13. 5. 3.   [7] *Dig.* 47. 20. 3. 2.

kidnappers of the same rank, for those who married beyond their station, and so on.[1]

As for *opus*, the earliest definite statement to the effect that a decurion should not suffer *opus publicum* is Caracalla's: 'Decurionem in opus publicum dari non oportere manifestum est.'[2] This was evidently a well-known fact (*manifestum est*). The same Emperor told Senecio that *metallum* and *opus publicum* were prohibited for sons of veterans.[3] Ulpian recorded that burglars (*effractores*) and plunderers (*expilatores*), corn speculators (*dardanarii*) and rustlers (*abigei*), were sentenced to *opus publicum* if they were *humiliores*, rather than *motio* or *relegatio*.[4] Much earlier is Pius' rescript to Apollonius on the subject of the punishment of the murderer of an adulterous wife.[5] If *humilis loci*, he was sentenced to *opus perpetuum*, if *honestior*, he was relegated to an island. But the *opus/relegatio* alternative probably goes back into the reign of Hadrian at least.

3 (a) Beating and the fine

est enim inconstans dicere eum, quem principales constitutiones fustibus subici prohibuerunt, in metallum dari posse.[6]

To judge from these words of Callistratus, *fustibus caedi* (*subici*), or beating, is to be grouped with the penalties for low-status criminals.[7]

What precisely did those who were exempted from beating escape? This question can be answered in two ways, in terms of

---

[1] *Dig.* 47. 17. 1 (theft); 47. 11. 10 (Nile); 48. 15. 7 (kidnapping—the penalty was once monetary, cf. *Coll.* 14. 3. 5); *CJ* 5. 5. 3. 1 ff. (319) (marriage); see also *PS* 1. 21. 4; ibid. 5; 2. 19. 9; 5. 19; 5. 19a; 5. 20. 2; ibid. 5; 5. 23. 4; ibid. 12; 14; 5. 25. 8; ibid. 10; 5. 26. 3; etc. Christians were frequently sent to the mines. See Tert. *apol.* 12. 5; 27. 7; *cult. fem.* 1. 5 praef.; Cypr. *ep.* 77; 76. 1–2 and 6, etc.; Eus. *EH* 8. 12. 10; 8. 13. 5; 9. 1. 7; *MP* 7. 2–3; 8. 1 and 13; 9. 1; 11. 6. H. Leclercq, *DACL* i. 467–74, s.v. *ad metalla*.

[2] *CJ* 9. 47. 3: 'It is plain that a decurion ought not to be sentenced to public labour.'

[3] Ibid. 5; cf. *Dig.* 49. 18. 3.

[4] *Dig.* 47. 18. 1. 2 (burglars); ibid. 1. 1 (plunderers); 47. 11. 6 praef. (corn speculators); 47. 14. 1. 3 (rustlers).

[5] *Dig.* 48. 5. 39. 8.

[6] *Dig.* 48. 19. 28. 5: 'It is inconsistent to say that he who has been exempted from beating by the constitutions of Emperors can be sentenced to the mines.'

[7] On beating see Mommsen, op. cit. 983 ff.; Brasiello, op. cit. 386 ff.; see also *JRS* 56 (1966), 167 ff.

the instrument of beating and the different levels of the punishment, and in terms of the different uses of beating in the legal system.

The military staff, *fustis*, replaced the rods, *virgae* (traditionally borne by the lictors), as the instrument of civilian beating, rather as the sword replaced the axe as the instrument of civilian execution.[1] A beating by *fustes* was not necessarily heavy, although it might be. *Verberare* is found with *fustes*, and *verberatio* is invariably a heavy beating.[2] Yet *castigatio* or *admonitio*, a light beating, can also be administered by *fustes*.[3] Anyone who was not liable to *fustibus caedi* was therefore free from both a heavy and a light beating.[4]

It would be unwise to insist upon a sharp contrast between beating as a *poena* and beating as an aspect of *coercitio*. This distinction had lost its precision long before the Severan era.[5] Nevertheless, it may be retained for the purpose of defining and characterizing the different uses of beating.

There was a group of minor offences, or *levia crimina*, which the governor was authorized to investigate and punish extrajudicially (*de plano*) by beating:

levia crimina audire et discutere de plano proconsulem oportet et vel liberare eos, quibus obiciuntur, vel fustibus castigare vel flagellis servos verberare.[6]

Governors also chastised freedmen on behalf of their patrons,

[1] Mommsen, op. cit. 983 and n. 4.
[2] *Dig.* 47. 10. 5 praef.–1 (contrast between *pulsatio* and *verberatio*); cf. ibid. 7. 2: 'leviter pulsaverit vel emendaverit' (but see ibid. 15. 38: one can *verberare* a slave to correct or reform him; and 47. 8. 4. 13—where *pulsare* and *verberare* are treated as synonyms); cf. 48. 6. 10. 1; 48. 7. 2. *Pulsare* by itself: *Dig.* 47. 10. 1. 2; ibid. 9 praef.; ibid. 15. 1.
[3] e.g. *Dig.* 1. 12. 1. 10; 1. 15. 3. 1; 1. 16. 9. 3; 47. 10. 15. 30; 47. 11. 7; 48. 2. 6; For *admonitio* see *Dig.* 48. 19. 7. *Verberatio* with fists (*pugnae*): *Dig.* 47. 10. 15. 40; *Coll.* 2. 6. 4.
[4] Whips (*flagella*) were normally used on slaves. See, e.g., *Dig.* 9. 2. 52. 1; 47. 9. 4. 1; 48. 2. 6; 48. 19. 10 praef.; *PS* 5. 4. 22. Cf. Philo, *in Flacc.* 78 ff.: different instruments of beating and different wielders of those instruments for Egyptians and for Alexandrians. Philo complained that Jewish 'councillors' were treated as if they were Egyptians of the lowest order.
[5] Ulpian wrote this of *poena*: '(cum) poena generale sit nomen omnium delictorum coercitio' (*Dig.* 50. 16. 131. 1).
[6] *Dig.* 48. 2. 6: 'The proconsul is authorized to hear and investigate petty offences extrajudicially, and either free the accused, or chastise them with rods (or if they are slaves, flay them with whips).' Such offences were barely 'crimes', according to Roman law.

either verbally or *fustium castigatione*.[1] They might also intervene in a civil disturbance to preserve order, with a swift act of *coercitio* which involved beating.[2]

Secondly, beating regularly preceded *opus publicum*[3] or *metallum*.[4] Beating before execution was an old-established practice.[5]

Finally, beating is found as an alternative to other punishments, *relegatio* and *opus* (Callistratus classed all three as *poenae ad existimationem*)[6] and the fine. The pairing of beating and the fine was especially apt. If beating was a handy punishment for any minor offence, a fine was levelled, according to Ulpian, 'when no special penalty was laid down'.[7] Of the two, beating was regarded as the more severe sanction,[8] principally because all forms of corporal punishment were held to be degrading. Yet the man of small means and little *dignitas* might well find beating preferable. In Republican times, when civil law knew only the monetary penalty (and when the *cognitio* procedure was unavailable), the poorer section of the population must have suffered considerable hardship when on the losing side in litigation. They were forced through debt to sell their meagre possessions, take out credit at unfavourable rates, and ultimately fall victim to the

---

[1] *Dig.* 1. 16. 9. 3; 47. 10. 7. 2 ('ceterum levem coercitionem utique patrono adversus libertum dabimus'); and see 37. 14. 1. The chastisement was not necessarily light. See *Dig.* 1. 16. 11 (the proconsul has *atrociter verberandi ius*).

[2] e.g. Tac. *Ann.* 1. 77 (*ius virgarum*); cf. Suet. *Div. Aug.* 45. 3; *PS* 5. 21. 1 (note the connection with expulsion); see also *Dig.* 48. 19. 28. 3; Acts 21: 33 (arrest of Paul). Beating in the course of interrogation (for intransigence, i.e. *contumacia* (?)): *Acta Maximi* (K–K, no. 12, p. 61; Decius) 2. 1.

[3] *Dig.* 47. 9. 4. 1; 47. 21. 2; 48. 19. 10 praef.; 49. 14. 18. 2; *PS* 5. 18. 1 = *Coll.* 11. 3.

[4] *Dig.* 47. 9. 4. 1; 49. 14. 12.

[5] Dion. Hal. 9. 40. 3; Sall. *Cat.* 51. 21; *Dig.* 47. 9. 9 (cf. Gai. *Inst.* 3. 189; Gellius 11. 18. 8); 48. 9. 9 praef.; Dio 54. 7. 6; Mark 15: 15; Matt. 27. 26; Jos. *BJ* 2. 306.

[6] *Dig.* 48. 19. 28. 1; cf. 50. 13. 5. 2. *Dig.* 48. 19. 10. 2 implies that beating was milder than *opus temporarium*. Flogging to death was a traditional punishment reserved for certain crimes. See Gellius, 10. 3. 5; 17. 21. 24; Livy 22. 57 (216 B.C.); Dion. Hal. 8. 89. 5; 9. 40. 4; Suet. *Nero* 49, with Aur. Vict. *epit.* 5. 7; Suet. *Dom.* 8. 3–4. The penalty was later regarded as illegal: *Dig.* 48. 19. 8. 3 (Ulp.). For Christians beaten to death see Leclercq, *DACL* 5. 1638–43, 'Flagellation'.

[7] *Dig.* 50. 16. 131. 1: 'quin immo multa ibi dicitur, ubi specialis poena non est imposita.'

[8] *Dig.* 48. 19. 10. 2 (Macer): '(quia et) solus fustium ictus gravior est quam pecuniaris damnatio.'

savage debt laws and forfeit their freedom. Under the Empire, however, beating replaced the fine for the free man of low status and little property, at least in the criminal courts.[1] Those delicts which were handled *extra ordinem* could also be punished with either a fine or a beating. The general principle was stated by Ulpian in these words: 'It is general policy, in the administration of the laws governing public trials or private crimes, for prefects or governors who judge *extra ordinem* to apply *extra ordinem* punishment to those who through poverty escape a monetary penalty.'[2] But the alternative of pecuniary or corporal punishment was established much earlier than the Severan age, when Ulpian was writing. An early example is found in the edict of L. Geta, the prefect of Egypt in A.D. 54, which ordered either a money payment or corporal punishment—ἢ ἀργυρικῶς ἢ σωματικῶς κολασθήσεται.[3] Geta was prescribing actual penalties.

Corporal punishment was traditionally used against slaves[4] and aliens.[5] This was written into the laws from the early second century B.C., when a *lex Porcia* granted to Roman citizens the right of appeal against beating as well as execution.[6] The clause was taken over into the Augustan *lex Iulia de vi publica*, and survived into the age of the classical lawyers.[7] As late as the reign of Commodus, the *coloni* of the saltus Burunitanus in Africa complained to the Emperor that *conductores* had had them flogged, although some of them were Roman citizens.[8]

---

[1] *Dig.* 2. 1. 7. 3 (Ulp.): 'in servos . . . et eos qui inopia laborant'; 47. 9. 9; 48. 1. 2; *CJ* 6. 1. 4. 2 (A.D. 317). For fining as an alternative to imprisonment (of one sort or another) see *Dig.* 11. 5. 1. 4. Fine by itself: *Dig.* 47. 12. 3. 5 (Hadr.; for magistrates and others unspecified).

[2] *Dig.* 48. 19. 1. 3: 'generaliter placet, in legibus publicorum iudiciorum vel privatorum criminum qui extra ordinem cognoscunt praefecti vel praesides, ut eis, qui poenam pecuniariam egentes eludunt, coercitionem extraordinariam inducant'; *CJ* 2. 11. 5 (A.D. 198): beating or *ignominia*.

[3] *OGIS* 2. 664.

[4] *Dig.* 49. 14. 12 (*verbera servilia*); Dion. Hal. 9. 40 (καθάπερ ἀνδράποδον); *Dig.* 47. 10. 7. 2. On *verberatio* for slaves see *Dig.* 4. 4. 24. 3 (slave or son); 9. 2. 52. 1; 21. 1. 17. 4; 44. 7. 34 praef.; 47. 8. 4. 13–16; 47. 10. 1. 7; ibid. 17. 4; and p. 137 n. 4.

[5] Tac. *Ann.* 1. 59. 4 (*virgas et securis*). See J. L. Strachan-Davidson, *Problems of the Roman Criminal Law* (1912), i. 126.

[6] *lex Porcia*: Sall. *Cat.* 51. 21 ff. and 40; Cic. *de rep.* 2. 53; Livy 10. 9.

[7] *lex Iulia de vi publica*: *Dig.* 48. 6. 7; *PS* 5. 26. 1 ff.

[8] *FIRA²* i, no. 103, p. 496, col. ii, ll. 10 ff. (A.D. 180–3).

This case should be read beside another, from Egypt.[1] In A.D. 153 the strategos of the Arsinoite nome had C. Mevius Apella, a veteran, soundly beaten by two guards. Apella is found in the papyrus instigating proceedings against the strategos before the prefect of Egypt. As nothing is preserved except a record of the event itself, it is not known whether breach of the *lex Iulia* was the basis of Apella's case, as it apparently was the basis of the complaint of the African peasants. It may seem unreasonable to doubt this. But Callistratus, writing under Septimius Severus and Caracalla, referred to rescripts of Emperors in which *honestiores* were specifically exempted from beating.[2] Callistratus at the same time gave the information that free men of low rank ('hi . . . qui liberi sunt et quidem tenuiores homines') were regularly beaten in his day. One rescript of this type is preserved. Issued in A.D. 198 by Severus and Caracalla, it began:' decuriones quidem, item filios decurionum, fustibus castigari prohibitum est.'[3] It must be firmly stated that the exemption of decurions did not date from A.D. 198. The sentence quoted should be read closely with the clause that follows. It runs: 'verum si iniuriam te fecisse proconsul vir clarissimus pronuntiavit, ignominia notatus es.'[4] Clearly there was nothing new or revolutionary in the opening sentence; the whole rescript was addressed to a particular situation. One Ambrosius, presumably a decurion, had apparently protested against a sentence passed on him by the proconsul, or had lodged an appeal against it. (Alternatively, he was simply complaining about harsh treatment suffered at the proconsul's hands). The Emperors gave their judgement on the basis of an established principle.[5] Similarly, the exemption of veterans and their sons from beating did not date from the time when Arrius

---

[1] *Aegyptus* 12 (1932), 129 ff. (H. Kortenbeutel).

[2] *Dig.* 48. 19. 28. 2.

[3] *CJ* 2. 11. 5: 'Beating is prohibited for decurions and sons of decurions.'

[4] 'But if the most distinguished proconsul ruled that you were guilty of injury, you have been branded with infamy.'

[5] Without Hadrian's constitution (*Dig.* 48. 19. 15) it would have been possible to hold that the ruling of the *divi fratres* (*Dig.* 48. 22. 6. 2) was novel. The *divi fratres* were addressing themselves to a specific case which had been referred to them, and gave their verdict with reference to an existing rule (which they summarized).

Menander put it on record that they were so privileged.¹ There is good reason for thinking that an exemption from beating for a status group that included decurions and veterans is implicit in a rescript of Hadrian of August, A.D. 119.²

The efficacy of the appeal laws is considered elsewhere.³ It may be claimed that they gave no protection to Roman citizens who were not protected for other reasons. Wealth afforded protection from beating, basically because the rich could pay a fine; beating was inflicted on those who could not. But the money payment in lieu of a beating must early have developed into a privilege. In general, the exemption from beating applied to all whose *honor* called forth *reverentia*.⁴

3 (b) Torture

Torture of *honestiores* was not permitted in the Antonine and Severan periods. But the direct evidence for their exemption is thin, and the few relevant texts are not easy to interpret. Paulus cited a rescript of Pius that is normally held to have excluded decurions from torture:

De decurione damnato non debere quaestionem haberi divus Pius rescripsit.⁵

¹ Cf. *Dig.* 49. 18. 1 (Arr. Men.); ibid. 3 (Marc.).
² *Dig.* 47. 21. 2; cf. *Coll.* 13. 3. 2; see Cardascia, art. cit. 468–9, and pp. 155 ff. below.
³ See pp. 82 ff., 268 ff.
⁴ *Dig.* 48. 19. 28. 5.
⁵ *Dig.* 50. 2. 14: 'Divine Pius ruled in a rescript that a decurion who has been condemned should not be tortured.' Paulus goes on: 'Whence, even if he has ceased to be a decurion, and is then condemned, he is not to be tortured, out of respectful memory of his former standing.' See Cardascia, art cit. 331, on the rescript. An item from the reign of the *divi fratres* is in apparent contradiction. In *Dig.* 48. 22. 6. 2 Priscus, presumably a decurion, is said to have confessed *ante quaestionem* to homicide and arson. The *ante* is temporal, and *quaestio* commonly means torture. (See *Dig.* 47. 10. 15. 41, Ulp.: '"Quaestionem" intellegere debemus tormenta et corporis dolorem ad eruendam veritatem.') Torture of accused men was irregular, although it is known in cases of treason. *Quaestio* regularly stands also for the whole investigation. It may do so here; or, and this is less probable, Priscus' confession anticipated the use of torture on *witnesses*.
    The section below deals with the torture of suspects and condemned men, and the arguments relating to the exemption of certain classes from torture. Torture of witnesses is treated elsewhere. See pp. 213 ff. Passages where the circumstances are not indicated precisely are mainly discussed below.

Ulpian in his *Public Disputations* apparently referred to the exemption of decurions and their sons from torture. This was observed by Diocletian and Maximian in a rescript which also cited a pronouncement of Marcus, excusing the descendants of *eminentissimi viri* and *perfectissimi viri* to the third generation from torture and plebeian penalties. The whole text runs:

> Divo Marco placuit eminentissimorum quidem nec non etiam perfectissimorum virorum usque ad pronepotes liberos plebeiorum poenis vel quaestionibus non subici, si tamen propioris gradus liberos, per quos id privilegium ad ulteriorem gradum transgreditur, nulla violati pudoris macula adspergit. In decurionibus autem et filiis eorum hoc observari vir prudentissimus Domitius Ulpianus in publicarum disputationum libris ad perennem scientiae memoriam refert.[1]

It may cause surprise that Marcus said nothing of immunity of any other class; also that Diocletian and Maximian cited a jurist rather than an Emperor for similar privileges possessed by decurions and their sons, a jurist, furthermore, as late as Ulpian.

To continue with the evidence for exemptions, a passage of Tarrutenus Paternus, who wrote in the second half of the second century, implies that soldiers were not tortured. Deserters and traitors were normally tortured and put to death on discharge, 'for they are treated as enemies, not as soldiers'.[2] A statement of the Severan jurist Modestinus is more straightforward. After giving the penalties that were inflicted on soldiers, he adds: 'for they will not be sentenced to the mines [*metallum*] or mine work [*opus metalli*], nor are they tortured.'[3]

Some ground had been lost by the fourth century. Decurions were subject to torture for *falsum*.[4] Anyone might be tortured for

---

[1] *CJ* 9. 41. 11: 'Divine Marcus ruled that children of *em. viri* and *perf. viri*, to their great-grandchildren, should not be subjected to plebeian penalties and tortures, if no stigma from the violation of propriety stains the children of the more nearly related grade through whom that privilege passes to the more remote grade. Moreover, in the books of his *Public Disputations*, set down for perpetuity in the records of jurisprudence, Domitius Ulpianus mentioned that this is observed in the case of decurions and their sons.'

[2] *Dig.* 49. 16. 7: 'nam pro hoste, non pro milite habentur.'

[3] Ibid. 3. 1: 'nam in metallum aut in opus metalli non dabuntur nec torquentur', cf. 3. 10.

[4] *CTh* 9. 19. 1 (= *CJ* 9. 22. 21), A.D. 316. See also ibid. 9. 35. 2. 1, A.D. 376.

magic (and astrology, soothsaying, and so on) or *maiestas*.[1] Ammianus[2] thought that torture of all ranks was permitted by law in treason cases from Sullan times. The fact that the early Emperors used torture on free men in investigating charges of treason and conspiracy does not support this contention. No clause in any law sanctioned this practice; an Emperor tortured with the same freedom as he executed or exiled.

The evidence for the use of torture against free men in the early Empire is in itself worth a brief survey; it may also help solve the problems raised by the rescripts of Pius and Diocletian.

The principle was by and large observed under the Republic that free men were not subject to torture. Augustan laws forbade the torture only of Roman citizens.[3] But this does not amount to a shift of policy at the outset of the Empire. The Julian law might simply have taken over this clause from Republican appeal laws: citizens may have held this legal guarantee, for what it was worth, also under the Republic. Besides, official policy under the Empire does not seem to have changed. Claudius, for example, swore not to torture any free men.[4] Even the torture of men suspected of or condemned for plotting against the life of the Emperor, a Julio-Claudian development, had its roots in the past: it was not far removed from some uses to which torture was put under the Republic.[5]

In 43 B.C. Q. Gallius, a praetor, was suspected of concealing a sword beneath his robe. He was tortured as if he had been a slave (*servilem in modum*).[6] An ominous remark was made by a senator in the course of the trial of Clutorius Priscus under Tiberius.

---

[1] *CTh* 9. 16. 6 (= *CJ* 9. 18. 7), A.D. 358 (magic, etc.); *Dig.* 48. 18. 10. 1; cf. *PS* 5. 29. 2; *CTh* 9. 5. 1 (= *CJ* 9. 8. 3), A.D. 314 (*maiestas*).
[2] Amm. Marc. 19. 12. 17; see Mommsen, op. cit. 407 n. 4.
[3] *Dig.* 48. 6. 7; *PS* 5. 26. 1.
[4] Dio 60. 15. 6. The Republican rule was adhered to, in general, in the early Empire. For torture of aliens see Jos. *BJ* 7. 450 (Jonathan); Philo, *in Flacc.* 84 (Flaccus and the Jews); etc.
[5] Torture against external enemies and opponents in civil war: Livy 26. 12. 17; 27. 3. 5 (Carthaginians and Campanians tortured in 2nd Punic War); Cic. *Phil.* 11. 5; Sen. *de Ira* 3. 18. 1; cf. Sen. *Suas.* 6. 10 (torture of civil war opponents); Livy 4. 50. 4; 7 (414 B.C.; mutinous soldiers tortured by M. Postumius Regillensis, a military tribune with consular power); Cic. *in Verr.* 5. 162 ff. (Verres).
[6] Suet. *Div. Aug.* 27. 4; for the crime cf. ibid. 19. 2; Suet. *Tib.* 19.

Priscus' alleged crime was the writing of a poem about Drusus during the latter's illness. From words of Marcus Lepidus it appears that if a man was found guilty of *maiestas* (of any kind), there was no limit to the punishment he might suffer. Unless he obtained quarter from the Emperor, he could expect not only imprisonment and the noose, but also servile tortures (*serviles cruciatus*).[1] Tiberius in his worst period used torture freely against free men and citizens (and so did Macro on his behalf).[2] The tale of the accidental torture of his old host from Rhodes was told by Suetonius as an illustration of the Emperor's characteristic behaviour. Suetonius went on to recount stories of Tiberius' activities on Capri in lurid detail.[3] At least some of them are likely to be true.

Gaius' sessions of torture were particularly well staged. Diners and revellers, says Suetonius, were treated to displays of inquisition by torture.[4] Seneca's is the most detailed account of Gaius' atrocities, but he reveals that Gaius did nothing to his victims which Sulla had not done to Marius.[5] Gaius tortured conspirators or those he suspected of conspiracy. On one day, according to Seneca, he disposed of the consular Sextus Papinius, his quaestor, the son of his procurator, and other senators and knights, having them tortured, 'not to extract information, but to satisfy an inclination'.[6]

Suetonius noted a streak of cruelty in Claudius. He too was a spectator to examinations by torture, as well as to the punishment of parricides.[7] Claudius had actually begun his reign with an oath that he would not torture free men. But he soon showed that he considered would-be assassins and rebels as a race apart. The crushing of the revolt of Camillus Scribonianus in the second

---

[1] Tac. *Ann.* 3. 50.
[2] See Dio 57. 19. 2; 58. 21. 3; 24. 2; 27. 2; and next note.
[3] Suet. *Tib.* 62.
[4] Suet. *Gaius* 32. 1: 'saepe in conspectu prandentis vel comisantis seriae quaestiones per tormenta habebantur.'
[5] Sen. *de Ira* 3. 18. 1.
[6] Ibid. 3: 'uno die flagellis cecidit torsit, non quaestionis sed animi causa'; cf. Dio 59. 25. 5b; see also 59. 26. 4.
[7] Suet. *Div. Cl.* 34: 'Tormenta quaestionum poenasque parricidarum repraesentabat exigebatque coram.'

year of his reign was marked by the torture of men of high birth, both aliens and citizens.[1] Tacitus knew of the torture of the equestrian Cn. Nonius, who was found with a sword when greeting Claudius. It was hoped that he would betray his 'accomplices'.[2] The use of torture is also recorded after the discovery of the conspiracy of Messalina and Silius; and, in the reign of Nero, in the context of the Pisonian conspiracy.[3]

Thus, when treason was the charge, no man was safe from torture, whether as a punishment or as a means of securing the names of possible confederates. The theory was that whoever threatened the life of the Emperor had forfeited his rights and privileges: he could be treated as a slave.

When we come to the second century, we find little in the legislation of Emperors to suggest that the traditional situation, that only slaves were to be tortured, no longer obtained.[4] With this in mind, we may turn again to the rescript of Pius with which we began.

Pius was considering the case of an ex-decurion, one who had been condemned and had lost his rank.[5] The question at issue was whether torture should be applied to him in his new condition. In stating that torture was not applicable, Pius was implying, of course, that decurions were not subject to torture. But the rescript can hardly be said to have in itself excluded decurions from torture. It merely serves to show that, at a time when torture was making further inroads into the legal system, decurions were still considered beyond its reach. Hence the rescript does not possess the authority and importance that has been claimed for it. This may be one reason why Diocletian and Maximian cited Ulpian for the privileges of decurions.[6]

What is the significance of Ulpian's statement? All that is known of it is that it covered roughly the same ground as Marcus'

---

[1] Dio 60. 15. 5–6: Dio blamed Messalina, Narcissus, and the other freedmen.
[2] Tac. *Ann.* 11. 22. 1.
[3] Dio 60. 31. 5 (Messalina and Silius); Tac. *Ann.* 15. 56; 16. 20 (Piso).
[4] See p. 215.
[5] Cf. *Dig.* 48. 18. 9. 2: 'De eo, qui in insulam deportatus est, quaestio habenda non est, ut divus Pius rescripsit.'
[6] Also, Pius' rescript had nothing to do with *poenae*. The Emperors may have been looking for a broader statement. Cf. next note.

146   THE DUAL-PENALTY SYSTEM

edict, but was concerned with decurions and their sons. The
genre of such observations of jurists is by now familiar. They
normally summarized the current situation. Sometimes, too, they
included a résumé of past rulings, if there were any. But if Ulpian
on this occasion had quoted or referred to any authorities, one
would have expected the Emperors to have cited those authorities.
One may also infer from the fact that the Emperors turned to
Ulpian that they had no knowledge from other sources of any
Imperial pronouncements relating to decurions and their sons
and their exemption from plebeian penalties and tortures.

It is conceivable that Marcus' edict was the first Imperial
constitution touching on torture which went beyond the conventional categories of slave and free;[1] yet it acknowledged the
immunity from torture and plebeian penalties of a very small category of people, descendants of a few leading equestrian officials.
The edict does not even contain an explicit reminder of the immunity of the equestrian officials themselves. Nor are there grounds
for positing a series of parallel constitutions covering those officials, and other groups within the *honestiores*. A more likely suggestion seems to be that this constitution was issued to affirm,
or re-affirm, privileges which had recently been challenged or
overlooked, presumably in the law courts. The privileged status
of the equestrian officials themselves (like that of senators) was
not open to question. But the position of their descendants, who
could not *ipso facto* be assumed to have belonged to any definite
social order,[2] may well have needed clarification.

The constitutions of Pius and Marcus protect fringe groups
whose standing was in doubt. Their wider significance is to show
that torture and the harsher penalties were increasingly used in
the administration of the law. Thus the rescript of Pius, for example,
suggests that torture was commonly applied to condemned men
of free birth who had retained their freedom.[3] And if the torture

---

[1] Of course, the edict is not solely about torture. *Plebeiorum poenae*, indeed,
comes first. For Marcus' (and Verus') other utterances on torture see *Dig.*
48. 18. 1. 3–4; 14; 27 (on *fides*); cf. 5; ibid. 17 praef. (slave against master).
[2] See pp. 241–2.
[3] Cf., of free witnesses, *Dig.* 48. 18. 15 praef. (p. 216 n. 2). Free Christians
were habitually tortured. See espec. *Pass. Jacobi et Marciani* (K–K, no. 15,

of men who had lately been decurions could even have been considered under Pius, it is not inconceivable that it could also have been countenanced for a grandson of a leading equestrian who had allegedly committed a capital crime. Marcus may have been recently reminded of this when he legislated.

3 (c) 'Custodia'

The word *custodia* has an extensive application. It covers the various ways in which a defendant might be held in custody before the trial or the execution of sentence. It stands for the imprisonment that is an act of *coercitio* by a magistrate. It refers to methods of punishment after sentence has been passed.

Lentulus and his fellow plotters in the Catilinarian conspiracy were placed in the care of magistrates and senators while waiting for the Senate's verdict. In the sources their situation is described as *libera custodia*, free custody.[1] This was a mild form of detention, one reserved (in Imperial times, at any rate) for men of high status. For Ulpian, in his *de officio proconsulis*, says that the governor chooses whether an accused man should be put in prison or entrusted to armed guards or guarantors 'or even to himself'; and he goes on to stress that the governor, in making his decision, should consider the rank and wealth of the accused as well as the gravity of the crime committed: 'Concerning the custody of accused men, the proconsul is accustomed to decide whether in each case the person should be put in prison, or handed over to a soldier, or entrusted to guarantors, or even to himself. He usually makes this decision in accordance with the kind of crime which is charged, or the standing of the person accused, or his great wealth, or his innocence, or his dignity.'[2] Pius in a rescript had laid down that if a man was prepared to provide guarantors, then

p. 67; Valerian) 5, 3 ff.; cf. *Acta Maximi* (K–K, no. 12, p. 60; Decius) 2. 1 ff.; *Acta Kononis* (K–K, no. 14, p. 64; Valerian (?)) 5. 5; etc.

[1] Sall. *Cat.* 47. 3: 'senatus decernit, uti abdicato magistratu Lentulus itemque ceteri in liberis custodiis habeantur.' See also Acts 28: 30 (St. Paul).

[2] *Dig.* 48. 3. 1: 'de custodia reorum proconsul aestimare solet, utrum in carcerem recipienda sit persona an militi tradenda vel fideiussoribus committenda vel etiam sibi. hoc autem vel pro criminis quod obicitur qualitate vel propter honorem aut propter amplissimas facultates vel pro innocentia personae vel pro dignitate eius qui accusatur facere solet.'

he should not be thrown into *vincula* (prison): 'The Divine Pius replied in Greek to a letter of the people of Antioch, that the man who was prepared to give guarantors should not be thrown into prison, unless it be agreed that his crime was so grave that he should not be entrusted either to guarantors or soldiers, but should be punished with imprisonment itself before death [or the proper penalty]'.[1] This was not out of key with Ulpian's advice, because normally only men of means, men with *amplissimae facultates*, would be able to fall back on guarantors. But Pius would not grant the privilege of guarantors in the case of a very serious crime. What did this mean in practice? Perhaps the Emperor had in mind capital crimes. Apparently decurions arrested for capital crimes were held in prison.[2]

So much for *custodia* in the sense of detention prior to trial, sentence, or punishment.[3] *Libera custodia* was also in practice a possible penalty. Julius Caesar proposed for Lentulus and the rest that their property should be confiscated, and that they should be held in Italian towns for the rest of their lives.[4] He urged this plan as an alternative to the execution which D. Iunius Silanus had advised. Silanus, however, changed his position after Caesar's powerful speech, and asserted that by the ultimate penalty (ἐσχάτην δίκην) which he had pressed for, he had meant the ultimate penalty for a Roman senator (ἐσχάτην δίκην ἀνδρὶ βουλευτῇ ʽΡωμαίων),

---

[1] *dig.* 48. 3. 3: 'divus Pius ad epistulam Antiochensium Graece rescripsit non esse in vincula coiciendum eum, qui fideiussores dare paratus est, nisi si tam grave scelus admisisse eum constet, ut neque fideiussoribus neque militibus committi debeat, verum hanc ipsam carceris poenam ante supplicium sustinere.'

[2] See, for example, *Dig.* 48. 19. 27. 1; 48. 22. 6. 1.

[3] See also *Dig.* 48. 3. 5; 48. 4. 4; *PS* 5. 26. 2 (*confessi*); *Dig.* 47. 10. 13. 2; *PS* 5. 26. 2 (*contumaces*, etc.). Imprisonment before execution for condemned persons during the Republic: Livy 29. 19. 5; 22. 7; 34. 44. 6; *per.* 61; Cic. *in Vat.* 11. 26; Sall. *Cat.* 55 (cf. Plut. *Cic.* 20. 3), etc. (all Romans); Plut. *Mar.* 12; Livy, *per.* 67; Dio 40. 41; Mommsen, op. cit. 930 n. 1 (distinguished foreigners). For the Empire see Suet. *Tib.* 61. 4 (in general); Tac. *Ann.* 3. 51. 1 (Clutorius Priscus); ibid. 4. 70. 5–6 (Titius Sabinus); ibid. 5. 9. 2 (children of Sejanus); ibid. 6. 39. 1 (Paconianus); ibid. 6. 40. 1 (Vibulenus Agrippa); Suet. *Tib.* 75. 2; cf. Dio 59. 6. 2 (prisoners on death of Tiberius). Dio 59. 18. 3 (victims of Gaius); Tac. *Ann.* 11. 2. 5 (Poppaea Sabina: voluntary death); *Agric.* 45 (Helvidius Priscus); Pliny, *Ep.* 2. 11. 8. Imprisonment before exile: *Dig.* 28. 3. 6. 7; 48. 19. 27. 2; 48. 22. 6. 1; 49. 4. 1 praef.

[4] Sall. *Cat.* 51. 43; cf. Plut. *Cic.* 21. 1.

which, he said, was imprisonment.[1] In Tiberius' reign Iunius
Gallio was brought back from exile and kept in Rome in the
houses of magistrates: 'custoditurque domibus magistratuum.'[2]
Over a century later, one Aelius Priscus, who was clearly insane,
murdered his mother. Marcus and Commodus judged him to be of
sufficient *locus* and *ordo* to be guarded privately: '. . . ut a suis vel
etiam in propria villa custodiatur'.[3] Finally, the consular Iulius
Paulinus, who annoyed Septimius Severus with his free talk and
frivolous gibing, was put in ἀδέσμῳ φυλακῇ.[4]

These cases indicate how easily imprisonment of whatever
kind might become a definite punishment or *poena*. In law it was
not a recognized penalty, but a coercive measure.[5] The official
position with regard to the use of imprisonment as a sanction
is stated by Ulpian in relation to incarceration. He complained
that governors were in the habit of condemning men to incarceration, and insisted that this was highly irregular: 'But this
they should not do. For penalties of this sort are forbidden.
Prison is properly regarded as a means of detaining men, not
punishing them.'[6] Ulpian disapproved, but nevertheless *vincula*
or *vincula publica* appears as a punishment alongside *relegatio*,
exilium, *deportatio*, *opus publicum*, and the money fine.[7] Here it is
Ulpian's position rather than the practice of governors and other
judges which calls for comment. The governors, in employing

---

[1] Ibid. 21. 3; cf. Sall. *Cat.* 50. 4. Cicero (*in Cat.* 4. 4. 7) sums up Caesar's
case for imprisonment as an alternative to death with these words: 'vincula vero,
et ea sempiterna, certe ad singularem poenam nefarii sceleris inventa sunt.' See
Greenidge, *Legal Procedure of Cicero's Time* (1901), 333, 514 ff., for the use of
imprisonment as a preventive penalty. Yet the Romans never officially accepted
imprisonment as a legal penalty, whether for life or for a short term. See n. 6
below.

[2] Tac. *Ann.* 6. 3. 3; Dio 58. 3. 5 (Gallus, ἐν φυλακῇ ἀδέσμῳ).

[3] *Dig.* 1. 18. 14.   [4] Dio 77. 11. 1a.

[5] Mommsen, op. cit. 48–9. See Gellius 13. 12. 6 (Varro). For the misuse of
imprisonment as *coercitio* see G. Chalon, *L'Édit de Tiberius Julius Alexander*
(1964), 27 ff. (text), ll. 15 ff.

[6] *Dig.* 48. 19. 8. 9: 'sed id eos facere non oportet. nam huiusmodi poenae
interdictae sunt. carcer enim ad continendos homines, non ad puniendos haberi
debet.' Hadrian regarded imprisonment for life as illegal. See *Dig.* 48. 19. 35.
Caracalla thought it hardly suitable even for slaves. See *CJ* 9. 47. 6 (A.D. 214);
cf. *Dig.* 48. 19. 8. 13. An example from the reign of Tiberius: Suet. *Tib.* 37. 3.

[7] *PS* 5. 21. 1; 5. 17. 2 (*relegatio*); ibid. (*exilium*); 5. 21. 2 (*deportatio*); 5. 17. 2
(*opus*); *Dig.* 11. 5. 1. 4 (fine); cf. *PS* 5. 18. 1; Cic. *de leg.* 3. 3. 6 ('multa vinclis
verberibusve').

imprisonment as a penalty, could be said to have shown a fuller understanding of the direction in which the penal system was evolving. *Cognitio* judges had devised a system of secondary penalties for low-status criminals which deprived them of their freedom of movement, temporarily or permanently. These penalties, involving forced labour, were clearly regarded as forms of custody.[1] It is curious that the most effective form of custody, incarceration, was denied official recognition.[2]

How were prisoners treated? Callistratus quoted *mandata* of one Emperor to a governor, which stated: 'You will hold them bound [*vinctos*].'[3] But were bonds normal? One problem is the ambiguity of words and phrases. Ulpian stated that to be *in carcere clausus* is not the same as to be *vinctus* or *in vinculis* 'nisi corpori eius vincula sint adhibita'.[4] This is hard to reconcile with what Callistratus has to say on the subject of *vincula*:

> vinculorum autem appellatio latius accipitur: nam etiam inclusos velut lautumiis vinctorum numero haberi placet, quia nihil intersit, parietibus an compedibus teneatur.[5]

---

[1] *Dig.* 48. 19. 28. 14: 'ita et in custodiis gradum servandum esse idem princeps rescripsit.' Even exiles, who were normally high-status criminals, were not always left to their own devices. They might be kept *in custodiis* on an island. See Suet. *Div. Aug.* 65. 4 (Agrippa Postumus); Dio 59. 8. 8 (Piso); cf. *Dig.* 48. 3. 1 (*militi tradenda*); Dio 55. 20. 5 (exile μετὰ φρουρᾶς, if necessary).

[2] There was no obvious 'legal' bar to the recognition of incarceration. As has been pointed out, the system of *cognitio*, the most important single feature of which was the discretionary power possessed by the judge, developed its own penalties. Most of these had their origin in acts of *coercitio*, sanctions which lacked a genuine judicial character. The result was the blurring of the line between penalties proper and magisterial *coercitio*.

On the origin of *vincula* as a penalty, there is some plausibility in the theory of Brasiello (op. cit. 367–73) that the penalty grew up by analogy with, or in derivation from, the sanction of *vincula* imposed upon slaves. For slaves, *Dig.* 48. 19. 8. 13; ibid. 10 praef.; ibid. 33; Gai. *Inst.* 1. 13; *PS* 5. 18. 1. For private *vincula* in cases of debt in early civil law see *XII Tables* (*FIRA*[2] i, p. 32), 3; *lex Urs.* (*FIRA*[2] i, p. 179) 61; cf. *Dig.* 50. 16. 224; Mommsen, op. cit. 960 n. 2, on *carcer privatus*).

[3] *Dig.* 48. 19. 27. 2: 'vinctos eos custodies.'

[4] 'unless chains are applied to the body', *Dig.* 50. 16. 216; cf. *Dig.* 11. 4. 1. 7: 'diligens custodia etiam vincire permittit'—*custodia* must be *diligens* for bonds to be used. Decurions were put in prison *diligentioris custodiae causa* (*Dig.* 28. 3. 6. 7), but it does not follow that they were bound. For *them*, incarceration was a severe sanction. The former passage concerns runaway slaves.

[5] *Dig.* 4. 6. 9: 'The name *vincula* is interpreted more broadly; for it seems good to regard those imprisoned in stone quarries as *vincti*, on the grounds that

This is a reminder that conditions in some prisons were harsher than in others. Apollonius of Tyana was placed by Domitian's praetorian prefect in 'the free prison' (τὸ ἐλευθέριον δεσμωτήριον).[1] He was one of about fifty inmates, all of whom feared for their lives as they awaited trial on a variety of charges.[2] The Emperor took a particular interest in Apollonius, and he was offered anything he desired.[3] The atmosphere changed after a private conversation between them. Apollonius was thrown into a different prison, where he was bound.[4] After two days he was permitted to return to the first prison for the five days that remained before his trial.

If an acknowledged tyrant like Domitian could refrain from chaining men on capital charges, it is not impossible that this was the norm, at any rate for men of wealth or position or fame. All the persons mentioned by Philostratus in the story are of this type.[5] The sources do not refer to any legal guarantee against chaining and other harsh treatment. At the most it might have been thought *adversus bonos mores* to chain *honestiores*.

But imprisonment itself, with or without chains, was clearly something to be avoided if possible.[6] We have seen that it was

---

it makes no difference whether men are confined by walls or by chains.' Mommsen (op. cit. 302 n. 3) read *lautumiae* as a generic term for 'das leichtere Gefängnis', but this is unconvincing. For *lautumiae* see also *Dig.* 11. 5. 1. 4; Sen. *Contr.* 7. 1. 22. Mommsen (op. cit. 960 n. 1) held that *carcer* and *vincula* were synonymous. This was refuted by Brasiello (op. cit. 407 n. 62). *Vincula* and *custodia* are not synonymous either (see *Dig.* 4. 6. 10 and 50. 16. 48; ibid. 224). Nor are *custodia* and *carcer* (see *Dig.* 47. 2. 52. 12).

[1] Philostr. *Ap.* 7. 22 and 40.
[2] Ibid. 7. 23: a Κίλιξ, for wealth, on the grounds that he acquired it μὴ ἐπ' ἀγαθῷ τῆς τυραννίδος; ibid. 24: the accused did not mention that Domitian was a son of Athene in public prayers at a public sacrifice in Tarentum; ibid. 25: the owner of property in Acarnania who had planted an island with vines and trees. Evidently the property was coveted by the Emperor. The charge was trumped up—he was alleged to have tried to escape from 'his crimes'; ibid. 42: an Arcadian from Messene of conspicuous beauty, in trouble for refusing to submit to Domitian.
[3] Ibid. 28: πᾶν, εἴ τι βούλοιο; cf. Jos. *AJ.* 18. 202–4 (Agrippa and Antonia).
[4] Ibid. 36; cf. 34. δεδέσθαι, in 23 fin. (cf. δεδέσθαι in 26, ed. Loeb, p. 222), is misleading, as it simply refers to imprisonment. Contrast Acts 21: 33; 22: 29.
[5] See n. 2 above.
[6] Fourth-century sources reveal the horrors of prisons at that time. See, e.g., Libanius, *Or.* 45; *CTh* 9. 3. 1, A.D. 320; cf. ibid. 7, A.D. 409. It is impossible to tell how far conditions deteriorated over three centuries. See Mommsen, op. cit. 303 ff.

generally possible for decurions and *honestiores* to secure a less rigorous form of *custodia*, unless the crime deserved a capital penalty. We possess no statement of an Emperor on the question earlier than that of Pius—which cannot be regarded as a major breakthrough, for it was little more than an instruction to governors to grant *libera custodia* more freely. The privileged group was a broad one—it included anyone 'who was ready to provide guarantors'—and it was left to Marcus and Commodus to introduce direct reference to the status of defendants.

Conclusion

In the second and third centuries there was a definite trend towards harsher penalties.[1] Most of the penalties that came to be regularly applied to criminals originated as irregular sanctions, with no basis in the criminal law. Formerly felt to be suitable almost exclusively for slaves, by the Antonine and Severan periods they are found in general use against *humiliores*. Indeed, by the late third and early fourth centuries, they were overtaking even the provincial aristocracy. In the preceding two centuries it was not their position and the position of *honestiores* in general which improved, but that of the *humiliores* which worsened. That is not of course to imply that *honestiores* and *humiliores* were ever on an equal footing in the sight of the law. The Antonine and Severan Emperors were not the first to employ a differential penalty system in favour of the higher orders: the character of the statements made by classical lawyers, and Emperors, makes this conclusion inescapable. The possibility remains that, although the system was inherited rather than created by the Antonines and Severans, they, and particularly the Severans, did give it a different basis in law. This matter cannot be judged until the various stages in the evolution of the dual-penalty system have been outlined.

[1] This development is analysed in greater detail in *Natural Law Forum*, 13 (1968), 141–62.

5

HADRIAN AND THE EVOLUTION OF
THE DUAL-PENALTY SYSTEM

In Severan practice a penalty belonged to one of two categories, and each category was aligned with one of two broad social groups, in such a way that severer penalties of servile origin were applied to criminals from the lower stratum of society and milder penalties to criminals from the upper stratum. It is impossible to describe the growth of this system with any precision, because of the limitations of the sources. In particular, certain crucial developments of the pre-Hadrianic period are known only in outline. The *Digest* and *Code* contain no pertinent material from the first century A.D., and the historical and biographical writers on whom we are thrust back had little interest in changes which occurred in the administration of the law during the period. What we can do is examine the relevant legal decisions of Hadrian, the earliest Emperor whose legislation or rulings are preserved in any number.[1] Hadrianic constitutions quoted earlier indicate that the penalties discussed by the Severan jurists were already in existence and graded within their distinct categories.[2] It would be profitable to investigate whether Hadrian recognized a correspondence between a category of penalties and a social group, and punished the guilty accordingly.[3] If this turns out to be the

---

[1] The attention of historians and jurists has been drawn to administrative developments in Hadrian's reign and to activity in the spheres of private law and jurisprudence. The criminal law has been largely ignored. Select bibliography: B. W. Henderson, *The Life and Principate of the Emperor Hadrian* (1923); F. Pringsheim, *JRS* 24 (1934), 141 ff.; A. A. Schiller, *Seminar* 7 (1949), 26 ff., espec. 37 ff.; B. d'Orgeval, *L'Empereur Hadrien, œuvre législative et administrative* (1950); A. d'Ors, *Les Empereurs romains d'Espagne* (1964), 147 ff.

[2] *Dig.* 48. 19. 28. 13–14, quoted p. 103.

[3] D'Orgeval's analysis (op. cit. 334–5) will not be discussed in detail here. He holds that Hadrian and his successors formulated legal distinctions, but believes that these distinctions did not become distinctions of *class* until Caracalla

ease, it may then be asked whether Hadrian's constitutions were any more instrumental than those of his successors in setting up the dual-penalty system.[1]

The dual scale of penalties

The argument for the existence of a dual scale of penalties in the reign of Hadrian depends in part on the edict and rescript already cited.[2] None of the penalties recorded were new. But the arrangement of them was novel, or at least not previously attested. What is striking in the arrangement is less the order in which the penalties within each group are graded (for *summum supplicium* was always more severe than *metallum*, *metallum* than *opus publicum*) than the fact that they are divided into distinct groups. The lack of overlap between the groups, the fact that there is no transition from *relegatio* to *opus publicum*, for example, or from *opus publicum* to *deportatio*, or from *deportatio* to *metallum*, makes it difficult to entertain seriously the possibility that there was only one ladder of penalties under Hadrian. The two rulings by themselves offer no enlightenment on the question of whether it was Hadrian's practice systematically to prescribe one set of penalties, the different grades of exile, to offenders of high social standing, and another set, the so-called *custodia* penalties, *metallum* and *opus*, to plebeians. But their silence on this point is hardly significant, for they dealt simply with the proper punishments for escaped convicts.[3]

virtually abolished the difference between citizens and aliens. But the *honestiores* and *humiliores* in Hadrian's time and in the rest of the second century were not, respectively, ' "cives Romani" et quelques assimilés' and 'le reste de la population'. D'Orgeval's hypothesis would only begin to be tenable if it were possible to show that Hadrian's various pronouncements did not contain any acknowledgement of status distinctions. To refute it one need not go beyond the several rescripts in which Hadrian instructed judges to give more weight to witnesses of high social rank than to their inferiors (*Dig.* 22. 5. 3. 1–4; 6).

[1] Cardascia (art. cit. 467–72) in his section on the evolution of the *honestiores*/ *humiliores* distinction briefly summarizes the growth of the dual-penalty system (472) and addresses himself chiefly to the passing of the variation of penalty from 'judicial practice' into 'law' through 'legislation'. The implications of his judicial practice/law dichotomy are explored later (ch. 6). Cardascia also rejects the idea that Hadrian's legislation has any relevance to *class* distinctions. See p. 155 n. 1 below.

[2] See p. 153 n. 2 above.

[3] On escape, Pliny, *Ep.* 10. 56–7; *Dig.* 48. 19. 8. 6–7; 50. 13. 5. 3.

The decree banning the execution of decurions for murder is central to the present argument.[1] For a complete system of distinctions is implied by this isolated enactment. It is a fair assumption that Hadrian regarded execution of a decurion for other 'ordinary' capital crimes as irregular also.[2] Further, the man who was not to be executed (*capite puniri*) presumably was meant to be immune from aggravated forms of the death penalty (*summum supplicium*). That is to say, not only death by the sword, but also death by fire, crucifixion, or wild animals was ruled out.[3] Again, if the secondary punishment for decurions was deportation (*poena legis Corneliae*), they were unlikely to be sentenced to labour in the mines. Lawyers considered both *metallum* and *deportatio* as alternatives to the death penalty, and both involved loss of citizenship. But of the two, only *metallum* deprived the condemned man of his liberty. The Romans balked at reducing decurions to a condition tantamount to slavery. Finally, if the most serious of the *serviles poenae* was not countenanced, it would have been inconsistent if decurions had been subject to other *serviles poenae* and to beating (*servilia verbera*).

As for non-decurions, or 'plebeians', it is not improbable that they were subject to death, *summum supplicium*, and to the *custodia* penalties as a whole.

A rescript of Hadrian of A.D. 119 on the moving of boundary stones was quoted by Callistratus. The text in the *Digest* is as follows:

divus Hadrianus in haec verba rescripsit: 'quin pessimum factum sit eorum, qui terminos finium causa positos propulerunt, dubitari non potest. de poena tamen modus ex condicione personae et mente facientis

---

[1] *Dig.* 48. 19. 15. Cardascia's interpretation of this is ambiguous: it represents discrimination, but not full discrimination according to class (art. cit. 331), which was not introduced into the law till the reign of Pius (ibid. 468). He misinterprets *Dig.* 48. 8. 16, holding that it contradicts 48. 19. 15 (ibid. 327 and n. 7), and elsewhere (ibid. 470 and n. 4) notes that 48. 22. 6. 2 confirms 48. 19. 15.

[2] I would class as 'ordinary' capital crimes those for which the statutory penalty or (in the case of crimes handled *extra ordinem*) normal penalty was *interdictio* or *deportatio*, and which were punished no more severely than this (in the case of *honestiores*) throughout our period. Examples include *falsum*, *vis publica*, arson (except in a city, for plunder), homicide.

[3] Death by the axe and noose and death by beating were also outlawed, *Dig.* 48. 19. 8. 1.

magis statui potest: nam si splendidiores personae sunt, quae convincuntur, non dubie occupandorum alienorum finium causa id admiserunt, et possunt in tempus, ut cuiusque patiatur aetas, relegari, id est si iuvenior, in longius, si senior, recisius. si vero alii negotium gesserunt et ministerio functi sunt, castigari et ad opus biennio dari. quod si per ignorantiam aut fortuito lapides furati sunt, sufficiet eos verberibus decidere.[1]

In the rescript there are different penalties for *splendidiores personae* and for *alii* (others). The former were relegated, the latter sentenced to two years' *opus* after a beating—or to beating alone, if it could be shown that the crime was committed in ignorance or by mistake.

Hadrian ordered the judge to take into consideration the *condicio personae* and the *mens facientis* when he came to decide on a penalty. The phrase *mens facientis* echoes a principle which left its mark on much of Hadrian's legislation: 'In crimes, it is the purpose, not the issue, which is tested.'[2] It was important that the judge should discover whether the offence was committed maliciously, or whether the offender was acting under orders, or whether the offence was committed accidentally. This would in-

---

[1] *Dig.* 47. 21. 2: 'Divine Hadrian issued the following rescript: "It cannot be doubted that the crime of those who move stones placed to mark boundaries is very serious. Yet on the question of penalty, a limit can be fixed in accordance with the status of the person and the motive: for if those convicted are men of high social station, without any doubt they committed the crime in order to seize the territory of other men. They can be relegated for a term, according as the age of each permits, that is to say, the younger man for a longer term, and the older for a shorter. But if others have done the deed and performed it as a service, they should be beaten and given over to public labour for two years. If they stole the stones out of ignorance or quite by chance, it will be enough to beat them."' Cardascia (art. cit. 468–9) rejected the *Digest* text as corrupt, preferring another version, *Coll.* 13. 3. 1–2. In the latter, *id est . . . castigari* is omitted. After *relegari* we read *et sic in biennium aut triennium ad opus publicum dari*. This does not make good sense. One might have expected the two penalties of *relegatio* and *opus* to have been separated by *aut*, for *in biennium aut triennium* belongs to *opus publicum*. Again, *et sic* suggests that something is missing before *opus publicum*. That *castigari* has fallen out is suggested by *sufficiet eos verberibus coerceri*. A beating before *opus* was regular. Moreover, there is a case for supplying a subject, as *relegari* is cut off from what follows, in *Coll.* Further, *splendidiores personae* seems to demand the presence of a second subject for purposes of comparison. This phrase, and *ex condicione personae*, points forward to the discriminatory ruling which follows.
[2] *Dig.* 48. 8. 14: 'in maleficiis voluntas spectatur, non exitus'; cf. ibid. 1. 3–4 (cf. *Coll.* 1. 6); ibid. 4. 1 (cf. *Coll.* 1. 11); 48. 21. 3. 5; *PS* 5. 23. 3; etc.

evitably bring him to consider the *condicio personae*. For, in the opinion of Hadrian, *splendidiores personae* were incapable of committing this particular offence without evil intent—invariably they were after another man's land. Thus their punishment was harsh, but only in relative terms. In comparison with their social inferiors they got off lightly—the penalty for *splendidiores personae* was a mild form of exile, while *alii* suffered a penalty drawn from the *custodia* group.[1] In sum, the judge decided how severe the penalty should be by inquiring into the motive of the offender; the *type* of penalty set depended on the status of the defendant.

The term *splendidiores personae* is surely an alternative for *honestiores*, and *alii* for *humiliores*. *Splendidiores personae* were apparently men of property, or *possessores*.[2] Such men in the Roman world tended to have high social standing as well as wealth—the adjective *splendidiores*, significantly, is a non-economic term. In the same way *alii*, perhaps largely peasants or employees of landowners, were for Hadrian men of low status.

This text is the only one of its kind from Hadrian's reign.[3] In some other decisions Hadrian apparently did not apply the principle of differential punishment according to status, and this might be thought significant. The provincial council of Baetica asked Hadrian for a judgement on the proper penalty for rustling. He replied:

abigei cum durissime puniuntur, ad gladium damnari solent. puniuntur autem durissime non ubique, sed ubi frequentius est hoc genus maleficii: alioquin et in opus et nonnumquam temporarium damnantur . . . aut si quis tam notus et tam gravis in abigendo fuit, ut prius ex hoc crimine aliqua poena affectus sit, hunc in metallum dari oportere.[4]

---

[1] Beating was commonly attached to penalties in the latter group. See pp. 136 ff.

[2] For *possessores* see p. 257.

[3] There are, in fact, very few texts of the same kind from the whole period. See pp. 162 ff.

[4] *Coll.* 11. 7. 1–2: 'When rustlers are punished very harshly, they are usually condemned to mortal combat. But they are not everywhere punished very harshly, but only where that kind of offence is fairly common: otherwise, they are sentenced to public labour, sometimes even only for a restricted time . . . or, if someone has been such a notorious and troublesome rustler that he has been punished in some way previously for the crime, he should be sent to the mines.' Cf. *Dig.* 47. 14. 1 praef.

Later in the century no man of *dignitas* would have suffered any of these penalties. Ulpian made this observation, when adding to the rescript the comment:

> quamquam autem Hadrianus metalli poenam temporari vel etiam gladii praestituerit, attamen qui honestiore loco nati sunt non debent ad hanc poenam pertinere, sed aut relegandi erunt aut removendi ordine.[1]

It should be emphatically stated that neither Hadrian nor Ulpian implied that *honestiores* suffered *opus* (for example) in the Hadrianic period. Hadrian might have replied differently to the council if Spanish decurions had been among those under arrest and if he had been informed of the fact. His rescript was designed for a concrete situation, and he evidently was not concerned with theoretical possibilities.[2] In contrast, Ulpian was giving advice of a general kind to governors. When looking for an authority to cite on the punishment of rustling he found this rescript. His legal mind discerned a potential loophole, and he could not quote the rescript uncorrected.

A second text, again from Ulpian's treatise on the duties of a proconsul, is in some ways comparable:

> idem divus Hadrianus rescripsit: 'Constitutum quidem est, ne spadones fierent, eos autem, qui hoc crimine arguerentur, Corneliae legis poena teneri eorumque bona merito fisco meo vindicari debere, sed et in servis, qui spadones fecerint, ultimo supplicio animadvertendum esse . . . nemo enim liberum servumve invitum sinentemve castrare debet, neve quis se sponte castrandum praebere debet. at si quis adversus edictum meum fecerit, medico quidem, qui exciderit, capitale erit, item ipsi qui se sponte excidendum praebuit.[3]

---

[1] *Coll.* 11. 8. 3: 'But although Hadrian laid down the penalties of the mines, temporary public work, and mortal combat, nevertheless those born of higher status should not receive such penalties, but should be relegated or expelled from their order.' Cf. *Dig.* 47. 14. 3. Ulpian found problems of interpretation in the rescript. See *Coll.* 11. 7. 3–4.

[2] Hadrian was giving the most serious penalties for a crime that decurions were not likely to commit, cf. 47. 14. 3. 3 (*receptores abigeorum* were perhaps more likely to include decurions). See *Coll.* 11. 3. 1; cf. 11. 4. 1 (fine of rustlers of status).

[3] *Dig.* 48. 8. 4. 2: 'Divine Hadrian also wrote in a rescript: "It was laid down, in order to end the practice of making eunuchs, that those who were convicted of this crime should be liable to the penalty laid down in the Cornelian law, and should forfeit their property deservedly to my fiscus, but that slaves who made people eunuchs should be punished with the ultimate punishment . . .

The rescript is in two parts. First, Hadrian refers to an earlier regulation (*constitutum est*), perhaps a senatorial decree of A.D. 97,[1] which laid down that castration was to be punished by the penalty of the Cornelian Law (deportation)[2] with confiscation, but that slaves who performed the operation were to be executed. Then, after reminding proconsuls of their responsibility for aiding victims of castration, he firmly states that the castration of any man, slave or free, willing or unwilling, is a crime, together with the act of offering oneself for castration. For both offences he names death as the penalty.

What does the edict reveal about judicial practice in Hadrian's reign, before and after it was issued? First, the mere fact that Hadrian cited the *S.C.* (if it was the *S.C.*) does not prove that his judges, when called upon to punish castrators or the castrated, had done so with an eye to that social division which the *S.C.* recognized (slave and free), and no other. The penalty set by the *S.C.* for free men was, of course, the traditional penalty for homicide and other crimes punishable under the Cornelian law. It is noteworthy that this penalty was still mentioned by jurists in the Severan period, and not always with an accompanying acknowledgement that Severan courts applied it not to all free men, but to members of the higher orders alone. So Marcianus stated simply that the penalty for *falsum* or *quasi-falsum* was *deportatio . . . et omnium bonorum publicatio*, adding that slaves were given *ultimum supplicium*.[3] It is necessary to turn to other jurists to discover that in the Severan age free men were thrown to the

For no one ought to castrate a free man or a slave whether unwilling or willing, nor ought anyone to offer himself voluntarily for castration. And if anyone acts against my edict, it will mean a capital penalty for the doctor who performs the operation, and the same for him who has offered himself voluntarily to be operated on.'

[1] A *S.C.* of A.D. 97 (for the date see R. Syme, *Tacitus*, App. 10 and 68) dealt with at least one aspect of the punishment of castration (*Dig.* 48. 8. 6), and no doubt other aspects too, about which nothing is known. See also Dio 68. 2. 4; cf. 67. 2. 3 and Suet. *Dom.* 7. 1. Despite Smallwood (*Latomus* 18 (1959), 334 ff.; 20 (1961), 92 ff.), it was not Hadrian who first assimilated castration to homicide.

[2] *Dig.* 48. 8. 3. 5: 'legis Corneliae de sicariis et veneficiis poena insulae deportatio est et omnium bonorum ademptio.'

[3] *Dig.* 48. 10. 1. 13. It has never been suggested that variation of penalty applied throughout the Severan system with the sole exception of the punishment of *falsum*. See next note.

beasts for one kind of *falsum*, and that decurions generally received milder penalties than plebeians for *falsum*.[1] Marcianus serves us better in his discussion of that Cornelian law with which we are at present concerned; the statement that the penalty of the law is deportation and confiscation is followed by the addendum: 'sed solent hodie capite puniri, nisi honestiore loco positi fuerint, ut poenam legis sustineant: humiliores enim solent vel bestiis subici, altiores vero deportantur in insulam.'[2] The omission of this comment might have left the situation somewhat confused.[3]

Could a jurist of the early second century have written a *sed solent hodie* clause? A rescript of Pius on the murder of an adulterer reads as follows:

ei, qui uxorem suam in adulterio deprehensam occidisse se non negat, ultimum supplicium remitti potest, cum sit difficillimum iustum dolorem temperare et quia plus fecerit, quam quia vindicare se non debuerit, puniendus sit. sufficiet igitur, si humilis loci sit, in opus perpetuum eum tradi, si qui honestior, in insulam relegari.[4]

Pius, then, prescribed discriminatory penalties for this kind of homicide, and presumably would have done so for any other form of homicide on which a ruling was required. Hadrian too issued a constitution on homicide which clearly envisaged different punishments for decurions and men of lower status: the former escaped the death penalty (and received the *poena legis Corneliae*), and by implication the latter succumbed to it.[5] Thus the contrast

---

[1] *Dig.* 48. 10. 8 (Ulp.; beasts); ibid. 13. 1 (Pap.; decurions/plebeians).

[2] *Dig.* 48. 8. 3. 5: 'But today they are customarily executed...'

[3] Marcianus wrote (ibid.): 'The penalty of the Cornelian law ... *is* deportation with loss of all property', and just before this: 'He who castrates a man out of lust or for gain *is punished* by the penalty of the Cornelian law, according to the *S.C.*' It was not uncommon for jurists to make reference to the 'penalty of the law' without either saying what it was or adding in parenthesis that it applied only to *honestiores*. Under the heading of *falsum* alone see *Dig.* 48. 10. 1 praef.; ibid. 1. 2; 2; 9. 3; 21; 27. 1; 32 praef.

[4] *Dig.* 48. 5. 39. 8 (Pap.): 'He who does not deny that he has killed his wife caught in adultery may be excused from the ultimate punishment, since it is very difficult for him to restrain his just anguish; and he should be punished because he has done more [sc. than he should have], rather than because he was not entitled to avenge himself.' Marcianus (48. 8. 1. 5) refers back to the rescript, but names different penalties. He has also substituted synonymous expressions for *humilis loci* and *honestior*. His version is only a paraphrase, while Papinian professes to quote the original. [5] *Dig.* 48. 19. 15.

implicit in the *sed solent hodie* clause of Marcianus was not between his day and the reigns of Hadrian and Pius.

Hence it is conceivable that, before Hadrian's edict the conventional division of slave and free was not the only division considered by judges in the punishment of castration.

What of Hadrian's own recommendations? At first sight they show no awareness of a status differential in relation to the full scale of penalties. However, in naming one penalty, death, Hadrian did not rule out discrimination between social groups in the punishment of this crime. There were different grades of the death penalty which judges were free to apply in accordance with the status of the accused, and Hadrian could not but have been aware of this.[1]

The only problem is to decide which social distinctions Hadrian expected his judges to observe. Here we can choose one of two alternatives: Hadrian had in mind either the punishment of all free men with a comparatively mild form of execution (*capite puniri*, decapitation), and that of slaves with an aggravated form of execution (*summum supplicium*, in one of its forms); or the punishment of members of high-status groups with the former penalty, and of all others with the latter penalty.[2] In the latter case, it would be possible to compare castration with parricide, for which there was no escape from the death penalty. If the edict itself is neutral between the two positions, the latter position seems preferable because of the supporting evidence.

Neither the rescript on rustling nor the edict on castration throw any doubt on the proposition that the use of the dual-penalty scale for discrimination according to status was known in the reign of Hadrian.[3] At the most, they cause one to hesitate before adopting the stronger thesis, that the dual scale was already

---

[1] Jewish rabbis who refused to accept the ban on circumcision were put to death, some with cruel torture (Smallwood, art. cit. 337 ff.). This is relevant, because Hadrian himself assimilated circumcision to castration (*Dig.* 48. 8. 5). Castration may itself have been punished by means of the harshest penalties.

[2] Unless there were three penalties, one each for two categories of free men, and one for slaves.

[3] Cardascia (art. cit. 470) cited *Dig.* 48. 19. 16. 3 (Claudius Saturninus) as further proof that Hadrian knew only the slave/free dichotomy. For Saturninus' dates, W. Kunkel, *Herkunft und soziale Stellung*, no. 46, 184–5 (post-Hadrian).

applied universally, in the punishment of every crime.[1] However, it would be premature to commit oneself to any view before investigating the post-Hadrianic period for innovations in the penal system.

Post-Hadrianic innovation

The contribution of Pius to the development of the system may be considered first. We may begin with two constitutions, one on the murder of an adulterer (quoted above), and one on theft from Imperial mines, both of which might be thought to be innovatory.

The rescript on the murder of an adulterer cannot be said to have in itself established the principle that criminals of high status should be punished differently. There was ample precedent in the practice of courts for over a century. Further, the opposition between exile and one of the *custodia* penalties was anticipated by Hadrian's decision on boundaries. Nor was Pius the first to prescribe different penalties in punishing homicide, as another constitution of Hadrian (on decurions) shows. In so far as there was innovation, it lay simply in the fixing of lighter penalties for one particular crime which fell under the Cornelian law on homicide. The reform was in a sense made necessary, and was certainly influenced, by actions of Pius' predecessor. Hadrian had dealt with a subject close to Pius', and with great leniency:

> item divus Hadrianus rescripsit eum, qui stuprum sibi vel suis per vim inferentem occidit, dimittendum.[2]

In general, by injecting into Roman law a concern for the *mens facientis*, Hadrian had made the law as a whole more flexible, but the state of the law on particular points uncertain. Hadrian had ruled that murder in revenge for *stuprum* was not to be punished as ordinary murder, but had made no specific statement on murder in revenge for adultery. Pius was perhaps asked to fill the gap, and did so, offering his own idea of leniency in the process.

The edict on thefts of gold and silver from Imperial mines is novel in a similar, restricted sense:

---

[1] See p. 164 n. 1 below.
[2] *Dig.* 48. 8. 1. 4: 'Likewise Divine Hadrian wrote that the murderer of the man who violated him or his own should be discharged.'

Si quis ex metallis Caesarianis aurum argentumve furatus fuerit, ex edicto divi Pii exilio vel metallo, prout dignitas personae, punitur.[1]

Presumably the penalty of exile was for men of standing, and low-status criminals were to be sent to the mines. Pius was perhaps extending a recognized system of penalties to a particular offence which had not been touched by the original lex Iulia peculatus (probably Augustan). Imperial mines were not unknown in the reign of Augustus. But they were rare, did not bear the common title metalla Caesariana, and were not an element in the pattern of punishment.[2] Alternatively, Pius might have been raising the penalties, either because the offence had become particularly troublesome, or because he considered it particularly serious.

Over one matter it may be possible to make a direct comparison between the attitudes of Hadrian and Pius. An edict of Hadrian and a rescript of Pius deal with the plundering of wrecks and ruins. The substance of Hadrian's ruling was that anyone found guilty of the crime would be treated as a bandit (latro) and given a heavy penalty (gravis sententia), the content of which was not revealed. Pius was asked specifically about penalties, perhaps because Hadrian had left them vague. The judge's first concern, he wrote, was to establish whether the offender was simply collecting 'perishables' (peritura) or maliciously seizing preservable property. He went on:

ideoque si gravior praeda vi adpetita videbitur, liberos quidem fustibus caesos in triennium relegabis aut, si sordidiores erunt, in opus publicum eiusdem temporis dabis: servos flagellis caesos in metallum damnabis.[3]

It would be rash to assume that Hadrian envisaged for this crime one penalty for all conditions of men. His edict stated neither that there were differential penalties nor that there were

---

[1] Dig. 48. 13. 8. 1: 'Whoever steals gold or silver from the Caesarian mines is punished with exile or the mines, depending on his dignity, according to an edict of Divine Pius.' Cf. 48. 19. 38 praef.

[2] F. Millar, JRS 53 (1963), 30, on Augustus and the Cyprian copper mines.

[3] Dig. 47. 9. 7 (Hadr.); ibid. 4. 1 (Pius): 'Thus, if it appears that comparatively valuable booty has been sought with violence, you will relegate free men for three years after beating them with rods, or, if they are of meaner origin, you will put them to public labour for the same term; slaves you will condemn to be whipped and sent to the mines.'

not.[1] He simply gave an assurance that the crime would be punished with severity. Pius' rescript is full of difficulties. *Relegatio* and *opus* are opposed, and this division is evidently correlated with a division in society. But with which division? Prima facie, with the division between free men, free men who were *sordidiores*, and slaves. The first group were 'relegated', the second sentenced to *opus*. But the former were beaten before going into exile, and this lessens the likelihood that they were, or included, *honestiores*. *Honestiores* were not beaten, at least from Hadrianic times.[2] Perhaps the truth is that Pius envisaged for the offence of plundering shipwrecks penalties graded in a way slightly different from that which was customary. It seems that Hadrian did not consider the possibility that decurions might try their hand at rustling. Similarly, Pius might have thought that *honestiores* did not loot shipwrecks.[3]

Finally, when Pius gave attention in a constitution to a sanction or penalty, it was usually to analyse and explain rather than to modify.[4] Torture and *metallum* are two possible exceptions. Pius introduced reforms in the use of torture. However, they were minor, and his motives were humanitarian rather than political.[5] For example, he ruled that children under fourteen should not be subjected to torture, except in treason cases.[6] In matters of more moment, Pius did not move from the position of his predecessors.

---

[1] Cf. *Dig.* 47. 12. 3. 5 (a fine, and no other penalty, is named by Hadrian for the crime of burying the dead within a city area; presumably, if the offender was unable to pay, he would be punished in another way); 48. 9. 9 praef. (*bestiae* alone is mentioned as an alternative to the traditional penalty for parricides. Would a decurion have suffered this penalty? See 48. 19. 15, which points, rather, to decapitation); 48. 19. 28. 7 (Pius prescribes *vincula publica*, apparently indiscriminately—but perhaps only those of low status would have been involved).

[2] See pp. 155 ff. If *liberi* included *honestiores* throughout the passage, then *honestiores* were beaten, whether the sum of money involved was great or small. When Pius dealt with cases where the amount was inconsiderable, he wrote only of two classes of criminals, *liberi* and *servi*: 'si non magnae pecuniae res fuerint, liberos fustibus, servos flagellis caesos dimittere poteris.'

[3] Nor does Paulus correct Pius after citing him. For the omission of *honestiores* see *Coll.* 11. 7. 1–2 (and pp. 157–8), 48. 10. 8 (and pp. 158 ff.), and n. 1 above.

[4] See, for example, *CJ* 9. 47. 1, on *deportatio* and *opus*.

[5] *Dig.* 29. 2. 86 praef.: 'quod et hic *humanitatis gratia* optinendum est' (condemned by Gradenwitz).

[6] *Dig.* 48. 18. 10 praef.; ibid. 15. 1.

As for *metallum*, it has been claimed, on the basis of a passage of Marcianus, that Pius significantly changed the condition of those condemned to the mines by creating, or recognizing officially, the 'new juridical condition' of 'slave of the penalty' (*servus poenae*). Pius appears to have denied the Imperial treasury, the Fiscus, right of ownership over any legacies left to men condemned to the Imperial mines.[1] This measure is hard to evaluate. It is uncertain whether there was any originality in his gesture, or even whether the gesture was truly magnanimous.[2] But the central point is that Pius did not change in the slightest the legal condition of the man condemned to the mines. It is not even certain that he invented the name *servus poenae*.[3]

In sum, Pius' legislative programme was not that of a great innovator.

A large number of constitutions are attributed in the sources to Marcus and Verus, Marcus, and Marcus and Commodus.[4] Few of them contain anything relevant to the issue of penalty

---

[1] See Brasiello, op. cit. 378, arguing from *Dig.* 34. 8. 3 praef., cf. 49. 14. 12. Other refs. to *servus poenae*: 28. 3. 6. 6–7; 29. 1. 13. 2; 29. 2. 25. 3; 40. 1. 8 praef.; 40. 5. 24. 6; 48. 19. 8. 8 and 12; ibid. 17 praef.; *PS* 3. 6. 29. See Brasiello, op. cit. 416 ff.

[2] *Originality*: the Biographer claims that Hadrian attempted to close the Fiscus to confiscated property (*SHA Hadr.* 7. 7; but cf. *Dig.* 48. 8. 4. 2; perhaps also 48. 20. 7. 3). The ruling, if not fictional, was not put into effect. All the juristic evidence shows that confiscated property went into the Fiscus. See F. Millar, art. cit. 37 n. 123; P. A. Brunt, *JRS* 56 (1966), 81–2.
Magnanimity: *bona caduca* (property lacking an heir) traditionally went to joint legatees with children, and to heirs with children (Ulp. *reg.* 17. 2; cf. 18. See Millar, art. cit. 34–6; Brunt, art. cit. 79–81). Otherwise, it went into the Aerarium, although already in the first century there were signs of encroachment from the Fiscus. If indeed beneficiaries with prior claim had been bypassed (sc. by procurators) and *bona caduca* had been deposited in the Fiscus, and if Pius was trying to stop this, then his action was both necessary and magnanimous. If, on the other hand, Pius was simply waiving the claims of the Fiscus as opposed to the Aerarium if there were no other beneficiaries, then his action possessed the degree of generosity of the measure ascribed to Hadrian (above).

[3] Some minor legislation shows that Pius was attentive to the lot of *servi poenae*. Condemnation to the mines was for life; but in special circumstances the condemned man might be released, provided he had kinsmen and had served at least ten years of his sentence (*Dig.* 48. 19. 22). Of course the Emperor could grant a reprieve through *restitutio* (ibid. 8. 12).

[4] They include *Dig.* 48. 22. 6. 2 (which draws on implications of 48. 19. 15); *Coll.* 4. 3. 6 (cf. *Dig.* 48. 5. 39. 8; 48. 8. 1. 5); *Dig.* 23. 1. 16 and 23. 2. 16 praef. (cf. ibid. 44 praef.). Other passages include 2. 14. 8; 60; 47. 18. 1 praef.; 2.

and status, and those that do, with one exception, basically repeat previous enactments. The exception is the edict of Marcus concerning the privileged status of the descendants of leading equestrian officials to the third generation.[1] Marcus was perhaps clarifying the position of a small group on the fringe of the privileged élite which was uncertain or which had been challenged. In Roman eyes status was inherited, and it was natural to believe that children benefited from any parental privileges awarded because of status. The situation of more remote agnate descendants was less clear; nor in the present case could they be assumed to belong *ipso facto* to any definite social class or status group. After the edict there could no longer be any doubt about their eligibility for privileged treatment in the law courts.

The relevant constitutions of the Severan Emperors may be divided into two groups. Three rescripts banned the use of certain penalties against children of veterans and decurions.[2] Two others directly concerned decurions.[3]

It is scarcely conceivable that any of the three rescripts in the first group conferred privileges which were not previously possessed. Thus, for example, it might be true that no Emperor before Caracalla stated that the children of veterans were exempt from 'plebeian' penalties, but this is without significance, given the Roman understanding that children inherited privileges derived from status.[4] Both rescripts in the second group show by their wording their lack of novelty.[5] Severus and Caracalla cited the rule (*prohibitum est*) that decurions were not to be beaten, while Caracalla stated that decurions patently (*manifestum est*) should not be sentenced to *opus*. Moreover, the rough contexts of the rescripts can be reconstructed with some plausibility, and the result is relevant. Severus and Caracalla were replying to one Ambrosius, apparently a decurion or the son of a decurion, who had presumably protested against a beating received at the hands

---

[1] *CJ* 9. 41. 11 praef.   [2] *CJ* 9. 47. 5; 9; 12; and see next note.
[3] *CJ* 2. 11. 5 (also on sons of decurions); 9. 47. 3.
[4] *CJ* 9. 47. 5.
[5] *CJ* 2. 11. 5: 'decuriones quidem, item filios decurionum fustibus castigari prohibitum est'; 9. 47. 3: 'decurionem in opus publicum dari non oportere manifestum est.'

of the proconsul. Similarly, the Geminius to whom Caracalla wrote was probably a decurion sentenced to forced labour. These rescripts, in company with the other Imperial legislation of the post-Hadrianic period, were designed less to establish a system of privilege than to preserve one which existed already.[1]

Hadrianic innovation

It remains to estimate Hadrian's own contribution to the development of the penal system, and to assess the degree to which he was an innovator. The matter turns on the interpretation of four constitutions. All of them have been introduced already into the discussion. They are the edict on exile and the rescript on the *custodia* penalties (*Dig.* 48. 19. 28. 13–14), the rescript on boundaries (*Dig.* 47. 21. 2), and the decree on decurions (*Dig.* 48. 19. 15). The first two, as has been said, indicate only that Hadrian was familiar with the penalties used later by the Severans, and that he classified them into two groups according to type. In the light of the rescript on boundaries this division of penalties takes on a new meaning. But how epoch-making was that rescript?

The pre-Hadrianic evidence shows that courts and judges which investigated crimes *extra ordinem* were always able to vary penalties, and that in Imperial times a greater number of penalties were at hand from which a choice could be made. As for the way in which the penalties were applied, the lower ranks of the free population, including citizens of low status, were sometimes, at least, awarded penalties from the *custodia* group. Moreover, it was considered highly irregular for senators or equestrians to suffer one of these penalties rather than deportation (for capital crimes, the *poena legis*, if there was a relevant *lex*) or a milder penalty of the same type. Hence Hadrian's rescript on boundaries is not

---

[1] It is unlikely that the rescripts of Marcus and Commodus (*Dig.* 1. 18. 14) and Pius (*Dig.* 48. 3. 3) on *custodia* were the first which recognized that prisoners of standing and means were treated more leniently than their social inferiors. A juristic observation of the Severan period points to an innovation belonging to the post-Hadrianic age. Ulpian (*Dig.* 48. 22. 6. 1) reports that the governor did not possess the *ius deportandi*. The loss of the right to deport, however, belongs to the realm of administration, and involved no change either in the nature of the penalty of *deportatio* or in the type of person to whom it was applied. For the background to the change see pp. 80 ff.

likely to have been the first judgement which split into two the category of the free, and set two penalties of different kinds—one mild, the other degrading. The novelty of the rescript lies in the setting of those particular penalties (exile, public labour) for that particular crime (the moving of boundary stones). The penalties still held good in Severan times.

The rescript on boundaries might have been the first of its type in another way. It has been suggested, largely on the basis of a passage in the *vita Macrini*, that Hadrian's rescripts were the first 'true' rescripts.[1] In the course of a sweeping attack on Imperial rescripts, Macrinus is said to have adduced in support of his arguments Trajan's alleged refusal to reply to *libelli*, petitions. Macrinus confused the issue, perhaps deliberately (*fuit in iure non incallidus*), by failing to distinguish between replies to the consultations of officials and replies to the petitions (*libelli*) of private individuals. Both were technically *rescripta*. Trajan's dissatisfaction must have been with the latter, not with the former, of which several examples survive.[2] The bulk of Hadrian's legislation was contained in rescripts to officials or in general edicts. His rescripts did not differ from Trajan's rescripts in kind.[3]

---

[1] A. d'Ors, op. cit. 152: 'des rescrits proprement dits'. See also J. Gaudement, 'L'Empereur, Interprète du Droit', *Festschr. für E. Rabel* (1954), ii. 169 ff. See *SHA Macr.* 13. The passage is suspect. See pp. 174 ff.

[2] Trajanic rescripts of the former type include, perhaps, *Dig.* 27. 1. 17. 6; 36. 1. 31. 5; 48. 17. 5. 2, and almost certainly 29. 1. 24; 48. 18. 1. 11–12 and 19; 48. 19. 5 praef.; 48. 22. 1; 49. 16. 4 praef. and 5. Some of his replies to Pliny as governor of Bithynia surely fit into this category. (For that matter, Trajan did read the *libelli* from *privati* sent on by Pliny, although these were not requesting legal rulings as such.) Other enactments of Trajan go under different names in the sources. The distinctions between the different types of constitutions are somewhat imprecise and I suspect in some cases illusory—see p. 174 n. 3. See *Dig.* 48. 13. 5. 4; Gai. *Inst.* 3. 72 ('constitutions'); *Dig.* 34. 9. 5. 20; 49. 14. 13 praef.; *CJ* 7. 6. 1. 12a; *IJ* 3. 7. 4 ('edicts'); *Dig.* 47. 14. 3. 3 (*epistula*); *Dig.* 48. 16. 10. 2 (*interpretatio*); *CJ* 5. 75. 5 (*S.C. auctore divo Traiano*); *Dig.* 29. 1. 1 praef. (a ruling, perhaps a *constitutio*—see ibid. 2—which was converted into *mandata*). For constitutions of pre-Trajanic Emperors see above, p. 8 n. 4.

[3] Even allowing for the bias of the *Digest* towards second- and third-century Emperors, it is likely that the volume of rescripts increased under Hadrian. This was a product of administrative reform and the greater prominence achieved by jurists (see Schiller, art. cit.). There are few examples of *libelli* sent by private persons to Hadrian and answered. See, for example, *Dig.* 42. 1. 33 (but this led to a rescript to *the governor*); 48. 20. 7. 3 (cf. Dio 69. 23. 2; also 56. 10).

Hadrian neither created the system of dual penalties nor invented a medium, the rescript, by which status distinctions were brought into the law. Did he, by his ruling on execution, broaden the privileged group so that it included decurions?

In the first place, the ruling does not *look* like a general edict which deliberately raised the status of decurions. Its application was limited—it contained no general statement about the inapplicability of the death penalty, and thus cannot be represented, for example, as one of a series of edicts exempting decurions from specific penalties. Rather, it concerned only the crime of murder, and prohibited the death penalty in murder cases alone. (This is all that is explicitly stated. It can be legitimately inferred that execution for other ordinary capital crimes was regarded as irregular, that capital exile was the highest penalty for such crimes, that decurions should be beyond the reach of all *custodia* penalties.) Again, there is no indication that the ruling announced or constituted a departure from previous policy. The Roman administration had always distinguished carefully between the local aristocracy and the mass of the people in the cities. Granted the wealth, social status, and political usefulness of the former, it was inevitable that the Roman citizenship, the judicial decuries, the equestrian order, and the Senate should have become accessible to them, and that the distinctions won by individuals within their ranks should have added to the prestige of the group as a whole. The actions and attitudes of courts had long reflected a respect for social prestige. Hence it was expected of judges that they would discriminate in favour of provincials of high status.[1] This brings us to consider the immediate context of the ruling. Hadrian's travels enabled him to see at first hand how the Empire was administered and the law enforced. He was notoriously interfering[2]—but no Emperor was more accessible to people with just complaints. As the Biographers reported, Hadrian did not hesitate to correct abuses when he found them. Amongst those called to account were governors,[3] and one of their misdeeds (*facta*), I would suggest, was to exceed the penalty of the law in

---

[1] See, for example, Pliny, *Ep.* 9. 5.   [2] Dio 69. 5. 1 (τὸ πολύπραγμον).
[3] *SHA Hadr.* 13. 10.

their punishment of decurions for capital offences. In so doing they were in effect denying that any distinction existed between decurions and the rest of the free population of the provinces. This clashed with the views of Roman aristocrats of the late first and early second centuries.

The upshot is that Hadrian did not so much raise decurions to a new status as confirm them in an old one, at a time when penalties were becoming harsher and the newer penalties more widely used, and when governors were no less inclined to arbitrary actions than their predecessors had been. On another level the decree is an indication that decurions had achieved Imperial recognition as a group worthy of protection.[1]

It seems that the penal system was no more transformed by self-conscious legislative acts in Hadrian's reign than in the succeeding period. Over-extravagant claims have been made about the background and purpose of rescripts of Emperors such as Hadrian, Pius, and Severus, and their true significance has been missed. The Hadrianic rescript on boundaries, for example, is principally important as an illustration of the advance which the criminal *cognitio* procedure was making at the expense of the formulary procedure of the civil law. Two laws, one of Julius Caesar (or of the Emperor Gaius), and one of Nerva, had dealt with the moving of boundary stones. But they had envisaged an action by which a plaintiff sued for a private penalty, a fine.[2] That is to say, the offence was still thought of as a delict for which compensation was sought in a private action. Perhaps for the first time under Hadrian the same offence was treated as a crime and

[1] It is sometimes stated that *Dig.* 48. 19. 15 (and 47. 21. 2) represents remedial legislation to compensate decurions for the heavy financial burdens imposed on them. See, recently, G. W. Bowersock, in *Phoenix* 18 (1964), 327–8, and *Augustus and the Greek World* (1965), 148 n. 3. A formal analysis of the rescripts as attempted above suggests that this is improbable. Further, although there are signs that the burdens on the decurions were increasing in the late first and early second centuries, it cannot be shown that their lot was sufficiently hard to warrant or necessitate Imperial intervention. In any case, it may be doubted whether the alleged concessions (now, according to the theory, given for the first time) could have served as, or have been taken as, a true palliative.

[2] *Dig.* 47. 21. 3 praef.–1. Cf. *FIRA*² i, no. 12, p. 138 (Julian agrarian law). The amount of the fine was 5,000 HS. By Nerva's law a slave was put to death unless his master paid compensation.

punished by the state *extra ordinem*. There is other evidence that *cognitio* was being used more widely about this time,[1] and one effect of the wider use of *cognitio*, as the rescript on boundaries bears witness, was that judges were given more frequent opportunity to discriminate in favour of rank.

Conclusion: From Augustus to the Severans

So far it has been suggested that the dual-penalty scale was not the creation of any second- or third-century Emperor or Emperors, but that it had already attained a considerable degree of maturity, if not full maturity, by the Hadrianic age. By this interpretation the crucial developments in the evolution of the penal system took place in the first century A.D. Unfortunately the inadequacy of the sources makes possible only a limited understanding of this formative period. What follows is necessarily only a sketchy outline of a complicated process.

Variation of penalty was practised from the time when the *cognitio* procedure was introduced. In the early stages discrimination was a matter of the selection of penalties of greater or lesser harshness for low-status or high-status criminals from a limited list of penalties including the payment of a fine, loss of status, various grades of exile, and execution. The next stage commenced perhaps in the reign of Tiberius. Severer sanctions, in origin mostly slave penalties, became available alongside the older conventional ones, and were increasingly employed against defendants of lower status. The use of these penalties was a precondition of the development of the mature penal system familiar to the classical lawyers. Judges chose penalties according to type as well as according to gravity. In the first century individual Emperors and governors in moments of excess applied degrading penalties to members of the higher orders. Early writers record with indignation or disapproval these isolated events, which showed a blatant disregard for judicial precedent. However, such periodic challenges did not break the immunity from 'servile'

---

[1] See *Dig.* 47. 9. 1 praef.; cf. ibid. 4 and 7 (*naufragium*, etc.); perhaps also *Coll.* 11. 6–8; cf. *Dig.* 47. 14. 1–2 (rustling was once treated as theft, but serious cases at any rate were punished *extra ordinem* by Hadrian's time). The urban prefect began to take *causae pecuniariae* in Hadrian's reign, *Dig.* 1. 12. 2.

and 'plebeian' penalties which the higher-status groups had gradually built up in judicial practice: they may even have helped to consolidate it. During the latter part of the century, aristocratic immunity gained both in value and in prominence, as the *cognitio* procedure (and therefore the variation of penalties) increased its hold on the criminal law and began to make inroads into the civil law.

The evidence for the second century enables us to follow the advance of *cognitio* in both the criminal and civil spheres, and also to see that the *de facto* privileges of status groups continued to be challenged, albeit sporadically. Now for the first time, thanks to the legal sources, the response of the highest authorities to such challenges is visible. Imperial constitutions, of which the first on record was Hadrian's on decurions, show the anxiety of Emperors to protect the higher orders. In addition, jurists warned governors in their treatises that they were expected to uphold and administer a status differential in the field of penalties.

More needs to be said on the subject of the Imperial constitutions (and the juristic statements) and their relation to the system of privilege. The above account, stressing that the dual-penalty system evolved by a continuous and natural process, which was unmarked by 'establishing legislation' at any stage, rejects by implication certain interpretations of the purpose of the constitutions, for example, the idea that they were intended to put the system on a new footing in law. This theory may now be discussed, together with the proposition that the constitutions did change the legal basis of the system of privilege, whether or not that consequence was intended.

6

THE LEGAL BASIS OF THE
DUAL-PENALTY SYSTEM

CARDASCIA remarks upon the appearance of 'class' distinctions in 'the law' from the time of Pius. Variation of penalty according to the class of the defendant (his argument runs) was a reality in 'judicial practice' before Pius' reign; from Augustan times a judge was free to vary the penalty according to the circumstances of the case, including the status of the accused. However, the judge was not obliged to pay attention to this factor. Pius, according to Cardascia, was the first to introduce class distinctions into 'the law'. After his reign variation of penalty became frequent in 'legislation', until under the Severans it took 'a general character'. As a result the independent initiative of the judge was sapped, and the Republican system of the fixed penalty gradually re-established.[1]

By 'the law' and 'legislation' are meant Imperial constitutions, the rescripts and edicts of Emperors.[2] The true *ius* stemmed from the Republican organs of state—the popular assembly and the magistrates. But comitial legislation had disappeared by the second century, and the *ius honorarium*, or magisterial legislation, was finally frozen by its codification under the supervision of Hadrian's jurist Julian, after a century in the course of which few innovations seem to have been introduced into it. As the old Republican legislative machinery ran down, an independent emender, interpreter, and creator of law was coming forward.[3] The Emperor gave

---

[1] Cardascia, art. cit. 467 ff.; cf. 307, 331. See also de Robertis, *ZSS* 59 (1939), 219 ff., on which Cardascia's analysis is partly based. On Cardascia and class see p. 234 n. 1.

[2] On Imperial legislation, G. Hänel, *Corpus legum* (1857); L. Wenger, *Die Quellen des römischen Rechts* (1953); H. Jolowicz, *Historical Introduction* (2nd edn., 1954), 374 ff.; Mason Hammond, *The Antonine Monarchy* (1959), ch. 10, 328–46; G. Gualandi, *Legislazione imperiale e giurisprudenza* (1963); R. Bonini, *I 'Libri de cognitionibus' di Callistrato* (1964), ch. 5, 35 ff.

[3] R. Orestano, *BIDR* 44 (1936–7), 272 ff., argues against Wlassak's view that Imperial edicts were merely interpretative. J. Gaudemet, *Festschr. für E. Rabel*, ii. 169 ff., has attempted to separate corrective, interpretative, and creative constitutions.

orders and made decisions by *edicta* and *decreta*.¹ *Mandata* were
instructions to officials, and were meant to be obeyed.² *Rescripta*
and *epistulae* too were treated as orders.³ They were replies to the
consultations of officials or the requests of private individuals.
An *ad hoc* decision might easily be transformed into an established
rule which was binding in other situations.⁴ Ulpian knew of an
opinion given by the jurist Neratius Priscus which Hadrian included in a rescript and which was treated as *ius* in his own day.⁵
Before the middle of the second century jurists were citing Imperial
rescripts in their works,⁶ and it was not long before collections
of constitutions were appearing. No judge could safely ignore them.
In the words of Marcianus, 'But if a judge neglects the constitutions of Emperors, he is punished.'⁷

The authority of the new law probably won only gradual acceptance. Curiously, the only hint of resistance comes comparatively
late, and from an unlikely source. According to the Biographer,
Macrinus, Emperor in A.D. 195, decided to abolish all rescripts
of past Emperors, on the grounds that they were not *ius*.⁸ The
jurists traced the Emperor's prerogative to make law to the *lex*

¹ *Edicta* were applicable throughout the Empire. *Decreta* were specific
judicial decisions which of course might be applied generally. See Hesky,
RE 4 (1901), 2289 ff., b 1, *decreta principis*; Ruggiero, *DE* 2 (1910), 1497 ff.,
decretum; 2 (1926), 2129 ff., *epistula*; Wilcken, *Hermes* 55 (1920), 1 ff.; Luzzatto,
Scritti di diritto romano in onore di C. Ferrini (ed. G. G. Archi, 1946), 265 ff.
² Kreller, *RE* 14 (1930), 1023 ff., iv. 2c, *mandata principum*. *Mandata* might
be published by the governor in an edict. See *Dig.* 48. 3. 6. 1; Pliny, *Ep.* 10. 96.
In *Ep.* 10. 110 it is not stated how the content of the *mandata* became known
to the *ecdicus* of Amisus.
³ Brassloff, *RE* 6 (1909), 204–10, *epistula*, identified *epistula* and *rescriptum*.
Cf. *DE* 2, 2129–35. For other views, Mason Hammond, op. cit. 339, Jolowicz,
op. cit. 379. No absolute distinctions can safely be made between the various
categories of enactments. See *Dig.* 5. 3. 25. 16 ('nam et divus Marcus . . .
decrevit . . . exemplo rescripti divi Marci'); 48. 8. 4. 2 ('idem divus Hadrianus
rescripsit . . . edictum meum'); etc. How is *Dig.* 39. 4. 4. 1 ('divus Hadrianus
praesidibus scripsit') to be classified? See also above, p. 168 n. 2.
⁴ As Trajan apparently appreciated, *SHA Macr.* 13. 1, p. 168 above.
⁵ 'extat Neratii sententia existimantis bona esse vendenda: et hoc rescripto
Hadriani continetur, quo iure utimur.' *Dig.* 42. 4. 7. 16; cf. 48. 13. 5. 4; 47.
12. 3. 5.   ⁶ *Dig.* 22. 3. 13; cf. 50. 17. 191 (Celsus).
⁷ 'sed et si iudex constitutiones principum neglexerit, punitur.' *Dig.* 48.
10. 1. 3.
⁸ *SHA Macr.* 13. 1. The authenticity of this anecdote is suspect. Rescripts
lost much of their authority in the fourth century (Jones, *Later Roman Empire*,
472), to which *SHA* belongs. Syme, *Ammianus and the Historia Augusta* (1969).

which gave him *imperium*.[1] But the *lex de imperio* does not seem to have conveyed any such power. Technically Macrinus was right: Imperial legislation had no more than a *de facto* validity in the 'restored Republic'. But Macrinus' protest was hopelessly out of date. Imperial constitutions were firmly established as sources of law. To abolish them would have been to bring havoc to the legal system; to question them would have been to challenge the authority of the person from whom they derived.[2]

Some of the relevant constitutions have been divided into two groups. To these groups (one concerned with privileges of children of decurions and others, one with those of decurions themselves, and each now increased in size with the addition of pre-Severan material)[3] a third may be added comprising three rescripts on the punishment of individual crimes—Hadrian's on the moving of boundary stones, and Pius' two on the murder of adulterers and on thefts from Imperial mines.[4] What has to be settled is the extent to which these rescripts, representing the law of Imperial constitutions, backed the dual-penalty system and changed its basis in law.

It is evident that the rescripts lack generality: they manifestly fail to cover the whole field of privileged categories, penalties and crimes.

First, on privileged categories, an Imperial rescript refers specifically to the fact that the sons of veterans were exiled rather than sent to forced labour, but only implies that veterans themselves were similarly favoured. No other rescript deals with veterans' privileges.[5] Again, it is nowhere stated explicitly by an

[1] Gai. *Inst.* 1. 5: *Dig.* 1. 4. 1 praef. (Ulp.); cf. *IJ* 1. 2. 6.

[2] On the validity of the edicts of Emperors see *StR* ii. 911 ff.; M. Wlassak, *Kritische Studien zur Theorie der Rechtsquellen* (1884), 133 ff.; R. Orestano, art. cit. 219 ff. Orestano argues, correctly, in my view, that the Imperial *ius edicendi* is different from the magisterial *ius edicendi* (229 ff.). The Emperor's power to legislate was an extension of his magisterial powers by *auctoritas*.

[3] Add to group one *CJ* 9. 41. 11 praef.; to group two, *Dig.* 48. 19. 15; 48. 22. 6. 2; *CJ* 9. 41. 8 praef.

[4] *Dig.* 47. 21. 2 (excluded by Cardascia, see art. cit. 468); 48. 5. 39. 8 (cf. 48. 8. 1. 5); 48. 13. 8. 1. *Dig.* 47. 18. 1. 2 is a text of a different kind, but perhaps could be included—the jurist's following comment shows that Marcus' punishment of an equestrian presupposes the use of the dual-penalty system.

[5] *CJ* 9. 47. 5: 'honor veteranis etiam in eo habitus est, ut liberi eorum usque ad primum dumtaxat gradum poena metalli vel operis publici non adficiantur,

Emperor that decurions were not to be condemned to the mines. But Alexander informed one Demetrianus that as his mother was a decurion's daughter she was not to suffer that fate.[1] Observations of lawyers supplement the rescripts to some extent, but even so the field is not fully covered. (Equestrians, for example, are hardly mentioned, and senators not at all.[2]) The lawyers, of course, are merely describing the current judicial practice for the benefit of contemporary legal practitioners and administrators.

Next, on crimes, we have not been able to find anything approaching a complete set of rescripts covering every crime and prescribing dual penalties. Only three judicial decisions of Emperors survive in which dual penalties are employed, and for other information we must turn to the descriptive comment of jurists on crime and punishment in their time.

Finally, on penalties, there are no general Imperial pronouncements about penalties containing directions which could be applied in the punishment of each offence as it came up. For less authoritative statements of this type it is necessary to have recourse once again to the jurists.

Thus if the alleged enhanced legality of the dual-penalty system depended on Imperial constitutions, we should have to conclude that some parts of the system had a higher status in law than other parts. The paradox is intensified when it is recognized that all the rescripts we have been discussing are concerned with the penal system, and that virtually all our information about discrimination in other spheres of the law comes directly from jurists, if from a legal source at all. The *Digest* contains hardly any explicit information on the subject of lower-level and higher-level tribunals; we have only Ulpian's note on the practice of referring to the Emperor capital cases involving decurions, and he cites no higher authority. Again, the praetorian practice of withholding actions against members of the aristocracy was no less

---

sed in insulam relegentur.' No rescript refers to the privileges of soldiers before Diocletian's *CJ* 9. 41. 8 praef.

[1] *CJ* 9. 47. 9: 'si matrem tuam decurionis filiam fuisse probatum fuerit, apparebit eam non oportuisse in ministerium metallicorum nec in opus metalli dari.'

[2] On equestrians, p. 175 n. 4 above.

'valid' because no Imperial rescript backed it openly. Conversely, Hadrian's rescripts on witnesses did not in any new and more authoritative way empower judges to discriminate in favour of witnesses of status.[1]

To resolve the dilemma it is necessary to go back to the rescripts, and see what can be said as to their purpose or purposes and the use made of them by the classical and post-classical jurists.

The nine rescripts in the first two groups were apparently aimed at repelling specific challenges to the privileges of high-status groups that had come to the notice of the Emperor. Some of them were picked up by the classical jurists and cited in their works to point to existing rules, or to show that specific contemporary practices had Imperial authority behind them. They were not necessarily cited because they were thought to be milestones in the evolution of legal discrimination. As was pointed out previously, the rescripts contain little that is creative, and in any case the jurists had no intention of describing the emergence of discrimination according to status. These rescripts appear in the *Digest* among other items loosely arranged under general headings without any regard to chronological order or historical context. Other rescripts appear in the *Codes* in an arrangement which is chronological but also lacking in historical sense.

The background of two of the three rescripts in the third group is uncertain; but the two rescripts of Pius were probably prompted, as the Hadrianic rescript certainly was, by requests for rulings on the proper penalties for specific crimes. Now Hadrian and Pius prescribed dual penalties for the three offences. By so doing they can certainly be said to have shown themselves in favour of the dual-penalty system, but not necessarily to have given it a legal standing which it did not have before. There can be no assurance that Hadrian's rescript was the first of its type. It was certainly not quoted because it was the first of its type. Ulpian's intention was simply to present precise information about the proper punishment of a specific crime for the benefit of Severan governors. In all probability there were rescripts or decrees of earlier

---

[1] *Dig.* 48. 22. 6. 1 (reference to Emperor); pp. 182 ff. below (withholding actions); *Dig.* 22. 5. 3 (witnesses).

Emperors on other matters, which might have survived in the legal sources, had chance allowed.

The early Empire saw the establishment in the criminal sphere of a system of dual law. Through penalty variation, judges and courts were able to deny to members of the lower orders, *de iure*, benefits and protection equal to that afforded members of the higher orders. Differential punishment as practised by judges was sanctioned by jurists and Emperors. It had as much 'legality' as the *cognitio* procedure with which it was closely associated; and *cognitio* arose from and was supported by the administrative (as opposed to legislative) action of the state.[1] The few Imperial constitutions of second- and third-century date did not 'establish' the dual-penalty system or give it increased 'validity'. At the most the constitutions confirmed its status as administrative law. While the 'appearance' of status discrimination in 'the law' has thus no intrinsic *legal* interest, it is nevertheless a significant historical phenomenon. It points to the difficulties experienced by the central administration in Rome in imposing its policies throughout the Empire. The constitutions are preoccupied with the privileges of decurions and veterans and their children because they were subject to the jurisdiction of those officials whom the Emperors were least able to control—the provincial governors. Similarly, the constitutions concentrate on the penal law because the privilege of milder penalties was the privilege most valuable, and most accessible, to the provincial aristocracy.

---

[1] For the Roman antipathy towards State legislation see F. Schulz, *Principles of Roman Law* (1936), 6 ff.

PART III

THE CIVIL SUIT

7

THE PRAETOR

UNDER the Republic and early Empire most civil actions were covered by the formulary procedure, which was regulated by the *ius ordinarium*, based on the praetor's edict.[1] A plaintiff approached a praetor at Rome (or a governor in the provinces) with a request for a suit. This led to a two-stage *actio*, *actio in iure* before a praetor, and *actio apud iudicem* before a judge. The judge was appointed with the agreement of both sides by the praetor, if he considered the plaintiff had a case. The praetor passed on to the judge a *formula*, or an instruction, setting out the factual and legal grounds on which the case was to be decided.

It is clear that the key figure in the launching of judicial proceedings was the praetor. Kelly has recently reopened the subject of the standards of the praetorship.[2] His thesis is that a decline in standards set in about the beginning of the last century of the Republic: from that time praetors showed greater susceptibility to political pressure, and to improper influence generally. The subject of this section is different. I shall be concerned with the wider question of praetorian discretion, and its use, especially in the initial stages of a private suit, in the interests of members of the higher orders.

The granting of an action

A civil *actio* began with *in ius vocatio*, the summoning of one man by another before the praetor to answer a charge. The legal

---

[1] F. Schulz, *Classical Roman Law* (1951), 19 ff.; W. W. Buckland, *Textbook of Roman Law*[3] (1963), 630 ff.; W. Kunkel, *Introduction to Roman Legal and Constitutional History* (1966), 84 ff.; M. Kaser, *Das römische Zivilprozessrecht* (1966), 107 ff. Some of the more important private claims which were settled by civil actions were claims of possession, breach of contract, damage, fraud, and injury.

[2] J. M. Kelly, *Roman Litigation* (1966).

texts reveal that *vocatio* was not permitted against parents, patrons, magistrates, priests, and certain other categories, without the consent of the praetor (*sine meo permissu*).[1] Yet one wonders whether Modestinus had in mind these or only these categories of persons when he remarked:

> generaliter eas personas, quibus reverentia praestanda est, sine iussu praetoris in ius vocare non possumus.[2]

It was Callistratus, an older contemporary of Modestinus, who said that *reverentia* was for *honor*, such *honor* as decurions, for example, possessed.[3] This prompts the question: was there any guarantee that the praetor would view sympathetically an attempt by an ordinary citizen to impeach a man of high rank? Here it is pertinent to refer to the jurist Labeo, whose comments on the action for fraud were cited by Modestinus' teacher Ulpian:

> et quibusdam personis non dabitur (actio), ut puta liberis vel libertis adversus parentes patronosve, cum sit famosa. sed nec humili adversus eum qui dignitate excellet debet dari: puta plebeio adversus consularem receptae auctoritatis, vel luxurioso atque prodigo aut alias vili adversus hominem vitae emendatioris. et ita Labeo.[4]

M. Antistius Labeo flourished in the age of Augustus.[5] How much of the quotation can be attributed to him? It might be argued that 'sed nec humili adversus eum qui dignitate excellet debet dari' is Ulpian's, because of the words used and the ideas expressed. The phrase 'is qui dignitate excellet' occurs nowhere else in the legal sources,[6] but it is Ciceronian Latin, and Labeo might

---

[1] *Dig.* 2. 4. 2 and 4.

[2] Ibid. 13: 'As a rule, we cannot summon to court without the praetor's permission those persons towards whom a high degree of respect should be displayed.'

[3] *Dig.* 48. 19. 28. 5; cf. 37. 15. 2 (*honori parentium ac patronorum*).

[4] *Dig.* 4. 3. 11. 1: 'An action will not be given to certain persons, for example, to sons or freedmen proceeding against parents or patrons, since it carries *infamia*. Nor, however, should it be given to a man of low status against someone pre-eminent in status—for example, to a commoner against a consular of assured prestige, or to a man of wanton and wasteful life, or someone worthless in some other way, against a man of faultless life. Labeo says this.'

[5] W. Kunkel, *Herkunft und soziale Stellung der römischen Juristen*[2] (1967), 114 ff., no. 1; cf. 32 ff., no. 53.

[6] *Qui dignitate inter eos praecellit* is part of a passage condemned by Gradenwitz. See *Dig.* 2. 14. 8.

have used it.[1] Ulpian and his contemporaries had frequent occasion to write of the men prominent in *dignitas*, but they used other expressions.[2] *Humilis*, standing alone in the positive form and as a status word, is unique in classical legal texts.[3] *Humilis persona* is known in Gaius and Callistratus,[4] while *humilis* qualifying a noun is common in non-legal Latin of the late Republic and early Empire.[5] Severan lawyers preferred to use the comparative *humiliores*, a form of the word that is rare in the classical prose writers. In sum, the use of *humilis* in the present text cannot be satisfactorily explained. But leaving this aside—and it is no argument for Ulpian's authorship of the sentence at issue—Labeo's authorship is not ruled out by any linguistic argument.

Nor can it be shown that the actual illustrations come more appropriately from Ulpian. Labeo, in discussing *iniuria*, uses the examples of father and patron—and an illustration from politics.[6] As for the two examples that illustrate the antithesis between the man of *dignitas* and the *humilis*, neither is precisely paralleled in other texts.[7] But there is no special reason for denying them to Labeo.

However, the *dignitas/humilis* clause is a stumbling-block, for ideological rather than linguistic reasons. Labeo seems to be credited with a conception of *humilitas* and *dignitas* which, for historical reasons, an Augustan lawyer could not have had. But this is not the inevitable consequence of ascribing the clause to Labeo. It is possible that the words, and therefore the whole

---

[1] Cic. *de imp. Pomp.* 41. For what it is worth, Labeo used the word *dignitas* in the course of his discussion of *iniuria*—if indeed the sentence in which it occurs is his and not Ulpian's. See *Dig.* 47. 10. 1. 2.

[2] e.g. *in aliqua dignitate positus, qui altioris dignitatis sunt*, etc. See pp. 224–5.

[3] *Humilis* in a moral sense is found in late texts, normally in company with another adjective with a moral sense, e.g. *CJ* 5. 27. 1 praef. (*vel humili vel abiecta*), and Cardascia, *Studi in memoria di Emilio Albertario*, ii. 663 ff. In *Dig.* 2. 13. 6. 1 (Ulp.) the clause containing *humilis et deploratus* is rightly rejected by Beseler as a late addition. The moral sense is not completely out of place in our text, but a word with a broader social reference plus moral overtones is surely more apt in a generalization which covers two examples, only one of which is moral. Cardascia, 'L'Apparition', 467, thought *et ita Labeo* covered only the moral example.

[4] Gaius, *Inst.* 3. 225; *Dig.* 48. 19. 28. 11 (Call.). Cf. *Dig.* 48. 5. 39. 8 (*humilis loci*); *PS* 5. 4. 10 (*humili loco natus*).

[5] See Lewis and Short, *humilis*, II A.   [6] *Dig.* 47. 10. 7. 8; cf. ibid. 7. 2.

[7] The *Vocabularium* does not contain entries for *prodigus* or *luxuriosus*. *Vilis* in the sense required is rare. *Dig.* 47. 10. 17. 13; 50. 2. 12.

clause, did not have the same meaning for the two lawyers. It should be remembered that in Labeo's day Roman citizenship was not the common property of the world, and thus the sphere of praetorian law was somewhat circumscribed; while Roman private law had more that a domestic significance for Ulpian, the lawyer of an empire. What did Labeo understand by 'qui dignitate excellet'? Labeo, a known political conservative of Roman or Italian stock, would probably have thought only of the aristocracy at Rome. For Ulpian, on the other hand, the Roman aristocracy was only part of a wider group, all members of which possessed *dignitas*.

To sum up, there are three possibilities: the ideas and expressions are all Labeo's; the whole is Ulpian's paraphrase of an original statement of Labeo; Ulpian transmitted Labeo's thoughts and words, but made additions. No additions have been located. Even allowing for some rewriting by Ulpian—and this can be suspected rather than detected—it is reasonable to conclude that Labeo introduced a notion of status into his interpretation of the praetorian edict.

A second conclusion follows almost automatically: as early as the Augustan period actions for fraud against certain types of people (fathers, patrons, magistrates, men of standing) were systematically refused when they were brought by certain other types (children, freedmen, private citizens, men of low rank, respectively). Those protected performed certain social or political functions—or were simply members of the higher orders. This inference is justified by what is known about the purpose of the commentaries on the edicts, and about the status of those commentaries. This is not the place to enlarge on the importance of the 'jurists' law', represented by the commentaries and by other central works of jurisprudence. The jurists played a vital role in the development of Roman law. It should not be forgotten that the *ius honorarium* was framed by the expert counsel of the jurists. But, in addition, commentaries such as Labeo's were written for the use of magistrates and legal practitioners.[1] There-

---

[1] On the *ius honorarium* see A. Berger, *Encycl. Dict. of Rom. Law*, 529. Emperors sometimes incorporated the *sententiae* of jurists in constitutions. See

fore it can be assumed that Labeo's advice on the administration of the *actio de dolo* was heeded by praetors of later generations, if not his own. Yet the advice is not likely to have been startlingly original. Jurists' comments were commonly based upon tendencies or norms already present in the legal system. That is to say, praetors already discriminated between parties on the basis of status in a quite open way.

No texts comparable to the passage of Labeo/Ulpian survive relating to other actions. Yet it is highly improbable that only the *actio de dolo* was regulated in this way. Labeo's words leave no doubt that the granting of the *actio* was restricted, not because of the nature of the offence of *dolus malus*, but because of the consequences of conviction for *dolus malus*, which included *infamia*.

Infamia has been referred to as the 'derogation of *dignitas*'.[1] The higher orders had good reason to fear *infamia*, having *dignitas* to lose. *Infamia* (or the *infamia* which followed conviction in an *actio famosa* such as the *actio de dolo*) involved, in addition to various procedural disabilities, disqualification from office-holding. For a senator, for example, this meant nothing less than the sudden end of a political career.

In addition to the *actio de dolo*, the actions for *iniuriae*, *furtum*, and *vi bona rapta* (and certain non-delictual fiduciary actions) were *famosae*. These actions were not given against parents or patrons, apparently on the grounds that they were an insult to their good name (*opinionem apud bonos mores suggillet*), and a denial of the respect (*reverentia*) to which they were entitled.[2] Praetors

---

Dig. 42. 4. 7. 16. The works of jurists were not unknown in the provinces. Ulpian's *de officio* (sc. *proconsulis*) is referred to in a Greek inscription from Ephesos: *JÖAI* 45 (1960), Beiblatt 82–4, no. 8, ll. 8–9.

[1] A. H. J. Greenidge, *Infamia* (1894), 4. On *infamia* see also M. Kaser, *ZSS* 73 (1956), 220–78; briefly, W. W. Buckland, op. cit. 91 ff.; A. Watson, *Tijdschrift voor Rechtsgeschiedenis* 31 (1963), 76 ff. *Infamia* is a useful but not a technical term.

[2] The principal texts relating to the immunity of parents and patrons are *Dig.* 37. 15. 2 praef.; ibid. 5 praef.–1; ibid. 7. 2; 44. 4. 4. 16. For the *actiones famosae* see *Dig.* 3. 2. 1; Gai. *Inst.* 4. 182; *tab. Herac.* 108 ff.; Lenel, *Das Edictum Perpetuum*[3] (1927), 77 ff. Watson (art. cit. in n. 1) argues that *infamia* as a result of condemnation in an *actio famosa* (mediate *infamia*) had ceased to exist in classical law. For the defendant in such an action avoided *infamia* by appointing a representative, *cognitor* (or *procurator*), against whom the *condemnatio* then lay. (The *cognitor* also escaped *infamia* if he lost the case, because he was acting *alieno nomine*.) This thesis seems to require qualification. Mediate

could have blocked all such actions against men of high social and political position for the same reasons. That there is no direct statement to this effect in the *Digest* would suggest, at the most, that discrimination of this kind was not officially acknowledged (a questionable assumption, considering the haphazard way the *Digest* was compiled); it does not show it was not practised.

One action carried especially disastrous consequences for members of the high-status groups—the action for debt. An adverse verdict in such an action brought *proscriptio* as well as *infamia*, that is to say, confiscation and sale of property as well as loss of status and political extinction. It is perhaps surprising that the governing élite took no special steps to avoid the action for debt until the closing years of the Republic—until this time they must have looked to the praetor to block such actions. Finally, a law of Julius Caesar permitted impoverished aristocrats to cede part of their land to their creditors without loss of status.[1] Moreover, under the early Empire a milder alternative to the *venditio bonorum* which was the lot of the ordinary debtor was established or confirmed by senatorial decree. This was *distractio bonorum*. By this procedure individual items of property were taken and sold under the supervision of a special agent, again without loss

---

infamia must have survived to some extent, because certain persons were not permitted to provide a *cognitor* (or act as one). The categories of the disqualified were doubtless spelt out in the Edict. We unfortunately have only partial knowledge of the relevant sections of the Edict. Besides, the Edict is not likely to have contained a complete list of those excluded. The decision in individual cases would have rested with the praetor, and if *Dig.* 4. 3. 11. 1 is a guide to the use he made of his discretion, the criteria for exclusion were broader than the Edict recognized. In addition, even supposing that the praetor did not reject a representative, it may not always have been easy to find a man to act as such in an *actio famosa* (cf. Watson, art. cit. 84). (The furnishing of a representative would always have raised financial problems for a poor man. See p. 188 n. 1.) Of course, *actiones famosae* were worth avoiding, even in those cases where condemnation did not automatically produce *infamia* in the defendant. One who lost such a case would suffer social disgrace (Watson, art. cit. 85), and practical disabilities not far removed from those involved in mediate *infamia*. See below.

[1] On *cessio bonorum*, E. Woess, *ZSS* 43 (1922), 485–529; M. W. Frederiksen, *JRS* 56 (1966), 128 ff. with bibl. Those lacking substantial property-holdings would not have been able to escape *venditio*. *Cessio* could be accomplished extra-judicially merely *per nuntium vel per epistulam* (*Dig.* 42. 3. 9; cf. *CJ* 7. 71. 6). This suggests that the ceders of property tended to be men with the high-status virtue of *fides*.

of status on the part of the owner. *Distractio bonorum* was available to *clarae personae*, especially members of the senatorial order. The pertinent text runs:

> curator ex senatus consulto constituitur, cum clara persona, veluti senatoris vel uxoris eius, in ea causa sit, ut eius bona venire debeant: nam ut honestius ex bonis eius quantum potest creditoribus solveretur, curator constituitur distrahendorum bonorum gratia vel a praetore vel in provinciis a praeside.[1]

Discriminatory rules or discriminatory practices, then, protected members of the higher orders from being taken to law in some circumstances. From the time of Julius Caesar bankruptcy suits could be avoided. This was accomplished by direct legislation, an exceptional remedy. In normal circumstances the praetor was approached by the plaintiff and had the responsibility of deciding whether the plaintiff had a case. If the plaintiff failed to satisfy the praetor, no judge was appointed. The evidence shows that a humble prosecutor might be rejected merely because of the quality of his opponent. This was standard practice in cases of alleged fraud. The same rule may have applied whenever the defendant was in danger of loss of status or reputation.

The acceptance of an action

An action, once granted, could not proceed if the defendant did not obey a summons, *in ius vocatio*, or send a representative, *vindex*, to guarantee his appearance at a later date. Only the rich were admissible as *vindices*, presumably because a *vindex* was liable to the plaintiff in the event of the subsequent non-appearance of the defendant.[2] Thus, as a general rule, only defendants who were themselves rich would have been able to furnish them. For the average defendant of low status and small means there was

---

[1] 'An agent is appointed by *S.C.* when a person of note, for example, a senator or his wife, is in the situation of having to sell his property. He is appointed by a praetor, or in the provinces by a governor, to divide up the property, so that as much of it as possible can be made over to the creditors in a relatively honourable fashion.' *Dig.* 27. 10. 5 (Gaius). *Distractio* was known to the Trajanic jurist Neratius (ibid. 9).

[2] Gaius, *Inst.* 4. 46: 'qui in ius vocatus neque venerit neque vindicem dederit'. For the *vindex* of Gaius the *Digest* substitutes *fideiussor iudicio sistendi causa datus*. For the wealth of a *vindex* see *Dig.* 2. 6. 1; 2. 8. 5; ibid. 10; *lex Urs.* 61.

probably no alternative to a personal appearance before the praetor in answer to a summons.[1]

By the principle of self-help, laid down in the *Twelve Tables*, and apparently not revoked in the Republican or classical period of Roman law, it was for the plaintiff, by the use of persuasion or force, to ensure that the defendant appeared before the praetor.[2] Here he might strike trouble, if his opponent was stronger than he and disposed to ignore the summons.

The case of L. Calpurnius Piso (*cos. suff.* 1 B.C.) and Urgulania in the reign of Tiberius shows that the problem was not merely a theoretical one. Piso, of noble birth, proud and defiant, had once threatened to abandon politics because of the prevalence of judicial corruption and other abuses. Tiberius had persuaded him with difficulty to change his mind. Tacitus continues: 'The same Piso before long gave just as vivid proof of his free and passionate spirit by summoning to court Urgulania, whose friendship with Augusta had lifted her beyond the reach of the law. Urgulania did not obey the summons, but, scorning Piso, rode in a carriage to the Emperor's house and took sanctuary there.'[3] More will be said later about the manner in which this dispute was resolved. It hardly needs saying that Piso did not pursue his opponent and seek to drag her before the praetor by force.

One might well wonder what attitude was taken up by the praetor towards a refractory defendant. *In ius vocatio* was in theory supported by certain legal sanctions.[4] But, in the view of Kelly, these were paper remedies. *In ius vocatio* might be reinforced by the ordering of *missio in possessionem*. But a plaintiff who could not carry out *vocatio* (the argument runs) was not likely to be able to enforce *missio*. Both would founder because of the lack of 'equal

---

[1] Other alternatives (for which see pp. 194 ff. below) were probably also out of his reach. A low-status defendant would have had difficulties also in providing a representative (*cognitor* or *procurator*) to take his place in an action. In such cases the payment of security was compulsory. See Gai. *Inst.* 4. 101.

[2] *XII Tables*, 1. 1–2: 'si in ius vocat, ni it, antestamino; igitur em capito. si calvitur pedemve struit, manum endo iacito.' See Kelly, op. cit. 6 n. 2.

[3] Tac. *Ann.* 2. 34; cf. 4. 21 ff. See pp. 195–6; and G. E. M. de Ste Croix, *British Journal of Sociology* 5 (1954), 42.

[4] Kelly, op. cit. 10 ff. On p. 9 Kelly dismisses the possibility that the praetor ever sent in his (small) police force to assist a plaintiff.

or greater power' (*par maiorve potestas*). *Missio* in turn might be backed up by an interdict or an *actio in factum*. But these involved another *in ius vocatio*, which would presumably be just as ineffective as the first.

All this leads Kelly to the following conclusion: the institution of self-help was inequitable and one-sided, and the praetor could not but have been aware of this. If, as it appears, he consistently failed to act with force on the side of the weaker plaintiff, this could only mean that, as a member of his order, he accepted the advantages which the system gave to the strong and socially elevated.

However, it should be pointed out that a plaintiff of low rank was not completely on his own.[1] In the first place, if he possessed a patron with greater influence and physical resources than himself, pressure could be brought to bear on an opponent who refused to go to court. The relationship between patron and client was a reciprocal one. The patron was expected to give both financial and legal aid when it was needed. A second ally of the plaintiff was the Roman social conscience. Romans in general considered it important to maintain their good name in the community, and their standing with the magistrates. Probably few men were prepared to flout convention and the law by refusing to obey a summons. There were exceptions: the Julian law on violence specifically provided for the indictment of those who resisted a summons with the aid of armed men.[2]

What chance had the plaintiff, when social pressures failed to bring his opponent to heel? The efficacy of the sanctions which were at the praetor's disposal should not be underrated. For example, the responsibility for carrying out *missio in possessionem* lay with the plaintiff, but he could call upon auctioneers, *coactores argentarii*, for aid. These were often significant and powerful men, who had a financial interest in the sale of the property which would follow seizure.[3] Again, the penalty of *infamia* was not to

---

[1] For some of the points which follow cf. M. W. Frederiksen, *JRS* 57 (1967), 254 ff.; J. Crook, R. Stone, *CR* 17 (1967), 83 (reviews of Kelly, op. cit.).

[2] *Dig.* 48. 7. 4 (Lex Iulia *de vi*, prob. Julius Caesar); pp. 192–3. On public opinion see pp. 191–2 below.

[3] Cic. *pro Caec.* 10 and 27. See Mommsen, *Hermes* 12 (1877), 94 ff., on the activities of *argentarii* at Pompeii; in general, *RE* 2, 708 ff. (1896). Later,

be despised, except perhaps by those who had little or nothing to lose.[1] There may have been a clause in the praetor's edict stating that a defendant who resisted summons could be declared *infamis*. Such a rule (as Kelly recognized) might easily have dropped out of the edict, together with other rules relating to *infamia*. Censorial *infamia* seems to have applied for this and similar offences, and praetorian rules on *infamia* were probably based on censorial rules.[2] Even if there was never any such clause in the edict, the resisting defendant might suffer restriction or suspension of his private and public rights. It was not beyond the praetor to refuse him access to the courts in the future, when he himself might wish to litigate. Thus a man who in one instance had considered himself above the laws (*supra leges*) might be denied legal remedies indefinitely. Additional acts of defiance would worsen his prospects. Successful resistance to the edict ordering *missio*, for example, would expose him to the suspension of further rights. It is known that those whose property had been (or would be) seized and put up for auction were ineligible for membership of a municipal senate. The candidacy of someone who had held on to his property by force in defiance of a *missio*-order was not likely to be considered seriously by the electoral officers; while if such a man was already a councillor, his expulsion from the council was certain. The situation in Rome (with the substitution of Roman Senate for municipal senate and Roman senators for municipal senators) would presumably have been identical.[3]

Thus a recalcitrant defendant would forfeit his standing with the magistrates, and risk informal, if not formal, curtailment of his

intervention *extra ordinem* was regular to support a *missio*. See *Dig*. 43. 4. 3 praef.–1 (Ulpian).

[1] Ulpian, *Dig*. 47. 10. 35, recognizes the possibility that some might 'despise an injury-suit, because of their (sc. moral) *infamia* and poverty' ('si quis iniuriam atrocem fecerit, qui contemnere iniuriarum iudicium possit ob infamiam suam et egestatem . . .'). The attitude of a man of means whose *existimatio* was still intact would have been otherwise.

[2] Kelly, op. cit. 24–7. On the relation of censorial to praetorian *infamia* see Greenidge, op. cit. 114 ff.

[3] *tab. Herac*. 115 ff. Greenidge (ibid. 116) calls this section of the 'Lex Iulia Municipalis' (= *tab. Herac*.) 'a codification of the most permanent portions of the censorial *infamia*', and notes that the grounds for disqualification in the Edict are closely comparable.

prerogatives. But there was a further consequence: he would suffer loss of reputation in the community at large. His position may be compared with that of the unjust father or patron in Julian, who was immune from the penalty of infamy (arising out of conviction for *dolus* or *iniuriae*), but who could not escape a *nota infamiae* arising out of what he had done (*re ipsa*) and public disapproval of it (*opinione hominum*).[1]

Lest the importance of public opinion in Rome and the cities of the Empire be underrated, some illustrations may be given of ways in which it could be actively harnessed in support of victims of injustice. A man threatened by injury or theft might seek help from the citizenry with the cry *fidem imploro Quirites (Quiritium)*, or variants.[2] Those who heard the cry (*quiritatio* or *comploratio*) bore a moral obligation to prevent the wrong being done, or to pursue and apprehend the wrongdoer.[3] *Quiritatio* was most suited to the small close-knit community, and was no answer to the more sophisticated and organized crimes of a large metropolis. But where crimes of violence or theft of movables were in question, it continued to be useful in late-Republican Rome. In any case, there were other ways of arousing popular support where an offence had not been witnessed, or where the offender was

---

[1] *Dig.* 37. 15. 2 praef. Cicero, *de leg.* 1. 19. 50–1, recognizes *infamia* of two kinds, that which results from condemnation from an offence, and *ipsa infamia* which springs from the committing of the offence. Cf. *ad Att.* 1. 16. 2.

[2] See Livy, 2. 23. 8; 3. 41. 4; 44. 7; 45. 9; Varro 6. 68; Sen. *Ep.* 15. 7. Those addressed include *Quirites* (texts above; Petr. 21; Apul. *Met.* 2. 27); *cives* (Plaut. *Amph.* 376; *Men.* 996 ff.); *populares* (Plaut. *Rud.* 615; Ter. *Ad.* 155); *populus* (Apul. *Met.* 4. 27; Cic. *Sext. Rosc. Am.* 29); *plebs* (Livy 2. 55. 7); neighbours (Plaut. *Rud.* 616; Cic. *Tull.* 50; Apul. *Met.* 7. 7); governor (ibid. 10. 28); consul and Senate (Cic. *de dom.* 12); Emperor (Apul. *Met.* 3. 29; 7. 7; 9. 42); gods (ibid. 8. 18; Livy 3. 45. 9; Cic. *Sex. Rosc. Am.* 29); judges (ibid.). Words for the cry include *implorare* (above); *plorare* (*leges regiae, Servius Tullius* 6; Plaut. *Aul.* 317–18); *comploratio* (Livy 3. 47. 6; 40. 8 ff.); *endoplorato* (Cic. *Tull.* 50 on *XII T.*; Fest. p. 77); *quiritare* or *quiritatio* (Livy 33. 28. 2–3; 40. 9. 7; Val. Max. 9. 2. 1; Varro 6. 68; Pliny, *Ep.* 6. 20. 14; *Pan.* 29; Apul. *Met.* 8. 6); *convocare* or *invocare* (Petr. 21; Apul. *Met.* 7. 7); *clamor* (*Dig.* 9. 2. 4. 1; Gaius on *XII T.*). See W. Schulze, *Kl. Schr.* (1934), 160 ff.; Wieacker, *Festschr. Wenger* i. 129 ff. On popular justice see G. Broggini, *Iudex Arbiterve* (1957), 40 ff.; A. W. Lintott, *Violence in Republican Rome* (1968), 6 ff. For the connection with *provocatio*, E. Staveley, *Hist.* 3 (1955), 418. For an example of an effective intervention by bystanders see Livy 3. 44 ff.

[3] Here the parallel with the Germanic 'gerüchte' and the early English 'hue and cry' breaks down. For a discussion of the evidence from comparative law see Schulze, art. cit.

apparently immune from indictment. If the victim was sure enough of the identity of his enemy, he might dog his footsteps, dressed in mourning clothes, with long hair and beard. That this practice was liable to punishment by an *actio iniuriarum* if entered upon maliciously is sufficient testimony to its effectiveness as a means of arousing at least the passive resentment, *invidia*, of citizens against the offender.[1] Alternatively, verbal defamation might be resorted to by the victim. The recital of defamatory songs (*occentare*) was recognized as a capital offence in the *Twelve Tables*, probably because such a procedure was likely to lead to a riot of the populace. From about the turn of the third century B.C. the offence was actionable as *convicium* under the *actio iniuriarum*. Our 'powerful and intractable defendant' would have had nothing but brute strength to turn against either a silent protest or systematic abuse.[2]

The Romans, then, did not practise a system of naked self-help, in which the strong lorded it over the weak. In the first place, a wronged man, whether weak or strong, was required to seek recovery of alleged losses, or compensation for alleged injuries, by judicial processes. Private vengeance was ruled out except in special circumstances. Secondly, a plaintiff, even if weak, might have the support of public opinion and individual backers in the community. Moreover, if his stronger opponent turned his back on the courts, he might hope for praetorian remedies, which, even if they did not include the intervention on his side of a police force, could nevertheless be efficacious.

The situation of the weaker plaintiff improved with the end of the Republic and the coming of the Empire. We have been concerned above with the position that arose when the efforts of the plaintiff were frustrated by the superior force of the defendant. By a clause of the Julian law on violence (of Julius Caesar or Augustus) it was made a crime to resist a summons by force:

legis Iuliae de vi privata crimen committitur, cum coetum aliquis et concursum fecisse dicitur, quo minus quis in ius produceretur.

[1] *Dig.* 47. 10. 15. 27.
[2] Defamatory songs: ibid.; *XII Tables* 8. 1; cf. Cic. *de rep.* 4. 10. 12 (in Aug. *de civit. Dei* 2. 9). Other vocal abuse: Tac. *Ann.* 3. 36 with *Dig.* 47. 10. 38. On the Roman law of defamation see D. Daube, *Atti del Congr. int. di dir. rom.* (1951), iii. 413–56.

For the plaintiff this carried the important consequence that the summoning of a defendant who offered physical resistance was taken out of his hands.[1] For in the case of a criminal offence the state and not the individual was responsible for summonses. Meanwhile there were grounds for hope that the defendant would retreat from the greater risk of a public prosecution,[2] and would allow the plaintiff to institute civil proceedings.

The clause in the *lex Iulia* had only a limited application. But there may have been ways of having a less violent kind of resistance to summons enrolled as a crime.[3] The Emperors further supplemented the system of private summons by making it a criminal offence to disobey the injunctions of magistrates (a form of *contumacia*). In addition, the *cognitio* procedure, which had its own method of summons, became more frequently employed for the settling of private disputes.[4]

When all this is said, it must be admitted that there were practical difficulties about private summons, difficulties which might become almost insuperable if the praetor himself were uncooperative. This is the crux. It cannot be assumed, for example, that the praetor was free with the grant of *missio* to plaintiffs of low standing. Of a man who hid to escape trial (*qui fraudationis causa latitabit*), the praetor stated in his edict that he would order his property to be confiscated and sold: 'si boni viri arbitratu non defendetur'.[5] That is to say, the intervention of men of good reputation and means on the side of the defendant was sufficient

---

[1] 'A crime against the Julian law on private violence is committed when someone is said to have assembled a company to prevent a man from being led off to face the law.' *Dig.* 48. 7. 4, quoted Kelly, op. cit. 11. Kelly dismisses the clause with the comment that the man of low status would find it exceedingly difficult to win his case anyway. This, however, is another point, and in making it Kelly has tacitly conceded that the vicious circle could be broken. On the *lex Iulia de vi* see Kunkel, *RE* 24 (1963), 771–2.

[2] Condemnation in a criminal case undoubtedly carried *infamia* (in addition to other penalties).

[3] e.g. an indictment for *iniuriae* under the *lex Cornelia* is a possibility. This is suggested, though only indirectly, by *Dig.* 48. 7. 4 fin.

[4] See pp. 170–1. On the punishment of *contumacia* see *Dig.* 48. 19. 5 praef.: 'adversus contumaces vero . . . secundum morem privatorum iudiciorum' (Trajan/Ulpian); cf. *CJ* 7. 43. 1 (Hadrian, Pius); Kipp, *RE* 4 (1901), 1165 ff. For civil measures against disobedience see *Dig.* 2. 3. 3 (praetor's edict, Labeo).

[5] *Dig.* 42. 4. 7. 1. See ibid. 2: Ulpian says that *latitatio* is the most common reason for the ordering of *missio*.

to hold up a *missio*. There was no more guarantee that a praetor would apply his sanction of *infamia* to a powerful defendant who would not obey summons (supposing that resistance to summons was not labelled *famosum* in the edict).[1] In short, the system of private summons might readily become in the hands of the praetor an instrument of status discrimination. While the praetor was well placed to assist the plaintiff who lacked the capacity to carry out a summons, it is unwise to assume that he did so.[2]

This section has been largely devoted to the problem of resistance to summons. It may conclude with a brief consideration of two ways of avoiding summons which did not involve flouting the law. Both took the form of extra-judicial agreements between the parties, normally before judicial proceedings began. The first was *vadimonium*, the second *transactio*.

A defendant who wished to avoid an immediate appearance before the praetor in response to a summons might bind himself by a promise, *vadimonium*, to appear in court at a future date.[3] *Vadimonium* was not necessarily accompanied by the payment of security, *satisdatio*; sometimes a verbal agreement, with or without an oath, was sufficient.[4] But it is unlikely that *vadimonium* without *satisdatio* (which in the case of a money dispute might amount to as much as one half of the sum at issue) was acceptable in the case of a defendant whose financial resources were meagre.[5] As a practical matter, therefore, low-status defendants were in all likelihood

---

[1] See p. 190, above.

[2] Problems did not vanish under *cognitio*. *Missio* was supported by *extra ordinem* intervention (*Dig.* 43. 4. 3 praef.; cf. ibid. 3. 1). But how readily was the intervention ordered by the judge? See also *Dig.* 5. 1. 72: a defendant who failed to respond to summons (*evocatio*) was sent a *peremptorium edictum* to inform him that the trial would go on in his absence. But up to three edicts might be sent, depending on the discretion of the judge. He made his decision after considering the 'condicio causae *vel personae* vel temporis'. Delay could of course be very useful. See also 5. 1. 68–71; 73. 3; *PS* 5. 5A. 6 (7).

[3] Cic. *pro Quinctio* 61. *Vadimonium* might also be made when proceedings *in iure* could not be concluded within the day. See Gaius, *Inst.* 4. 184.

[4] Ibid. 185.

[5] Exempted were men of *fides* (*Dig.* 40. 5. 4. 8) and *honestas* (26. 4. 5. 1), and owners of immovable property (2. 8. 15 praef.: *possessores immobilium rerum*). These texts show the narrowness of Gaius, *Inst.* 4. 102 (*suspectae personae* were required to provide *satisdatio*).

barred from both of the two recognized ways of postponing court proceedings, the provision of a *vindex*, and the making of a *vadimonium*.

Transactio (*transigere*), or *decisio* (*decidere*), stands for a settlement out of court.[1] The class of defendants who sought *transactio* was probably quite substantial in number. Defendants of high rank, especially when their *existimatio* or *dignitas* was at stake, might have been ready to strike a bargain with plaintiffs. If a plaintiff was unwilling (he may have to settle for a slightly smaller sum than he was claiming), he might perhaps be reminded of the anxieties and expense of a long-drawn-out battle in the courts, which might in any case end in his defeat. All the inconvenience and risk could be avoided by a quick settlement and an immediate composition payment.[2] He might not see reason. Cicero knew how stubborn provincial plaintiffs could be, even when their opponents were senators, who were certain to demand and obtain a trial in Rome.[3] Perhaps only the application of pressure of a different kind would bring results, especially if the parties were of unequal strength.

Few plaintiffs could have been subjected to greater pressure than was L. Piso, who summoned Urgulania to appear before the praetor to recover a debt.[4] It will be remembered that Urgulania refused to go to court and sought refuge in the palace, in the knowledge that Livia would protect her. The passage in the *Annals* goes on:

But Piso held his ground, despite Augusta's complaint that her majesty was being dragged in the dust. Tiberius, thinking that he should so far gratify his mother as to say that he would go to the praetor's tribunal and support Urgulania, set out from the Palatium. His soldiers had orders to follow at a distance. The mob rushed up to look, as Tiberius, his face composed, and pausing every now and then for

---

[1] See Kelly, op. cit. 132–52, on the differences between *transactio* and *pactum*.

[2] Alternatively, the defendant might promise, by *stipulatio*, to pay at some date. Kelly argues persuasively for the possibility of *transactio* both during the *apud iudicem* stage and after the judge had made his decision, *post rem iudicatam*, ibid. 147–52.

[3] e.g. Cic. *ad fam.* 13. 26 and 55.

[4] Tac. *Ann.* 2. 34. See p. 188.

conversation, made his leisurely way, until, Piso's relations being unable to restrain Piso, Augusta issued orders for the payment of the money he was claiming. This ended an affair from which Piso emerged with glory, and Caesar with an enhanced reputation.

Tacitus told the story to illustrate Piso's courage and tenacity. He was not interested in procedural details. But it was surely an extra-judicial settlement which terminated the dispute. Of course the case was not a typical one, and the settlement differed from run-of-the-mill settlements. Here settlement was probably the aim of the prosecutor rather than of the defendant. For the defence was striving after nothing less than the outright withdrawal of the charge; while Piso probably realized that full judicial proceedings were out of the question, but would accept nothing less than a settlement. Tiberius' role is ambiguous. He may have thought that Piso, though unmoved by the pleas of his relatives, would withdraw when he intervened. But Piso's intransigence seems to have forced Tiberius to patch up a compromise.

Although there seems to have been little restriction on settlements (which indeed were permitted, if not encouraged, from the early Republic),[1] not all defendants were able to negotiate them with impunity. In the language of the lawyers, while *transactiones* (or *decisiones*) could be entered into without unhappy consequences for the defendant, *pacta* carried *infamia*, or disabilities analogous to *infamia*.[2]

Ulpian defines the two terms in this way:

qui transigit, quasi de re dubia et lite incerta neque finita transigit. qui vero paciscitur, donationis causa rem certam et indubitatam liberalitate remittit.[3]

The distinction presents no difficulties on paper. *Transactio* could take place only where the issue was unclear and the guilt of the defendant was contested; the defendant who *paciscitur*,

---

[1] See *XII Tables* 8. 16 (*duplione damnum decidito*); 12. 3; *Dig.* 2. 14. 7. 14; 4. 4. 9. 2.

[2] *Dig.* 3. 2. 4. 5; ibid. 6. 3; *Tab. Herc.* 108 ff.

[3] *Dig.* 2. 15. 1: 'He who makes a *transactio* makes it, as it were, over a doubtful claim, a legal dispute which is uncertain and uncompleted. But he who makes a *pactum* is abandoning out of generosity, as a present to his opponent, a case which is certain and sure.'

on the other hand, declares 'no contest', and in such a way as
openly or tacitly to acknowledge his guilt. But how important
was the distinction in practice? If high-status defendants rather
than low-status defendants tended to seek settlements because of
their greater financial resources and their greater fear of *infamia*,
one may wonder how many defendants were sufficiently 'generous'
(*liberalitate*) to confess their guilt, where loss of status was a certain consequence. It may be that Ulpian's definition of *pactum* is
over-simplified, and that *transactio* was not allowed to defendants
whose guilt was 'certain'. If this was so, it would not be surprising if the praetor's concept of 'certainty' (for surely the decision lay with the praetor) turned out to be both vague and
flexible; if his decision was made with reference not just to the
facts of the case, but also to the person of the defendant; if
praetorian discretion in this sphere as well as others was used to
protect the *dignitas* of defendants of rank.[1]

The Formula: 'condemnatio'

Once the parties were in court the plaintiff announced the
nature of his claim and requested a specific *formula* from the praetor. The proposed *formula* would then be debated by the parties
and finally given approval, whether in its original or an amended
form, by the praetor. After the appointment of a *iudex* who was
acceptable to both parties, the proceedings *in iure* came to an
end with the *litis contestatio*, or the final agreement of the parties
on the *formula*.

All *formulae* apart from those of 'prejudicial' actions, in which
the judge was required merely to settle a legal fact, contained
a *condemnatio*. This might specify a definite sum of money, or a
maximum, or no definite sum.[2]

A clause of the first kind occurred in *formulae* for *actiones
certae creditae pecuniae*, or actions for the recovery of a specific
sum of money.

[1] In matters of inheritance and legacy *transactio* was *allowed* even to the
poor, but only under the praetor's strict supervision. In contrast, a man *honesti-
oris loci* could do without a praetor, *Dig.* 2. 15. 8. 7–8; 11; 23.
[2] On the parts of the *formula* see Gaius, *Inst.* 4. 39 ff.; on *condemnatio*,
4. 48–52.

In contrast, *formulae petitoriae* such as were used in *actiones in rem*, where what was at issue was ownership of a thing, stated that the defendant, if condemned, was to pay the cash equivalent (unspecified) of the thing disputed, unless the defendant restored it to the plaintiff to the satisfaction of the judge: '(si) . . . neque ea res arbitrio iudicis Aulo Agerio restituetur.' It may be said in passing that the existence of this *clausula arbitraria*, with the opportunity it gave for avoiding *condemnatio pecuniaria* as well as *actiones in rem*, weakens the argument that the universal monetary penalty was instituted by the wealthy with the deliberate aim of oppressing the poor.[1]

The second kind of *condemnatio* is most relevant to the present discussion. It is found in *formulae* of certain *actiones in factum*, in which the *condemnatio* contained a clause such as the following:

> quantam pecuniam recuperatoribus [*or* iudici] bonum et aequum videbitur ob eam rem Numerium Negidium Aulo Agerio condemnari, tantam pecuniam dumtaxat sestertium [   ] milia.

The praetor, then, set a maximum figure for damages, and left the judge to determine the precise amount according to what was fair and equitable. It is important to decide how the sum which served as the maximum was arrived at. In investigating this we may take one of the more common of the actions under consideration, the *actio iniuriarum*.[2]

Gaius ends the third book of the *Institutes* with an account of the punishment of *iniuriae*. Excluding the case of *membrum ruptum*, where private vengeance in the form of *talio* was permitted, the *Twelve Tables* set a sum for *os fractum* (300 asses if a free man was injured, 150 if a slave) and for other injuries (25 asses, presumably

---

[1] The argument of Kelly (op. cit. 69–84) that monetary prestation weighed more heavily on the poor than any other kind of prestation would is unconvincing. Any time that damages have to be paid the poor are in a worse position than the rich, but this is so whether money or services or goods have to be rendered. On the *clausula arbitraria* see, for example, Buckland, op. cit. 659–61; cf. Kelly, op. cit. 81 n. 1.

[2] *Iniuriae* might involve physical injuries or offences against the good name of a person. Actions with *formulae* of a similar kind include *actiones rei uxoriae*, *funerariae*, *sepulchri violati*, and the action against the judge *qui litem suam facit*. See A. Berger, *Encycl. Dict. of Rom. Law* 346–7, with bibl. On (*bonum et*) *aequum* see, for example, M. Kaser, *Das römische Privatrecht* (1955), 172–3, 526, with bibl.; Berger, op. cit. 354–5.

for injury to a free man). These amounts, he explains, were once
thought substantial. As for his own time (*sed nunc alio iure utimur*),
it seems that the praetor estimated the compensation due for an
injury, and that the judge was not allowed to exceed that estimate
(nor, in the case of severe injury, *iniuria atrox*, was he expected
to reduce it).

However, Gaius does not explain the principles on which the
praetor based his calculations. The *Twelve Tables* (above) bore
a trace of a 'wergeld' system such as was operated in Western
Europe in the Late Roman period and the Early Middle Ages,
whereby differences between ranks were numerically calculated,
and compensation payments for injury were graded accordingly.
It is not out of the question that Romans of a later period maintained a system of this kind, if a flexible and informal one. A
text from the late third century lays down penalties for injury
which were applicable when that offence was tried *extra ordinem*.
Slaves were struck with whips, free men of low rank with rods,
and *ceteri*, that is, presumably, men of high status, were banished
for a time, or denied access to certain honours or exercise of
certain rights.[1] These penalties were, of course, imprecise. The
number of strokes of whip or rod, the time of banishment, and
so on, could be regulated according to the gravity of the injury
and the status of the injured party. A comparable text for injury
as tried by the formulary process (which knew only pecuniary
penalties) might have laid down for the same three social groups
three maximum and minimum levels of composition. No such
text survives, if it ever existed; Ulpian merely writes in his commentary on the edict that certain injuries are mild when inflicted
by free men, and serious when inflicted by slaves.[2]

Be that as it may, the above texts at least indicate that the
Romans had not abandoned the general principle that the gravity
of the penalty inflicted on the agent or accused should depend, to a

[1] *Dig.* 47. 10. 45: de iniuria nunc extra ordinem ex causa et persona statui
solet. et servi quidem flagellis caesi dominis restituuntur, liberi vero humilioris
quidem loci fustibus subiciuntur, ceteri autem vel exilio temporali vel inter-
dictione certae rei coercentur' (Hermogenianus).

[2] Ibid. 17. 3: 'quaedam iniuriae a liberis hominibus factae leves (non nullius
momenti) videntur, enimvero a servis graves sunt. crescit enim contumelia ex
persona eius qui contumeliam fecit.'

certain extent, on the social position of both the agent and the injured party. This point can be further documented from earlier texts, especially from passages which treat *iniuria atrox*.[1]

Cicero in *de inventione* discussed the case of a Roman knight who lost his hand in a scuffle with armed men and brought an action for injury.[2] The plea of the defence for an *exceptio* (*extra quam in reum capitis praeiudicium fiat*) was dismissed by the praetor, on the grounds that the crime was so serious (*atrox*) that the case had to be brought to trial as quickly as possible. Why was the injury judged to be *atrox*? Was it just because of the violence of the deed (*qualitas rei*), or also because of the status of the injured man (*condicio personae*)? Cicero gives no clue to the correct answer, and the matter may be disputed. At any rate, it is certain that in the early Empire the principle had won acceptance that the *persona* of the injured party might convert a mere action for injury into an action for 'grave' injury, *iniuria atrox*. The only point of issue is what the early jurists understood by *persona*.

When discussing *iniuria atrox*, Ulpian cited Labeo, the Augustan jurist:

atrocem autem iniuriam aut persona aut tempore aut re ipsa fieri Labeo ait.

Ulpian continued:

persona atrocior iniuria fit, ut cum magistratui, cum parenti patrono fiat.

[1] Non-legal literary texts have little to say on the subject of *iniuriae*. We have record of two cases tried *extra ordinem*, both involving verbal injury. Vespasian's *decretum*, 'non oportere maledici senatoribus, remaledici civile fasque esse' (Suet. *Vesp.* 9. 2), may seem to imply that any citizen, of whatever rank, could return a senator's abuse with impunity. But the context is the trial of an equestrian, not of a plebeian, and Vespasian may have had in mind only exchanges between equestrians and senators (who, in his eyes, were not far apart in rank, see p. 89). See previous note, *fin.* The summary treatment given Annia Rufilla (Tac. *Ann.* 3. 36, and see pp. 31–2) has already been discussed. We can perhaps say that she would have been punished less precipitately if she had been a lady of higher rank.

[2] Cic. *de inv.* 2. 20. 59–60. This is Cicero's earliest work, written about 84 B.C. when he was 22. It is a rhetorical essay setting down the conventional forms and distinctions which he had been taught. The case before us is probably a type case, and not a historical event. But, if anything, this makes the choice of an equestrian as the injured party more significant. On *atrocitas*, Quint. *Inst. Or.* 6. 1. 15.

It would appear, then, that Labeo did not think beyond the conventional social relationships of father/son and patron/freedman, and the standard political relationship of magistrate/private citizen.[1]

But a comparison of Labeo's statement as reported by Ulpian with that of Claudius Saturninus, a jurist of the second half of the second century, should arouse our suspicions. Of *persona*, Saturninus wrote:

> persona dupliciter spectatur, eius qui facit et eius qui passus est: aliter enim puniuntur ex isdem facinoribus servi quam liberi, et aliter, qui quid in dominum parentemve ausus est quam qui in extraneum, in magistratum vel in privatum.[2]

It will be seen that the examples chosen by Labeo and Saturninus are almost identical. Yet Saturninus, at any rate, might have furnished additional ones. He might, for instance, have followed Gaius, probably his older contemporary, who said that injury to a senator *ab humili persona* was *atrox*.[3]

Nor was Gaius' account as full as it might have been. This will be seen if it is set beside two parallel passages from post-classical works. The text of Gaius runs as follows:

> atrox autem iniuria aestimatur vel ex facto . . . vel ex loco . . . vel ex persona, veluti si magistratus iniuriam passus fuerit, vel senatori ab humili persona facta sit iniuria.

The author of the late third-century work *Paul's Sentences* wrote:

> atrox iniuria aestimatur aut loco aut tempore aut persona . . . persona, quotiens senatori vel equiti Romano decurionive vel alias

---

[1] *Dig.* 47. 10. 7. 8: 'Labeo says that an injury becomes grave because of the person injured, the time of the injury, and the nature of the injury itself. An injury is grave because of the person injured when, for instance, the victim is a magistrate, a parent, or a patron.' Cf. 1. 12. 1. 10 (*iniuriae* by a freedman to his patron; the penalties given were *castigatio* or *exilium temporarium* or *metallum*); 37. 14. 1. See also, for the criminal law, 48. 19. 28. 8: 'omnia admissa in patronum patronive filium patrem propinquum maritum uxorem ceterasque necessitudines gravius vindicanda sunt quam in extraneos.'

[2] Ibid. 16. 3: 'Person has a double reference, both to the agent and to the victim. Slaves and free men are punished differently for the same crimes; so are offenders against a master and a parent on the one hand and a stranger on the other, or against a magistrate on the one hand and a private citizen on the other.'

[3] Gaius, *Inst.* 3. 225: 'Injury is judged to be grave because of what is done, or the place where it is done, or the person to whom it is done . . . because of the person to whom it is done, as when a magistrate has suffered an injury, or a senator at the hands of a man of low status.'

spectatae auctoritatis viro: et si plebeius vel humili loco natus senatori vel equiti Romano, decurioni vel magistratui vel aedili vel iudici, quilibet horum, vel si his omnibus plebeius.[1]

Finally, we read in the *Institutes* of Justinian:

> atrox iniuria aestimatur . . . vel ex persona, veluti si magistratus iniuriam passus fuerit vel si senatori ab humili iniuria facta sit, aut parenti patronoque fiat a liberis vel libertis: aliter enim senatoris et parentis patronique, aliter extranei et humilis personae iniuria aestimatur.[2]

Justinian's account is quite derivative. His concept of *persona* is no advance on that of Gaius, who was probably his main source. Nor is his statement exhaustive. This is proved by the fact that he has ignored the more detailed treatment in *Paul's Sentences*. But even the list in that work is selective. This is shown by a rescript of Valerian and Gallienus, issued in A.D. 259. They judged injury to a provincial priest to be *atrox*

> cum esses in sacerdotio et dignitatis habitum et ornamenta proferres.[3]

But the author of *Paul's Sentences*, in choosing his examples, does seem to have considered social status as well as social and political functions.

Justinian did not completely omit consideration of social status, for he took over Gaius' example of an assault on a senator by a *humilis persona*. There is no reason for supposing that Gaius could not have produced as comprehensive an analysis as that of the author of *Paul's Sentences*. He might, for example, have included the provincial aristocracy. *Paul's Sentences* does not contain the first reference to provincials in the context of injury. Apart from

---

[1] *PS* 5. 4. 10: 'An injury is judged to be grave because of the place where it is done, the time when it is done, or the person to whom it is done . . . because of the person to whom it is done, when the victim is a senator or equestrian or decurion or someone else of conspicuous prestige; and if a senator or equestrian, a decurion, a magistrate, aedile, or judge has suffered at the hands of a plebeian or someone of humble birth.'

[2] *IJ* 4. 4. 9: 'An injury is judged to be grave . . . because of the person to whom it is done if, for example, a magistrate has suffered an injury, or a senator at the hands of a man of low status, or a parent or patron at the hands of children or freedmen: injury is judged differently depending upon whether it is done to a senator, parent, and patron, or to a stranger and man of low status.'

[3] *CJ* 9. 35. 4: 'since you were holding the office of priest and were displaying the dress and decorations which go with the office.'

the rescript of A.D. 259 referred to above, there is an edict of Caracalla, partly preserved on papyrus.[1] The edict does not go very far, but it at least shows that injury to decurions was viewed seriously. If the accused was another decurion, he would lose his rank and suffer *ignominia*.[2] Presumably a non-decurion would have suffered a harsher penalty. There is good evidence that in Gaius' day (the mid second century), not only senators (and equestrians), but also decurions as offenders, received milder punishments than ordinary citizens.[3] It would have been strange if, in addition, injury to a decurion by a plebeian had not been regarded as more serious than injury to a plebeian by a plebeian.

If Gaius was not seeking to be exhaustive (as is obvious in any case from his exclusion of some conventional examples), no more was Claudius Saturninus. The latter might just as well have spoken of injury to a member of the higher orders (by one of low status) as of injury to a master (by a slave), to a father (by a son), or to a magistrate (by a private citizen). This brings us back to Labeo. I would regard Cicero's illustration of the equestrian who lost his hand as an indication that Labeo's account need not have been confined to conventional examples. But leaving this aside, and even supposing that Labeo had not himself encountered cases of unequal treatment of men of unequal status condemned for *iniuriae* (an unlikely assumption), there is still a strong probability that Labeo's view of *persona* was not a limited one. If we can be guided by his definition of *iniuriae*, as pertaining *aut ad dignitatem aut ad infamiam*,[4] and by the attitude he took over the prosecution of members of the aristocracy for fraud,[5] it seems reasonable to hold that he might have admitted into his discussion of *iniuria atrox* (and simple injury) the notion of social status.[6]

---

[1] *P. Oxy.* 1406; cf. *CJ* 2. 11. 5 (A.D. 198), where the injured party was perhaps a decurion.

[2] See *Dig.* 47. 10. 40 (Severus/Macer): a penalty of *motio ordine* (expulsion from the order) for a decurion convicted of *atrox iniuria*.

[3] See, for example, *Dig.* 48. 22. 6. 2.   [4] *Dig.* 47. 10. 1. 2.

[5] *Dig.* 4. 3. 11. 1.

[6] Gellius, *Noct. Att.* 7. 14, on punishment 'for the preservation of prestige', is very relevant to the preceding discussion. Gellius in effect gives a justification for differential punishment for injury. See pp. 1 ff.

Execution of judgement

Execution of judgement followed the defendant's condemnation in an *actio iudicati*.[1] Alternatively, if the candidate did not consent to co-operate in the *actio iudicati*, the praetor might order *missio in possessionem* as a preliminary to *venditio bonorum*.[2]

The weaker plaintiff was up against the same problems in executing judgement as he was in carrying out summons, that is, the likelihood of physical resistance to summons or refusal to obey summons (preparatory, on this occasion, to the *actio iudicati*), and physical resistance to *missio*. It may be that on isolated occasions praetors in Rome, or governors in the provinces, gave assistance, in the form of an armed troop, to successful plaintiffs for the execution of judgement. However, aid of this kind was probably granted only to influential individuals or their agents as a personal favour, and was not made available to plaintiffs of lesser significance.[3] The weaker plaintiff's problems were eased as courts and tribunals became available which settled claims *extra ordinem* and he was relieved of the burden of execution as well as of summons. There is, to my knowledge, no direct evidence that the praetor was ever instructed to intervene in strength in support of a plaintiff who had won a civil suit by the formulary process.[4]

[1] On execution and the *actio iudicati* see, e.g., Buckland, op. cit. 642 ff. If the defendant disputed the validity of the judgement, *litis contestatio* and another trial would follow. This might gain the defendant additional time— but condemnation carried double damages.

[2] Execution *in personam* (involving private imprisonment still, but probably no longer sale or death) persisted into the Empire (see *lex Urs.* 61; Gellius 20. 1. 51; E. Woess, *ZSS* 43 (1922), 485 ff.), but was presumably not within the capability of a weaker plaintiff whose stronger opponent was avoiding the *actio iudicati*. Hence it is disregarded here.

[3] The M. Scaptius who secured a *praefectura* for debt collection from Appius, governor of Cilicia and Cyprus, and was refused one by the next governor, Cicero, was an agent of Brutus. Cic. *ad Att.* 5. 21. 10.

[4] Kelly (op. cit. 29) holds that such instructions were issued first by Antoninus Pius in a rescript to the magistrates of Rome: 'a divo Pio rescriptum est magistratibus populi Romani, ut iudicum a se datorum vel arbitrorum sententiam exsequantur hi qui eos dederunt' (*Dig.* 42. 1. 15 praef.). But the rescript refers to civil disputes settled by *cognitio* by judges appointed (*datus*) by magistrates, and especially by the consuls. The citation comes, in fact, from Ulpian's *de officio consulis*. The other texts cited by Kelly seem no more relevant to execution under the formulary process.

It is proper to ask whether the difficulties in the way of execution were in fact insuperable before the Emperors introduced an alternative procedure in civil law. As with summons, so with execution, the weaker plaintiff's position might in reality have been less unfavourable than appearances would suggest. It is unlikely that more than a handful of desperate men were able to resist execution successfully and were prepared to accept the probable consequences of their actions, exclusion from public affairs, community life, and, of course, the law courts.

It remains a fact that the law itself provided no mechanism for redressing the balance between two parties of unequal strength. The praetor played no active part in enforcing either the judgement of a court or his own edicts. If a stubborn defendant was brought to accept the judgement of a court, this was achieved by the combination of social pressures and the intervention of such private supporters as the plaintiff was fortunate enough to possess. It is also significant, though in no way remarkable, that the praetor, as a representative of the ruling oligarchy, did nothing to eradicate the undoubted structural weaknesses of the formulary system. It remained for the disguised monarchy, whose intolerance of disorder and extra-legal or illegal activity was at least as strong as its aristocratic prejudices, to supply in the *cognitio* procedure what was at least a partial remedy.

Conclusion

There is little recognition in the legal sources of the fact that the praetor had regard for status distinctions in his administration of the civil law. It stands to reason that only those distinctions which were overtly acknowledged by the legal authorities are actually demonstrable. Less formal distinctions, that is, distinctions which were made, as far as we know, without official acknowledgement but at the praetor's discretion, can be inferred from these, although naturally their prevalence cannot be accurately assessed. Finally, examples were found of *de facto* inequality; in such cases, advantages fell to those having the capacity to exploit inequitable aspects of the formulary system which successive praetors had allowed to stand.

No lengthy or sophisticated explanation is required of the praetor's preferential treatment of members of the higher orders. He had the opportunity to discriminate against the weaker party as the controller of the sanctions behind *in ius vocatio* and execution, as the granter or withholder of actions, and as the magistrate who controlled the composition of the *formula* for the instruction of the judge. And he shared the feelings and prejudices of his rank.

8

THE JUDGE

I T could be said of the Roman legal system that its pervasion by improper influences made equality before the law unattainable.[1] This section is designed to show that the judicial system at its best was still far from equitable, because it was permeated by influences which, in Roman eyes, were perfectly proper.

The ground covered will be the actual judicial proceedings, especially the hearing of the parties and their advocates and witnesses, and the impact of these persons on the judge.[2] In a subsection the torture of witnesses will be discussed.

Proper and improper influences

Cicero recognized three forces which had an adverse effect on the working of the law: *gratia, potentia, pecunia.*

quod enim est ius civile? quod neque inflecti gratia neque perfringi potentia neque adulterari pecunia possit.[3]

Pecunia stands for judicial bribery, which of course was never accorded social approval. On the other hand, the possession of wealth, *facultates*,[4] as distinct from its use for corrupt purposes, was a definite advantage in a law court, and this fact did win both official acceptance and public recognition. An example from the realm of private law and the rules of guardianship will illustrate this point. The *praetor tutelaris* might or might not require a guardian to present a *satisdatio*, security. In Ulpian's view no *satisdatio* was necessary for a guardian having *honestas*, respectability.

---

[1] This is Kelly's theme (op. cit. 31 ff.).

[2] The discussion is relevant to proceedings in either civil or criminal courts.

[3] Cic. *pro Caec.* 73 (quoted Kelly, op. cit. 33): 'What is the civil law? That which can be neither perverted by favour nor violated by influence nor falsified by money.'

[4] *Pecunia* may refer simply to the possession of money (Cic. *de inv.* 2. 59. 177), but another term is adopted here to avoid ambiguity.

Apparently the owner of *substantia modica*, some property, had this quality: 'But it is better for the praetor to decide by judicial investigation whether or not a patron and his sons ought to give security; so that, if he is respectable, he should be excused security, and especially if he has some property, while if he is common and less respectable, it should be said that there is reason for payment of security. Thus security is called for either by reason of the kind of guardianship, or its cause, or the character of the guardian.'[1] On the other hand, Ulpian was ready to affirm that poverty in a guardian was not sufficient cause for his dismissal. It must have been a common assumption of judges that a poor man's character was adversely affected by his economic position.[2]

Potentia (power) is defined by Cicero in cold-blooded but non-violent terms: 'Power is the possession of resources sufficient for preserving one's own interests and weakening those of another.'[3] *Potentia* may be paired with *auctoritas* (prestige). The *potentior* or *vir potens* threatens force; the *vir spectatae auctoritatis* is impressive with moral power. Quintilian wrote of the embarrassment caused to advocates by the presence of *personae potentes*, who had to be chastised verbally if the case was to be won.[4] Tiberius' attempt to render ineffective the prayers of the powerful (*potentium preces*) won from Tacitus ambiguous praise: 'Truth was being served, but freedom undermined.'[5] Tacitus' interest, if not passion, was the conflict of *principatus* and *libertas*. The incompatibility of *potentia* and *veritas* (or *aequitas*) was for him of less moment.

Pliny praised his friend Calestrius Tiro for his success, as governor, in honouring *dignitas* without displaying *gratia*.[6] *Gra-*

---

[1] *Dig.* 26. 4. 5. 1.

[2] See *Dig.* 26. 10. 8: 'suspectum tutorem eum putamus, qui *moribus talis* est, ut suspectus sit; enimvero tutor quamvis pauper est, fidelis tamen et diligens, removendus non est quasi suspectus.' In Cic. *de inv.* 2. 59. 177 wealth is one of the *extraneae virtutes*. Cf. *Auct. ad Herenn.* 1. 5. 8; 3. 6. 10. See also pp. 232–3.

[3] 'potentia est ad sua conservanda et alterius adtenuanda idonearum rerum facultas.' Cic. *de inv.* 2. 56. 169. *Potentia* is soon afterwards presented as one of the *extraneae virtutes* (ibid. 2. 59. 177).

[4] Quint. *Inst. Or.* 9. 2. 68.

[5] Tac. *Ann.* 1. 75: 'set dum veritati consulitur, libertas corrumpebatur.' The freedom is presumably that of the influential to apply pressure, and that of judges to submit to that pressure.

[6] Pliny, *Ep.* 9. 5 (quoted pp. 77–8).

tia is closely related to *potentia*. Indeed the passage in Suetonius' *Life* which runs parallel to the account in Tacitus' *Annals* of Tiberius' interference in trials identifies the evil that Tiberius was combating as *gratia*.[1] *Gratia* may be defined as 'excessive favour'.[2] In the judicial context, it is the favourable response in a judge or jury to *potentia*, to the pressure applied by men of influence. The counterpart of *gratia* (to pursue the same example) is the good impression made on the judge or jury by the moral qualities and elevated social position of the defendant. The response is one of *benevolentia* or *respectus dignitatis* (or *reverentia honoris*). This might affect the character of the penalty or the harshness of the verdict in a trial conducted *extra ordinem*, or even the nature of the verdict itself in any kind of trial.

Arguments from the *persona* of the accused were regularly used at any stage of the trial, and indeed might be employed before the trial itself. There is plenty of evidence that Cicero the politician and patron used his influence well before the trial stage on behalf of friends and clients who found themselves involved in legal disputes.[3] Cicero the rhetorician provided a stock speech for the use of the defendant whose case was slipping away, and whose only hope of saving the day was to lodge a plea for pardon. He could plead his good record and the services (*beneficia*) performed by his ancestors:

Afterwards, if there is an opportunity, he will demonstrate that he is either of the same blood as great men and leaders, or that his family have been their friends from early times. He will show how deep is his own good will, how noble the breeding and how high the rank of those who want to see him safe, and that he possesses all the other things which are associated with personal honour and distinction. His plea will be forceful, but not arrogant.[4]

[1] Suet. *Tib.* 33.

[2] Of course *gratia* does not always have a pejorative sense. See, for example, Cic. *ad Att.* 3. 10. 2; 11. 2; 4. 1. 3; etc. (non-judicial contexts).

[3] Cic. *ad fam.* 13. 26; cf. 28A (a governor at Cicero's request defends the interests of a senator in contests over property of which he is the heir. The property was originally fraudulently appropriated); 54 (prevention of a prosecution); etc. Such requests normally include a face-saving clause such as 'sicuti tua fides et meus pudor postulat' (ibid. 58). See also Fronto, *ad am.* 1. 1 (ed. van den Hout, p. 164); and G. E. M. de Ste Croix, art. cit. (p. 188 n. 3), 42 ff.

[4] Cic. *de inv.* 2. 35. 107. In the opposing speech nothing is said against the argument from the *persona*.

The influence that the *personae* of the parties might have on the judge is nowhere more vividly revealed than in a passage of Aulus Gellius describing his own experience as a private judge in a money dispute.[1] Gellius found that he was in sympathy with one party and hostile to the other. The basis of the contrast between the two men was character, although Gellius also had in mind their social and economic situations.[2] In any case, character, or way of life, in the Roman view, was intimately connected with social position: *boni mores*, good character, were nothing less than the virtues of the higher orders.[3]

Gellius frankly admitted that the arguments of the claimant were thin, unsubstantiated as they were by documentary evidence of any sort, or by witnesses.[4] But he was a fine and upright man, while his opponent was a scoundrel.[5] The character contrast between the two men must have been brought up in court, for at one point the defendant protested, reasonably enough (in our eyes), that the matter was quite irrelevant. 'The dispute', he maintained, 'is over money and before a private judge, not over morals and before censors.'[6] The *consilium* of jurisconsults recommended judgement for the defendant, but Gellius rejected their advice and ordered an adjournment: 'For when I thought about the two men, the absolute trustworthiness of the one and the sheer wickedness of the other, his life so utterly foul and iniquitous, nothing could persuade me to acquit.'[7] Gellius then went to consult the

---

[1] Gellius, *Noct. Att.* 14. 2.

[2] Yet see n. 5 below, and p. 211 n. 1.

[3] See Quintilian's comment (*Inst. Or.* 5. 10. 24) to the effect that there is sometimes a causal connection between birth (*genus*) and manner of life ('et nonnumquam ad honeste turpiterque vivendum inde causae fluunt'). Cf. *Dig.* 47. 2. 52. 21, where *honestus vir* is synonymous with *vir locuples*. In general, it is interesting that a word with a primarily moral meaning, *honestus*, should have been chosen to describe men of high social status, *honestiores*. For a fuller discussion of this question see pp. 223; 231 ff.

[4] § 4: 'argumentis admodum exilibus nitebatur.'

[5] Gellius also calls the claimant *non bonae rei*, which should be translated 'not possessed of good fortune'. See § 6.

[6] § 8: 'rem enim de petenda pecunia apud iudicem privatum agi, non apud censores de moribus.'

[7] § 10: 'sed enim ego homines cum considerabam, alterum fidei, alterum probri plenum spurcissimaeque vitae ac defamatissimae, nequaquam adduci potui ad absolvendum.' Notice the emphasis on *fides*, a high-status virtue; cf. p. 227 below.

sophist Favorinus. Favorinus cited words of Marcus Cato, spoken as an advocate in a trial. Cato had said that if the cause was evenly balanced, the judge should be asked to decide 'which of the two parties was the better man'.[1] The decision was to be in favour of the defendant only if there was nothing to choose between the two men. This, Cato added, was not a private opinion of his own, but a traditional Roman attitude.[2]

One might have thought, as Favorinus did, that Gellius' course was now clear. But, to his credit, Gellius did not declare for the claimant. He preferred to back out of the case, with an oath that the matter 'was not clear to him' (*mihi non liquere*), pleading that his years were few and his merit slight.

Cato had held that the issue should hang on the characters of the two parties only if there were no witnesses. There were none in Gellius' case.[3] Where witnesses were available, their characters and social position were just as relevant as the quality of their evidence.

A list of those who could not act as witnesses (*intestabiles*) was included in the Julian law on violence, and is preserved in excerpts from both Ulpian and Callistratus.[4] But there were some doubtful categories which were not specifically mentioned in this law or other laws. Papinian discussed the case of the man convicted of *calumnia* in a *iudicium publicum*. His comment was that judges should show *religio* (scrupulousness) in weighing the testimony of someone with this background, and, for that matter, in weighing the testimony of any witness: 'But what is omitted by the laws will not be omitted by scrupulous judges [*religione iudicantium*], whose duty it is to examine the reliability [*fidem*] even of the evidence given by a man of honest exterior'.[5] The key word is *fides*, reliability or trustworthiness. 'The trustworthiness of

---

[1] § 21: 'uter ex his vir melior esset'. *Melior* does not have a narrow moral reference.
[2] § 21: 'ita esse a maioribus traditum observatumque ait'.
[3] § 22.
[4] *Coll.* 9. 2 (Ulp.); *Dig.* 22. 5. 3. 5; (Call.); cf. ibid. 20 (Ven. Sat.); ibid. 21. 2; 1 praef. (Arc. Char.); and see Buckland, op. cit. 92.
[5] *Dig.* 22. 5. 13 (Pap.): 'verumtamen quod legibus omissum est, non omittetur religione iudicantium ad quorum officium pertinet eius quoque testimonii fidem, quod integrae frontis homo dixerit, perpendere.'

witnesses should be carefully scrutinized', wrote Callistratus,[1] and the following sentences indicate the factors which in his mind made for trustworthiness: 'It is especially important to examine the status of each man, to see whether he is a decurion or a commoner; to ask whether his life is virtuous or marred by vice, whether he is rich or poor (for poverty might imply that he is out for gain), and whether he is personally hostile to the man against whom he is witnessing, or friendly to the man whose cause he is advocating . . .'

The investigation of a witness, then, did not aim at establishing his interest or lack of interest in the trial. His character, his position in society, and his economic condition were all thought to have a bearing on the degree to which he could be trusted.[2]

Callistratus went on to quote a series of rescripts of Hadrian which provided the authority for his statements. Hadrian would not accept written *testimonia*, but insisted on interrogating witnesses. If none were sent to him, he would remit the whole case to the relevant governor (if the suit involved provincials), for him to inquire into the *fides* of the witnesses. The theme of the other rescripts is that *dignitas*, *existimatio*, and *auctoritas* in a witness (three virtues of the higher orders) stood him in good stead.[3]

Thus, *auctoritas* in accusers,[4] defendants, and witnesses might influence the decision of the judge. Specifically, he might condemn or acquit or avoid a verdict unjustly; or, in cases where the *formula* instructed him to fix damages in conformity with standards

---

[1] *Dig.* 22. 5. 3 praef.

[2] Courts of law in modern democratic societies would, theoretically, regard these last factors as extraneous (unless a previous conviction for perjury should bring the defendant's character into consideration).

[3] *Dig.* 22. 5. 3. 3; cf. 3. 4. Ibid. 3. 1; ibid. 3. 2 (*dignitas*); ibid. 3. 1 (*existimatio*); ibid. 3. 2; 3. 4 (*auctoritas*). All references are to Hadrianic rescripts. It should be stressed that as long as there had been law courts (and rhetorical schools) attention had been drawn to the *persona* of the witness. See, e.g., *Auct. ad Herenn.* 2. 6. 9: 'a testibus dicemus secundum auctoritatem et vitam testium et constantiam testimoniorum.' Cf. Quint. *Inst. Or.* 5. 7. 24; see J. Ph. Lévy, *Studi in onore di Biondo Biondi* (1965), ii. 29 ff.

[4] *Dig.* 48. 2. 16 (Ulp.): 'si plures existant, qui eum in publicis iudiciis accusare colunt, iudex eligere debet eum qui accuset, causa scilicet cognita aestimatis accusatorum personis vel de dignitate, vel ex eo quod interest, vel aetate vel moribus vel alia iusta de causa.' Clearly a whole class of people might be overlooked on these criteria, quite apart from those who did not possess the *ius accusandi*; see *Coll.* 4. 4.

of justice and equity (*bonum et aequum*),[1] he might decide upon a greater or lesser sum in accordance with the prestige of the injured party, and the gap between his prestige and the prestige of the agent. It was considered perfectly proper that verdicts should be affected in this way: justice and equity were thought thereby to have been achieved rather than compromised. In general, it caused the Romans no concern that there was a divergence between the law as it was written and the law as it was applied. Equity was not the same as the letter of the law; it was on a different, higher plane. The remark of Papinian, made in the context of a discussion on witnesses, can be given a general application: the omissions of the laws were rectified by the directives of Emperors, the interpretations of jurists—and the scrupulousness of judges (*religio iudicantium*).[2]

The torture of witnesses

In some criminal trials the torture of witnesses was permitted, but, in theory, free men were exempt. In Athens and Rhodes, according to Cicero, not only free men, but also citizens, were tortured.[3] So far was this from being the case in Rome that it was a common manœuvre to manumit one's slaves so that they might avoid torture.[4] The *legis lator* of the Lex Aelia Sentia made it his business to close this loophole in the law;[5] but he could not have been entirely successful, because Pius returned to the matter in a rescript.[6]

In line with the principle established under the Republic, when torture was applied to witnesses in the Julio-Claudian

[1] See p. 198.
[2] *Dig.* 22. 5. 13 (quoted p. 211 n. 5). On equity and the law see Cic. *de inv.* 2. 46. 136; cf. 2. 45. 131: the place of equity is in an argument 'ex ingenio eius qui contra legem fecerit, non ex lege'.
[3] Cic. *part. or.* 118. On torture see Mommsen, *Straf.* 405 ff.; Ehrhardt, *RE* 6A (1937), 1775-94, s.v. *tormenta*.
[4] Cic. *pro Cael.* 68; *pro Mil.* 57.
[5] *Dig.* 40. 9. 12 praef. (Ulp.). When evidence from a slave was admitted, it was taken normally by torture (*Dig.* 48. 18. 9 praef.; 20; *CJ* 3. 32. 10 (A.D. 290); Mommsen, op. cit. 412 ff.; Buckland, *Roman Law of Slavery* (1908), 87). It was probably inadmissible otherwise (*Dig.* 48. 18. 1. 16).
[6] *Dig.* 48. 18. 1. 13. See also *PS* 5. 16. 9; *CJ* 9. 41. 10 (A.D. 290). Inquiry *super statu ingenuitatis* of a possible witness still took place under Diocletian and Maximian. See *CJ* 9. 41. 9 (A.D. 290); cf. *Dig.* 48. 18. 12 (Hadr./Ulp.); 48. 5. 28. 5.

period, the witnesses were slaves.[1] Augustus countenanced the
use of torture on slaves in cases of gravity when there seemed no
other way of arriving at the truth: 'I consider that tortures should
not always be resorted to, in respect of every case and person.
When the more serious and capital crimes cannot be examined
and investigated otherwise than by the torture of slaves, I believe
torture is the most effective way of discovering the truth, and
resolve that it should be used.'[2] But there was one practical exception to the rule that only slaves were tortured—*maiestas*. The
reason was obvious enough: the Emperor's life might be in danger.
In time, it became a rule that anyone involved in a treason trial
might be tortured. Arcadius Charisius wrote in the late third or
early fourth century: 'But when the charge is treason, which concerns the lives of Emperors, all without exception are tortured,
if they are called to give evidence, and when the case requires it.'[3]
The torture of free men is well enough documented, but in some
cases it is not clear whether any of the men involved were witnesses.
For example, Dio[4] says that after Germanicus' death in A.D. 20,
Tiberius began to torture free men and citizens, as well as slaves,
in treason trials. No examples are given. Again, Macro is said to
have employed torture as praetorian prefect, perhaps mainly in
the interrogation of suspects.[5] Under Nero a freedman testified,
when tortured, against his patron, an ex-praetor, suspected of
complicity in the Pisonian conspiracy.[6] An equestrian, Antonius
Natalis, and a senator, Flavius Scaevinus, revealed the names of
the leaders of that plot against Nero's life.[7] Nero's predecessor,
Claudius, had sworn to torture no free man,[8] but he too considered
that conspirators were an exception.[9]

At the end of the century, the position was no different: slaves

---

[1] Tac. *Ann.* 2. 30; 3. 14; 3. 22; 3. 67; etc. The status of the witnesses is not always reported; e.g. ibid. 1. 74 (Granius Marcellus). On the condition of such slaves see *Dig.* 48. 5. 28. 11–14.

[2] *Dig.* 48. 18. 8 praef.

[3] *Dig.* 48. 18. 10. 1 (Arc. Char.); cf. *PS* 5. 29. 2; *CTh* 9. 5. 1 = *CJ* 9. 8. 3 (A.D. 314).

[4] Dio 57. 19. 2.   [5] Ibid. 58. 21. 3; 24. 2; 27. 2.

[6] Tac. *Ann.* 16. 20.   [7] Ibid. 15. 56.

[8] Dio 60. 15. 6.

[9] Ibid. 60. 31. 5 (Silius/Messallina affair): Tac. *Ann.* 11. 22 (Cn. Nonius, an equestrian).

alone might be tortured.[1] It was as if Claudius' oath stood, for every successive Emperor. Hadrian again ruled out torture of the free.[2] He shared Augustus' scepticism about the *fides* of a witness who had been examined under torture.[3] Again, Hadrian rejected the use of the testimony of slaves against their masters.[4] This was no new departure—there was an old *senatusconsultum* on the subject.[5] A problem arose if slaves were tortured as 'accomplices' and in the process gave information which damned their masters. Trajan left the matter to the judge's discretion: 'he should rule as the case demands.'[6] Ulpian thought this rule worked to the disadvantage of the master, and observed that subsequent constitutions had improved his position. One was issued by Hadrian.[7]

Pius' position was virtually identical with Hadrian's at every point. Torture was not to be used on the free man; if a slave had been freed specifically to enable him to escape torture, torture could be applied to him.[8] Pius also discouraged the hasty use of torture.[9] As for the torture of a slave against his master, on this subject Pius reiterated Hadrian's words.[10]

[1] From the Flavian period there is nothing to record apart from the torture of witnesses during the trial of an ex-praetor who was involved in the disgrace of Cornelia, the chief Vestal Virgin (Suet. *Dom.* 8. 4).

[2] *Dig.* 48. 18. 12 (indirect).

[3] See *Dig.* 48. 18. 1 praef.–2; ibid. 1. 4 (Marcus and Verus). Other evidence was needed before notice was taken of the testimony of a slave (*Dig.* 48. 18. 18. 3; *CJ* 9. 41. 8; *PS* 5. 14. 4). Note the sarcasm of Cicero when he speaks of the 'value' of torturing slaves (*pro Mil.* 60; but cf. *Deiot.* 3). The whole subject is treated at length by Ulpian (*Dig.* 48. 18. 1. 23–7); see also Val. Max. 8. 4; *Auct. ad Herenn.* 2. 7. 10 (arguments for and against); Quintilian (*Inst. Or.* 5. 4. 1) commented briefly that the speeches *veterum ac novorum* were full of the topic.

[4] *Dig.* 48. 18. 1. 5; cf. ibid. 9. 1; 17. 2; 1. 12. 1. 8; 29. 5. 6. 1; *CJ* 4. 20. 8 (A.D. 294); *PS* 1. 12. 3; 5. 13. 3; 5. 16. 4 = *Dig.* 48. 18. 5; 5. 16. 5.

[5] Tac. *Ann.* 2. 30. There were exceptions, such as incest (Cic. *part. or.* 118; *pro Mil.* 59; *de n.d.* 3. 30. 74; Val. Max. 6. 8. 1; Ascon. *in Mil.* p. 46; Suet. *Dom.* 8. 4; *Dig.* 48. 18. 4–5), treason (Cic. *part. or.* 118; see R. S. Rogers, *TAPA* 64 (1933), 18 ff., for references from Tac. *Ann.*; *Dig.* 48. 4. 7. 2; 48. 18. 10. 1; *CJ* 9. 41. 1 (A.D. 196); 9. 8. 6. 1; *PS* 5. 13. 3), adultery (from the time of Marcus: *Dig.* 48. 18. 17 praef.; cf. *CJ* 9. 41. 1; *Dig.* 40. 9. 12. 1–2; 48. 5. 28. 6; ibid. 28. 8–13; 48. 18. 5; Tac. *Ann.* 14. 60), *fraudatus census* (*CJ* 9. 41. 1), *falsum testimonium* (*Dig.* 48. 18. 6. 1), forgery of coins (*Dig.* 5. 1. 53), etc.

[6] *Dig.* 48. 18. 1. 19: 'prout causa exegerit, ita pronuntiare eum debere.'

[7] Ibid. 1. 5; cf. ibid. 1. 22.   [8] Ibid. 1. 13.

[9] *Dig.* 29. 5. 1. 5. This was not intended as a general comment, but concerned specifically the torture of '(is) cui fideicommissa libertas pure debetur'.

[10] *Dig.* 48. 18. 1. 5.

But there are signs that torture was becoming more common. The torture of slaves in pecuniary cases was introduced. Pius issued the ruling: 'Torture may be applied to slaves in a pecuniary case if the truth cannot otherwise be discovered.'[1] Another text suggests that free men were sometimes tortured. The authority is Callistratus, the Severan lawyer: 'It is not right to torture a free man when his evidence does not waver.'[2] The implication is, that torture was applied, whether the witness's testimony wavered or not. Finally, by the turn of the fourth century or soon after, it was regular for decurions to be tortured for *falsum*, and all alike to be tortured for magic as well as treason.[3] This seems to have been a post-classical extension. In the period of the classical lawyers, except in the case of treason, *honestiores* seem to have been exempt from torture.

Conclusion: the social status of defendants

Given the obstacles confronting a plaintiff who lacked power and rank in his attempt to bring to justice an opponent of higher standing, it is reasonable to ask whether such suits ever occurred.[4]

In a well-known case in the elder Seneca's *Controversiae*, a rich man mocks a poor man for being unwilling to prosecute him for the murder of his father. He is made to say: 'Why don't you accuse me, why don't you take me to court?' It seems that the poor man is not unable to take the rich man before a magistrate, but that, even if he should do so, the rich man would have no cause for anxiety: 'This rich man was powerful and influential, as not even he denies, and thought he never had anything to fear, even as a defendant . . .' The source of the poor man's frustration (he is made to exclaim: 'Am I, a poor man, to accuse a rich man?')

---

[1] 'posse de servis haberi quaestionem in pecuniaria causa, si aliter veritas inveniri non possit' (*Dig.* 48. 18. 9 praef.). This was confirmed by Severus. Augustus had restricted the use of torture to *capitalia et atrociora maleficia*. See *Dig.* 48. 18. 8 praef. (A.D. 8). In a pecuniary case the issue was payment of a sum of money, e.g. as fine or damages.

[2] 'ex libero homine pro testimonio non vacillante quaestionem haberi non oportet' (ibid. 15 praef.).

[3] See pp. 142–3.

[4] Kelly (op. cit. 62 ff.) has suggested that the average lawsuit was either between equals or was brought by a plaintiff of superior social status and power against an inferior.

was not that he could never effect a summons, but that he could
not hope to secure a conviction. It turns out that his father had
been murdered for having had the effrontery to engage the rich
man in litigation. The rich man all but exclaimed: 'What would
I not be ready to do to you if you impeached me, I who saw to the
death of a man who merely engaged in litigation with me?'[1]

To judge from this story, the possibility of suits brought by men
of comparatively humble origin and position against men of
rank cannot be ruled out; but they are unlikely to have been a
frequent occurrence. This was not because of the existence of
powerful, intractable defendants who, caring little for their public
reputation, refused to submit to trial. This class was probably
small, for three reasons. First, the desire even of the strong to
be respected in society, and to stay on the right side of the magistrates and the law, should not be underestimated. Second, the
threat of penalties and disabilities, and later, of criminal prosecution, might have succeeded where social pressures failed in
persuading a potential resister of the wisdom of going to law.
Third, as the story in Seneca demonstrates, a strong defendant
might consent to face praetor and judge, in the knowledge that he
stood a good chance of winning his case against an enemy of lower
status, because of the partiality of the courts. Moreover, and this
is the other side, if it is conceivable that a powerful defendant was
ready to go to law because he was confident of his prospects, it is
much more likely that a man of low rank who had suffered at his
hands would be discouraged from seeking redress by litigation,
because he knew, or suspected (from his own previous experiences
or from those of acquaintances), that a court would decide against
him. Another factor which might discourage him was the threat of
retaliation from the potential defendant, who might, in extreme
cases, do him physical harm, and, in any event, was likely to be in
a position to damage his interests. In addition, he was unlikely

---

[1] Sen. *Contr.* 10. 1 (30); Kelly, op. cit. 49–50; Daube, art. cit. 433 ff. *Controversiae* cannot be totally disregarded as evidence for contemporary practices,
although they have to be approached with circumspection. They would lose
their point if they strayed too far from the possible and credible. A safer historical source perhaps is Cicero's *Letters*. Provincials were not averse to bringing
suits against Romans of various ranks, including senators, as Cicero well knew.
See *ad fam.* 13. 26, espec. § 3; cf. 28a; 55; 69; etc.

to make any showing in front of a court without legal assistance and representation. We should like to know how easy it was for men of low rank to find jurisconsults, or jurisconsults of any quality, who were prepared to take on their cases. These were men of high social rank, who drew their clientele from their peers through informal social contacts, and were conversant chiefly with the legal problems normally faced by the higher orders. Nor should the possibility be overlooked that ignorance of the law might hold back a man of low status from consulting jurisprudents, or, for that matter, from attempting to sue at all. Doubtless there were some patrons who were ready to provide their clients with most of what they lacked, contacts, money, and knowledge. But it may be conjectured that, in general, patrons were most faithful to those of their clients who were well placed to offer worthwhile reciprocal services, and that meant clients whose social and economic station was not far below their own. Finally, if a would-be plaintiff did try to initiate legal proceedings, it was quite possible that the praetor would reject his application for a suit, especially if the particular action requested put a defendant's status in jeopardy.

To sum up, the impeachment of defendants of high status by plaintiffs of low status through the formulary system was impeded, first, by the aristocratic bias of both praetor and judge, and second, by the *de facto* incapacity of the lower orders, through insufficient education, resources, and initiative, to use the legal system. The weaker plaintiff may have gained in some respects when he was able to approach with his claim a magistrate or official who adjudicated *extra ordinem*. At least summons and execution would then cease to be a problem for him, as they were effected by the state. On the other hand, the state apparatus for punishing breaches of the law was not self-initiating, and there clearly could be no substantial improvement in the condition of the lower orders while they were held back, by their own disabilities, from initiating action at law. Further, there was no assurance that a judge who investigated by *cognitio*, and who was appointed by the state, would give the weaker plaintiff a fairer hearing than a private judge appointed by the praetor with the consent of both parties.

PART IV

THE *HONESTIORES*

9

THE VOCABULARY OF PRIVILEGE

THE jurists of the classical period of Roman law presented Imperial society as divided into two main groups, of higher and lower status.[1]. This is commonly referred to as the *honestiores/humiliores* distinction.

This particular formula is in fact only one of several that occur in the sources. It is by far the most popular one in *Paul's Sentences*, but that is a late third-century work.[2] In texts from the Severan period or before there is no single occurrence of the terms *honestiores* and *humiliores* in combination.[3] Papinian, reporting a rescript of Pius, used *honestior* and *humilioris loci*, a close approximation.[4] Again, Marcianus, writing of the Cornelian law *de sicariis et veneficiis*, contrasted the penalty for *honestiore loco positi* or *altiores* with that for *humiliores*.[5] It is normal for *honestiores* or *humiliores* to be balanced by another phrase altogether; or a cognate adjective is found qualifying a noun,[6] sometimes in a participial construction,[7] sometimes in a full clause.[8]

When lawyers dealt in general terms with the subject of legal discrimination, they preferred to say that consideration was given, or should be given, to the *persona*—in particular to the *persona* of

---

[1] Other divisions are also given recognition, e.g. the division between free men and slaves. See pp. 260–1.

[2] Refs. in Cardascia, art. cit. 324 n. 1 (*honestiores*); 325 n. 9 (*humiliores*). See G. G. Archi (and others), *Pauli Sententiarum fragmentum Leidense* (1956), 57 (R. Marichal), for the date.

[3] Cardascia, art. cit. 324, thinks of *Paul's Sentences* as Severan in date.

[4] *Dig.* 48. 5. 39. 8. Note the singular *honestior* (cf. 47. 18. 1. 2), and the use of a noun with *humilis* (cf. Gai. *Inst.* 3. 225; *Dig.* 48. 19. 28. 11). See also *Dig.* 47. 9. 12 and 47. 12. 11 = *PS* 5. 19A (both *humilior*); 2. 15. 8. 23; 48. 8. 3. 5; 48. 13. 7 (all *honestior*). For the superlative, again with a noun, *Coll.* 12. 5. 1 (*humillimus*). For *humilis* standing alone see *Dig.* 4. 3. 11. 1.

[5] *Dig.* 48. 8. 3. 5.   [6] See n. 4 above.

[7] *Dig.* 48. 8. 1. 5 (*humiliore loco positum*); Pliny, *Ep.* 8. 6. 16 (*honesto loco nati*).

[8] *Dig.* 47. 14. 1. 3 = *Coll.* 11. 8. 3 (*qui honestiore loco nati sunt*); cf. *Dig.* 48. 13. 7 (*si h. l. natus sit*).

the accused. Penalties for crimes, for example, were awarded in part *pro persona*.[1] Sometimes the word *persona* is understood:[2] *pro dignitate* is shorthand for *pro dignitate personae*, *pro condicione* for *pro condicione personae*, and so on. In the same way, *personae* should be supplied with *honestiores* and *humiliores*. The notion of *persona*, then, is primary.

'Humiliores' and synonyms. Words or phrases which stand for *humiliores* include (*qui*) *humiliores loco positi* (*nati*) (*sunt*),[3] *plebeii*, *tenuiores*,[4] and variants on these.[5] *Liberi plebeii* and *humiles personae* have similar meanings.[6]

What is a *plebeius*? Gaius' definition of *plebs* is broad: the rest of the citizenry excluding senators (*ceteri cives sine senatoribus*).[7] If this statement were given a provincial or municipal setting, 'plebeians' would turn out to be the bulk of the citizen population, excluding the decurions.[8] There is a clear contrast in legal texts between penalties for decurions and those for plebeians.[9] Indeed, a whole group of penalties is labelled *plebeiorum poenae*.[10] These are the sorts of penalties which might be applied to slaves.[11] In addition, *plebeius* is found opposite *consularis receptae auctoritatis*,[12] *honestior*,[13] and (in company with *humiliore loco natus*) a long list of officials.[14]

Tenuiores[15] is rare in the classical period but common in later texts, where it stands for free men of low status, habitually subject to oppression by *potentiores*. Such oppression was not, however,

---

[1] *Dig.* 47. 21. 3. 2 (Call.); cf. 48. 19. 16. 1 ff. (Cl. Sat.). See also Gai. *Inst.* 3. 225; *IJ* 4. 4. 9.

[2] It is explicit in *PS* 1. 21. 5 and 12; 2. 19. 9; etc.

[3] See p. 221 nn. 4–5, 7–8 above.

[4] See nn. 7–15 below.

[5] Add (*liberi*) *sordidiores* (*Dig.* 47. 9. 4. 1).

[6] *Dig.* 48. 19. 28. 11.

[7] *Dig.* 50. 16. 238 praef. The editor bracketed *senatoribus*.

[8] Gaius' definition has an archaic flavour, perhaps due to the fact that his work is a commentary on the *XII Tables*. It would have been out of place under the Empire to call an equestrian a 'plebeian'.

[9] *Dig.* 48. 19. 10. 2; 50. 2. 2. 2.

[10] *CJ* 9. 41. 11 praef.

[11] *Dig.* 48. 19. 28. 11.

[12] *Dig.* 4. 3. 11. 1.

[13] *Dig.* 47. 18. 1. 2.

[14] *PS* 5. 4. 10.

[15] *Dig.* 48. 19. 28. 2 (*liberi* . . . *et* . . . *tenuiores homines/honestiores*). See Cardascia, art. cit. 308 n. 2. Note *Dig.* 50. 4. 6 praef., where *tenues* is used of impoverished decurions.

a peculiar feature of the late Empire.[1] The references of *potentiores* and *honestiores* are not identical.[2]

'*Honestiores*'.[3] *Honestiores* is connected with *honor* or *honos*. The noun itself appears occasionally in phrases that describe the privileged groups, such as *in honore aliquo positi*.[4] Here the word *honor* seems to refer quite closely to an official position or office.[5] Again, *propter honorem*, high-status defendants are granted a freer kind of *custodia*.[6] The reference is apparently to the 'honour' or esteem which attaches to a member of the higher orders, whether for offices held or for high social standing. Finally, veterans and decurions are held in like *honor*, presumably because their social position is thought to be comparable:

> veteranis et liberis veteranorum idem honor habetur, qui et decurionibus.[7]

Political and social predominance are closely linked with moral ascendancy.[8] *Honestus* and *honestior* have a definite moral flavour. In Cicero's description of an *honestus* in the *Brutus*, moral superiority is nicely combined with success in politics:

> cum honos sit praemium virtutis iudicio studioque civium delatum ad aliquem, qui eum sententiis, qui suffragiis adeptus est, is mihi et honestus et honoratus videtur.[9]

The addition of *et honoratus* underlines the respect which is due to the man of the type described.

---

[1] *Dig.* 1. 18. 6. 2; 5; 47. 22. 1 praef.; ibid. 3. 2 (*collegia tenuiorum*); 48. 19. 28. 7.

[2] On *potentiores* see Cardascia, art. cit. 308–9; J. Gagé, *Les Classes sociales dans l'Empire romain* (1964), 417–24; J. Gaudemet, *The Irish Jurist* i, N.S. 1 (1966), 128.

[3] The earliest uses of *honestiores* in a social sense are to be found in Seneca (*Ep.* 47. 15) and Petronius (*Sat.* 34. 7). Among rare synonyms are *altiores* (*Dig.* 48. 8. 3. 5); *splendidiores personae* (*Dig.* 47. 21. 2); from the fourth century, *maiores personae* (*Coll.* 15. 3. 7); *honorati* (ibid.); cf. ἐπιφανέστεροι/ἐλάττονες (Dio 71. 27. 3²).

[4] *Dig.* 48. 8. 16; cf. *CTh* 9. 16. 6 = *CJ* 9. 18. 7 (A.D. 358) (*honoribus praediti*).

[5] *Dig.* 50. 4. 14 praef. (*honor municipalis*); 50. 2. 2. 2 (*honor decurionis*); cf. 50. 5. 5 (*a decurionatu, quamvis hic quoque honor est*).

[6] *Dig.* 48. 3. 1.

[7] *Dig.* 49. 18. 3; cf. 48. 19. 28. 5 (*honoris reverentiam*).   [8] See below.

[9] Cic. *Brutus* 281: 'Since honour is the prize given for virtue by the citizenry out of esteem and affection, he who has won it by their judgement and approbation is in my eyes both honourable and honoured.'

'*Dignitas*'. Cicero provides a definition:

dignitas est alicuius honesta et cultu et honore et verecundia digna auctoritas.[1]

In this heavily loaded sentence, the emphasis is placed on moral qualities, manner of life, and the esteem which these evoke—or rather command, for *auctoritas* is a full-blooded word, meaning influence or power, the authority which in the Roman context is derived from political leadership.[2] The word *dignitas* may stand for a particular office, and in this sense it is found in both the singular and the plural.[3] Valerian and Gallienus dealt with a case of injury to a priest who was actually wearing the *dignitatis habitum et ornamenta* at the time.[4] Position or office is perhaps central in *in aliqua dignitate positus*, which is contrasted with *humiliore loco positus*,[5] or *humiliores*.[6] But it is often impossible to separate the various shades of meaning possessed by the word: the office itself, the prestige that is acquired through office, the rank in society that an office holder attains to, the quality of his life.

The word was sometimes used with reference to decurions.[7] Paulus, reporting Pius' ruling that an ex-decurion should not be tortured, commented that the concession was given *in memoriam prioris dignitatis*.[8] It would be idle to try to decide which sense of the word is the dominant one here. All are in play. While service in the local senate might be called an *honor* in the sense of 'office',[9] the word *decurio* did not simply designate a particular kind of functionary. It was also an honorific title. *Dignitas* was a suitable word for another reason. *Dignitas* was non-transient and inheritable;[10]

---

[1] Cic. *de inv.* 2. 166: 'Dignity is honourable prestige. It merits respect, honour, and reverence.' Of words of similar meaning, such as *auctoritas*, *amplitudo*, *maiestas*, only the first features in the legal texts.

[2] See p. 227.

[3] See *Dig.* 50. 2. 12. The plural does not always mean 'offices'. See *Dig.* 50. 4. 3. 15.

[4] *CJ* 9. 35. 4 (A.D. 259).   [5] *Dig.* 48. 8. 1. 5.

[6] *Dig.* 26. 10. 3. 16.

[7] *Dig.* 48. 10. 13. 1; 50. 1. 15 praef. Cf., not specifically of decurions, *Dig.* 48. 23. 3; 50. 1. 17. 12; ibid. 22. 6; 50. 2. 12; 50. 4. 14 praef.–1; cf. *Dig.* 1. 9. 6. 1; ibid. 7. 2; ibid. 9; 23. 2. 34. 3 (*dignitas senatoria*).

[8] *Dig.* 50. 2. 14.   [9] *Dig.* 50. 5. 5.

[10] Ch. Wirszubski, *Libertas as a Political Idea* (1950), 37. *Dignitas* in a wife is derived from her husband: *vat. fr.* 104 (Paulus); cf. *Dig.* 1. 9. 1 praef.–1 (*consularis femina*).

a decurion served for life, and, by the Severan epoch, was normally succeeded by his son.[1]

Another fringe case where an attempt to categorize achieves little is the employment of *hi qui altioris dignitatis sunt* (opposed to *inferioris dignitatis homines*) and *hi qui inferioris dignitatis sunt* (opposed to *antecedentis gradus homines*).[2] And is the normal sense of *dignitas* rather than the social sense paramount in the passages which describe the virtues of reliable witnesses: *dignitas, fides, mores, gravitas*?[3] A text concerning the *actio de dolo* shows how closely the three senses of *dignitas* are connected:

> sed nec humili adversus eum qui dignitate excellet debet dari (sc. actio): puta plebeio adversus consularem receptae auctoritatis, vel luxurioso atque prodigo aut alias vili adversus hominem vitae emendatioris.[4]

Consular office and rank, the influence in the community which this brings, and the virtuous life all indicate *dignitas*.

'Condicio'. Condicio appears in many contexts;[5] in some it stands for social rank. For example, some are debarred from accusing *propter condicionem suam* (*ut libertini contra patronos*);[6] in crimes relating to the pilfering of shipwrecks, as in other cases, the penalty is to be decided *ex personarum condicione* (*et rerum qualitate*).[7] Torture is permissible as a last resort, *si personarum condicio pateretur*.[8] Those who tamper with the levée-banks of the Nile are punished *pro condicione sua* (*et pro admissi mensura*).[9]

---

[1] See pp. 243 ff., on the social status of decurions.

[2] *Dig.* 23. 2. 49 (Marcellus). Other occurrences of the word in the *Dig.* in a similar sense include: *Dig.* 1. 5. 20; 1. 9. 1 praef.; 23. 2. 66 praef.; 25. 4. 1. 13; 35. 3. 3. 5; 47. 11. 10; 48. 13. 8. 1; 48. 19. 28. 9; 50. 13. 5. 2.

[3] *Dig.* 22. 5. 2; ibid. 3. 1; 3. 2; *PS* 5. 15. 1. See J. Ph. Lévy, op. cit. (p. 212 n. 3), ii. 29 ff.

[4] *Dig.* 4. 3. 11. 1 (Ulp.): 'Nor should the action be granted to a man of low rank against one of conspicuous dignity, to a commoner, for example, against a consular of acknowledged prestige, or to a man whose life is wanton and wasteful, or in some other way worthless, against one of exemplary life.'

[5] Quint. *Inst.* 5. 10. 26: 'condicionis etiam distantia est: nam clarus an obscurus, magistratus an privatus, pater an filius, civis an peregrinus, liber an servus, maritus an caelebs, parens liberorum an orbus sit, plurimum distat.'

[6] *Dig.* 48. 2. 8; cf. *CJ* 9. 21. 1 praef. (*libertina condicio*).

[7] *Dig.* 47. 9. 4. 1.

[8] *CJ* 9. 41. 8. 2 (Diocl. and Max.).

[9] *Dig.* 47. 11. 10.

An attempt has been made by Cardascia to show that *condicio* was not used in any phrase that is relevant to the *honestiores/ humiliores* distinction.[1] When *pro condicione personae* appears, the argument runs, it is the dichotomy of free men and slaves, or a trichotomy of *honestiores, humiliores*, and slaves, which is in question. Yet in *Dig.* 47. 11. 10 *pro condicione sua* is echoed by *secundum suam dignitatem.* The latter formula, and therefore the former, is one of the many that point to the *honestiores/humiliores* distinction. Moreover, there is no reference here to slaves and to free men. The trichotomy referred to above occurs in *Dig.* 47. 9. 4. 1, where Paulus quotes a rescript of Pius (the interpretation of which is disputed).[2] Again, the comment that follows the quotation has a wider application than the one case to which the Emperor addressed himself. The words are:

> et omnino ut in ceteris, ita huiusmodi causis ex personarum condicione et rerum qualitate diligenter sunt aestimandae.[3]

Two possible exceptions are dismissed by Cardascia on inadequate grounds. In *PS.* 5. 25. 10 there is no hint of a distinction between slaves and free. The second text, *Dig.* 22. 5. 3 praef., runs:

> exploranda . . . condicio cuiusque, utrum quis decurio an plebeius sit.[4]

This is considered irrelevant because the opposition here is allegedly between 'orders' rather than 'classes'. At this point Cardascia's discussion is coloured by his theory about the nature of the categories of *honestiores* and *humiliores.* He claims that the terms represent 'classes' rather than 'estates': *condicio* is held to be the technical term for 'estates'. At this juncture, it is only necessary to say that Cardascia's theory gains no support from the use of the word *condicio* in the legal texts.[5]

---

[1] Cardascia, art. cit. 336, and n. 1.　　　　　[2] See pp. 163–4.

[3] 'In general, in cases of this kind, as in the other cases, a careful assessment should be made on the basis of the status of the person and the nature of the goods.' One of the *ceterae causae* is provided by Modestinus. In *Dig.* 47. 21. 1 he states that there is no longer a fine for moving boundary-stones, 'sed pro condicione admittentium coercitione transigendum'.

[4] 'The status of each man ... should be investigated, to ascertain whether he is a decurion or a commoner.' See also *CJ* 12. 1. 1 (*privata condicio . . . clarissima*).

[5] Cardascia, art. cit. 332 ff.; see p. 234 n. 1 for criticisms of his theory of the nature of the categories.

Brasiello gave Cardascia a starting-point for his argument, by distinguishing between *condicio* and *status* on the one hand, and *dignitas* on the other. The former, it is argued, stands for personal *condicio* or 'capacità', the latter for social *condicio* or 'stimà'.[1] The above discussion has given grounds for thinking that the distinction was not all-pervasive. *Condicio* and *dignitas* are virtual synonyms in passages that describe preferential treatment, or a difference of penalty.[2]

'*Auctoritas*', '*gravitas*', '*fides*'. *Auctoritas*, as has been noted, is associated with *dignitas* and is closely connected with office holding.[3] Injury is *atrox* when the injured man is a senator, a knight, a decurion, or a man 'signally prestigious in some other way' (*vel alias spectatae auctoritatis viro*).[4] The last phrase covers such officials as magistrates, aediles, and judges. Again, an action for fraud was not given to a plebeian against a consular 'of acknowledged prestige' (*receptae auctoritatis*).[5] *Auctoritas* is a quality in a witness which recommends itself to judges.[6] Another is *gravitas* which denotes constancy, stability, trustworthiness, or *fides*.[7]

'*Existimatio*'.[8] It is another characteristic of a good witness that he should possess *existimatio*, reputation or good name; it also

---

[1] U. Brasiello, op. cit. 552 ff.; *IJ* 1. 16. 5 shows that *status* and *dignitas* are not synonymous—perhaps *Dig.* 1. 5. 20 does too—but not that there is 'opposition' between the two (just as in the latter text *magistratus* and *potestas* are not opposed). *Status* is commonly used when the condition of a slave is contrasted with that of a free man. e.g. *CJ* 9. 21. 1 praef.; *Dig.* 1. 5 *pass.* This applies equally to *Dig.* 40. 15. 3: 'ante quinquennium defuncto status honestior, quam mortis tempore fuisse existimatur, vindicari non prohibetur. idcirco et si quis in servitute moriatur, post quinquennium liber decessisse probari potest.' Despite Cardascia (art. cit. 336 n. 1, incorrect reference), the status of a *liber* is loftier (*honestior*) than that of a *servus* in the same sense that a decurion's surpasses a plebeian's.

[2] *CJ* 9. 41. 8. 2 with *PS* 5. 29. 2; *Dig.* 48. 8. 1. 2 with 49. 16. 6. 1.

[3] See above, p. 224; cf. Lévy, op. cit. 63 ff.; F. Schulz, *Principles of Roman Law* (1936), 164 ff., with bibl.

[4] *PS* 5. 4. 10.

[5] *Dig.* 4. 3. 11. 1 (Ulpian/Labeo).

[6] *Dig.* 22. 5. 3. 2; 4.

[7] Ibid. 2. See Lévy, op. cit. 48 ff. *Gravitas* and *fides* are moral qualities; ibid. 92: 'Gravitas n'a aucune signification juridique.'

[8] *Dig.* 22. 5. 3. 1; cf. 48. 18. 10. 5. See Brasiello, op. cit. 546. Other words of similar meaning occur primarily in non-legal sources: *fama, laus, decus, nomen, gloria,* etc.

connotes status, which stands or falls with *dignitas*. Callistratus writes:

existimatio est dignitatis inlaesae status, legibus ac moribus comprobatus, qui ex delicto nostro auctoritate legum aut minuitur aut consumitur.[1]

Callistratus claims for *existimatio* the approbation of law and custom. He does not say that it rests on them, or derives from them.

'*Qualitas*'. Qualitas acts as a variant for *dignitas* or *condicio*, in *proqualitate personae*,[2] and similar phrases.[3]

'*Gradus*'. This is another term for social rank. *Humiliore loco* is found opposed to *in aliquo gradu*,[4] and *in honore aliquo positi* opposed to *secundo gradu*.[5]

'*Locus*', '*ordo*'. These are also status terms. Marcus and Commodus found one Aelius Priscus

tali . . loco atque ordine esse, ut a suis vel etiam in propria villa custodiatur.

He was thus saved from a sojourn in prison in chains.[6] Phrases such as *honestiore loco natus* are common.[7]

'*Fortuna*'. In the legal sources there is one relevant passage:

humilioris quidem fortunae summo supplicio adficiuntur, honestiores in insulam deportantur.[8]

Loci might have been written for *fortunae*.[9]

---

[1] *Dig.* 50. 13. 5. 1: 'Good name is a condition of unimpaired dignity. It is upheld by law and custom, but again, by the authority of the laws, is diminished or destroyed through our offences.'

[2] *Dig.* 48. 13. 7; cf. *PS* 1. 21. 12; *CJ* 9. 39. 1 (A.D. 374).

[3] *PS* 1. 21. 5 (*pro personarum qualitate*); *Coll.* 11. 3. 1; *PS* 5. 18. 1 (*pro qualitate eius*); *PS* 5. 22. 1 = *Dig.* 48. 19. 38. 2 (*pro qualitate dignitatis*).

[4] *Dig.* 47. 9. 12; cf. *Coll.* 12. 5. 1 (*humillimo loco/in aliquo gradu*).

[5] *Dig.* 48. 8. 16; cf. 23. 2. 49, and see Cardascia, art. cit. 326 n. 8.

[6] *Dig.* 1. 18. 14: 'is of sufficient status and rank to be guarded by his own family and in his own house.' For *ordo* see also *CJ* 5. 4. 10 (Diocl.): *claritas/secundi ordinis virum*. Cardascia (art. cit. 336) found the term *ordo* irrelevant to the *honestiores/humiliores* distinction (cf. *condicio* and *status*).

[7] *Dig.* 47. 9. 12. 1; 47. 14. 1. 3 = *Coll.* 11. 8. 3; 48. 8. 3. 5; 48. 13. 7; *Coll.* 12. 5. 1; cf. *Dig.* 47. 10. 45 and 48. 5. 39. 8.

[8] *PS* 5. 19A = *Dig.* 47. 12. 11: 'Those defendants who are of humble circumstances are given the ultimate penalty, while men of rank are deported to an island.' Cf. Tac. *Ann.* 2. 72 (Germanicus).

[9] For the broad application of the word *fortuna* see Cic. *de inv.* 1. 24. 34–5;

'Genus', 'mores', 'facultates'

For the rhetoricians birth, moral qualities, and wealth were three of the more important aspects of a person from which arguments in law courts could be drawn.[1] The legal documents reflect this.

'Genus'. In the *Acta Hermaisci*, the Emperor Trajan is represented as provoked by the insults of a defendant, the Alexandrian gymnasiarch Hermaiscus, into crying out: 'You answer me wilfully, trusting in your birth (sc. to protect you)' (αὐθαδῆς ἀποκρίνῃ πεποιθὼς τῷ σεαυτοῦ γένει). This was Trajan's second warning. It is uncertain whether Hermaiscus thought his lineage would influence Trajan in his favour. The Emperor at least was aware of it.[2]

In the *Digest*, high birth is mentioned among qualifications for privilege, in formulae such as *qui honestiore loco nati sunt*.[3] In addition, there are a number of texts in which sons of decurions, veterans, and others are specifically protected from 'plebeian' penalties.[4] The implication may be that the principle that privilege was inheritable was not universally accepted; but it does seem to presuppose the existence of the principle.

2. 9. 30. Still under the heading *persona*, the age of a defendant sometimes secured a milder penalty: *Dig.* 47. 21. 2; 48. 13. 7; 48. 19. 16. 3; or, for that matter, it might disqualify a man from accusing: *Dig.* 48. 2. 8. Sex could carry the same advantages and disadvantages: *Dig.* 48. 13. 7; cf. 48. 2. 8; and see 1. 5. 9. But wives of *honestiores* could probably expect privileged treatment, see *vat. fr.* 104 (Paulus); so could daughters (e.g. *CJ* 9. 47. 9), if they did not marry below their station: *Dig.* 1. 9. 8 (daughter of senator); cf. ibid. 6. 1 (son of senator).

[1] *Genus*: Quint. *Inst. Or.* 5. 10. 24 ff.; Cic. *de inv.* 2. 35. 107; 1. 24. 34–5; *Auct. ad Herenn.* 3. 6. 10; 13. *Mores*: Quint. *Inst. Or.* 5. 10. 24 ff.; 7. 2. 33. *Facultates*: ibid. 5. 10. 26; Cic. *de inv.* 1. 24. 34; *Auct. ad Herenn.* 3. 6. 10.

[2] *Acta Hermaisci*, P. Oxy. 1242, col. iii, l. 44, in H. A. Musurillo, *Acts of the Pagan Martyrs* (1954), viii. 45 (text) and 177 (comm.); cf. *Acta Athenodori*, P. Oxy. 2177, fr. 2, col. ii, l. 55, in *Acts* x. 61; and *Acta Appiani*, P. Oxy. 33, col. iv–v, ll. 15 ff., in *Acts*, xi. 67.

[3] Similarly, low birth was a disqualification: *Dig.* 47. 14. 1. 3 = *Coll.* 11. 8. 3; 48. 13. 7 fin.; *CJ* 9. 41. 9 (A.D. 290): 'ne alieni forte sordidae stirpis splendidis et ingenuis natalibus audeant subrogari.' ἀγενής/εὐγενής: *CJ* 2. 11. 16 (A.D. 240); cf. *Acta Athenodori* and *Acta Appiani* (last note). *Genus*: *CTh* 9. 35. 1 = *CJ* 9. 8. 4 (A.D. 369).

[4] Decurions: *Dig.* 50. 2. 2. 2; *CJ* 9. 41. 11. 1; 9. 47. 9 (daughter). Veterans: *Dig.* 49. 18. 3; *CJ* 9. 41. 8; 9. 47. 5.
Eminentissimi viri, perfectissimi viri: *CJ* 9. 41. 11 praef. (sons, grandsons, and great-grandsons).

'*Mores*'. According to Quintilian, there is sometimes a causal connection between birth and manner of life:

genus, nam similes parentibus et maioribus filii plerumque creduntur, et nonnumquam ad honeste turpiterque vivendum inde causae fluunt.[1]

Ulpian underlined the word *nonnumquam* with an example of a base father who produced an upright son. It is significant that Ulpian considered that a son's traditional subservience to a father before the law[2] could be waived if there was a dispute between them:

interdum tamen putamus . . . iniuriarum actionem filio dandam, ut puta si patris persona vilis abiectaque sit, filii honesta.[3]

That public *mores* exercised a regulative function in Roman society hardly needs stating. There is a recognition of this in a rescript of Caracalla, in which *mores* is placed beside *leges* and *constitutiones*:

pacta, quae contra leges constitutionesque vel contra bonos mores fiunt, nullam vim habere indubitati iuris est.[4]

But *mores* played this role already under the Republic. It was written in the praetor's edict that an *actio iniuriarum* would be given for *convicium* (abuse) which was judged to be *adversus bonos mores*.[5] A ruling of Severus illustrates how *mores* could supplement *leges*. There was nothing illegal about the marriage of a freedman with his patroness, or with the daughter, wife, granddaughter, or great-granddaughter of his patron. But Severus considered it out of keeping with the *mores* of his times.[6]

---

[1] Quint. *Inst. Or.* 5. 10. 24: 'with regard to birth, sons are commonly thought to be like their parents and ancestors, and sometimes this is the reason for the honourable or dishonourable quality of their lives.' If possible, the defendant's counsel should demonstrate his client's *vita integra*. See *Auct. ad Herenn.* 2. 3. 5; cf. Quint. *Inst. Or.* 7. 2. 27 ff.

[2] e.g. *Dig.* 48. 19. 16. 3; cf. *IJ* 4. 4. 9 (*atrox iniuria*); *Dig.* 4. 3. 11. 1 (*actio doli*). For the unequal relationship of *libertus* and *patronus* see *Dig.* 4. 3. 11. 1; *IJ* 4. 4. 9; *Dig.* 47. 10. 7. 2 and ibid. 11. 7; *CJ* 5. 4. 3. Cf. *PS* 2. 19. 9.

[3] *Dig.* 47. 10. 17. 13: 'We can imagine the situation arising on occasion where an action for injury should be granted to a son, as when the father's character is base and worthless, and the son's honourable.'

[4] *CJ* 2. 3. 6 (A.D. 213): 'It is undoubtedly part of law that settlements which are made contrary to enactments and constitutions and canons of good conduct have no force.'

[5] *Dig.* 47. 10. 15. 2; 5; 6; 20; 23; 34; 39; cf. 4. 2. 3. 1.

[6] *CJ* 5. 4. 3 (A.D. 196).

The *mores* of a potential accuser,[1] and also of a witness,[2] were subject to scrutiny by the judge. In the case of a witness, the judge was urged to make inquiry 'et an honestae et inculpatae vitae, an vero notatus quis et reprehensibilis'.[3] Some would-be witnesses were ruled out 'propter notam et infamiam vitae suae'.[4] This last statement of Callistratus follows the citation of a section of the Julian law on violence. The law contained a list of those prohibited from giving testimony. The *intestabiles* are mostly *infames*, that is, they belonged to a category of persons who lacked various legal prerogatives which citizens normally possessed. Either a criminal record or the exercise of certain sordid practices had placed them in this category.[5] Apart from legal disqualifications, harsher penalties were traditionally their lot, according to Callistratus:

> maiores nostri in omni supplicio severius servos quam liberos, famosos quam integrae famae homines punierunt.[6]

The terms *infames* and *famosi* are apparently coextensive.[7]

The concept of a man *honestae et inculpatae vitae* as one who has not besmirched his name is somewhat negative. Other texts mention more positive attributes.[8] More interesting for present purposes is the use with a moral sense of the adjective *honestus*—and also of the noun *honestas*, for *honestas* and *existimatio* are put forward as qualities of a trustworthy witness.[9] In Ulpian's hypothetical confrontation of father against son the *persona vilis abiectaque* of the one is pitted against the *honesta (persona)* of the other. Again, *honestum* appears as an antonym of *adversus bonos mores*, in a passage that recalls in subject-matter the rescripts of

---

[1] *Dig.* 48. 2. 16 (accusers); see also Gellius 14. 2. 5 ff.; 10 ff.; 21 ff. (both parties). See pp. 210–11.
[2] *Dig.* 22. 5. 2.
[3] Ibid. 3 praef.: 'whether the man was of honourable and blameless life, or whether he had suffered disgrace and was deserving of censure'.
[4] Ibid. 3. 5: 'because of the shame and notoriety of their lives'.
[5] *Infames*: see, for a brief discussion, W. W. Buckland, *Text-Book of Roman Law*³ (1963), 91 ff.
[6] *Dig.* 48. 19. 28. 16: 'Our ancestors, in every case of punishment, have awarded harsher penalties to slaves than to free men and to men of bad reputation than to men of unblemished name.'
[7] See, e.g., *Dig.* 48. 2. 13; 48. 4. 7 praef. (*famosi*); cf. *Coll.* 4. 4 (*infames*).
[8] *Dig.* 22. 5. 3 praef.   [9] Ibid. 21. 3.

Caracalla and Severus quoted above. Modestinus ruled out certain types of marriage partners for the daughter of a senator with the words:

> semper in coniunctionibus non solum quid liceat considerandum est, sed et quid honestum sit.[1]

That a word with a basically moral meaning, *honestus*, should have been chosen to describe men of distinguished social position, *honestiores*, demonstrates that, in Roman eyes, there was more than a contingent connection between social position and moral values.[2]

'*Facultates*'. *Honestus vir* is synonymous with *vir locuples* in a passage of Ulpian:

> cum Titio honesto viro pecuniam credere vellem, subiecisti mihi alium Titium egenum, quasi ille esset locuples, et nummos acceptos cum eo divisisti: furti tenearis . . .[3]

Idoneus is used for *honestus* in a parallel passage, and is perhaps the more common word in such contexts.[4]

Amplissimae facultates might keep a man out of prison.[5] A wealthy defendant could be entrusted to *fideiussores*, no doubt partly because he would be less inclined to run away and abandon his estate. Again, a rich man could expect not to be beaten.[6] This exemption was not granted simply because he could pay damages; it was a prerogative accorded to status.

In contrast with *honestus* and *idoneus*, *locuples*[7] (*locupletior*)

---

[1] *Dig.* 23. 2. 42: 'With regard to marriages, it is always necessary to consider not only what is lawful, but also what is honourable.' Cf. 50. 4. 6 praef.; Tac. *Dial.* 10. 5; Pliny, *Ep.* 10. 31. 3; etc.

[2] Moral words were commonly used in the Republic to describe political groups, e.g. *boni, optimates, improbi*. See Cic. *ad Att.* 1. 13. 2–3; 14. 1 and 5–6; 16. 3 and 5–7; etc.

[3] *Dig.* 47. 2. 52. 21: '(Suppose that) when I wanted to entrust some money to an honourable man, you provided me with someone who was poor, pretending the while that he was rich, and you then divided the money received with him. You could be sued for theft.'

[4] Ibid. 67. 4; cf. 47. 9. 9, and perhaps, 48. 10. 18. See espec. *Auct. ad Herenn.* 3. 4. 7 ('ab idoneis hominibus . . . honestiori ordini'). The Greek counterpart of *locuples/idoneus* is εὔπορος/ἐπιτήδειος. See *P. Oxy.* 1405, ll. 22–3 (A.D. 200); cf. *PSI* 1160 (first cent. B.C.).

[5] *Dig.* 48. 3. 1.   [6] See pp. 138 ff.

[7] e.g. *Dig.* 22. 5. 3 praef. (*locuples/egens*).

and *possessor*[1] are relatively neutral, descriptive terms. The use of the first two for men of means illustrates the well-known truth that the possession of wealth gave access to the governing élite; the use of the last two testifies to the significance of wealth in the eyes of the law.

[1] *Dig.* 50. 9. 1. See p. 257.

10

PRIVILEGED GROUPS

FROM the preceding discussion, it can be seen that the jurists, with the assistance of the rhetoricians and others, have left us an adequate account of the criteria required for legal privilege. They were, briefly, the possession of *honor* or *dignitas*, which derived from character, birth, office, and wealth.

However, the criteria were not presented in any coherent way. In particular, they were not included in any definition of the *honestiores*. There is, in fact, no theoretical definition of the term *honestiores* in the *Digest*; nor can a practical definition, that is, a list of those who made up the *honestiores*, be found.

Not surprisingly, the consequence has been drawn from this that 'the privileged class' was vague and indefinable; lawyers gave no list of its membership because there could not be such a list; the two terms *honestiores* and *humiliores* were relative, subjective notions, and not names for juridical categories.[1]

This analysis might seem to draw strength from *PS* 5. 4. 10 on *iniuria atrox*. In that passage the list of privileged persons ends with the phrase *vel alias spectatae auctoritatis viro* ('or a man conspicuous in authority in some other way'). The choice of this

---

[1] Cardascia, art. cit. 327, 330 (practical definitions impossible); 336 (subjective); 326 (not juridical). Cardascia argues that *honestiores* and *humiliores* were classes rather than estates (*états*). One may question the appropriateness both of the term 'class', with its economic connotations (passed over by Cardascia, art. cit. 332–3), and of 'estate', which has reference to features peculiar to medieval society. But in any case the argument seems to rest on the untenable premiss that Roman society was made up of two large, essentially homogeneous groups. On gradations within the *honestiores* see ch. 12; and within the *humiliores*, see pp. 260–3. On weaknesses of the idea of a dichotomic social structure see S. Ossowski, *Class Structure and the Social Consciousness* (1963), 32 ff.; for reasons why the idea might appeal to a privileged stratum, ibid. 35.

On *honestiores* see C. Jullian, *DS* 3 (1900), 235–6, v. *Honestiores, Humiliores*; F. M. de Robertis, *RISG* 1939, 59–110; G. Cardascia, art. cit. 305–37, 461–85; U. Brasiello, *Novissimo digesto italiano* 8 (1962), 108, v. *Honestiores e humiliores*.

phrase might mean that the author was unable to complete the
list; he could go no further in his catalogue of the privileged than
'senator, equestrian, decurion'. But it should be noted that the
author did not include all those groups whose privileged status
was not in doubt, for example, veterans. Moreover, a list of those
for whom *iniuria* was automatically *atrox* is not equivalent to a
list of those who made up the *honestiores*.

The point to stress is that there were publicly recognized or
recognizable criteria on the basis of which those with privileges
could be identified. The lack of a definition in the sources is hardly
crucial, for the Romans were suspicious of definition, and avoided
it where possible.[1] Moreover, while the jurists did not link the
criteria with particular social groups in a systematic way, they
did take an easily identifiable group, the decurions, and state that
they were to be regarded as representative of a wider group, composed of those with matching *dignitas* and *honor* in the community.
An informed observer would have had little difficulty in deducing
who belonged to this category, and who did not. The jurists
themselves are to be seen as uniquely placed observers, who could,
moreover, by their theorizing, increase the status consciousness
of their society and make the criteria more clear-cut. The modern
historian has some chance of reconstructing the membership of
the *honestiores*, although the information at his disposal is limited.

Senators[2]

There is little in the legal texts to illustrate the obvious fact that
senators were privileged before the law. Gaius and later the
compiler of *Paul's Sentences* both indicated that *iniuria* became
atrox if suffered by a senator at the hands of a *humilis persona*.[3]
Similarly, it is known that no plebeian could sue a consular for
fraud, and this rule may well have applied to all senators and for

---

[1] *Dig.* 50. 17. 202 (Iavolenus).
[2] Select bibliography: Mommsen, *StR* iii, e.g. 867–904; M. Gelzer, *Die
Nobilität der römischen Republik* (1912) (= *Kl. Schr.* i. 17–135); M. Gelzer,
'Die Nobilität der Kaiserzeit', *Hermes* 50 (1915), 393–415 (= *Kl. Schr.* i.
136–53); O'Brien Moore, *RE* S. 6 (1935), 660 ff., s.v. *senatus*, esp. 760 ff. (Principate); J. Gagé, *Les Classes sociales dans l'Empire romain* (1964), ch. 2, 82–106.
[3] Gai. *Inst.* 3. 225; *PS* 5. 4. 10. See pp. 201 ff.

some other charges in civil law.[1] *Distractio bonorum* was a means by which senators, in particular, could satisfy their creditors without loss of status.[2] As for penalties suffered by senators, one *clarissimus iuvenis*, or the son of a senator, was deported by Severus and Caracalla for a crime punishable with death under the Julian law on peculation.[3] Deportation was the penalty awarded to *honestiore loco nati* for such crimes.[4]

The deficiency of the legal sources is made up in some degree by the historical sources. In the matter of penalties, the statements of Silanus (in the context of the Catilinarian conspiracy) and Thrasea Paetus (towards the close of the Julio-Claudian epoch) assert or imply that the death penalty was excluded for senators.[5] Silanus was unable to prevent the execution of the conspirators which he had at first himself advocated, and Paetus avoided execution only by suicide. This was because armed rebellion against the state and violation of the Emperor's *maiestas* were never included in the practical immunity of senators from execution. In other respects, that immunity must have been virtually guaranteed senators under the Republic by senatorial control through the magistrates of the execution of penalties: voluntary exile was always open to them as a means of escaping the death penalty. Under the Empire, senators were in general protected from harsh penalties, in both capital and non-capital cases, by their privilege of trial before the Senate.[6] The Senate regularly discriminated against low-status defendants and accusers alike, both in reaching verdicts and in issuing sentences.[7]

It was predictable that the political supremacy of the Senate in Republican times would be reflected in the administration of the law. But both then and later, under the Empire, the source of their legal privileges was no less their social position than their political prominence. The senatorial order was an exclusive group

---

[1] *Dig.* 4. 3. 11. 1. The consular may have been taken simply as an example. See pp. 182 ff.

[2] *Dig.* 27. 10. 5.   [3] *Dig.* 48. 13. 12. 1.   [4] Ibid. 7.

[5] See p. 105.

[6] There is some evidence that senators could count on the revocation to Rome of legal disputes which had been launched by provincials against them. See p. 195.

[7] See pp. 34 ff.

by Republican tradition. Augustus emphasized its social superiority by forbidding marriage between senators and freedwomen or women of low connection.[1] A similar rule applied in the case of women of senatorial rank and freedmen. The *lex Iulia* of 18 B.C. also laid down that senators and agnatic descendants to the third generation and their wives were of senatorial rank.[2] Membership of the order was denoted by the adjective *clarissimus(a)*, with *vir, femina, iuvenis, puer*, and *puella*. The title was first written in full, and later in abbreviated form, as one would expect with a regular formula. Abbreviations do not occur in the inscriptions until the Trajanic period—indeed *clarissimus vir* did not become an established title, excluding others, until about that time.[3]

Equestrians

'Senators and equestrians have special property qualifications, not because they differ in nature from other men, but, just as they enjoy precedence in place, rank, and dignity, so they should enjoy it also in these things which make for mental peace and physical well-being.'[4] This is Tacitus' report of part of a speech of Asinius

[1] *Dig.* 23. 2. 44 praef.–1. There was no change during the period of the classical lawyers. See ibid. 23 (Celsus); ibid. 58 (Pius/Marc.); ibid. 16 praef. (Marcus/Paulus); ibid. 42. 1 (Mod.). Marcellus wrote (ibid. 49): 'observandum est, ut inferioris gradus homines ducant uxores eas, quas hi qui altioris dignitatis sunt ducere legibus propter dignitatem prohibentur: at contra antecedentis gradus homines non possunt eas ducere, quas his qui inferioris dignitatis sunt ducere non licet.' These words are unlikely to be a reference to the *honestiores/humiliores* distinction, or if they are, the chances that Marcellus was correct are small. Extension of the rule to other groups apart from senators is known from pronouncements of Constantine: *CTh* 12. 1. 6, A.D. 319; cf. *CJ* 5. 5. 3. 1 (decurions); *CTh* 4. 6. 3, A.D. 336; cf. *CJ* 5. 27. 1 praef. (senators, *viri perfectissimi, duoviri*, provincial priests). See Cardascia, *Studi in memoria di Emilio Albertario* (1953), 655–67.

[2] *Dig.* 23. 2. 44 praef.; cf. 50. 1. 22. 5 (but see *Dig.* 1. 9. 10); *StR* iii. 468–9. For the status of wives, *Dig.* 1. 9. 8.

[3] *StR* iii. 471; O. Hirschfeld, 'Die Rangtitel der römischen Kaiserzeit,' *Sitzungsb. der Berl. Ak.* (1901), 579–610 (= *Kl. Schr.* 646–81); L. Friedländer, *Darstellung aus der Sittengeschichte Roms* (1910), 279, 403–5. *Clarissimus vir* was used as an official title as early as A.D. 56 (*C* x 1401). See also *C* x 7852 (A.D. 69). *C(larissimus) p(uer)* is used of the great-grandson of Antonius Felix, L. Anneius Domitius Proculus (*C* v 34, early Trajan); *c(larissimus) i(uvenis)* of the jurist Aburnius Valens (*C* vi 1421, A.D. 118); *c(larissimus) v(ir)* of the legate Catullinus at Lambaesis (*C* viii 2532, A.D. 128). Cf. *C* viii 98 ('[pro]cos. c.v.'; Hadrian); 11451 = 270 (= *FIRA*² i, no. 47, p. 291) ('Lucili Africani c.v.'; A.D. 138).

[4] Tac. *Ann.* 2. 33. 5: 'Distinctos senatus et equitum census, non quia diversi

Gallus, a prominent senator in the age of Tiberius. He went on to say that those who undertook 'cares' and exposed themselves to 'greater dangers' had the right to expect 'privileges'. Gallus was putting forward the proposition that extravagance could only be properly measured in relation to the fortune of the individual. This debate, and Gallus' success in scotching a *senatusconsultum* restricting luxury and extravagant expenditure, is a small illustration of the truth of a significant aside of the younger Pliny: 'when I observe the public practices and laws of a state, which hold that the financial qualifications of men should be given special attention . . .'[1] A respect for wealth had found its way into both the customs and the laws of states. Perhaps in a different context an Asinius Gallus would have argued that the justice of a sentence of a law court depended on the 'place', 'rank', 'dignity', and 'means' of the defendant.

Gallus spoke of senators and equestrians in the same breath. His opponent in a debate in the same year, Cnaeus Piso, stated the opinion that public business ought to go on, although the Emperor had announced he would be absent, 'so that the ability of the Senate and equestrians to carry out their proper duties in the absence of the Emperor should bring honour to the state'.[2] Our interest is less in this 'show of liberty' (*species libertatis*) than in the image of two sets of officials working side by side, each performing a part of the business of state. This *concordia ordinum* (harmony between the orders),[3] envisaged in late Republican times, was largely an Augustan creation. Augustus looked to a refurbished equestrian order to provide jurors, financial agents and tax collectors, army officers and provincial governors, senators

natura, sed, ut locis ordinibus dignationibus antistent, ita iis quae ad requiem animi aut salubritatem corporum parentur . . .'

[1] Pliny, *Ep.* 1. 14. 9: 'cum publicos mores atque etiam leges civitatis intueor, quae vel in primis census hominum spectandos arbitrantur . . .'

[2] Tac. *Ann.* 2. 35: 'ut absente principe senatum et equites posse sua munia sustinere decorum rei publicae foret.'

[3] On *concordia ordinum* see Nicolet, *L'Ordre équestre à l'époque républicaine* (1966), 633 ff. In 253 ff., he argues for the existence and importance of social contacts and alliances between senators and equestrians in the late Republic. But he cannot deny the reality of the political conflict between the two orders at that time. On the use of the adjective *honestus* of equestrians see p. 239 n. 7 and Nicolet, op. cit. 235 ff.

and magistrates. Moreover, the social conservatism which had placed a reconstructed senatorial order in a position of political, social, and moral leadership also attempted to establish the equestrian order as a second aristocracy. Existing privileges and distinctions were confirmed and extended; the membership of the *ordo* was reviewed and scrutinized; social legislation designed to give the Senate a moral superiority over the lower orders was extended to cover equestrians.[1] *Concordia ordinum* was thus both a social and a political phenomenon. If the newer *cursus honorum* was able to attract men who might have chosen the older, traditional one, if there could be a Mela and a Crispinus (described by Tacitus as 'equestrians of senatorial dignity'), then the social gap between the two orders was certainly narrow.[2] The division of plebeians/senators, of which Gaius spoke in his commentary on the *Twelve Tables*, does not do justice to the enhanced standing of the 'second order'.[3] The closing of the gap is reflected in terminology. After the senatorial decree relating to scenic and gladiatorial performances and equestrians, Augustus exhibited no man who was *honeste natum*.[4] *Honesto loco ortum* and *nobilium familiarum posteros* in similar contexts in Tacitus refer to equestrians, as well as to those of senatorial rank.[5] Among the *multos honesti ordinis* maltreated by Gaius were some equestrians.[6] Finally, Vespasian was of equestrian stock—his mother was *honesto genere orta*.[7]

The comparative unity of the higher orders is also reflected in the sphere of trial and punishment. But before the evidence for the legal privileges of the equestrian order is summarized, an

---

[1] Equestrians filled gaps in magistracies: Dio 54. 26. 5; 54. 30. 2; 56. 27. 1; Suet. *Div. Aug.* 40. 1. For their privileges see pp. 240 ff. Review and scrutiny: Suet. *Div. Aug.* 37; 38. 3; 39. Social legislation: Dio 48. 43. 3; etc. (senators); Suet. *Div. Aug.* 43. 3; Dio 56. 25. 7; cf. Dio 51. 22. 4; Tac. *Ann.* 2. 85. 1; Suet. *Tib.* 35 (equestrians). Other refs. to knights appearing on the stage, etc.: Dio 55. 10. 11; 55. 33. 4; 60. 7. 1.

[2] Tac. *Ann.* 16. 17. 1.

[3] *Dig.* 50. 16. 238 praef. ('senatoribus' is bracketed by edd.). Contrast *Res Gestae* 35. 1: 'sena[tus et e]quester ordo populusq[ue] Romanus universus'. See *StR* iii. 461 n. 3.

[4] Suet. *Div. Aug.* 43. 3.   [5] Tac. *Ann.* 14. 21. 2; 14. 14. 5.

[6] Suet. *Gaius* 27. 4.

[7] Suet. *Div. Vesp.* 1. 3. *Honestus* is used of equestrians in the late Republic. See Cic. *ad fam.* 13. 14. 1; 13. 31. 1; 13. 62; *pro lege Man.* 17 (*publicani*); Caesar, *b.c.* 1. 51. 3; etc.

attempt should be made to specify what was meant by the equestrian order.

Equester ordo originally denoted *equites equo publico*, eighteen hundred young men who were entitled to a 'public horse' and who voted in the eighteen centuries of *equites equo publico* in the centuriate assembly.[1] *Equester ordo* in this sense is still found in the early Principate, although the *ordo* by then had grown in number. The composition of the order in Imperial times is disputed. The basic point at issue is whether citizens of equestrian census (*cives equestri censu*), that is, citizens who possessed 400,000 HS but who had not been awarded the gold ring and other privileges, were recognized as members of the order. On one side, it is held that the distinction in the epigraphical sources between equestrians adlected into the *turmae equitum* (or those given the *equus publicus*) and other equestrians is only apparent, the latter being identical with the former. By this view, all who claim equestrian rank in inscriptions have received this rank by a specific grant of the Emperor or a subordinate in his name. Some may feel that this is to postulate a greater degree of control from the centre than is evidenced or plausible: it might be argued that, if a provincial with the required census and free birth dubbed himself an equestrian, there would be no one to contest his claim on the grounds that he lacked all the qualifications laid down in the Tiberian legislation.[2]

Whatever the truth of the matter, those equestrians who resided at home were the wealthiest citizens of their cities, wealthier than the average decurion (although many decurions were equestrians). Other equestrians of provincial origin were not content with the social prestige which equestrian rank brought them in the provinces, but took up careers in the Imperial service or in the army.

More is revealed about equestrian legal privilege in literary non-legal sources than in legal sources. First, some instances are known of a conspicuous lack of preferential treatment for equestrians. Marius Priscus, proconsul of Africa, for a fee had an

---

[1] Select bibliography: A. Stein, *Der römische Ritterstand* (1927); P. A. Brunt, *JRS* 51 (1961), 71 ff.; M. I. Henderson, *JRS* 53 (1963), 61 ff.; J. Gagé, op. cit. 107–22; C. Nicolet, op. cit.; R. P. Duncan-Jones, *PBSR* 22 (1967), 147–88.

[2] Pliny, *n.h.* 33. 32.

equestrian beaten, condemned to the mines, and strangled in prison (and another exiled, for a lower price); Gessius Florus, procurator of Judaea, flogged and crucified Jewish equestrians; the Emperor Gaius threw an equestrian to the beasts.[1] Such arbitrary actions taken against equestrians attracted attention because of their novelty. (They were breaches of convention and precedent rather than law, for no law exempted equestrians from the crueller punishments.)[2] Second, some evidence was found earlier for the trial of equestrian defendants before, first, the Senate, and second, the Emperor, and it was suggested that in both courts they were favoured above defendants of lower rank.[3]

The jurists often write of the influence of wealth in the administration of the law, but rarely mention equestrians as such. *Iniuria* against equestrians was judged *atrox* when committed by a member of the lower orders.[4] An equestrian burglar (*effractor*) was banished from Rome, Italy, and Africa by the Emperor Marcus— a plebeian would have suffered any penalty up to *opus publicum* for the same offence.[5] Finally, Marcus ruled that the descendants of *eminentissimi viri* and *perfectissimi viri* were not subject to 'plebeian' penalties or tortures, as far as the third generation.[6] (Strictly, the first title was borne only by praetorian prefects, the second by leading officials in the Imperial secretariat together with other prefects.)[7]

On the basis of Marcus' edict,[8] at least a superficial comparison

---

[1] Pliny, *Ep.* 2. 11. 8 (Priscus); Jos. *BJ* 2. 308 (Florus); Suet. *Gaius* 27. 4 (Gaius); cf. *Tib.* 51 (equestrian condemned to treadmill).

[2] Gaius' victim proclaimed his innocence, not the illegality of the action; Florus did 'what no one previously dared to do'.

[3] See pp. 85 ff.   [4] *PS* 5. 4. 10.   [5] *Dig.* 47. 18. 1. 2.

[6] *CJ* 9. 41. 11 praef.

[7] See indexes in H. G. Pflaum, *Les Procurateurs équestres sous le Haut-Empire romain* (1950), and *Les Carrières procuratoriennes équestres sous le Haut-Empire romain* (1960–1). Pflaum shows that from the reign of Septimius Severus the title *eminentissimus vir* was allowed to some prefects of the watch (*praefecti vigilum*), presumably because of the fact that praetorian prefects had been given increased status. The first man so honoured of whom there is record was Cn. Marcius Rustius Rufinus (A.D. 205–7), as a result of the award of consular *ornamenta* to Fulvius Plautianus before his adlection into the senate (*Les Carrières*, ii, no. 234, pp. 625 ff.).

[8] The edict has been variously interpreted. Mommsen (*Straf.* 1033) thought, for example, that equestrian status became hereditary with its publication. Cf. Kübler, *RE* 6 (1909), 295, s.v. *equites Romani*. As Stein (op. cit. 78) pointed out,

between the position of top equestrians and that of senators can be made. Rules respecting senators affected their agnate descendants to the third generation—legal benefits possessed by leading equestrian officials carried as far. Families of equestrians of lower rank, *egregii viri*[1] and *equites Romani*, were perhaps protected only to the first generation, as was the case with the families of decurions (below).

Decurions

Decurions may be briefly described as members of the local councils in the cities of the Empire.[2] In the legal sources decurions are contrasted with 'plebeians'.[3] Veterans are said to bear the same *honor* as decurions,[4] *honor* which is the source of *dignitas*, *auctoritas*, and *reverentia*.[5] Decurions were exiled rather than executed for capital crimes, and by Severan times no capital punishment could be inflicted on them without a previous inquiry by the Emperor.[6] Crucifixion, exposure to wild beasts, work in the mines and other public labour, chastisement and torture, in short, all

---

Marcus was clearly not concerned in the edict with the whole equestrian order, but only with its upper stratum. Gagé (op. cit. 115) contrasted the senatorial order, where 'le rang est devenu transmissible', with the equestrian order, where 'le brevet . . . demeure personnel'. Stein's distinction (op. cit. 76) between 'Geburtsadel' and 'Personaladel' is similar. But Stein admits (ibid. 75, cf. 175–89) that the whole equestrian order possessed 'eine faktische Erblichkeit'. This is important: the son of an equestrian was not *ipso facto* an equestrian, but neither was the son of a senator a senator. Both were in a good position to take over their fathers' positions. It was of course difficult for the son of an *e.v.* to become an *e.v.*, because there were very few *e.v(iri)*. But he would have to lack all merit and initiative to fail to become an equestrian functionary of some kind. Moreover, a man of his birth would be strongly placed to strike for the Senate. As to whether the son of an *e.v.* called himself *e. i(uvenis)* or *e. p(uer)*, Hirschfeld (*Kl. Schr.* 654 and nn.) produces a few examples of these titles, but not enough to satisfy himself that they were in general use. Stein (op. cit. 76 ff.) dismisses even these, and others, not always with ease (see, e.g., the discussion on *C* III 14403a of A.D. 144, p. 80). It is still important that sons and daughters mention their exalted parentage, even if they do not take their father's title as their own.

[1] See Duncan-Jones, art. cit. 185–6.
[2] See *RE* 4 (1901), 2319 ff., s.v. *decurio* (Kübler); *DE* 2. 2 (1910), 1515 ff. (Mancini).   [3] *Dig.* 48. 19. 9. 14–15; ibid. 10. 2; 50. 2. 2. 2.
[4] *Dig.* 49. 18. 3.
[5] e.g. *Dig.* 48. 10. 13 (*dignitas*); *PS* 5. 4. 10 (*auctoritas*); *Dig.* 48. 19. 28. 5.
[6] Ibid. 15; 48. 22. 6. 2 (exile instead of execution); 28. 3. 6. 7; 48. 8. 16; 48. 19. 9. 11; ibid. 27. 1; 48. 21. 2. 1; 48. 22. 6. 1; 49. 4. 1 praef. (Imperial inquiry).

'plebeian' penalties and tortures, were ruled out for themselves and their children.[1]

An explanation of how decurions qualified for legal privileges should begin with an analysis of their social position. Members of the *ordo* were selected on the basis of their social background and financial situation. A dishonourable profession, or a criminal record, barred a man from the *ordo* of decurions.[2] In addition, free birth was a requirement, at least from the reign of Tiberius.[3] Some freedmen managed to gain admission, perhaps because they were particularly wealthy or particularly generous, but normally freedmen could win only the special benefits which decurions enjoyed, without securing full membership of the *ordo*.[4] (The political ambitions of their sons were not similarly frustrated.[5]) There was a census requirement for membership in Sicily in the late Republic, but otherwise no trace of one survives in the sources before the reign of Trajan, when Pliny recorded a qualification of 100,000 HS at Comum.[6] (This sum was a quarter of the qualification for an equestrian, and less than a tenth of that for a senator.)[7] The same amount may have been required elsewhere, but good evidence for this is lacking.[8]

Other local rules and customs ensured that all local politicians were men of means.[9] Candidates for some offices (later, for all

---

[1] *Crux*: *Dig.* 48. 19. 9. 11 (*furca*). *Vivus exuri*: ibid. *Bestiae*: *CJ* 9. 47. 12; *Dig.* 49. 18. 3. *Metallum*: *CJ* 9. 47. 9; *Dig.* 48. 19. 9. 11; ibid. 28. 5; *Dig.* 49. 18. 3; 50. 2. 2. 2. *Opus publicum*: *CJ* 9. 47. 3; *Dig.* 49. 18. 3. *Fustibus caedi*: *CJ* 2. 11. 5; *Dig.* 48. 19. 28. 5; 49. 18. 3; 50. 2. 2. 2. Plebeian penalties and torture: *CJ* 9. 41. 11. 1. Many of the texts are specifically about the children of decurions.

[2] *tab. Herac.*, 110 ff., 118 ff.; Fronto, *ad am.* 2. 7. 12 (ed. van den Hout, p. 183); *Dig.* 47. 10. 40; 50. 2. 6. 3; ibid. 12. [3] *CJ* 9. 21. 1.

[4] For a freedman decurion see *AE* 1966, 75. Other examples are less sure.

[5] On the freedman's son see M. L. Gordon, *JRS* 21 (1931), 65 ff. For a son who capitalized on the benefactions of his father (who won limited advantages for himself) see *C* x 4760 = *ILS* 6296.

[6] Cic. *in Verr.* 2. 120; 122 (Sicily); Pliny, *Ep.* 1. 19. 2 (Comum).

[7] For the senatorial census Dio gives the figure of 1,000,000 HS (54. 17. 3), and Suetonius 1,200,000 HS (*Div. Aug.* 41. 1). The latter figure is preferable. See Dio 55. 13. 6, better evidence for the census than Dio 54. 30. 2, and Tac. *Ann.* 1. 75. 3; 2. 37. 1.

[8] See Petr. *Sat.* 44; Dio 72. 16. 3; Cat. 23. 26–7. None of the references shows conclusively that the Comum figure applied elsewhere in Italy, or beyond.

[9] G. Charles-Picard, *La Civilisation de l'Afrique romaine* (1959), 118 ff., tried to estimate the wealth of decurions from the size of the entry fee. Cf. R. Duncan-Jones, *PBSR* 17 (1962), 69 ff., on private fortunes and incomes.

R

offices) were required to provide sureties and securities.[1] Decurions, who were not paid, were compelled to own a house within the city of a certain standard of opulence, or pay a fine.[2] Moreover, decurions (and magistrates) were expected to be benefactors.[3] New magistrates, in Africa at any rate, regularly promised to spend a definite amount, most often on a specific project, and just as regularly spent more. Again, from about the turn of the first century a fee for entry into the council was payable by all decurions.[4] Finally, the responsibility of decurions for public liturgies (*munera*) and magistracies (*honores*) involved additional expenditure.[5] In short, the cities were heavily dependent on their leading citizens, the decurions, for their financial well-being.

The privileges of decurions in the cities were comparable with those of senators at Rome.[6] They sat in special seats at the games and in the theatre; they dined at public expense; they used public water free of charge; they received more than others in a distribution of gifts; they wore distinctive dress; high-sounding epithets were applied to the order as a whole.

The effect of such benefits and status symbols was to surround the order of decurions with a certain mystique, and to set it apart from the rest of the populace as a privileged aristocracy. Nor was its prominence lost on outsiders. In a passage of Epictetus the distance between decurion and commoner is seen as comparable with that between a general and a rank-and-file soldier and a magistrate and a private individual.[7] Pliny the Younger, in a speech at Comum, spoke of the senate house as a refuge against the unruly

---

[1] *lex mun. Tar.* 1–25; *lex Mal.* 60; cf. E. Bormann, *JÖAI* 9 (1906), 315 ff. (Caracalla's charter on Lauriacum).

[2] *lex mun. Tar.* 26 ff.; *lex Urs.* 91.

[3] R. Duncan-Jones, *PBSR* 18 (1963), 159 ff. (Africa); 20 (1965), 189 ff. (Italy).

[4] It is commonly taken for granted that decurions always paid an entry fee. Only Mancini (*DE* 2 (1910), 1527 ff.) saw the significance of Pliny, *Ep.* 10. 112–13, which reveals that there was no entry fee for decurions in Bithynia before Trajan's reign. The matter is treated in a forthcoming article in *Historia*.

[5] See pp. 274 ff.

[6] In general see *RE* 4 (1901), 2330 ff. (Kübler).

[7] Epict. 3. 24. 99: τίνα με θέλεις εἶναι; ἄρχοντα ἢ ἰδιώτην, βουλευτὴν ἢ δημότην, στρατιώτην ἢ στρατηγόν . . .;

plebs.[1] It was Pliny who advised his governor friend Calestrius Tiro to continue preserving 'the differences between the ranks and degrees of dignity' in his province.[2] How such a policy could work out in practice is shown by a third-century Martyr Act. The discovery that Romanos was the son of a decurion (πατρόβουλος) put an end to the governor of Syria's preparations for his torture and cremation. It was only after submitting to long harangues and relentless abuse from the saint that the exasperated governor resumed his original plan.[3]

Legal privilege, in the eyes of governors such as Pliny, Tiro, and Asclepiades (the governor of Syria), was due to decurions and their families because of their status. Curial privilege was not a crude *quid pro quo* designed to compensate decurions for additional expenditures.[4] The Imperial constitutions which defended those privileges (for they defended rather than instituted them) reveal a sensitivity, at the highest level, to both the honorific and the functional aspects of the decurionate. In other words, they were a response to curial status, and to the functions which decurions were performing, and must continue to perform, if the Empire was to prosper.[5]

Veterans and soldiers

An extract from the *de re militari* of Ulpian's contemporary, Arrius Menander, establishes the privileged status of veterans:

veteranorum privilegium inter cetera etiam in delictis habet praerogativam, ut separentur a ceteris in poenis. nec ad bestias itaque veteranus datur nec fustibus caeditur.[6]

[1] Pliny, *Ep.* 1. 8. 16–17.
[2] Ibid. 9. 5: 'ut discrimina ordinum dignitatumque custodias . . .' (quoted pp. 77–8).
[3] See H. Delehaye, *Anal. Boll.* 50 (1932), 241 ff.
[4] See p. 170 n. 1.
[5] The grant of *Latium maius* (Gai. *Inst.* 1. 96; *ILS* 6780 (Gigthis)) should be seen in the same light. Through this concession decurions of 'Latin' cities were able to win Roman citizenship automatically on their entry into the council. See p. 266 below.
[6] *Dig.* 49. 18. 1: 'The privilege of veterans, which extends, amongst other things, to the area of delicts, gives them the prerogative of standing apart from the rest in respect of punishments. Thus a veteran is not sent to the beasts or beaten.'

Marcianus, writing a little later, put veterans and their sons on a par with decurions:

> veteranis et liberis veteranorum idem honor habetur, qui et decurioni- bus: igitur nec in metallum damnabuntur nec in opus publicum vel ad bestias, nec fustibus caeduntur.[1]

The position of soldiers is more open to doubt.[2] A passage of Menander indicates that soldiers were subject to beating, which Callistratus (who claims support from unspecified and unquoted Imperial rescripts) rules out for *honestiores*.[3] Again, it has been thought relevant that deserters were not exempt from low-status punishments.[4]

The second argument amounts to little. In his *de re militari* Tarrutenus Paternus commented:

> proditores transfugae plerumque capite puniuntur et exauctorati torquentur: nam pro hoste, non pro milite habentur.[5]

That is to say, a soldier suffered plebeian penalties and tortures only if he acted like a foe. This is stated quite emphatically by Modestinus:

> is, qui ad hostem confugit et rediit, torquebitur ad bestiasque vel in furcam damnabitur, quamvis milites nihil eorum patiantur.[6]

Earlier, the same jurist had specifically excluded *metallum, opus metalli*, and torture from sanctions to which soldiers were subject.[7]

That soldiers could be beaten while *honestiores* were exempt

---

[1] *Dig.* 49. 18. 3: 'Veterans and their sons are held in the same honour as decurions: thus they will not be condemned to the mines or public labour or beasts, nor are they beaten.'

[2] Or so thought Cardascia, art. cit. 328 and n. 2. Mommsen (op. cit. 1034) considered soldiers and veterans to be *honestiores*; cf. E. Cuq, *Manuel des instituts juridiques des Romains*[2] (1928), 108 n. 1: veterans and their sons are *honestiores*; soldiers are 'à quelques égards'.

[3] *Dig.* 49. 16. 3. 16 (Men.); 48. 19. 28. 2 (Call.).

[4] *Dig.* 49. 16. 3. 10 and 16.

[5] Ibid. 7: 'Traitors and deserters are mostly tortured and executed after being cashiered. For they are treated as enemies, not soldiers.' Paternus was *ab epistulis* of Marcus and praetorian prefect of Commodus, at whose hands he lost his life; see Kunkel, *Herkunft und soziale Stellung* 219 ff., no. 54.

[6] Ibid. 3. 10: 'The man who flees to the enemy and returns will be tortured and thrown to the beasts or condemned to the fork, although soldiers suffer none of these penalties.' For *damnatio ad bestias* cf. ibid. 4. 1.

[7] Ibid. 3. 1; cf. *CJ* 9. 41. 8 praef. (Diocl.; soldiers); 9. 47. 5 (Carac.; veterans and sons). Deportation of soldiers: *Dig.* 48. 5. 12 praef.; 49. 16. 5. 4; ibid. 13. 6.

from beating is interesting but unimportant. The beating designed to curb lack of discipline, a specifically military problem,[1] is not strictly comparable to the beating imposed in a non-military court on a man of low status, as an alternative to (for example) the fine exacted from a man of rank.[2] It is clear that a soldier might be either fined or beaten.[3]

Proponents of the view that soldiers were excluded from the *honestiores* might have made something of the frequent use of the death penalty. Soldiers were put to death for outright desertion,[4] and for sundry actions which were held to threaten the safety of the state. Cowardice, indiscipline, and insubordination cover most cases. The offences include leaving one's post, losing one's weapons, stirring up mutiny, disobeying orders, and abusing or assaulting officers.[5] It should be noticed, however, that the context is almost always war. With national security so obviously at stake, it is easy to see why behaviour which jeopardized it was severely punished. For the soldier, this was an occupational hazard.

In short, that soldiers do not quite fit into the *honestiores* in respect of punishment is an effect of circumstance, which does not alter the fact that theirs was a privileged position before the law.[6]

The subject of Juvenal's last satire was the rewards of the military life (*praemia militiae*), and the bulk of the surviving portion deals with the advantage of the soldier over the civilian in a legal dispute between them. A civilian never had the nerve to strike a soldier, Juvenal says, or to approach a magistrate, if roles were reversed and a soldier was the attacker. For:

> Bardaicus iudex datur haec punire volenti
> calceus et grandes magna ad subsellia surae,
> legibus antiquis castrorum et more Camilli
> servato, miles ne vallum litiget extra
> et procul a signis.[7]

---

[1] Ibid. 3. 1; 5; 16; ibid. 13. 4; 14. 1.   [2] See pp. 138 ff.
[3] Ibid. 3. 1; cf. Gellius 11. 1. 6 (fine).
[4] *Dig.* 49. 16. 5. 3; ibid. 3. 11; 5. 1; 6. 4; 6. 9; 13. 5.
[5] Ibid. 3. 4; 3. 22; 6. 3; 10 praef. (leaving post); ibid. 3. 13 (losing weapons); ibid. 3. 19; 16. 1 (mutiny); ibid. 3. 15 (disobedience); ibid. 13. 4 (abuse); ibid. 6. 1 (assault).
[6] On soldiers' crimes and punishments see Mommsen, op. cit. 30 ff.
[7] Juv. 16. 13 ff.: 'If he seek redress, he is given as judge a hob-nailed

This was not an ordinary civil case before a regular magistrate—
it was a court martial. Moreover, the hostility of the court to
anyone daring enough to bring a suit was assured. As for prospective witnesses, they would keep their distance.[1]

The general principle that a military court for military offenders
benefited soldiers can be accepted. More doubt might be entertained
about Juvenal's further assertion, that soldiers possessed a virtual
immunity from prosecution or 'vengeance' (*ultio*). There were,
none the less, occasions when officicls, both local and Imperial,
connived at acts of violence and lawlessness of soldiers, especially
the illegal requisitioning by force of animals, boats, food, and men.[2]
As for retired soldiers, public officials in Egypt knew they were
not easy to deal with, even without their weapons.[3] One strategos,
presumably irritated beyond control, had a veteran beaten up
in Philadelphia, a village in the Arsinoite nome. But the veteran
soon sought redress at the court of the prefect.[4]

Juvenal went on to make the general point that the soldier could
obtain swift justice, while the civilian was forced to put up with
the long-drawn-out processes of ordinary law (ll. 35–50). He then
turned to the subject of the soldier's status in private law. The
text breaks off in the middle of a discussion of a privilege which
went back to Augustus, if not to Julius Caesar:

> solis praeterea testandi militibus ius
> vivo patre datur.[5]

This was a unique privilege. Not even a consul, if he was a *filius-*
familias, had full possession of his property and rights of disposal

centurion with a row of jurors with big calves sitting before a big bench. For
the old camp law and the rule of Camillus still holds good that forbids a soldier
to attend court outside the camp and far from the standards.'

[1] Juv. 16. 29 ff.

[2] See *P. Lond.* iii. 1171 *v*, p. 107 (A.D. 42); *PSI* 5. 446 (A.D. 133–7); *IGBulg.*
iv. 2236 (= A–J, no. 139, p. 467; A.D. 238, Scaptopara); A–J, no. 141, p. 476
(A.D. 244–7, Aragua); P. Herrmann, *Neue Inschriften zur historischen Landeskunde*
von Lydien und angrenzenden Gebieten (1959), pp. 11–12.

[3] L. Mitteis and U. Wilcken, *Grundzüge und Chrestomathie der Papyruskunde*
(1912), i. 461 (beg. 3rd cent.).

[4] H. Kortenbeutel, *Aegyptus* 12 (1932), 129–40.

[5] ll. 51–2. Cf. *Dig.* 14. 6. 2. See 29. 1. 1 praef. (*factio testamenti*: Caesar,
Titus, Domitian, Nerva, Trajan); Ulp. *Reg.* 23. 10; *FIRA*[2] i, no. 78, p. 428
(A.D. 119: Hadrian permitted sons to petition for their inheritance).

over it.[1] Moreover, the soldier under the Empire had something to
bequeath—a *peculium castrense*,[2] which included whatever was
saved from pay, donatives, booty, slaves, legacies, and also profits
from any land which the soldier had leased in the *territorium* of
the legion.[3] If partial immunity from taxation and burdens is
added, it can be seen that the Emperors were attentive to the
economic situation of the soldier and veteran.[4] Finally, the gift
of land on discharge—as an alternative to a sum of money—
put an ex-soldier in a position to play a leading part in local
politics.[5]

Veterans were socially and politically prominent, in the main,
in smaller cities of recent foundation, for example in Syria and
Pannonia. Veteran colonies had faded out about the time of
Hadrian, but settlement was not hindered—veterans were well
placed to acquire land at little or no cost, especially in frontier
districts.[6] In a period when legions moved rarely, veterans had
little desire to leave the area in which they had seen long service
as soldiers, especially as most had formed unofficial marriage

[1] *Dig.* 14. 6. 1. 3. Note 28. 3. 6. 6 (Ulp.): soldiers but not civilians could make
a will (by military law) even after a death sentence was passed on them.
[2] Defined by Macer in *Dig.* 49. 17. 11.
[3] Slaves: R. MacMullen, *Soldier and Civilian in the Later Roman Empire*
(1963), 91, 106 ff. Land leased: A. Alföldi, *Arch. Ért.* 1 (1940), 230 ff.; E.
Sander, *Rhein. Mus.* 101 (1958), 193 ff. (from at least the time of Trajan, although
for praetorians at least from A.D. 79). For Pannonia, A. Mócsy, *Acta Arch.* 3
(1953), 179–99; P. Oliva, *Pannonia and the Onset of Crisis in the Roman Empire*
(1962), 312–18; E. Swoboda, *Carnuntum*[4] (1964), 48, 61, etc.
[4] On these and other privileges see, for veterans, *FIRA*[2] i, no. 56, p. 315
(31 B.C.); ibid., no. 76, p. 424 (A.D. 88–9); Gai. *Inst.* 1. 57; Mitteis and Wilcken,
op. cit. i. 459 (= *BGU* i. 265; A.D. 148); ibid. 396 (= *BGU* i. 180; A.D. 172);
Dig. 50. 5. 7 (Sev.); *CTh* 7. 20. 2 = *CJ* 12. 46. 1 (A.D. 320). For soldiers see
Ulp. *Reg.* 3. 5 (*vigiles*, Tiberius); *P. Fouad* 21 (A.D. 63); *Dig.* 29. 1. 24 (Trajan);
Gai. *Inst.* 2. 109–10; *Dig.* 38. 2. 22 (Hadr.; cf. 37. 14. 8 and 49. 17. 13); Sander,
art. cit. 203 ff.; MacMullen, op. cit. 107 ff.
[5] The average amount of land given on discharge was, according to H. Schmitz
(*Stadt und Imperium: Köln in römischer Zeit* (1948), 140 ff.), about one square
kilometre, which, in the view of Mócsy (*Die Bevölkerung von Pannonien bis
zu den Markomannenkriegen* (1959), 91), corresponded to the average holding of
a decurion. On payments in cash see, recently, P. A. Brunt, *PBSR* 5 (1950),
50 ff.; G. R. Watson, *Historia* 5 (1956), 332 ff.
[6] In general, see J. C. Mann, *The Settlement of Veterans in the Roman Empire*,
unpubl. Ph.D. thesis, London, 1956; J. Lesquier, *L'Armée romaine d'Égypte
d'Auguste à Dioclétien* (1918), 328 ff., for Egypt; E. Kornemann, *Klio* 11 (1911),
390 ff., for the West. See also *Dig.* 6. 1. 15. 2; 21. 2. 11 praef.

alliances with women of the neighbourhood.[1] The authorities had long recognized and not discouraged these unions, which produced many of the recruits for the army.[2] Indeed, in the first part of the second century, steps were taken to ensure that sons born *castris* followed their fathers into the army: citizenship was acquired by the son not on his father's discharge, but on his own enrolment into the army.[3] This change is reflected in *diplomata* issued to auxiliary troops.[4]

It is impossible to calculate the extent to which Roman armies from about Flavian times were drawn from the municipal aristocracy.[5] There was nothing to prevent a veteran passing into

---

[1] e.g. Tac. *Ann.* 14. 27: veterans planted in Tarentum, Antium (and Puteoli?) drift back to the provinces. The settlement of veterans in Italy was abandoned in the reign of Trajan. Note *C* III 11223 (early 2nd cent.): a veteran of *XIV Gemina* was a decurion at Claudius' colony Savaria, but was buried at Carnuntum; cf. *C* VIII 2699 (end of 2nd cent.): a veteran of *III Augusta* was a decurion of Thamugadi, but was buried at Lambaesis.

[2] It is generally held that the marriage of soldiers was forbidden until Septimius Severus abolished the ban. Herodian 3. 8. 5 ((sc. αὐτοῖς . . . ἐπέτρεψε γυναιξί τε συνοικεῖν) may refer to legal marriage—or merely to cohabitation. Legal texts thought to be relevant are ambiguous or pre-Severan in origin or reference. Third-century diplomas, which continue to award *conubium*, strongly suggest there was no change in the legal position regarding marriage under Severus. See Mommsen, *C* III, pp. 2011–12; R. Cagnat, *L'Armée romaine d'Afrique* (1913), 369 ff.; J. Lesquier, op. cit. 262 ff.; M. Durry, *Les Cohortes prétoriennes* (1938), 292 ff.; E. Sander, art. cit. 152 ff.; R. MacMullen, op. cit. 126–7; G. R. Watson, *The Roman Soldier* (1969), 133 ff. The matter is discussed in *Calif. Stud. Class. Ant.* (forthcoming).

[3] The recruitment of sons of soldiers is known earliest on any scale in Egypt. See Lesquier, op. cit. 210–16. It is also known for Africa (see, e.g., *C* VIII 18084), for Pannonia (e.g. III 11218), and Moesia (e.g. III 6188; v 48.

[4] See K. Kraft, *Rekrutierung der Alen und Kohorten an Rhein und Donau* (1951), 112 ff.: H. Nesselhauf, *Historia* 8 (1959), 434 ff. The position of children changed between A.D. 139 and 144: contrast *C* XVI, n. 87 (A.D. 139): 'ipsis liberis posteris(que) eoru(m)', and ibid. n. 90 (A.D. 144), where the phrase does not appear. Regular conscription cannot be proved for the early third century. Menander the jurist, when he wrote of the *mutato statu militiae* (*Dig.* 49. 16. 4. 10), was thinking of the contrast between the Republican citizen call-up and the Imperial (largely) voluntary recruitment into a long-service army. Conscription from the civilian body increased with the chaos of the mid-third century. By the fourth century, conscription had become regular, also in the frontier zones. See *CTh* 7. 22. 1 (A.D. 313) and ibid. 2 (A.D. 326); A. H. M. Jones, *The Later Roman Empire* (1964), ii. 614 ff.

[5] See *Dig.* 49. 18. 5. 2. On the social status of soldiers see Durry, op. cit. 302 ff.; E. R. Birley, *Roman Britain and the Roman Army* (1953), ch. 3, 133 ff.: G. Forni, *Il reclutamento delle legioni da Augusto a Diocleziano* (1953), 113 ff., espec. 119–29; Mann, op. cit.; MacMullen, op. cit., ch. 5, 99 ff. Forni makes

the curial order, and this is sufficient justification for Marcianus' statement: 'Veterans and sons of veterans are held in the same honour as decurions.'[1] Veterans were on the same social plane as decurions, and for this reason (*igitur*) were similarly favoured in the law courts. The ultimate responsibility for this state of affairs rested with the Emperor. It was expedient for him to look after the soldiers. He was commander-in-chief, and they (the soldiers) created Emperors.[2]

'Magistratus', 'aedilis', 'iudex'

In the statement on *atrox iniuria* which comes in *Paul's Sentences* the *magistratus*, *aedilis*, and *iudex* are apparently cited after the senator, equestrian and decurion, as examples of the *vir spectatae auctoritatis*.[3] It might be thought to follow from this first, that the magistrate, the aedile, and the judge were not decurions (for example), and secondly, that they were none the less *honestiores*.

Neither suggestion is justified on the basis of this text. Protection against injury might be given for two distinct reasons: first, because the protected person either held a position of authority, or exercised a political, judicial, or social function (as magistrates, judges, and parents respectively);[4] and secondly, because the protected person had personal *dignitas*. Members of the higher orders possessed this *dignitas* whether or not they were holding public offices at the time.[5] Similarly, a man holding a position of authority as parent might not have this *dignitas*. Therefore a list of those who were automatically entitled to an action for *iniuria atrox* would not necessarily be identical with a list of members of

the point that when recruitment came to be concentrated in the provinces rather than in Italy, there was a noticeable improvement in the social ranking of the recruits. Italian recruits were of poor quality (see Tac. *Ann.* 4. 4. 2), although they were almost invariably of citizen rank.

[1] *Dig.* 49. 18. 3.

[2] See J. W. B. Barns, *JEA* 52 (1966), 141; in general, Sander, art. cit. 232 ff.

[3] *PS* 5. 4. 10: 'atrox iniuria aestimatur aut loco aut tempore aut persona: . . . persona, quotiens senatori vel equiti Romano decurionive vel alias spectatae auctoritatis viro.'

[4] e.g. *Dig.* 47. 10. 7. 8.

[5] Neither senators nor many equestrians nor decurions can be adequately described as functionaries or officials with a circumscribed term of office.

the *honestiores*. Further, as magistrates, aediles, and judges were office holders, and were mentioned as such, this passage cannot by itself constitute proof that members of the curial order were never magistrates, aediles, and judges.

It is implied in some legal texts that the decurions were representatives of a wider group of privileged persons who possessed exemptions from plebeian penalties. For example, Callistratus wrote:

> et ut generaliter dixerim, omnes, qui fustibus caedi prohibentur, eandem habere honoris reverentiam debent, quam decuriones habent.[1]

It is worth inquiring from what source 'magistrates, aediles, and judges' were drawn. There might have been a category of extra-curial families with credentials of the sort which would win for them preferential treatment in the law courts.

'*Iudex*'. In Rome the *iudex*, whether juryman or judge, was traditionally appointed from the higher orders.[2] Under the Empire the minimum requirement for membership of the judicial decuries was 200,000 HS, that is, only half as much as the property qualification for equestrian status.[3] But that was a nominal figure: the membership of the decuries and the equestrian order overlapped to a considerable extent.[4]

The provincial juryman was also a man of status and means, although the only qualification of which we have record, 7,500 denarii for membership of the *consilium iudicum* of Cyrene in the Augustan age, fell far short of even the sum required for membership of the decurionate.[5] About the qualification for sitting as a judge, that is, a *iudex pedaneus* or *iudex datus* (the successor of the *iudex privatus*),[6] nothing is known directly.

---

[1] *Dig.* 48. 19. 28. 5: 'And, to speak generally, all who are excluded from beating ought to be given the same respect for honour as decurions are given.'

[2] On *iudex* see Steinwenter, *RE* 9 (1916), 2464 ff.; and s. 5 (1931), 350–6. The *iudex* was not a magistrate but acted as a *privatus*. He lacked *imperium* (e.g. *Dig.* 5. 1. 58).

[3] *StR* iii. 535.

[4] R. Duncan-Jones, *PBSR* 22 (1967), 159 ff.

[5] *EJ* 311. i; cf. Cic. *in Verr.* 2. 32 (*ex conventu civium Romanorum*).

[6] See *RE* 9. 2470. The *iudices pedanei* were delegated minor cases (*CTh* 1. 16. 8: *negotia humiliora*) by the governor. See *CJ* 3. 3; 9. 22. 11; *Dig.* 2. 7. 3. 1; 3. 1. 1. 6; 26. 5. 4; *PS* 5. 28.

Iudicare is described by the jurists both as a 'public liturgy' (*munus publicum*) and a 'private liturgy' (*munus personale*) for citizens of the cities.[1] Decurions must have acted as judges, as they bore the brunt of liturgies. There is indirect evidence that it was at least common for judges to be decurions. A text in *Paul's Sentences* prescribes expulsion from the *ordo* as a punishment for corrupt judges:

> iudices pedanei si pecunia corrupti dicantur, plerumque a praeside *aut curia submoventur* aut in exilium mittuntur aut ad tempus relegantur.[2]

It would be surprising if *iudices* were not all drawn from the aristocracy in the provinces. However, some members of the provincial aristocracy may not have been decurions.

'*Aedilis*'. In Rome the aedile was a minor magistrate with administrative responsibilities and jurisdiction in minor matters.[3] In Italian towns he was a municipal magistrate. Juvenal characterized him as a 'nobody' whose time was spent on trivia.[4] *Aedilis* in *Paul's Sentences* might refer to either the Roman or the municipal aedile, or both. In each context he was a minor magistrate, in Rome, with senatorial dignity, in a *municipium*, normally without full membership of the council, although likely to advance into it on the strength of his magistracy. Much of the section on the magistrate which follows will be relevant to the condition of the aedile.

'*Magistratus*'. The clearest statement about the relationship of magistracies to the decurionate is to be found in *Paul's Sentences*:

> is, qui non sit decurio, duumviratu vel aliis honoribus fungi non potest, quia decurionum honoribus plebeii fungi prohibentur.[5]

---

[1] *Dig.* 5. 1. 78 (public); *Dig.* 50. 4. 18. 14 (private).

[2] *PS* 5. 28: 'If petty judges are said to have been bribed, they are mostly expelled from the senate house, or sent into exile, or relegated for a time by the governor.' The last two penalties are also for men of high status (cf. *PS* 5. 23. 11: *deportatio*).

[3] For the aedile's edict see *Dig.* 21. 1; cf. Gai. *Inst.* 1. 6. For his jurisdiction, at Rome, *StR* ii. 491 ff.; in the cities, *lex Urs.* 94; *lex Mal.* 66; *C* XII 1377 (Vasio); VIII 972 (Neapolis, Africa).

[4] Juv. 10. 102; cf. Pers. 1. 130.

[5] *Dig.* 50. 2. 7. 2 (*PS*): 'He who is not a decurion cannot hold the duumvirate or other offices, because plebeians are barred from holding curial offices.'

This principle may well have held in some areas of the West towards the close of our period. The presence of thirty-two *pedani* (decurions who had held no office) in the *album* of Canusium of A.D. 223 suggests that there the holding of even the minor offices followed election into the order.[1] But the above principle clashed with the older, traditional one, that some magistracies, far from being the reserve of decurions, actually gave access to the *ordo decurionum*. By the latter principle it was possible to distinguish between major magistracies held by decurions and minor magistracies accessible to commoners.[2] Thus the situation envisaged in *Paul's Sentences* did not by any means exist in every period. Without indulging in speculation about the process by which constitutional practice evolved in the cities, we can say with assurance, that in the earlier stages of that evolution, there existed a small number of families which possessed the property qualification for the decurionate, had not yet achieved that honour, but were seeking to win it. However, it is equally certain that we must look elsewhere, if we are seeking to locate a sizeable, wealthy, independent group of magistrates and ex-magistrates outside the council who were a force to be reckoned with in the cities and provinces.

Some time ago Lévy drew attention to a peculiarity of the local scene in the East, the existence of 'une sorte de classe de magistrats', which dominated the council from without as a 'collège de fonctionnaires supérieurs'.[3] Lévy supported his case with evidence of the quasi-liturgical nature of many Eastern magistracies. The basic qualification for office holding was wealth, and as wealth was hereditary, offices tended to be hereditary. A *cursus honorum* can barely be said to have existed.

Lévy's theory is neither confirmed nor refuted by the epigraphical evidence. A magistrate or ex-magistrate whose honorific

[1] *C* IX 338.
[2] For the distinction, Pliny, *Ep.* 10. 79. A strict *cursus honorum* was not always observed. Apart from the evidence of inscriptions, *Dig.* 50. 4. 11 praef. (Pius) and ibid. 14. 5 (Call.) show indirectly that offices were sometimes held out of order. There is no assurance that the offices which plebeians were urged or forced to undertake in Severan times (ibid. 14. 4) were *minor* magistracies.
[3] I. Lévy, 'Études sur la vie municipale de l'Asie Mineure sous les Antonins', *REG* 12 (1899), 265, 269.

inscription omits any mention of membership of the *ordo* might still have been a decurion. Similarly, it is hard to believe that only those officials of Egyptian *metropoleis* who are specifically stated in the papyri to have been councillors were councillors. Again, in some places there are signs of an awareness of a distinction between offices open to decurions and other offices—although it can still be asked whether the dividing line was ever rigid, or anything other than theoretical.[1]

The problem is a complex one, because of the slow but thorough transformation which overtook Greek institutions in the East in the course of the Antonine and Severan periods. The assembly faded out as a political force. Magistrates lost power to a council which at one time had a temporary membership, but which became a permanent body, containing, more and more, the richest and most distinguished men of the city. Yet, through much of the period, there may well have been a division between independent

---

[1] A. H. M. Jones (*Greek City* (1940), 342 n. 47) quotes *IGRR* iii. 623 (Xanthos) as evidence that the dictum in *PS* applied to Greek as well as Latin cities. The inscription indicates that there was at least a theoretical distinction between a δημοτικὴ ἀρχή and a βουλευτικὴ ἀρχή. (Cf. *SB* 7261, where βουλευτικαὶ λειτουργίαι are contrasted with δημοτικαὶ ὑπηρεσίαι.) It is one thing for such a distinction to exist, and another thing for it to be enforced. (Incidentally, if the *PS* dictum did apply, it is a little odd that a δημοτικὴ ἀρχή was mentioned at all, unless ἀρχή had completely lost its original meaning.) Next, he refers to *JEA* 21 (1935), 224 ff. (c. A.D. 250, Arsinoe). The prefect asks the prytanis: ἰδιῷ[ται γίγνον]ται πα[ρ'] ἡμεῖν (sc. ὑμῖν) [κο]σμη[τ]αὶ ἢ καὶ [β]ουλε[υτ]αί; ἀπεκρ(ίνατο) ἰδ[ι]ῶται (l. 69). The words ἢ καὶ [β]ουλε[υ]ταί are interlinear. The implication is that βουλευταί were never chosen as cosmete (cf. l. 61). Some parts of the text are not easy to decipher. But it is absolutely clear that villagers, rather than private individuals in the city, had appealed to the prefect. They produced a decision of Severus which ruled that villagers should not be called to μητροπολειτικαὶ λειτουργείαι (l. 83). The qualification for the office of cosmete was wealth: a man was nominated ὁπ[όται]ν ἔχῃ εὐπορίαν (l. 70). 'How many Arsinoites (? are in this category)?' The prytanis replies: 'Over 300'. The next few lines are unintelligible. The sense must be that the 'over 300', who, from the context, do not appear to be the βουλευταί, had already served as cosmete, or were serving in other magistracies (the ἀγορανομία and perhaps the δεκαπρωτεία are mentioned in this connection). It seems that the councillors of Arsinoe had unloaded as many of their burdens as they could onto private citizens, both city-men and villagers. So little were they interested in maintaining a strict division between βουλευτικαὶ and δημοτικαὶ λειτουργίαι or ἀρχαί, although in theory there may have been such a division. Lévy (art. cit. 266 ff.) distinguishes between powerful and less powerful magistrates within the 'bureau' of magistrates (headed by the scribe of the people), and also between 'political' and eponymous magistrates, but makes no case for a regular progression from lower to higher ranks.

and extra-curial magistracies, and curial magistracies. Some magistracies were in the virtual possession of single families, and they were not abolished overnight, nor were they quickly robbed of their power. Of the *dignitas* and social influence of the holders there can be no doubt. Moreover, priesthoods were often hereditary, and they are likely to have stood outside the council.

By the fourth century both priests and magistrates seem to have been councillors.[1] The earlier division between magistrates had now shifted within the council itself, where the top stratum, the *principales*, did their best to oppress their weaker colleagues.[2]

The extra-curial families in the second and third centuries are difficult to pin down. They might be sought, for example, among the members of the gerusia, an aristocratic club which is found in many Eastern cities. Half the foundation members of the gerusia in Sidyma were δημόται (commoners), and half were βουλευταί (councillors).[3] If this gerusia was not eccentric, birth and wealth were important qualifications for membership.[4] At Pergamum, where numbers were restricted, aspirants for membership were favoured if they had been magistrates or priests.[5] Might not they have been among the δημόται enrolled at Sidyma?

Callistratus may have given a further clue when he referred to *mandata* 'de decurionibus et principalibus civitatium'.[6] This may

---

[1] For the fourth century see the *album* of Thamugadi, *C* VIII 2403+17824, partly reproduced in *ILS* 6122, and improved by L. Leschi in *REA* 50 (1948), 71 ff.

[2] *CTh* 11. 16. 4 (A.D. 328); cf. 12. 3. 2 (A.D. 423); Symm. *Ep.* 9. 10; A. F. Norman, *JRS* 48 (1958), 79 ff., espec. 83 ff.; Jones, *Later Roman Empire*, ii. 731 and nn. The term *principales* (*civitatium*) was known to Callistratus (*Dig.* 48. 19. 27. 1), but on that passage see below. There were, of course, divisions in the *ordo* before the fourth century. See *Dig.* 50. 4. 6 praef.; 50. 7. 5. 5.

[3] *TAM* ii. 175–6 (A.D. 185–92). On the gerusia in general see Jones, *Greek City*, 225–6; E. G. Turner, *Archiv* 12 (1937), 179; J. H. Oliver, *Hesperia Suppl.* 6 (1941).

[4] Membership by wealth: there was an entry fee at Pergamum (H. Hepding, *Ath. Mitt.* 32 (1907), nn. 18–19, 294–5, 298–9) and Hyettus (*Syll.*³ 1112, pre-A.D. 212). Membership by birth: see the inscriptions from Pergamum and Hyettus, and the list at Sebaste in A.D. 99 (W. M. Ramsay, *Cities and Bishoprics of Phrygia* (1895–7), 602). Membership was a family matter at Sebaste, with father, mother, and five children represented.

[5] For ex-priests see Hepding, art. cit.

[6] *Dig.* 48. 19. 27. 1. Callistratus' origin is commonly thought to have been Greek. See Kunkel, *Herkunft und soziale Stellung*², 235, no. 61.

imply that not all the influential men were in the *ordo*. Another section of the same *mandata* mentions *qui ex principalibus alicuius civitatis*. There is no contradiction, if decurions were among the *principales*.[1]

Finally, Ulpian said that the choice of doctors (perhaps for exemption from burdens) lay not with the provincial governor, '. . . sed ordini et possessoribus cuiusque civitatis'.[2] A fragmentary inscription from North Africa records a meeting of the *possessores* and *decuriones* of a certain town.[3] Evidently *ordo* (*decuriones*) and *possessores* are not coextensive terms, and *possessores* seem to have had a power and influence which was not derived directly from office.[4] *Possessores* might include decurions: in an inscription from the vicus Vindonianus within the territory of Aquincum in Pannonia a group of *possessores* includes a priest who was a decurion, another decurion, an equestrian, and a veteran.[5] Not enough of the inscription is legible for it to be possible to determine whether the other men on the list had similar backgrounds. In North Africa groups of small landowners who were veterans or of veteran stock styled themselves *possessores*.[6]

It is therefore possible to assert that there were prominent provincials apart from decurions, whose prestige in the community would have compared favourably with that of decurions, and who for that reason—if we remember some words of Callistratus quoted earlier[7]—might have been given preferential treatment in law courts. Some were veterans. Others came from magisterial or priestly families. Moreover, there were doubtless some wealthy landed gentry, in every period, who were well-enough established

---

[1] *Acta Carpi Papyli et Agath.* (Decius), K–K, no. 2, p. 8, § 3. The proconsul said to Papylus: *principalis es?* He replied *civis*. In the Greek version the question is βουλευτὴς εἶ; and the answer πολίτης εἰμί.

[2] *Dig.* 50. 9. 1.

[3] A–J, no. 146, p. 483 (A.D. 186). Add *C* XI 15: *erga ordinem possessores et cives*.

[4] See also *Dig.* 7. 1. 27. 3 and 50. 4. 18. 25 (cf. 50. 1. 8). In 2. 8. 15 praef. *possessores immobilium rerum* are exempted from a security payment or *vadimonium*. So are men of *fides* (40. 5. 4. 8) and *honestas* (26. 4. 5. 1).

[5] *C* III 10570. Cf. *IGBulg.* iv. 2236 (A.D. 238, Scaptopara). Aurelius Pyrrhus, presumably a veteran of a praetorian cohort, goes on an embassy for the citizens. He is described as *convicanus et conpossessor*. And see *Dig.* 49. 18. 4 praef.

[6] See H. d'Escurac-Doisy, *Ant. afric.* 1 (1967), 59–71.

[7] *Dig.* 48. 19. 28. 5 (quoted above, p. 252.)

not to be desirous of office, and sufficiently powerful to be able to resist pressure to accept office, or to buy immunity from it.[1]

Conclusion

To the Romans the source of legal privilege was *dignitas* (*honor*, prestige). *Dignitas* was derived from political position or influence, style of life (character, moral values, education, etc.), and wealth. Each of the privileged groups discussed above possessed these attributes in some measure.

This view may be accepted with two qualifications. First, it should be recognized that differences in power, status, and wealth within the *honestiores* were reflected in the value of the privileges afforded.[2] Secondly, there were channels to legal privilege other than those which led through prestige, and were overtly recognized and sanctioned by the legal authorities. The legal privileges of Imperial freedmen are to be explained purely in terms of their proximity to the seat of power.[3] They were gained independently of *dignitas* or a social standing which would be acknowledged by judges and officials. Similarly, these privileges did not gain for the freedmen a status which could be justified in terms of the prevailing social values. Imperial freedmen were not held to be *honestiores*. Again, the section on civil law provided examples of power and wealth as direct sources of *de facto* legal privilege. The institution of self-help favoured the powerful, and the rules governing the provision of bail and guarantors benefited the rich.[4] Thus it

---

[1] Cardascia (art. cit. 328 ff.) argued that *negotiatores* were not *honestiores*. Ulpian wrote of the punishment of *dardanii*: 'nam plerumque, si negotiantes sunt, negotiatione eis tantum interdicitur, interdum et relegari solent, humiliores ad opus publicum dari' (*Dig.* 47. 11. 6 praef.). Cardascia saw that this passage does not justify the inclusion of *negotiatores* among the *honestiores*, but gave himself difficulties by seeing a 'literal opposition' between *negotiantes* and *humiliores*. There is a break in the sense after *interdicitur*; *interdum et relegari solent* is balanced by the *humiliores* clause, and Ulpian might just as well have written *honestiores relegari solent*. Cardascia's theory that some of the traders would have possessed the equestrian census and qualified for milder punishment in that way may well be correct. (Yet Cardascia does not believe that possession of the equestrian census in itself meant that a man would be punished with *relegatio* rather that *opus publicum*.) Constantine declared that *negotiantes* were equestrians (*CTh* 13. 5. 16).

[2] This fact, which is passed over by the jurists, is examined below, ch. 12.
[3] See pp. 85 ff. above.   [4] See ch. 7 above.

might be suggested that *dignitas* was the source of legal privilege only in so far as the distribution of prestige reflected the realities of the Roman social and political structure.

It might be argued, in addition, that citizenship should be placed alongside power, style of life, and wealth as a source of legal privilege. This suggestion raises important questions, and may be considered in detail.[1]

[1] The conceptual problems involved in such a view are discussed by W. G. Runciman, in *Social Stratification* (ed. J. A. Jackson, 1968), 34 ff.

11

CITIZENS AND *HONESTIORES*

THE *honestiores/humiliores* distinction was not the only distinction of which Romans took account in administering the law. Callistratus wrote that slaves were traditionally punished more severely than free men, and men of bad reputation (*famosi*) more severely than men of good reputation (*integrae famae homines*).[1] The latter division is clearly not the distinction between *honestiores* and *humiliores* in one of its guises: the differential punishment of *famosi* and *integrae famae homines* reveals something about the moral and social attitudes of the Romans, but nothing directly about their view of status.[2] The former division was, according to Gaius, the basic one in the law of persons:

> et quidem summa divisio de iure personarum haec est, quod omnes homines aut liberi sunt aut servi.[3]

Callistratus' statement that slave criminals were treated more severely than free men needs no elaborate comment.[4] Certain

---

[1] *Dig.* 48. 19. 28. 16: 'maiores nostri in omni supplicio severius servos quam liberos, famosos quam integrae famae homines punierunt.'

[2] Cf. Dio 56. 10. 1: different penalties for bachelors and for married men. This is relevant to a discussion of Augustan social legislation, but not to the Roman view of status.

[3] Gai. *Inst.* 1. 9: 'This is the basic division in the law of persons, that all men are either free or slaves.' *Servus/liber*: see Gellius, 11. 18. 8 = *XII Tables* 8, 14; *Coll.* 2. 5. 5 = *XII Tables* 8, 3; *Dig.* 47. 9. 4. 1; 48. 10. 8; 48. 19. 10 praef.; *CJ* 9. 47. 6; *FIRA*² i, no. 104, p. 498, §§ 5–7 (*lex metalli dicta*; Hadrian). *Servus/ingenuus*: *CTh* 9. 18. 1 = *CJ* 9. 20. 16 (A.D. 315). *Servi/liberi/sordidiores* (sc. *liberi*): *Dig.* 47. 9. 4. 1. *servi/liberi plebeii et humiles personae*: *Dig.* 48. 19. 28. 11. *Servi/honestiores/humiliores*: *PS* 5. 25. 1. *Servi/liberi humilioris loci/ceteri* (sc. *honestiores*): *Dig.* 47. 10. 45. For the division between slave and free in Alexandrian law of the third century B.C. see *P. Hal.* i, ll. 186–213 (= Hunt and Edgar, *Select Papyri* ii, no. 202), espec. 186 ff., 196 ff. (injury).

[4] On the unequal punishment of the free and unfree see Mommsen, *Strafr.* 1032–3. In Imperial times it was not completely true that the slave was *pro nullo* in civil and praetorian law. But he was only brought into court to be punished or to witness under torture. See Buckland, op. cit. 64; *Dig.* 28. 1. 20. 7; 28. 8. 1 praef.; 50. 17. 32. See also *Dig.* 48. 2. 12. 3–4 (slaves in public courts); *Dig.*

penalties were traditionally 'servile',[1] though, significantly, some of them came to be applied to free men of low status.[2] But the division between slave and free is too broad for our purposes. There are other divisions that neither Gaius nor Callistratus touches upon.

In A.D. 17 when the senate rounded on astrologers, the citizens among them were exiled, but the foreigners were put to death.[3] Again, during the reign of Marcus the governor of Lugdunensis separated Christian citizens from aliens, and after consulting the Emperor about their punishment, sent only the latter to the beasts, with the exception of Attalus, a citizen.[4] Citizens, then, might secure a milder penalty than aliens for the same offence.

Further, it was a basic principle of Roman law that aliens, being outside the *ius civile*, were subject to magisterial coercion (*coercitio*). Citizens, on the other hand, could in theory seek the aid of a tribune or exercise the right of appeal (*provocatio*) against magistrates. St. Paul's cry, 'Is it lawful for you to scourge a Roman citizen, uncondemned?' alarmed the tribune and enabled him to escape a beating in Jerusalem during the reign of Nero. Previously he had caused embarrassment to the local magistrates of Philippi by revealing his citizen status after suffering a beating and imprisonment.[5] Much later, in the reign of Commodus peasants from an African Imperial estate sent a petition to the Emperor, complaining of ill-treatment from a government official and from their overseers. They had been, among other things, beaten, although some of them were Roman citizens.[6] Two or three decades later Ulpian cited the clause of the Julian law on public

---

48. 8. 11. 2 (slaves sent to the beasts only with the permission of a magistrate); *Coll.* 3. 3; cf. *Dig.* 1. 6. 2 (Pius); Gai. *Inst.* 1. 53 (Pius); *Coll.* 3. 2 (*PS*); *CTh.* 9. 12. 1. 2 (A.D. 326) (all four references show that the restrictions on the master were extended).

[1] Tac. *Ann.* 15. 60. 1, for the phrase *serviles poenae*; and see, e.g., p. 127.

[2] *Dig.* 48. 19. 28. 11; *CJ* 9. 47. 6 (A.D. 214, illegally used); ibid. 11.

[3] *Coll.* 15. 2. 1; cf. Dio 57. 15. 8; Tac. *Ann.* 2. 32. 3. On citizenship see A. N. Sherwin-White, *The Roman Citizenship* (1939), and Kornemann, *RE* s. 1 (1903), 304 ff., s.v. *civitas*. On aliens (*peregrini*) see Buckland, op. cit. 96 ff.

[4] Eus. *EH* 5. 1. 47.

[5] St. Paul: Acts 22: 24 (Jerusalem); 16: 37 (Philippi).

[6] *FIRA²* i, no. 103, p. 496, 11, ll. 10 ff.

violence which dealt with appeal.[1] Further, the subject of appeal is treated at length in the *Digest*. So the peasants were correct in believing that officially, at any rate, appeal was not obsolete in the late Antonine age.

Discrimination in favour of citizens as opposed to aliens was thus a permanent feature of the Roman judicial system. It was practised in all spheres of law where aliens were technically excluded, as from the *ius civile*, and where they were not, as in criminal law as administered by the *cognitio* procedure.

Within the citizen body itself there were some who possessed restricted rights, for example, the *infames* and *intestabiles*, who have already been identified. Larger and more significant than either of these groups is a third, the freedmen.[2] Inequalities with regard to family rights affecting freedmen were the logical result of the laws relating to slavery, and were not corrected until the second century A.D. As for intermarriage, by Augustus' regulations senators were not permitted to marry women of slave origin.[3] Augustus had thus abandoned what appears to have been the Republican practice of preventing marriages between freedmen (and freedwomen) and all other Roman citizens.[4] In public law, freedmen could not hold Roman magistracies and priesthoods or vote in elections, were forbidden access to the legions, the praetorian guard, and the urban cohorts, and could not rise into the curial and equestrian orders.[5] In criminal law, the feeling that freedmen were inferior is reflected in punishments awarded by judges proceeding *extra ordinem*. Under Tiberius an attack was made on those who practised Jewish and Egyptian rites in Italy. The free-born were threatened with exile if they did not abandon their practices; freedmen were banished at once.[6] The failure of

---

[1] *Dig.* 48. 6. 7.

[2] Buckland, op. cit. 91–2 (*infames*); 92 (*intestabiles*); 87 ff.; cf. A. Watson, *Law of Persons in the Later Roman Republic* (1967), 226 ff. (freedmen).

[3] *Dig.* 23. 2. 44 praef.

[4] Livy 39. 19. 5; Dio 54. 16. 1–2. The reason given by Dio for Augustus' change was the shortage of well-born women. Marriage between freedmen and free-born women was less popular with the authorities. Severus forbade it within the freedman/patron relationship (*CJ* 5. 4. 3). See Watson, op. cit. 32 ff.

[5] A. M. Duff, *Freedmen in the Early Roman Empire*[2] (1958), 66–7, and refs.

[6] Tac. *Ann.* 2. 85. 4; Jos. *AJ* 18. 65 ff.

the attempt to incriminate Agrippina, the mother of Nero, ended in the relegation of Calvisius and Iturius, presumably free-born citizens, and the execution of Atimetus the freedman.[1] When Otho wreaked vengeance on the principal supporters of Galba, he had the courage to execute publicly only one of the two powers behind the throne; the other was assassinated before he could reach the island to which he had been exiled. The latter was an equestrian, Cornelius Laco, praetorian prefect; the former a mere freedman, Icelus.[2] Finally, the weakness of the freedman's position was exposed if his patron was murdered: he could be tortured and put to death.[3]

If ordinary citizens were favoured above freedmen, citizens of high status were favoured above rank-and-file citizens. This becomes apparent when we consider, first, courts, and second, punishments.

It was suggested in an earlier discussion[4] that defendants from the senatorial, equestrian, and curial orders gained advantages from trial before the Senate (especially in the case of senators) and before the Emperor. It was observed that 'ordinary' provincials of citizen rank were sometimes tried before Roman courts, but seldom in situations which were favourable to them, and seldom by their own choice. Those provincials who won a sympathetic hearing from the Emperor, whether as defendants or as accusers, seem to have taken the initiative and approached him in person, or to have gained access to him through a governor or through friends in Rome. But they were not exclusively citizens, and those who were citizens had other assets in addition to citizenship. Under the Empire, citizenship itself did not carry with it influence with the governor or connections in Rome, or even the capacity to bear the expense of travel to Rome. Now at an earlier stage, when citizens in the provinces were socially and economically a smaller and more select band, it is possible that the right of *reiectio Romam* was associated with citizenship. That is to say,

---

[1] Tac. *Ann.* 13. 22.   [2] Tac. *Hist.* 1. 46.
[3] See Tac. *Ann.* 13. 32. 1 (*S.C. Claudianum* of A.D. 57); 14. 42 ff. (murder of Pedanius Secundus, A.D. 61); Pliny, *Ep.* 8. 14. 12 ff. (murder of Afranius Dexter, A.D. 105).
[4] See chs. 1–3.

citizens might have been entitled to choose between trial at Rome and trial by the local courts. However, the sources give the impression that *reiectio Romam* was far from being a universal prerogative of citizens in the late Republic and early Empire, if it had been at any stage. It seems that by the Ciceronian age, in any particular case (and very few are known), the governor was not compelled to grant the request for reference to Rome, and that only members of the Roman aristocracy domiciled or with interests abroad, and a few individuals who had received the right as a special privilege, were likely to lodge a successful petition.[1]

In the sphere of penalties, the legal sources make clear that citizenship did not carry much weight. This may be shown with reference to beating and execution. The African peasants protested at being beaten, but they might have expected it. They were representatives of a group in whose welfare the Emperors might seem to have lost interest long before, *homines rustici tenues*. This phrase, which the peasants applied to themselves, finds an echo in Callistratus, who stated unambiguously that 'hi . . . qui liberi sunt et quidem tenuiores homines' (free men and men of low rank) were liable to be beaten, and that only *honestiores* were exempt. The statement is authoritative, for it repeats the substance of Imperial rescripts.[2] A rescript of Septimius Severus may have been one of those which Callistratus had in mind. It read:

> decuriones quidem, item filios decurionum fustibus castigari prohibitum est.[3]

Neither jurist nor Emperor was writing of a post-Commodan development. The exemption of decurions from beating was a long-standing rule (*prohibitum est*).[4] The plea of the peasants for a recognition of their rights was thus pathetically anachronistic.

Secondly, with respect to the death sentence, citizens could hold up the execution of the penalty of death by appealing to a higher judge. However, the position of decurions and other

---

[1] *Reiectio Romam* is discussed at greater length in *JRS* 68 (1968), pp. 56–7.
[2] *Dig.* 48. 19. 28. 2.
[3] *CJ* 2. 11. 5 (A.D. 198): 'The beating of decurions and sons of decurions has been prohibited.'
[4] *Dig.* 47. 21. 2 (Hadr.) is relevant. See pp. 155 ff.

honestiores was preferable: they were not subject to the death penalty at all, except in the case of a few very serious offences such as *maiestas*.

In general, an explanation is required for the absence of reference to citizenship among the criteria for legal privilege which can be assembled from the juristic writings. Perhaps this omission is not attributable to the classical jurists themselves, but to their successors, and above all, to the compilers of the *Digest* who excerpted the writings of the classical jurists, not without alteration and condensation. This suggestion is worth careful study, especially in the light of the history of the transmission of the text of the Fabian law on kidnapping. The Fabian law seems to have been designed originally (perhaps in the second century B.C.) to protect Roman citizens and freedmen who had gained their liberty in Italy.[1] But there is no mention of either of these categories in the section of the *Digest* devoted to the law; 'Gaius' and 'Ulpian' wrote of the *liber homo*, and 'Callistratus' of the *homo ingenuus et libertinus*.[2] The corruption can be traced fairly securely to the sixth century, as the versions of the law given in *Paul's Sentences* (late third century) and the *Collatio* (late fourth) are evidently closer to the original.[3] But the argument that the texts dealing with legal privileges were systematically rewritten is less convincing. The texts are several and scattered, and the task of purging anachronisms was thus less straightforward. (Although the compilers professed to be bent on bringing the jurists up to date, it can be shown that they fell far short of their goal.) It is as likely that the texts with which we are concerned are virtually untouched as that they are rewritten. In any case, our knowledge of the system

---

[1] On the Fabian law, Mommsen, op. cit. 780 ff. For the favourable position of freedmen emancipated in Italy, Petr. *Sat.* 57 (exemption from poll-tax and land-tax).

[2] *Dig.* 48. 15. 4 (Gaius); ibid. 1 (Ulpian); ibid. 6. 2 (Call.).

[3] *Coll.* 14. 3. 4: 'lege autem Fabia tenetur, qui civem Romanum eumve, qui in Italia liberatus sit, celaverit vinxerit vinctumve habuerit, vendiderit emerit, quive in eam rem socius fuerit . . .' Cf. the less detailed and less accurate *PS* 5. 30B. 1 (= *Coll.* 14. 2. 1): 'lege Fabia tenetur, qui civem Romanum ingenuum libertinum servumve alienum celaverit vendiderit vinxerit comparaverit.' It is perhaps curious that these late compilations retain categories which were no longer significant. The occurrence of a concept in a legal text is of course no guarantee of its contemporary relevance.

of privilege is not derived entirely from the *Digest*. The information contributed by the *Digest* complements, and is completely compatible with, the information drawn from other sources. Possession of citizenship did not ensure privileged treatment in the law courts: there were citizens amongst the *humiliores*.

In addition, possession of citizenship was not necessary for admission into the ranks of the privileged. Just as citizens were not *ipso facto* recipients of privilege, so non-citizens were included in their number. For not all decurions were citizens; none the less, decurions were a privileged group before the law.[1]

All members of local councils of 'Roman' cities were citizens. However, until the early second century A.D. decurions of cities of 'Latin' right gained the citizenship only by taking up a magistracy. The situation changed, perhaps in Hadrian's reign, with the introduction of *Latium maius*, now opposed to *Latium minus*.[2] Decurions of a city which had successfully sued for *Latium maius* (for the Roman authorities do not seem to have granted this status to all 'Latin' cities by decree) became Roman citizens from the time of entry into the council. The reform, however, left quite untouched the mass of cities in the East, which had not adopted Roman forms of local government (and were thus neither *coloniae* nor *municipia*). Citizenship was distributed altogether more sparsely in the East than in the West, because it was given piecemeal to individuals and families rather than *en bloc* to whole cities or ruling élites. Many of the Eastern councillors would have received such *ad hominem* grants, or inherited citizenship from their ancestors; but citizenship could not have come universally to councillors until the Emperor Caracalla conferred it on virtually the whole free population of the Empire.[3]

Thus the *honestiores/humiliores* distinction cuts across the citizen/alien distinction: there were citizens (and aliens) on both sides of the dividing line.

---

[1] There is no suggestion in any source that only decurions who were citizens were privileged in the sight of the law. For other aliens with *dignitas* see Dio 49. 22. 6 (Antigonus; M. Antonius' treatment of him was unprecedented and reprehensible); cf. 50. 13. 7 (Iamblichos, Arabian king; executed by M. Antonius after torture); Tac. *Ann.* 6. 40. 2 (Tigranes; succumbed to *supplicia civium*).

[2] Gai. *Inst.* 1. 96; *ILS* 6780 (Gigthis, N. Africa); Mommsen, *GS* iii. 33 ff.

[3] See Chr. Sasse, *Die Constitutio Antoniniana* (1958).

We must now consider the common belief that the former distinction replaced the latter. The citizen/alien distinction, so the argument runs, was pre-eminent in the first century of the Empire, and was overshadowed, or replaced, by that of the *honestiores/ humiliores* in the early second century.[1]

This doctrine rests principally on two theories. According to the first, the decline of *provocatio*—with which the Julian law that dealt with appeal was peculiarly associated—was complete by about the Trajanic period. A new appeal system, *appellatio*, which grew up soon afterwards, was available to *honestiores* but not to citizens in general. According to the second theory, rescripts of Hadrian and Pius herald the emergence of the *honestiores/ humiliores* distinction.

I have argued elsewhere that so-called *provocatio* and so-called *appellatio* were one and the same, and that the clauses in the Julian law applied to 'both', and had not lost their efficacy (such efficacy as they had in the first century) by the early second or late second century.[2] As for the emergence of the *honestiores/humiliores* distinction, the 'legislation' of Hadrian and Pius relates only to the differential-penalty system, and discrimination in favour of status involved more than this. Moreover, this 'legislation' did not institute the differential-penalty system, which was in existence in essentials by the reign of Hadrian.[3]

Thus the 'replacement' of the citizen/alien distinction by the *honestiores/humiliores* distinction cannot be dated to the early second century, or not by the arguments considered above. But

---

[1] A. H. M. Jones, *Studies in Roman Government and Law* (1960), 64–5; A. N. Sherwin-White, *Roman Society and Roman Law in the New Testament* (1963), 174.

[2] *JRS* 56 (1966), 167 ff., *pass.*, against Jones, op. cit. 53 ff. No sharp contrast can be drawn between appeal in the first century and appeal in the second. The evidence, such as it is, suggests that a more complicated system might have been evolved in the second century to handle the mounting volume of business which came before the appellate courts—but that is all. For a discussion of the two alleged appeal cases found by Jones in the pre-Hadrianic period see pp. 75–6 (with *JRS* 56, 182–5), and pp. 74–5 (with *JRS* 56, 181–2) (St. Paul; Bithynian Christians). Sherwin-White added four more cases: *EJ* 311. ii. 42–7; Pliny, *Ep.* 6. 31. 3; Tac. *Ann.* 16. 10. 2 (*Roman Society*, 60); Dio 60. 24. 4 (*Roman Citizenship*, 214). On the view that appeal became available to *honestiores* only see *JRS* 58 (1968), 54.

[3] See ch. 5.

did such a development occur at any stage? If so, it would follow that the former distinction was once as fundamental as the latter 'became'; and, conversely, that the latter distinction was at one stage unimportant.

How did citizens fare in the early Empire? There are signs that the Roman authorities were not oblivious of the safety of their citizens in the provinces. Cyzicus lost its liberty once, perhaps twice, and Rhodes once, for committing violence against Romans or for putting them to death. (The status of the citizens involved is unknown.)[1] In a Roman colony it appears that arrest, beating, and imprisonment were normal for aliens, but that it was potentially dangerous to give citizens the same treatment. Citizens may also have had a freer choice of court, even under the early Empire. So much is indicated by the career of St. Paul.[2] It was of course not always possible to keep governors in check. Fonteius Capito made a mockery of the institution of appeal by judging an appeal lodged against himself. Galba crucified a citizen for poisoning, ignoring the man's invocation of 'the laws' and his cry that he was a Roman citizen.[3] Their acts were reminiscent of Verres' treatment of Gavius, which, in Cicero's mind, shattered the hopes of all *homines tenues* who held the citizenship.[4] The disapproval which colours the narratives of Cicero, Suetonius, and Dio may suggest that the events they describe were unusual. The comparative respect which Pliny on one occasion showed for the citizenship may have been more typical of the attitude of governors: he separated the citizen Christians from the rest, who were arbitrarily executed.[5]

The concentration of the bulk of the references of this kind in the period from the 70s B.C. to the turn of the first century A.D.

[1] Cyzicus: Dio 54. 7. 6; 57. 24. 6; Tac. *Ann.* 4. 36. 2–3; cf. Suet. *Tib.* 37. 3. Dio records loss of freedom under 20 B.C. and again under A.D. 25, where he uses the word αὖθις ('again'). Rhodes: Dio 60. 24. 4. Miletus may have lost its freedom also (*IBM* 921a), but perhaps because of *stasis*.
[2] Acts 16: 22 ff.; 22: 24–5 and 29; 2 Cor. 11: 25. On the sending of Paul to Rome, a possible survival of *reiectio Romam*, see above, p. 76.
[3] Capito: Dio 64. 2. 3 and *JRS* 56 (1966), 176 n. 91. He was put to death, but not for this action (as Dio implied). See Tac. *Hist.* 1. 7. Galba: Suet. *Galba* 11.
[4] Cic. *in Verr.* 5. 167; cf. *ad fam.* 10. 32. 2 (Balbus).
[5] Pliny, *Ep.* 10. 96, and above, p. 74.

may indicate that citizenship was afforded more respect then than later. Tacitus, writing under Trajan and Hadrian, remarked on a slackening of standards in the award of citizenship—which he appears to link with the growth in the citizen population.[1] The truth behind this partisan, senatorial complaint (which contrasts with the eulogy of citizenship of the provincial Aristides) is that the privileges of citizenship were the property of a broader section of the population of the Empire than ever before. It is not our concern to judge whether the moral tone of citizenship was lowered as a result; but its privileges had evidently become less tangible. For example, appeal, and the less well authenticated *reiectio Romam*, probably worked smoothly only when the citizen population abroad had the character of a closely-knit, exclusive élite. The former institution alone seems to have survived the late Republic, and its working became less and less effective: the Romans never evolved a machinery adequate to cope with the additional appeals which necessarily accompanied a large increase in the number of citizens. Meanwhile, in Rome in the early Empire, institutional changes had contributed to the downgrading of the citizen. The substitution of courts with overlapping jurisdictions for a uniform court system, and of a flexible for an inflexible penalty structure, gave judges more opportunity to exploit the social divisions within the population. The result was the widening of the gap between the privileged groups and the lower orders, whether citizens or aliens.

However, the decline of citizenship took place over several centuries, and was not confined to the period from the Ciceronian age to the reign of Trajan.[2] Moreover, it may be merely an accident of the sources that the evidence of consideration (and conspicuous lack of consideration) for citizens falls mainly within those 175 years. A solitary piece of information from a non-contemporary source (Eusebius, *EH* 5. 1) confirms that the differential treatment of citizens and aliens persisted into the Antonine period. Pliny's action referred to above was matched by that of the governor of

---

[1] Tac. *Ann.* 3. 40. 2: citizenship was once 'rare and given solely as a reward for virtue'. Cf. Pliny, *Pan.* 37. 25.

[2] See p. 270 n. 2.

Lugdunensis in Marcus' reign in decapitating citizen Christians and sending aliens to the beasts. In fact, the citizen/alien distinction was (largely) set aside by the judicial authorities only after the edict of Caracalla was issued. In any case, the consideration given to citizenship in the early Empire appears insubstantial, when set beside the benefits granted in the same period to those with other attributes. Praetors and judges in administering the civil law used their discretionary power to discriminate in favour of men of means and social standing; judges investigating cases *extra ordinem* awarded differential penalties on the basis of status; the courts of the Senate and the Emperor were more accessible and favourable to the aristocracy than to the lower orders.[1] In all these ways citizenship was shown not to hold the key to the most significant legal privileges. In the first century as in the second *tenuiores*, members of the lower orders, did not count for much in comparison with men of rank, whether or not these were citizens.

To sum up: it is permissible to speak of a decline in the value of citizenship in the period from Augustus to Caracalla, as long as two points are kept in mind. First, there were some practical advantages in being a Roman citizen throughout the period under discussion. The eagerness of individuals and whole communities to obtain Roman status in the second century, as well as in the first, is undeniable, and it would be wrong to imagine that the petitioners were moved simply by an empty, snobbish wish to be Roman.[2] Second, citizens of high status and citizens of low status were at no stage in the period on an equal footing. Gradations within the body of citizens made equality, whether political or judicial or economic, impossible to attain. Just as magistracies were not in practice open to all citizens, but only to those who were qualified financially, similarly only a minority of citizens were eligible for

[1] In general, the interest of an Emperor in the welfare of citizens in the provinces does not make it any less likely that he would aid free aliens. For the Cnidos case see *FIRA*[2] iii, no. 185, p. 582. Only some of the African peasants who petitioned Commodus (see p. 261 n. 6 above) were citizens. *Dig.* 48. 6. 6 may be relevant: Pius instructed a governor to investigate a physical attack on a young man whose name indicates he was a citizen, but who is described by the Emperor simply as 'freeborn' (*ingenuus*).

[2] On both the decline of citizenship and the continued enthusiasm of would-be citizens for it see Sherwin-White, *Roman Citizenship*, chs. 9–10, *pass.*

preferential treatment in the law courts. In Roman society legal and political capacity depended, not only upon the *persona* or character of the individual as defined or recognized by the civil law (free or slave, citizen or alien), but also upon his background or status.[1]

[1] On the relationship between the concepts of citizenship, class, and status see T. H. Marshall, *Citizenship and Social Class and Other Essays* (1950), 28 ff.; also W. G. Runciman, op. cit. (p. 259 n. 2), 34 ff.

12

DIFFERENCES IN RANK AND THE
VALUE OF LEGAL PRIVILEGE

THE jurists took the curial order as the point of division between
the privileged and non-privileged. For them the decurions formed
a standard group, the basis of whose privilege could be easily
investigated. They recognized the existence of groups such as
veterans, which were of equal standing, but did not trouble to
point out that superior dignity and prestige were possessed by
higher orders. However, if the jurists passed over the gradations
within the *honestiores*, judges were fully conscious of the fact that
the *honestiores* were not a homogeneous group. This should be
borne in mind as we consider whether legal privilege was a thing
of value or just another mark of social eminence.

Legal privilege, to be at all useful, had to be respected by judges.
The immunity of senators and equestrian officials from certain
punishments could, in the normal scheme of things, be disregarded
only by an Emperor, and an oppressive act of an Emperor would
not pass unnoticed. On the other hand, it was the responsibility of
a governor to arrest, try, and punish a member of the provincial
gentry. Only in one circumstance was the Emperor required to be
consulted before the governor proceeded to the punishment,
when decurions were on trial for capital offences; and this seems to
have been a late second-century development. Otherwise, decurions, in theory, had no more access to the Emperor's court than
had any other provincial citizen.

Why did the Emperor intervene when decurions were defendants in capital cases? This was not bureaucratic interference
for its own sake. There is only one satisfactory explanation:
decurions and members of curial families had been deported
unjustly, and this had been brought to the Emperor's notice. If it
is asked why the Emperors intervened only so far and no further,
the answer, presumably, is not that governors behaved differently

when the charge was not capital, but that the Emperor's court was not equipped to handle every case involving provincial aristocrats.

Deportation was a permitted punishment for defendants of curial rank. What of the so-called 'plebeian' penalties from which they were immune? The Ambrosius to whom Severus and Caracalla addressed a rescript in A.D. 198 was apparently a decurion, or the son of one, and it is a fair assumption that the proconsul had subjected him to corporal punishment. Caracalla wrote to Geminius that decurions were not to be sentenced to forced labour. Geminius might have been a governor, in which case Caracalla was presumably reprimanding him for breaking this rule. It is more probable that he was a decurion, who had been set to do forced labour. The Emperor Severus Alexander was approached by the son of a woman who clearly had been put to work in the mines. Alexander ruled that this was irregular, as she was the daughter of a decurion. It would be interesting to know how many cases of this kind reached the Emperor. A governor was quite capable of obstructing appeals by force, as is demonstrated by a letter of Severus Alexander to the Bithynian provincial council. Some provincial notables might well have finished their days in chain-gangs in the mines.[1]

A governor might take the further step of depriving a decurion of his life. The Marius Priscus affair of Trajan's reign is unlikely to have been the last of its kind. Governors no doubt continued to be influenced by pressure groups, which were ready to pay for the disposal of rivals and enemies. Members of the provincial nobility could be caught up on either side, as plotters or as victims.[2] In intrigues of this sort the stronger did not always prevail, for the weaker might become strong with the aid of a powerful ally. Patronage was an important factor in local politics in all periods.[3]

---

[1] CJ 2. 11. 5 (Sev. and Carac.); 9. 47. 3 (Carac.); ibid. 9 (Sev. Al.: the tense of *oportuisse* shows that the sentence had been carried out); *Dig.* 49. 1. 25 (=*P. Oxy.* 2104; Sev. Al. to the Bithynians).

[2] In the Priscus case (Pliny, *Ep.* 2. 11) the victims were two equestrians and seven friends (of one of them) of unknown status. As for the plotters, Marcianus was a decurion of Lepcis; nothing is known of Honoratus.

[3] For the evidence from the third century and later see A. H. M. Jones, *Later Roman Empire*, 503–4, referring to CJ 2. 13. 1 (A.D. 293), CTh 2. 14. 1 (A.D. 400), 2. 13. 1 (A.D. 422).

To sum up, the extent of Imperial control over officials in the provinces should not be overestimated. There was always the danger that governors might take arbitrary action at the expense of members of the provincial aristocracy. Imperial rescripts and juristic treatises which emphasized the legal immunities of decurions and their families did not improve their situation, if the Emperor's authority could not be enforced. Indeed, the issuing and reissuing of Imperial rulings, and the comments of the jurists, only underline the fact that the decurions were further from their Imperial protector than was safe. In contrast, the privileged status of senators was seldom referred to in the legal texts. There was no need to mention it, much less give it stress.

The provincial aristocracy, similarly, was more exposed than the Roman aristocracy to the rising tide of higher penalties. In the late third-century work, *Paul's Sentences*, where this development is most clearly attested, reference is made to *honestiores* as a whole, and no hint is given that decurions were the first to succumb.[1] But again, their lack of political influence and their remoteness from Rome probably told against them.

In another way senators and equestrians were better placed. They, in company with certain other favoured individuals or groups (soldiers, for instance), were excused municipal liturgies. Veterans had lost their exemption from 'patrimonial' liturgies—which involved financial expenditure—but retained an immunity from 'personal' liturgies—which did not involve expense. Above all, they were not required to join the local council. This is the implication of a rescript of Severus Alexander to one Felicianus: 'Veterans who, when they might have safeguarded the advantages gained for them by immunity, preferred to become decurions in their city cannot return to the state of immunity which they abandoned . . .' A terse comment of the jurist Paulus belongs to about the same period: 'But veterans who allowed themselves to be enrolled into the council are compelled to perform liturgies.' Callistratus, citing the Emperor Pertinax, issued a similar warning to traders.[2]

---

[1] However, Constantine permitted a *corrector* to torture a decurion in a forgery case. See *CTh* 9. 19. 1; cf. *CJ* 9. 22. 21 (A.D. 316).

[2] *CJ* 10. 44. 1 (Sev. Al.); *Dig.* 49. 18. 5. 2 (Paulus); 50. 6. 6. 13 (Call.).

It appears that at one time it had been possible for those with immunity to gain the decurionate and avoid the liturgies that later went with it. Veratius Severianus of Naples volunteered for the offices of aedile and duumvir in his city, and in addition offered himself for liturgies, even though he could have claimed exemption because he held a priesthood. His adlection to the council is recorded separately, and not as another instance of his unwilling-ness to make use of his immunity. It seems reasonable to suppose that he might have remained an ordinary decurion and still preserved his exemption. The inscription recording his career belongs to the first half of the second century A.D.[1]

The inscription and the legal texts cited above lend support to a proposition which might be argued in detail, that the position of decurions altered in a fundamental way in the course of the second century. Decurions, as the leaders of their communities, had always borne the brunt of public liturgies. The prestige of curial office was generally felt to be sufficient compensation for the expenditure of time, energy, and money involved.[2] There were genuine patriots among them, men like Plutarch, who supervised the measuring of tiles and the delivering of stones and concrete 'not for myself . . . but for my native city'.[3] But, by the Severan period at least, some considered that the financial costs of membership of the council outweighed its benefits. Those of the immune who were politically ambitious evidently now thought twice about joining the council, since they could not carry their exemptions with them. Others were less fortunate—they were forced to take on office.[4]

The process of transformation in local government was a gradual one. It would be quite impossible to measure, within a given period, the increase in the cost of curial burdens, or the rate at which office holding in the cities lost its voluntary nature. But our inability to make these calculations and others of the same kind does not prevent us from weighing the benefits of legal privilege against the benefits of immunity from liturgies. No

---

[1] *C* x 3704 = *ILS* 5054.
[2] There were some in all ages who thought otherwise. For an early reference (Augustan) see *Dig.* 47. 10. 13. 5; cf. Apul. *Met.* 4. 8 (Antonine).
[3] Plutarch, *Mor.* 811 B–C.
[4] See, e.g., *Dig.* 50. 2. 6. 4; cf. 50. 1. 38. 6 (magistracies).

T

decurion would have been in any doubt as to which possessed the greater intrinsic value. Public liturgies were generally costly, and they came round fairly frequently. Legal privilege, on the other hand, was rarely needed and rarely used. Most decurions, it can be assumed, stayed out of the law courts. Legal privilege was thus, at best, a form of insurance, which its holder was able to fall back upon if things went wrong.

It is not difficult to understand why the privileges of decurions were legal rather than financial. While immunities before the law were awarded for social prestige and wealth, immunity from burdens, when it was not granted by the Emperor's special favour, was usually an indication of power and influence. That decurions lacked financial concessions of any kind was a measure of their political impotence.

CONCLUSION

THIS book is built around the hypothesis that the legal system in Rome favoured the interests of the higher orders in Roman society. There is nothing original about this proposition, and few perhaps would dispute it. But it is too general as it stands to be very informative. I have attempted to give it substance by asking two basic questions: What were the characteristic features of the Roman system of legal privilege? Which groups gained preferential treatment in the law courts, and why?

To answer the first question it was necessary first to identify specific ways in which favouritism was shown to privileged groups. This investigation, in which attention was focused on legal procedure, produced evidence of both *de iure* inequality (or legal discrimination) and *de facto* inequality. The former is that type of inequality which resulted directly from the prejudice and partiality of Roman judges and officials. Both the practice of sending high-status and low-status defendants to different courts and the differential punishment of condemned men according to their status fall into this category; with them can be classified the praetor's denial of certain civil actions to would-be plaintiffs of low standing and the preference shown by judges and juries for defendants (or accusers) of high standing. On the other hand, some features of the legal procedures themselves, independently of interference from judicial officials, constituted barriers to the enjoyment of theoretical legal remedies. For example, the institution of self-help which was a feature of the formulary procedure in civil law favoured the rich and influential, because they monopolized the material resources necessary to effect summons and execution in the face of opposition. In general, the unequal distribution of wealth, influence, and knowledge of the law prevented the lower orders from making full use of the legal system, and neither the formulary system nor the officials presiding over it made allowances for this fact.

A second point concerns the legal status of the Roman system of privilege. By definition *de facto* inequality was not openly recognized by judicial or political authorities. *De iure* inequality, on the other hand, was officially acknowledged, but was none the less informal in nature. The patterns of discrimination which characterized the legal system under the Empire did not owe their origin or validity to legislative enactments, which the Romans rarely employed; rather, they evolved gradually in administrative practice over a period of time. The conclusiveness of this finding is limited by the nature of the evidence. It may be simply an accident of the sources that no statutes or decrees survive which, for instance, assigned defendants in criminal trials to courts according to their status and position. On the other hand, it is hard to believe that legislation created the division between upper-level and lower-level tribunals, when the evidence shows that the division was not at all strongly marked under the early Emperors, but became more sharply delineated while probably never rigid as time went on. Similarly, the idea that an early Imperial law or edict created a penalty differential, or, for that matter, the *cognitio* procedure of which it was an outgrowth, is implausible; while the argument that the dual-penalty system familiar to the Severan jurists was transformed and given enhanced validity by rescripts of Hadrian and his successors becomes unconvincing once the content and context of the rescripts are examined. The rescripts seem to serve no more important *legal* function than to confirm the status of the system in administrative law. Meanwhile their value as historical evidence has not been fully appreciated. The rescripts, in the first place, testify to a growing uniformity of legal procedure. This is illustrated by the advances made by *cognitio* in the area of private as well as public law. In addition, they reveal that the penal system was becoming increasingly rigorous. The rescripts from which we derive much of our knowledge of the dual-penalty system were largely issued with the purpose of protecting the privileged status of the local aristocracy, which was threatened by the arbitrary actions of officials and the increasing harshness of penalties. In other words, it is the development of a more severe structure of penalties in the period under consideration which, in large measure, accounts for the picture of legal discrimination we find in the legal sources.

The second question refers to the nature and membership of the privileged groups. Four points seem worth repeating in this concluding summary. First, the principal criterion of legal privilege in the eyes of the Romans was *dignitas* or *honor* derived from power, style of life, and wealth. This view accounts for the legal privilege that was recognized and administered by judges and magistrates, but does not accommodate *de facto* inequality. For example, structural weaknesses in the formulary system gave advantages to the powerful and rich independently of *dignitas*. The dispensability of *dignitas* is shown in addition by the case of the Imperial freedmen. This is an indication that inequalities of power, wealth, and prestige in Roman society did not coincide in all respects.

Secondly, the privileged groups, or *honestiores*, are not defined in the sources, but this does not mean that they cannot be identified. The principal categories can be recovered largely on the basis of a few texts: a senator's son receives exile at the hands of Severus and Caracalla for a crime punishable with death, an equestrian burglar is exiled rather than sentenced to manual labour by Marcus, and veterans and decurions are stated to be exempt from the crueller and more degrading punishments. Moreover, the criteria for legal privilege are firmly laid down; magistrates and judges had only to apply them to settle any incipient doubts as to which parties were deserving of preferential treatment.

Thirdly, the substitution of monarchy for oligarchy brought changes in judicial institutions and consequently in patterns of discrimination; but there is every indication that the categories of privileged persons remained constant from the late Republic to the Severan age. Thus decurions were not added to the circle of the privileged in the early second century, as is sometimes supposed. This assumption is based on a mistaken view of the nature and purpose of a particular Hadrianic constitution. The governing aristocracy in Rome consistently favoured the interests of the local gentry over an extended period of time in both political and legal matters. Again, the fact that citizenship underwent a gradual devaluation as a result of its extension throughout the Empire does not provide grounds for the belief that citizens at some point ceased to constitute a category of the privileged. At no stage in the period under survey was citizenship as such a source of privilege. Citizenship bestowed certain formal rights on its holders as full members of the Roman community, but provided no guarantee of their exercise. In any case, those rights were not commensurate with the benefits enjoyed by *honestiores*.

Finally, *honestiores* and *humiliores* do not represent large homogeneous groups. This dichotomy, like the conventional division of members of societies into 'haves' and 'have-nots', is a theoretical construct, which conceals the complex nature of the Roman social order. Moreover, in the field of law it conflicts with the realities of the administration of justice. Senators, equestrians, veterans, and decurions did not have equal access to legal privileges and remedies. Nor were freeborn citizens, freedmen, free aliens, and slaves in equally disadvantageous positions before the law. The terms *honestiores* and *humiliores*, and their more commonly used variants, normally occur in the primary sources with a restricted sphere of reference. In the juristic writings, for example, they are used in a limited range of instances which relate almost entirely to the administration of the criminal law in the provinces. Hence decurions are treated by the jurists as representative of the membership of the *honestiores*. This clearly they were not. Their privileges were less secure and less substantial than those of the higher orders based on Rome. In law, as in other aspects of Roman society, the principal benefits and rewards were available to those groups most advantageously placed in the stratification system by reason of their greater property, power, and prestige.

BIBLIOGRAPHY

This is not a complete bibliography of the subjects touched upon in this book, but is a list of modern books and articles to which explicit reference has been made. Standard works of reference have been omitted.

ALFÖLDI, A. 'Epigraphica III', *Arch. Ért.* 1 (1940), 230, no. 11.

ARCHI, G. G. (and others). *Pauli Sententiarum fragmentum Leidense* (Leiden, 1956).

—— 'Rescrits impériaux et littérature jurisprudentielle dans le développement du droit criminel', *RIDA* N.S. 4 (1957), 221.

AURIGEMMA, S. *I Mosaici di Zliten* (Roma, 1926).

—— *L'Italia in Africa: Le scoperte archeologiche 1911–43: Tripolitania,* i, pts. i–ii (Roma, 1960).

BARNES, T. D. 'Pre-Decian *Acta Martyrum*', *Jl. Theol. St.* 19 (1968), 509.

BARNS, J. W. B. 'A letter of Severus Alexander', *JEA* 52 (1966), 141.

BAUMAN, R. A. *The Crimen Maiestatis in the Roman Republic and Augustan Principate* (Johannesburg, 1967).

—— 'Some remarks on the structure and survival of the *Quaestio de Adulteriis*', *Antichthon* 2 (1968), 68.

BIRLEY, A. R. 'The oath not to put senators to death', *CR* 12 (1962), 197.

BIRLEY, E. *Roman Britain and the Roman army: Collected papers* (Kendal, 1953).

BLEICKEN, J. *Senatsgericht und Kaisergericht*, Abh. Akad. Wiss. Göttingen, Phil.-Hist. Klasse III, 53 (Göttingen, 1962).

BONINI, R. *I 'Libri de cognitionibus' di Callistrato: Ricerche sull'elaborazione giurisprudenziale della 'cognitio extra ordinem'* (Milano, 1964).

BORMANN, E. 'Bronzeinschrift aus Lauriacum', *JÖAI* 9 (1906), 315.

BOULANGER, A. *Aelius Aristide, et la sophistique dans la province d'Asie au IIᵉ siècle de notre ère* (Paris, 1923).

BOWERSOCK, G. W. *Augustus and the Greek World* (Oxford, 1965).

BRASIELLO, U. *La repressione penale in diritto romano* (Napoli, 1937).

BROGGINI, G. *Iudex Arbiterve: prolegomena zum officium des römischen Privatrichters* (Köln, 1957).

BRUNT, P. A. 'Pay and superannuation in the Roman army', *PBSR* 5 (1950), 50.

—— 'The Lex Valeria Cornelia', *JRS* 51 (1961), 71.

—— 'Charges of provincial maladministration under the early Principate', *Historia* 10 (1961), 189.

—— Review of W. Kunkel, *Zur Entwicklung des römischen Kriminalverfahrens in vorsullanischer Zeit. Tijdschrift voor Rechtsgeschiedenis* 32 (1964), 445.

BRUNT, P. A. 'The Equites in the late Republic', *Second International*

BRUNT, P. A. (*cont.*):
Conference of Economic History, 1962 (1965), i. 117 ff. = The crisis of the Roman Republic, ed. R. Seager (Cambridge, 1969), 83.
—— 'The "Fiscus" and its development', *JRS* 56 (1966), 75.
—— 'Procuratorial jurisdiction', *Latomus* 25 (1966), 461.
BUCKLAND, W. W. *The Roman law of slavery* (Cambridge, 1908).
—— 'Interpolations in the *Digest*: A criticism of criticism', *Harvard Law Review* 54 (1941), 1273.
—— *A text-book of Roman law from Augustus to Justinian*³ (Cambridge, 1963).
CADOUX, T. J. Review of G. Vitucci, *Ricerche sulla praefectura urbi in età imperiale sec. I–III*, *JRS* 49 (1959), 152.
CAGNAT, R. *L'Armée romaine d'Afrique et l'occupation militaire d'Afrique sous les empereurs* (Paris, 1913).
CARDASCIA, G. 'L'apparition dans le droit des classes d'"honestiores" et d'"humiliores" ', *RHDFE* 27 (1950), 305–37, 461–85.
—— 'La distinction entre "honestiores" et "humiliores" et le droit matrimonial', *Studi in memoria di Emilio Albertario*, ii (Milano, 1953), 665.
CHALON, G. *L'Édit de Tiberius Iulius Alexander* (Olten–Lausanne, 1964).
CHILTON, C. W. 'The Roman law of treason under the early Principate', *JRS* 45 (1955), 73.
CONDURACHI, E. 'La Costituzione Antoniniana e la sua applicazione nell'Impero Romano', *Dacia* N.S. 2 (1958), 281.
CROOK, J. *Consilium Principis* (Cambridge, 1955).
—— Review of J. M. Kelly, *Roman litigation*, *CR* 17 (1967), 83 (with R. Stone).
—— *Law and life of Rome* (London, 1967).
CUQ, E. *Manuel des instituts juridiques des romains*² (Paris, 1917).
DAUBE, D. ' "Ne quid infamandi causa fiat": The Roman law of defamation', *Atti del Congresso internazionale di diritto romano e di storia del diritto* (Verona), iii (Milano, 1951), 413.
—— *The defence of superior orders in Roman law* (Oxford, 1956).
DELEHAYE, H. 'S. Romain, martyr d'Antioche', *Anal. Boll.* 50 (1932), 241.
DUFF, A. M. *Freedmen in the early Roman Empire*² (Oxford, 1958).
DURRY, M. *Les Cohortes prétoriennes* (Paris, 1938).
DUNCAN-JONES, R. P. 'Costs, outlays and summae honorariae from Roman Africa', *PBSR* 17 (1962), 47.
—— 'Wealth and munificence in Roman Africa', ibid. 18 (1963), 159.
—— 'An epigraphic survey of costs in Roman Italy', ibid. 20 (1965), 189.
—— 'Equestrian rank in the cities of the African provinces under the Principate: An epigraphic survey', ibid. 22 (1967), 147.
D'ESCURAC-DOISY, H. 'Notes sur le phénomène associatif dans le monde paysan à l'époque du Haut-Empire', *Antiquités africaines* 1 (1967), 59.
FORNI, G. *Il reclutamento delle legioni da Augusto a Diocleziano* (Milano, 1953).
FREDERIKSEN, M. W. 'Caesar, Cicero and the problem of debt', *JRS* 56 (1966), 128.
—— Review of J. M. Kelly, *Roman litigation*, *JRS* 57 (1967), 254.

FREND, W. H. C. *Martyrdom and persecution in the early Church* (Oxford, 1965).

FRIEDLÄNDER, L. *Darstellungen aus der Sittengeschichte Roms⁹* (Leipzig, 1910).

GAGÉ, J. *Les Classes sociales dans l'empire romain* (Paris, 1964).

GARNSEY, P. 'The Lex Iulia and appeal under the Empire', *JRS* 56 (1966), 167.

—— 'Adultery trials and the survival of the Quaestiones in the Severan Age', *JRS* 57 (1967), 56.

—— 'The criminal jurisdiction of governors', *JRS* 58 (1968), 51.

—— 'Why penalties become harsher: the Roman case, late Republic to fourth-century Empire', *Natural Law Forum* 13 (1968), 141.

GAUDEMET, J. 'L'empereur, interprète du droit', *Festschr. für E. Rabel*, ii (Tübingen, 1954), 169.

—— 'Les abus des "Potentes" au Bas Empire', *The Irish Jurist* i, N.S. 1 (1966), 128.

GELZER, M. *Die Nobilität der römischen Republik* (1912) = *Kleine Schriften* i (Wiesbaden, 1962), 17.

—— 'Die Nobilität der Kaiserzeit', *Hermes* 50 (1915), 395 = *Kleine Schriften* i. 136.

GORDON, M. L. 'The Ordo of Pompeii', *JRS* 17 (1927), 165.

—— 'The freedman's son in municipal life', ibid. 21 (1931), 65.

GREENIDGE, A. H. J. *Infamia: Its place in Roman public and private law* (Oxford, 1894).

—— *The legal procedure of Cicero's time* (Oxford, 1901).

GUALANDI, G. *Legislazione imperiale e giurisprudenza* (Milano, 1963).

HÄNEL, G. *Corpus legum ab imperatoribus Romanis ante Iustinianum latarum, quae extra constitutionum codices supersunt* (Leipzig, 1857).

HARRISON, A. R. W. 'Aristotle's Nicomachean Ethics, Book V, and the law of Athens', *JHS* 77 (1957), 42.

HAMMOND, MASON. *The Antonine Monarchy* (Am. Acad., Rome, 1959).

HENDERSON, B. W. *The life and principate of the Emperor Hadrian: 78–138 A.D.* (London, 1923).

HENDERSON, M. I. 'The process "de repetundis" ', *JRS* 41 (1951), 71.

—— 'The establishment of the Equester Ordo', *JRS* 53 (1963), 61.

HEPDING, H. 'Die Arbeiten in Pergamum 1904–1905, II: Die Inschriften', *Ath. Mitt.* 32 (1907), 241.

HERRMANN, P. *Neue Inschriften zur historischen Landeskunde von Lydien und angrenzenden Gebieten*, Öst. Akad. Wiss. Phil.-Hist. Klasse (Wien, 1965).

HIRSCHFELD, O. 'Die Sicherheitspolizei im römischen Kaiserreich', *Sitz. Berl. Akad.* 1891, 845 = *Kleine Schriften* (Berlin, 1913), 576.

—— 'Die Rangtitel der römischen Kaiserzeit', *Sitz. Berl. Akad.* 1901, 579 = *Kleine Schriften*, 646.

HONORÉ, A. M. *Gaius* (Oxford, 1962).

—— 'The Severan lawyers: A preliminary survey', *Studia et documenta historiae et iuris* 28 (1962), 162.

HÜTTL, W. *Antoninus Pius* (Prague, 1933–6).

HUNT, A. S., EDGAR, C. C. *Select Papyri*, ii (ed. Loeb, 1934).

JARRETT, M. G. *A study of the municipal aristocracies of the Roman Empire in the West, with special reference to North Africa*, unpubl. Ph.D. thesis (Durham, 1958).

JOLOWICZ, H. F. *Historical introduction to the study of Roman law²* (Cambridge, 1952).

JONES, A. H. M. *The Greek city from Augustus to Justinian* (Oxford, 1940).

—— *Studies in Roman government and law* (Oxford, 1960).

—— *The later Roman Empire, 284–602: A social, economic, and administrative survey* (Oxford, 1964).

KASER, M. 'Infamia und ignominia in den römischen Rechtsquellen, *ZSS* 73 (1956), 220.

—— *Das römische Privatrecht*, Handbuch d. Altertumswiss., X. 3. 3. 1 (München, 1955).

—— *Das römische Zivilprozessrecht*, Handbuch d. Altertumswiss., X. 3. 4 (München, 1966).

KELLY, J. M. *Princeps iudex: eine Untersuchung zur Entwicklung und zu den Grundlagen der kaiserlichen Gerichtsbarkeit*, Diss., Heidelberg (Weimar, 1957).

—— *Roman litigation* (Oxford, 1966).

KORTENBEUTEL, H. 'Ein Kaisereid', *Aegyptus* 12 (1932), 129.

KRAFT, K. *Rekrutierung der Alen und Kohorten an Rhein und Donau* (Bern, 1951).

KUNKEL, W. *Herkunft und soziale Stellung der römischen Juristen²* (Weimar, 1967).

—— *Zur Entwicklung des römischen Kriminalverfahrens in vorsullanischer Zeit*, Bay. Akad. Wiss., Phil.-Hist. Klasse (München, 1962).

—— *An introduction to Roman legal and constitutional history*, tr. J. M. Kelly (Oxford, 1966).

LEMOSSE, M. *Cognitio, étude sur le rôle du juge dans l'instruction du procès civil antique* (Paris, 1944).

LENEL, O. *Das Edictum Perpetuum³* (Leipzig, 1927).

LESCHI, L. 'L'album municipal de Timgad et l'"ordo Salutationis" du consulaire Ulpius Mariscianus', *REA* 50 (1948), 71.

LESQUIER, J. *L'Armée romaine d'Égypte d'Auguste à Dioclétien* (Cairo, 1918).

LEVY, E. *Die römische Kapitalstrafe*, Sb. Heidelb. Akad. Wiss. (Heidelberg, 1931) = *Gesammelte Schriften* (Köln, 1963), 325.

LÉVY, I. 'Études sur la vie municipale de l'Asie Mineure sous les Antonins', pt. 1, *REG* 8 (1895), 203; pt. 2, ibid. 10 (1899), 255.

LÉVY, J. Ph. 'Dignitas, gravitas, auctoritas testium', *Studi in onore di Biondo Biondi*, ii (Milano, 1965), 29.

LINTOTT, A. W. *Violence in Republican Rome* (Oxford, 1968).

LUZZATTO, G. I. 'Richerche sull'applicazione delle costituzioni imperiali nelle provincie', *Scritti di diritto romano in onore di C. Ferrini*, ed. G. G. Archi (Pavia, 1946), 265.

MACMULLEN, R. *Soldier and civilian in the later Roman Empire* (Cambridge, Mass., 1963).

—— *Enemies of the Roman order* (Cambridge, Mass., 1967).

MANN, J. C. *The settlement of veterans in the Roman Empire*, unpubl. Ph.D. thesis (London, 1956).

MARSHALL, T. H. *Citizenship and social class and other essays* (Cambridge, 1950).

MILLAR, F. 'The Fiscus in the first two centuries', *JRS* 53 (1963), 29.

—— *A study of Cassius Dio* (Oxford, 1964).

—— 'Some evidence on the meaning of Tacitus *Annals* xii, 60', *Historia* 13 (1964), 180.

—— 'The development of jurisdiction by Imperial Procurators; further evidence', *Historia* 14 (1965), 362.

—— 'The Emperor, the Senate, and the provinces', *JRS* 56 (1966), 156.

—— 'Emperors at work', *JRS* 57 (1967), 9.

—— *The Roman Empire and its neighbours* (London, 1967).

MITTEIS, L., WILCKEN, U. *Grundzüge und Chrestomathie der Papyruskunde* (Leipzig–Berlin, 1912).

MÓCSY, A. 'Das Territorium Legionis und die Canabae in Pannonien', *Acta Arch. Acad. Sc. Hung.* 5 (1953), 179.

—— *Die Bevölkerung von Pannonien bis zu den Markomannenkriegen* (Budapest, 1959).

MOMMSEN, Th. 'Die pompeianischen Quittungstafeln des L. Caecilius Iucundus', *Hermes* 12 (1877), 94.

—— *Römisches Staatsrecht* (Leipzig, 1887–8).

—— *Römisches Strafrecht* (Leipzig, 1899).

—— 'Die Rechtsverhältnisse des Apostels Paulus', *Zeitschr. für die neutestam. Wiss.* ii (1901), 81 = *Ges. Schr.* iii (Berlin, 1907), 431.

—— 'Latium maius', *ZSS* 23 (1902) 46, = *Ges. Schr.* iii, 33.

MUSURILLO, H. A. *Acts of the pagan martyrs: Acta Alexandrinorum* (Oxford, 1954).

NESSELHAUF, H. 'Das Bürgerrecht der Soldatenkinder', *Historia* 8 (1959), 434.

NICOLET, C. *L'Ordre équestre à l'époque républicaine* (Paris, 1966).

NORMAN, A. F. 'Gradations in later municipal society', *JRS* 48 (1958), 79.

OLIVA, P. *Pannonia and the onset of crisis in the Roman Empire* (Prague, 1962).

OLIVER, J. H. 'The sacred Gerusia', *Hesperia Suppl.* 6 (1941).

—— *The ruling power: A study of the Roman Empire in the second century after Christ through the Roman oration of Aelius Aristides*, Trans. Am. Phil. Soc. N.S. 43. 4 (Philadelphia, 1953), 871.

ORESTANO, R. 'Gli editti imperiali: contributo alla teoria della loro validità ed efficacia nel diritto romano classico', *BIDR* N.S. 3, 44 (1936–37), 219.

—— 'Augusto e la cognitio extra ordinem', *Studi economico-giuridici dell'Università di Cagliari* 26 (1938), 153.

D'ORGEVAL, B. *L'empereur Hadrien, œuvre législative et administrative* (Paris, 1950).

D'ORS, A. 'La signification de l'œuvre d'Hadrien dans l'histoire du droit romain', *Les Empereurs romains d'Espagne*, Madrid-Italica, 1964 (Paris, 1965), 147.

Ossowski, S. *Class structure in the social consciousness* (London, 1963).

Pflaum, H. G. *Les Procurateurs équestres sous le Haut-Empire romain* (Paris, 1950).

—— *Les Carrières procuratoriennes équestres sous le Haut-Empire romain* (Paris, 1960–1).

Picard, G.-Ch. *La Civilisation de l'Afrique romaine* (Paris, 1959).

Pringsheim, F. 'The legal policy and reforms of Hadrian', *JRS* 24 (1934), 141.

Ramsay, W. M. *Cities and bishoprics of Phrygia* (Oxford, 1895–7).

de Robertis, F. M. 'Arbitrium judicantis e statuizioni imperiali; pena discrezionale e pena fissa nella *cognitio extra ordinem*', *ZSS* 59 (1939), 219.

—— 'La variazione della pena 'pro qualitate personarum' nel diritto penale romano', *RISG* 1939, 59.

—— 'Sulla efficacia normativa delle costituzioni imperiali', *Annali della fac. di giurispr. della R. Univ. di Bari*, N.S. 4 (1941), 1–100, 281–374.

Rogers, R. S. 'Ignorance of the law in Tacitus and Dio', *TAPA* 64 (1933), 18.

—— *Criminal trials and criminal legislation under Tiberius* (Middletown, Conn., 1935).

—— 'Treason in the early Empire', *JRS* 49 (1959), 90.

Roussel, P. 'Un Syrien au service de Rome et d'Octave', *Syria* 15 (1934), 33.

Runciman, W. G. 'Class, status and power?' in *Social stratification*, ed. J. A. Jackson (London, 1968), 25.

de Ste Croix, G. E. M. 'Suffragium: from vote to patronage', *British Journal of Sociology* 5 (1954), 33.

Sander, E. 'Das Recht des römischen Soldaten', *Rhein. Mus.* 101 (1958), 152–91, 193–234.

Sasse, Chr. *Die Constitutio Antoniniana* (Wiesbaden, 1958).

Schiller, A. A. 'Bureaucracy and the Roman law', *Seminar* 7 (1949), 26.

Schmitz, H. *Stadt und Imperium: Köln in römischer Zeit* (Köln, 1948).

Schulz, F. *Principles of Roman law* (Oxford, 1936).

—— *Classical Roman law* (Oxford, 1951).

Schulze, W. 'Beiträge zur Wort und Sittengeschichte, II', *Sitz. Berl. Akad.* = *Kleine Schriften* (Göttingen, 1934), 160.

Seager, R. (ed.). *The crisis of the Roman Republic* (Cambridge, 1969).

Sherwin-White, A. N. *The Roman citizenship* (Oxford, 1939).

—— 'Poena legis repetundarum', *PBSR* 4 (1949), 5.

—— Review of J. Bleicken, *Senatsgericht und Kaisergericht*, *JRS* 53 (1963), 203.

—— *Roman society and Roman law in the New Testament* (Oxford, 1963).

—— *The letters of Pliny: A historical and social commentary* (Oxford, 1966).

Skeat, T. C., Wegener, E. P. 'A trial before the prefect of Egypt Appius Sabinus, *c.* 250 A.D.', *JEA* 21 (1935), 224.

Smallwood, E. M. 'Some comments on Tacitus *Annals* xii, 54', *Latomus* 18 (1959), 560.

—— 'The legislation of Hadrian and Antoninus Pius against circumcision', ibid. 18 (1959), 334.
—— 'The legislation of Hadrian and Antoninus Pius against circumcision: an addendum', ibid. 20 (1961), 92.
STAVELEY, E. S. 'Provocatio during the fourth and fifth centuries B.C.', *Historia* 3 (1955), 418.
STEIN, A. *Der römische Ritterstand* (München, 1927).
STRACHAN-DAVIDSON, J. L. *Problems of the Roman criminal law* (Oxford, 1912).
SWOBODA, E. *Karnuntum: seine Geschichte und seine Denkmäler⁴* (Graz, 1964).
SYME, R. *The Roman revolution* (Oxford, 1939).
—— *Tacitus* i, ii (Oxford, 1958).
—— *Ammianus and the Historia Augusta* (Oxford, 1968).
TURNER, E. G. 'The Gerousia of Oxyrhynchus', *Archiv* 12 (1937), 179.
DE VISSCHER, F. *Les édits d'Auguste découverts à Cyrène*, Rec. de trav. d'hist. et de phil. 3, i (Louvain, 1940).
VITUCCI, G. *Ricerche sulla praefectura urbi in età imperiale sec. I–III* (Roma, 1956).
WATSON, W. A. J. 'Some cases of distortion by the past in classical Roman law', *Tijdschrift voor Rechtsgeschiedenis* 31 (1963), 69.
—— *The law of obligation in the later Roman Republic* (Oxford, 1965).
—— *The law of persons in the later Roman Republic* (Oxford, 1967).
WATSON, G. R. 'The pay of the Roman army', *Historia* 5 (1956), 332.
—— *The Roman soldier* (London, 1969).
WEBER, M. *Economy and society* (ed. G. Roth, C. Wittich, N.Y. 1968).
WENGER, L. *Die Quellen des römischen Rechts* (Wien, 1953).
WIEACKER, F. 'Endoplorare. Diebstahlsverfolgung und Gerüft im altrömischen Recht', *Festschrift für Leopold Wenger* i, (München, 1944), 129.
WILCKEN, U. 'Zu den Kaiserrescripten', *Hermes* 50 (1920), 1.
WILLIAMS, W. 'Antoninus Pius and the control of provincial embassies', *Historia* 16 (1967), 470.
WIRSZUBSKI, CH. *Libertas as a political idea at Rome during the late Republic and early Principate* (Cambridge, 1950).
WLASSAK, M. *Kritische Studien zur Theorie der Rechtsquellen im Zeitalter der klassischen Juristen* (Graz, 1884).
VON WOESS, F. 'Personalexekution und cessio bonorum im römischen Reichsrecht', *ZSS* 43 (1922), 485.

INDEX OF SOURCES

LITERARY TEXTS

INSCRIPTIONS

PAPYRI

GENERAL INDEX